The Trail Guide to BOB MARSHALL COUNTRY

by
Erik Molvar

Helena, Montana

Falcon Press is continually expanding its list of recreational guidebooks using the same general format as this book. All books include detailed descriptions, accurate maps, and all information necessary for enjoyable trips. You can order extra copies of this book and get information and prices for other Falcon books by writing Falcon Press, P.O. Box 1718, Helena, MT 59624. Also, please ask for a free copy of our current catalog.

ISBN 1-56044-254-9

Printed in the United States of America.

All black-and-white photos by the author.
Cover photo by Rick Graetz.
Maps by Eric West.
Layout and design by Chris Stamper.

Text pages are printed on recycled paper.

CONTENTS

CAUTION

Outdoor recreation activities are by their very nature potentially hazardous. All participants in such activities must assume the responsibility for their own actions and safety. The information contained in this guidebook cannot replace sound judgment and good decision-making skills, which help reduce risk exposure, nor does the scope of this book allow for disclosure of all the potential hazards and risks involved in such activities.

Learn as much as possible about the outdoor recreation activities you participate in, prepare for the unexpected, and be safe and cautious. The reward will be a safer and more enjoyable experience.

This book is dedicated to Erick and Dave Nyquest, who got there first, and Ed Zink, who will get there yet.

Pergé!

ACKNOWLEDGMENTS

I would like to thank the wilderness managers of the Lewis and Clark, Flathead, Lolo, and Helena national forests for providing information on trail status, local history, and unique features of the backcountry areas covered in this book, as well as providing assistance in the editing process. Kraig Lang, Ray Mills, and Jim Blackburn were especially helpful in this process. Thanks also to the fire lookouts, wilderness rangers, and trail crews who provided up-to-the-minute trail information in the backcountry. I appreciate the support of friends and relatives, particularly Chad Williams, Brian Connolly, Little Joe Manley, and the Newton Clan, as well as John and Virginia Lenihan. I owe a particular debt of thanks to the spelunkers, loggers, teachers, Canadians, and other hikers who gave me a lift as I traveled between remote trailheads while researching the book. Phi Gamma Delta and the library staff at the University of Montana provided valuable assistance in gathering map and distance information.

OVERVIEW MAP

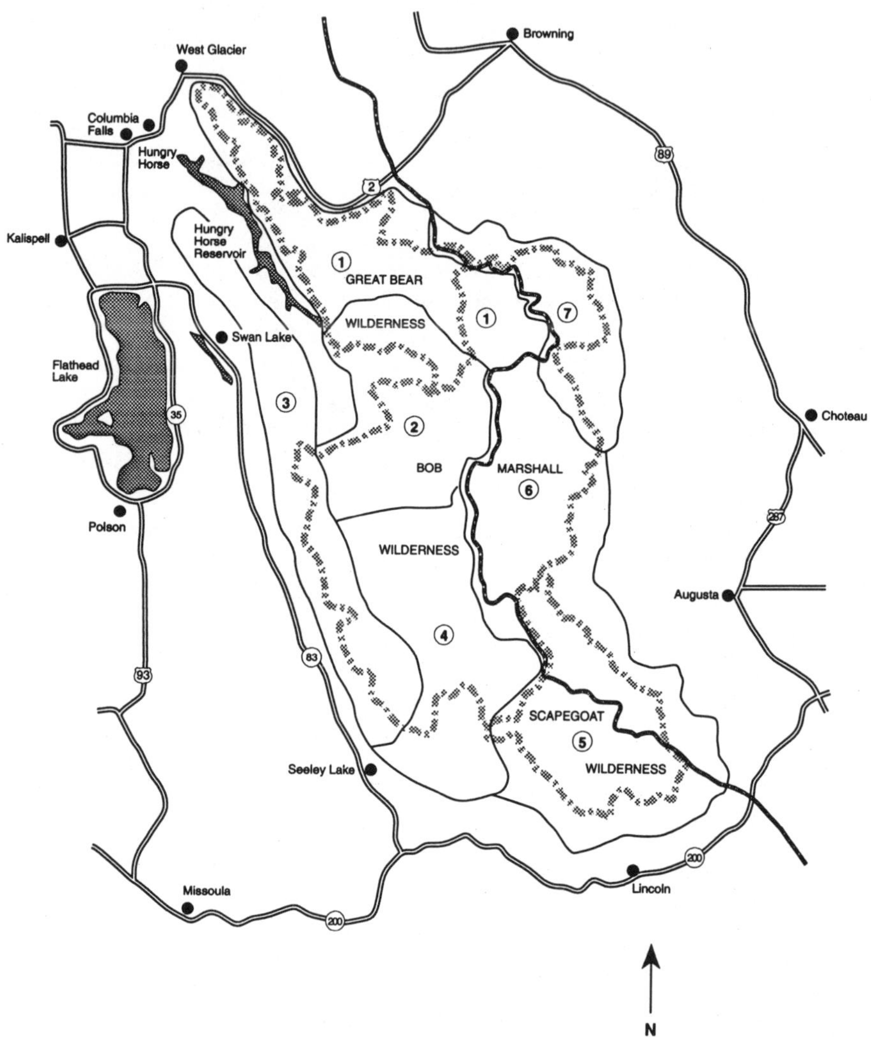

USGS TOPOGRAPHIC MAPS

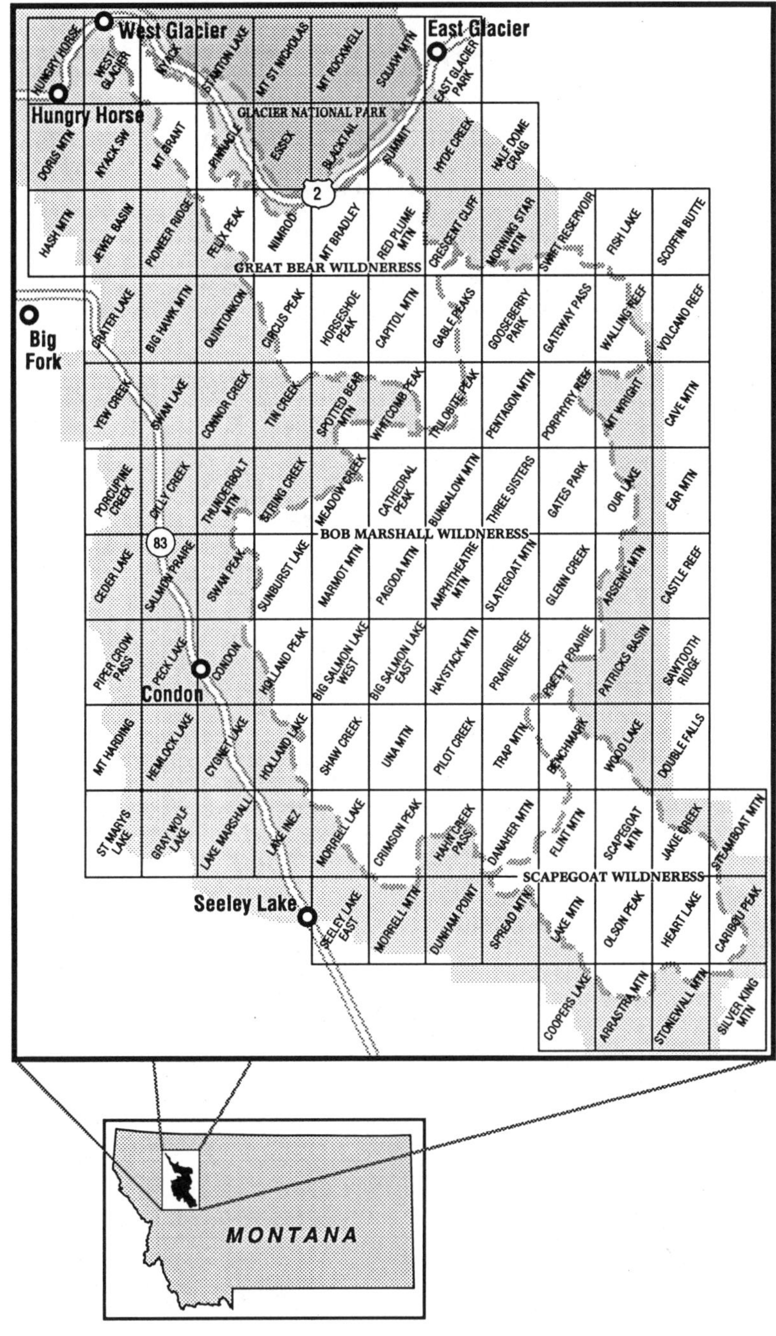

LEGEND

CONTINENTAL DIVIDE
WILDERNESS BOUNDARY
PAVED ROAD
INTERSTATE HIGHWAY
DIRT/GRAVEL ROAD
POWERLINE
RAILROAD
CREEK
NATIONAL FOREST BOUNDARY
STATE BOUNDARY
RIVERS
DESCRIBED TRAIL
OTHER TRAIL
UNMAINTAINED TRAIL
GLACIER
LAKE
x 7524 MOUNTAIN PEAK
CAMPSITE
RANGER STATION
PASS/SADDLE
BRIDGE
BUILDING
178 FOREST ROAD
TRAILHEAD
4 STATE ROAD
2 US HIGHWAY
PERMANENTLY LOCKED GATE
SEASONALLY LOCKED GATE

INTRODUCTION

Robert Marshall was an almost legendary figure in the movement to protect wilderness areas in the United States. He began his career with the Forest Service in the 1920s, and soon gained notoriety for his penchant for long solo trips into the backcountry. Marshall considered a thirty-five-mile trek to be a healthy day hike, and was known to cover more than seventy miles on foot in a single day. Marshall reached the pinnacle of his influence in the 1930s, advocating the preservation of 45 million acres of forest land for recreational purposes. Central to his plan was the protection of "primeval" and "wilderness" areas, places where a person could "spend at least a week or two of travel in them without crossing his own tracks." In response to his urgings, over five million acres were set aside as wilderness areas, where man was to be no more than a passing visitor.

It is quite fitting that in 1941, two years after Marshall's death, the South Fork, Pentagon, and Sun River wilderness areas were together commemorated as the Bob Marshall Wilderness Area. The later additions of the Great Bear and Scapegoat wilderness areas in the 1970s preserved a continuous tract of wild country that is widely known as the crown jewel of the American wilderness system. Entire ranges and basins lie rank on rank, stretching for mile after mile of untrammeled country. The opportunities for escape from the "civilization" that Marshall abhorred abound here, with opportunities and challenges for visitors with a wide range of abilities and

Looking down the valley of Crazy Creek.

View of Red Butte to the west of Prairie Reef.

skills. Here is one of the last great remnants of primeval North America, a window on a simpler and more primitive time. Enjoy its wildness and grandeur, and leave no trace of your passage to mar its primeval perfection.

PLANNING YOUR TRIP

It is important to gather as much current information as possible before starting out on a wilderness expedition. Permits are not required for expeditions into the Bob Marshall country, although it is wise to check in with a local ranger station to get the latest report on trail conditions. Ask for the trail supervisor or wilderness manager, who will be best equipped to answer your questions. A list of addresses and phone numbers for these ranger stations in provided in Appendix C. There are no designated camping spots in the wilderness areas, and campers are asked to practice minimum impact camping techniques as outlined later in this chapter. In the wilderness, man is a passing visitor and should leave no trace of camping spots to mar the wilderness experience of other travelers. Another Falcon Press book, *Wild Country Campanion*, is a good source for no-trace techniques and wildnerness safety.

The key to a quality hiking experience is good planning. Hikers who underestimate the distance or time required in completing a trip may find themselves hiking in the dark, a dangerous proposition at best. An experienced hiker traveling at a fast clip without rest stops can generally make three miles per hour on any terrain, and perhaps more if the distance is all downhill. Novices and hikers in poor physical condition generally have a maximum speed of 2.5 miles per hour. Note that these rates do not include stops for rest and refreshment, which add tremendously to the hiker's enjoyment and appreciation of the surroundings. Eight miles a day is a good goal for travelers new to backpacking, while old hands can generally cover at least twelve miles comfortably. We recommend traveling below top speed, focussing more attention on the surrounding natural beauty and less on the exercise of hiking itself.

A FEW WORDS OF CAUTION

WEATHER

Weather patterns in the mountains of the Bob Marshall country change frequently and without warning. Cold temperatures can occur even during the height of summer, and nighttime temperatures routinely dip into the 40s and even 30s on clear nights. Sudden thunderstorms may change cloudless days into drenching misery, so appropriate rain gear should be carried at all times. Ponchos are generally sufficient for day hikes, but backpackers should carry full rain suits, because water from drenched vegetation will quickly soak travelers who rely solely on ponchos for protection. Snowfall is always a distinct possibility in the high country, and overnight

Crown Mountain covered by "summer snow."

overnight expeditions should carry clothing and gear with this possibility in mind. Detailed short range forecasts are available at ranger stations and are usually reliable.

In general, snows linger in the high country into early June. This month traditionally receives the heaviest rainfall, with drier weather coming in late July and August. The first snowstorms visit the high country in early September, and a deep blanket of snow sometimes covers the passes by the end of the month. Temperatures are generally higher east of the divide, especially in the low basin of the Sun River, where daily high temperatures in the 90 degree range are not uncommon in July and August. The eastern side of the wilderness usually receives less rainfall as well, but heavy storms in late August and early September often unleash torrents of rain or deep blankets of snow.

WATER SUPPLIES

The pristine streams and lakes of the Bob Marshall country are quite refreshing, but may contain a microorganism called *Giardia lamblia*, which causes severe diarrhea and dehydration in humans. The microorganism is spread through the feces of wild mammals, especially the beavers that inhabit many of the low-elevation stream systems. The water can be rendered safe by boiling it for at least five minutes or by passing it through a filter system with a mesh no larger than five micrometers. Iodine tablets and other purification additives are not considered effective against *Giardia*. Any surface water supply is a potential source of this organism, and hikers that drink from lakes and streams undertake the risk of contracting the painful symptoms associated with this pestiferous microbe.

GRIZZLY BEARS

Grizzly bears are the original residents of Montana's mountain wilderness, and you will be passing through their territory during the course of day hikes and backpacks. By exercising precautions and treating the bears with respect, travelers can minimize the chances of a harmful encounter. It is easy to avoid an unpleasant confrontation with these wild and beautiful creatures by following a few common sense rules of thumb. Give bears a wide berth, as a direct approach is often perceived as threatening. Many a photographer has met trouble while trying to get just a little closer for that perfect shot. Females with cubs are particularly sensitive to intrusions by humans. In areas of dense brush along the trail, it will be necessary to announce your presence to bears. Bear bells may be worn for this purpose; clapping and shouting at appropriate times work just as well.

It is important to remember that a bear will attempt to avoid contact with humans, so if you meet a bear along the trail, the odds are that it will turn and flee. In the event of a human-bear confrontation, the best course of action is to talk in a firm, unexcited voice to the bear while waving your arms slowly and backing away. Do not try to run away from the bear, because doing this will trigger the bear's predatory instincts. It will then identify you as prey and give chase. Reaching speeds of nearly forty miles per hour, a grizzly can easily catch a running person if it wants to. Climbing a tree is a means of escape if an appropriate tree is nearby and one has sufficient time to get up into it (which is rarely the case). Playing dead (covering the neck and stomach) should be used as a last resort after the bear has decided to attack and may save the victim from mortal wounds. It is easier by far to avoid a bear encounter than to get out of one.

Many travelers in the Bob Marshall carry some sort of weapon to use against marauding bears. Killing a bear is no easy task: Their thick skulls can deflect a bullet, and their bulky mass reveals no obvious target for an instant kill. A much more practical anti-bear device is the cayenne pepper-based bear spray that is widely available at sporting goods stores. This spray has a range of about twenty feet and disable the bear with a stinging mist that irritates the eyes, nose, and mouth.The false sense of security of a gun might prove dangerous in itself. In all my travels in Alaska and the Northern Rockies, I have never carried a firearm or bear spray. Because I am defenseless against a determined bear, I feel more motivated to avoid them than I might if I was carrying a weapon.

OTHER ANIMALS

Black bears are in many respects as dangerous as their larger cousins. These bears have an innate curiosity that often brings them into camp and are not as shy of humans as are grizzlies. In addition, black bears are able climbers and will be able to raid food containers that are hung too close to the tree trunk. Other animals are more a nuisance than a danger. Deer often hang around camp sites and will chew on sweat-soaked clothing and saddle tack. At higher elevations, rodents dwelling in rockslides may chew their way into a pack in search of food or salt. There are no poisonous snakes in the Bob Marshall country, even in the semi-arid hills of the Front Range.

SHARING THE TRAIL

Visitors should expect to encounter a wide variety of different user groups in Bob Marshall country. This magnificent wilderness is a magnet for hunters, anglers, and solitude seekers of all descriptions. In the interest of a safe and pleasant wilderness experience for all, exercise consideration and good manners when meeting other parties on the trail. Respect for others is the cornerstone of the traditional western ethic, a code which is still in force in the wilderness areas of Montana. A few common-sense guidelines will help you avoid bad experiences when encountering other wilderness visitors.

Backpackers must share the trail with stock users of several types. Because pack and saddle stock are less maneuverable than foot travelers, hikers should yield to horse parties when the two meet on a trail. In such a situation, the best thing that a hiker can do is to hike up the hillside above the trail for at least twenty feet and allow the stock to pass. It often helps to talk to the animals in reassuring tones as they pass by. This keeps the animals from panicking and tangling up the pack string. Bear in mind that the main valley-bottom trails receive the heaviest stock use; visitors on foot can avoid the horse droppings and churned-up bogs by sticking to more remote paths.

When two stock parties meet, it is generally the longer and more heavily-laden string that has the right of way. When horse and llama parties meet on the trail, special problems may arise. Horses unaccustomed to llamas may panic and rear if the two groups come into close contact. Horse users should avoid this problem by introducing their stock to llamas in the controlled environment of their own corrals. Once the horses have learned that the llamas pose no threat, the two kinds of animals can pass on a trail with little difficulty.

SELECTING A CAMP SPOT

Wilderness visitors should choose a camping spot that is both resistant to impacts and away from trails. Shorelines of lakes and stream banks are particularly sensitive to disturbance, and all camping spots should be located at least two hundred yards away from the nearest lake or stream. Alpine meadows are also very fragile and should be avoided by campers. Try to locate your camp on a dry site within a mature forest. Such a site will be more difficult to damage. In addition, locate all camping spots away from high traffic areas—this will increase your own seclusion and help other parties preserve the sense that they are traveling through wild and untrammeled country.

When leaving a camping site, be sure that the area is returned to its natural state. Every item which was brought in should be removed, and any evidence of your presence should be erased. The USDA Forest Service discourages the building of cache poles and latrine sites, and any such structures must be dismantled upon departure. Parties who cut poles for wall tents and wish to leave them for later use should lean them against a tree far away from the nearest trail. Bear in mind that it is illegal to cut down a living tree without a permit (which is essentially impossible to obtain). Special minimum impact techniques for horse parties will be discussed later in this section.

In camp, all food must be stowed in a bear-proof manner. This practice may be required by law as early as 1994, and violators may be subject to stiff fines. Food which is hung must be placed at least ten feet above the ground and at least three feet away from the bole of the nearest tree. Alternately, food containers that are proven to be bear-proof can be used for food storage on the ground. A list of bear-resistant food containers that are acceptable under this new regulation will be available at the local Forest Service visitor centers.

The logic behind these new regulations is simple. Once a bear gets food from campers, it will look upon camps as a source of food and lose its natural fear of people. Such bears, which are habituated to the presence of humans, become very dangerous and may later attack other wilderness visitors in their quest for food. Each visitor to Bob Marshall country is responsible for ensuring that this cycle of habituation never gets started. Remember that your carelessness in this matter could cost another visitor his or her life.

In camp, cook all food at least one hundred yards from your tent site, as the odors produced by cooking may attract scavenging bears. Do not keep odor-producing goods, like toothpaste and soap, in a tent where it might attract a curious bear. It is a good idea to avoid wearing scented deodorants or perfumes, and avoid spilling food on your clothes while cooking and eating. Backpacks, saddle gear, and clothing should also be secured out of reach of varmints; the local deer and squirrels are notorious for chewing anything around camp that might contain salt.

Pack train at Gateway Pass.

MINIMUM IMPACT TECHNIQUES FOR STOCK USERS

Stock users must be particularly careful to minimize their impacts when in the backcountry, because poorly-managed stock can be particularly damaging to the environment. On the trail, it is imperative to keep all stock in a single-file line so that the original trail can be maintained in good shape. When approaching a mudhole, try to stick to the center of the trail bed unless there is a great risk of injury to the pack animals. If possible, use llamas rather than horses or mules for carrying supplies. These animals weigh less and have more surface area on their hooves, and thus do less damage to the trails. As an added bonus, the foreign smell of llamas reportedly frightens away curious bears.

In camp, make certain that pack and saddle stock are tied up in a responsible manner. Pack animals should never be tied directly to trees, because they will dig and paw around the base of the trunk, killing the roots and thus the entire tree itself. Instead, set up a "high-line," which is a length of rope tied between two trees. The stock can then be secured at intervals to this rope. Remember to locate the high-line on dry ground and change its location every day if you are camping in the same spot for any length of time.

Animals which are turned out to graze in natural openings should be hobbled or picketed. The locations of picket pins should be rotated every several hours, so that the animal does not have a chance to severely damage any one area. Portable electric fences are a favored method for maintaining stock in one place. The weight of the fence and the installing equipment is typically less than twenty pounds for a fence that will surround a one-acre plot. Remember that these fences must also be moved around frequently to prevent a concentration of damage to one spot. When using an electric fence, train the stock with it at home before coming into the backcountry. It is also a good idea to picket or hobble the leader among the animals, in case the fence is knocked down by passing deer.

Feeding stock animals in the wilderness is one of the greatest challenges faced by stock users. Finding adequate forage in the backcountry is always a problem, and stock parties should bring along sufficient feed for their livestock in case grazing cannot be found. Hay is one of the best feeds, but is heavy and bulky, and thus impractical for short-term expeditions. In addition, hay must be certified to be free of weed seeds; Montana is currently experiencing outbreaks of such noxious weeds as leafy spurge and spotted knapweed, and it would be a disaster if these pests spread into our wilderness areas. It is a good idea to feed stock animals weed-free hay for several days before entering the wilderness, to allow all seeds to move out of the digestive tract. Pelletized rations are popular and contain all the nutrition needed by livestock. However, pelleted feeds do not fill animals up so as to satisfy their hunger and should be supplemented by grazing the animals. Remember that a hungry animal will paw restlessly and damage the environment, while a content animal will do much less damage.

FORDING STREAMS AND RIVERS

In the Bob Marshall country, bridges are rare, and stream and river crossings are most frequently made by fording. Streams are typically highest in early summer, when snowmelt swells the watercourses with silty discharge. Water levels also rise following rainstorms. This phenomenon is especially evident on the Middle Fork of the Flathead River and the Birch Creek drainage, where the 1964 flood stripped away soil and vegetation that once slowed the flow of water into streams. Stream crossings should always be approached with caution; even a shallow stream can harbor slippery stones that can cause a sprained ankle, or worse. However, wilderness travelers can almost always make safe crossings by exercising good judgement and employing a few simple techniques.

When you get to the water's edge, the first thing you'll probably think is, "this is going to be really cold!" It will be even colder if you try to cross barefooted. Since most folks don't like to hike around in wet boots all day, I recommend bringing a pair of lightweight canvas sneakers specifically for the purpose of fording streams. Wearing something on your feet will prevent heat from being conducted from your feet to the stream cobbles, and will give you superior traction for a safer crossing. Walking staffs add additional stability when wading streams. Some manufacturers make special staffs for wading with metal tips, and some even telescope down to manageable proportions. If you use one of these, remember not to lean too hard on it; your legs should be taking most of the burden under all circumstances.

Before entering the stream, unclip your hip belt and other restrictive straps so that you can shuck your pack in case of an emergency. You'll probably never get into a situation where you have to bail out of your pack, but if you do, having the straps undone could save you from drowning. Water up to knee-depth can usually be forded without much difficulty; mid-thigh is the greatest safe depth for crossing unless the water is barely moving. Once you get in up to your crotch, your body starts giving the current a broad profile to push against, and you can bet that it won't be long before you are swimming.

When wading, discipline yourself to take tiny steps. The water will be cold, and your first impulse will be to rush across and get warm again, but this kind of carelessness frequently results in a dunking. While inching your way across, your feet should be seeking the lowest possible footing, so that it is impossible to slip downward any farther. Use boulders sticking out of the streambed as braces for your feet; these boulders will have tiny underwater eddies on their upstream and downstream sides, and thus the force of the current against you will be reduced by a fraction. When emerging from the water, dry off as quickly as possible with an absorbent piece of clothing. If you let the water evaporate from your body, it will take with it additional heat that you could have used to warm up.

Some streams will be narrow, with boulders sticking up from the water beckoning you to hopscotch across without getting your feet wet. Be careful, because you are in prime ankle-spraining country. Rocks that are damp at all may have a film of slippery algae on them, and even dry rocks might be unstable and roll out from underfoot. To avoid calamity, step only on boulders that are completely dry, and do not jump onto an untested boulder, as it may give way. The best policy is to keep one foot on the rocks at all times, so that you have firm footing to fall back on in case a foothold proves to be unstable.

HOW TO FOLLOW A FAINT TRAIL

Many of the trails that appear on maps of the Bob Marshall Wilderness complex are faint or even nonexistent. Visitors to this remote country should have a few elementary trail-finding skills in their bag of tricks in case a trail peters out or a snowfall covers the pathway. A topographic map and compass, and the ability to use them, are essential insurance against disaster when a trail takes a wrong turn or disappears completely. There are also a few tricks that may aid a traveler in such a time of need.

Maintained trails in the Bob Marshall complex are marked in a variety of ways. Signs bearing the name and number of the trail are present at most trail junctions, although weathering and inconsiderate visitors sometimes remove these plaques. The trail signs are usually fashioned of plain wood, with the script carved into them but not painted. They blend in well with the surrounding forest and may go unnoticed at junctions where a major trail meets a lightly-traveled one. These signs rarely contain mileage information, and where they do, the information is often inaccurate.

Along the trail, several kinds of markers indicate the location of maintained trails. In forested areas, cuts in the bark of living trees, known as "blazes," are made immediately beside the path. For a number of years, the USDA Forest Service has used a blaze in the form of an upside-down exclamation point to mark its trails. Visitors should be aware that hunters also use blazes to mark the routes to their kills, but these blazes rarely take the form of the inverted exclamation point. In spots where a trail crosses a gravel streambed or rock outcrop, piles of rocks called "cairns" mark the route. These cairns are typically constructed of three or more stones placed one on top of the other, a formation that almost never occurs naturally.

In the case of an extremely overgrown trail, markings of any kind may be impossible to find. On such a trail, the techniques used to build the trail serve as clues to its location. Well-constructed trails have rather wide, flat beds. Let your feet seek the flat spots when traveling through tall brush, and you will almost always find yourself on the trail. Old sawed logs from previous trail maintenance can be used to navigate in spots where the trail bed is obscured; if you find a sawed log, then you must be on a trail that was maintained at some point in time. Switchbacks are also a sure sign of an official trail; wild game travel in straight lines, and horsemen traveling off-trail seldom bother to zigzag across hillsides.

Trail specifications often call for the clearing of all trees and branches for several feet on each side of a trail. In a forest situation, this results in a distinct "hall of trees" effect, where a corridor of cleared vegetation extends continuously through the woods. Trees grow randomly in a natural situation, so a long, thin clearing bordered by tree trunks usually indicates an old trail bed. On more open ground, look for trees that have lost all of their lower branches on only one side. Such trees often indicate a spot where the old trail once passed close to a lone tree.

When attempting to find a trail that has disappeared, ask yourself where the most logical place would be to build a trail given its source and destination. Trailbuilders tend to seek level ground where it is available and often follow the natural contours of streamcourses and ridgelines. Bear in mind that most Forest Service trails avoid up-and-down motion in favor of long, sustained grades culminating in major passes or hilltops. Old trail beds can sometimes be spotted from a distance as they cut across hillsides at a constant angle.

Previous travelers can also leave clues to the location of old trails. Foot prints and horseshoe marks are the most obvious signs. The presence of clover in a trail bed is a good sign that horses have been there. This plant is not native to Montana and arrives in the wilderness via the feces of traveling pack animals.

Forest Service blaze on a tree trunk.

The "hall-of-trees" effect.

A lone tree lost its branches on one side to accommodate the trail.

A Forest Service trail crew constructs rock cribbing to prevent rockslides.

USING THE GUIDE

The primary intent of this guide is to provide information that will help hikers choose backpacking trips according to their desires and abilities, as well to provide a detailed description of the trail system for interpretation of the natural features found along the trails. This guide is intended to be used in conjunction with topographic maps, which can be purchased at ranger stations, local gift and sporting goods stores, or through the U.S. Geological Survey, Denver, CO 80225. A 1:100,000 scale topo map of the entire wilderness complex gives a general impression of the landforms that will be encountered; 1:24,000 scale quadrangle maps are available for those desiring greater detail. The appropriate quadrangle maps are listed for each featured hike in the Guide.

Each trail description begins with an outline describing the physical characteristics of the trail for quick and easy reference. Distances are listed first in miles, followed by a brief section describing the hike type: day hike, backpack, extended trip, or wilderness route. Extended trips cannot be reached by road, while wilderness routes represent abandoned trails and cross-country routes, where the only indication of a trail might be an occasional blazed tree. This description is followed by a difficulty rating. The difficulty rating can be interpreted as follows: *Easy* trails can be completed without difficulty by hikers of all abilities. Hikes rated *Moderate* will challenge novices. *Moderately Strenuous* hikes will tax even experienced hikers, and *Strenuous* trails will push the physical limits of the most Herculean hiker.

Trail maintenance level is divided into four categories. *Yearly* maintenance is performed early in the summer, and these trails are easy to find and have no obstructions to passage. Trails receiving *frequent* maintenance are cleared at least every other year; one might expect to find a bit of downed timber on such a trail, but the path is generally obvious and easy to follow. Trails maintained on an *occasional* basis are cleared on a three- to four-year rotation and are typically rather overgrown and may be a bit tricky to follow. Downed timber is often common on such trails, and horse parties should probably avoid them. Trails receiving *rare* maintenance, on a five or more year rotation, have often disappeared entirely in sections and are usually choked with brush and downed trees.

The traffic that a trail receives is recorded as an adaptation of the Forest Service Opportunity Class system. This information was gathered through monitoring the numbers of encounters that USDA Forest Service personnel had with other visitors on the trail. Trails receiving *very light* use offer an eighty percent chance of having no encounters with other visitors in a day of traveling. *Light* use indicates an eighty percent probability of meeting one party, or none, in a day. *Moderate* traffic indicates an eighty percent chance of meeting three or fewer parties, while *heavy*-use trails offer an eighty percent probability of seeing five or fewer other groups. This information should be taken into account when planning a trip: Trails that receive heavy use are usually muddy in wet weather, while solitude seekers will want to find trails that receive light or very light use. Finally, altitude gain and loss, maximum trail elevation, topo maps required for the hike, and directions to the trailhead are listed.

Following this statistical section is a mile-by-mile description of landmarks, trail junctions, and gradient changes. Distances were developed using an instrument called a planimeter, which measures two-dimensional distances on a topographic map. These distances were then corrected for altitude gain or loss. The resulting mileages should be looked upon as conservative estimates, because they do not account for small-scale twists and turns or minor ups and downs. These mileages are, however, more reliable than the distances posted on the few old trail signs that are scattered at random throughout the wilderness complex.

The reference section is followed by a detailed interpretive description of the trail, including geologic and ecological features, fishing opportunities, campsites, and other important information. Photographs have been included to give the reader a visual preview of some of the prominent features seen along the trail. An elevation profile accompanies each trail description and provides a schematic look at the major elevation gains and losses incurred during the trip.

North Boundary

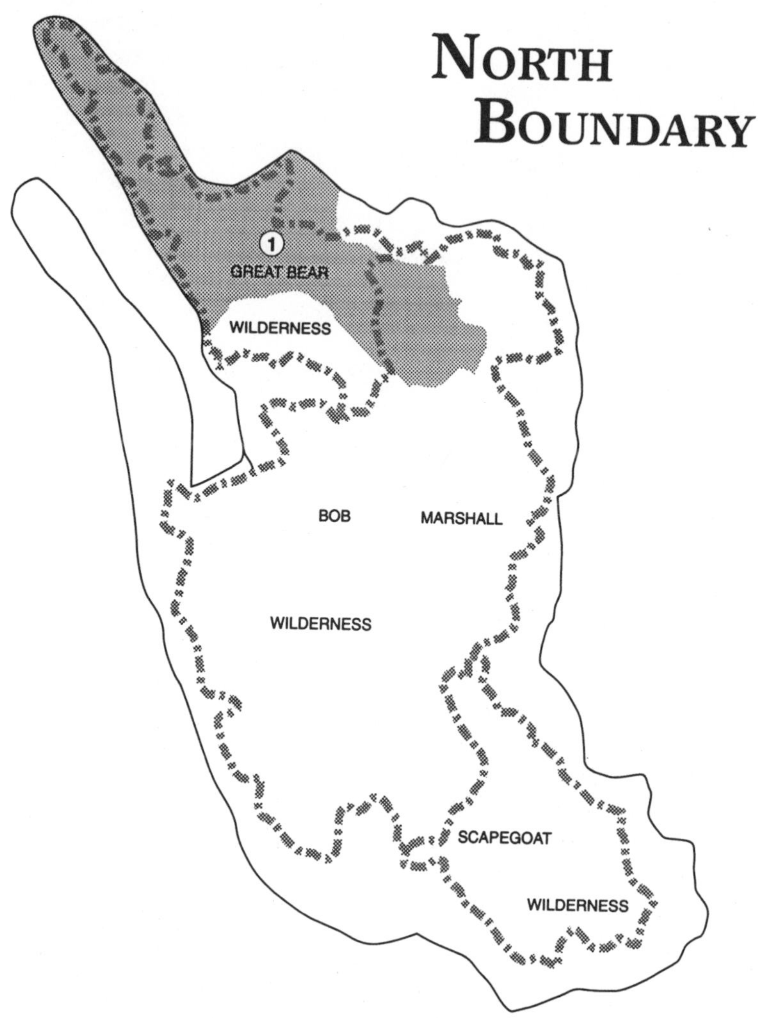

The northern part of the Bob Marshall country is defined by the valley of the Middle Fork of the Flathead River. This mighty stream, sometimes referred to as the "Big River," drains a basin some millions of acres in extent, including the majority of the Great Bear Wilderness, a small portion of the Bob Marshall, and the southwestern part of Glacier National Park. Many of the hikes featured here require travelers to ford the Middle Fork, which is a hazardous proposition even when conditions are favorable. The river runs high and discolored through June, as the snowpack in the surrounding mountains melts and feeds the raging torrent. Both foot and stock parties should plan trips across the river between mid-summer and late fall, when low water levels make safe crossings possible. Even so, the river responds quickly to rainstorms, becoming impassable for several days following a sustained downpour. If your trip takes you across this river, plan alternate routes out and pack extra food in case you have to wait a few days to cross.

The Flathead Range dominates the lower valley of the Middle Fork, with its peaks rising sheer 4,000 feet above the valley floor. This range creates its own climate, with abundant rainfall that sustains a lush growth of vegetation in its glacier-carved valleys. Forest openings tend to be brushy, and trails that are maintained infrequently tend to get swallowed up in a jungle of greenery. Visibility is often a problem on these trails, so remember to make lots of noise to warn bears of your presence. The upper basin of the Middle Fork is quite a bit drier, with forested hills to the north and the craggy Trilobite Range to the south. Lodgepole pines cover the well-drained slopes of the upper basin, while spruce forests dominate the moister bottomlands.

Travelers can find most services in Hungry Horse and West Glacier, while the nearest outlet for backpacking supplies is in Columbia Falls. The town of Essex is really little more than an elaborate hotel and resort, while there are roadside cafes and gas stations scattered along the length of U.S. Highway 2. Most of the trails discussed in this chapter fall under the jurisdiction of the Hungry Horse Ranger District, although the Middle Fork valley above Granite Creek is administered by the Spotted Bear Ranger District. There is a USDA Forest Service cabin at the Geifer Creek trailhead which is rented out to visitors; call the Hungry Horse Ranger Station for more information on reservations.

TRAIL 1 *OUSEL PEAK*

Trail 331
General description: A stiff day hike from the highway to timberline on Ousel Peak, 2.6 mi. (4.2 km).
Difficulty: Strenuous
Trail maintenance: Occasional
Traffic: Very Light
Elevation gain: 3,260 ft.
Maximum elevation: 6,600 ft.
Topo maps: West Glacier, Nyack.
Finding the trailhead: The trail begins at a trailhead sign on a blind corner at mile 159.6 on U. S. Highway 2, 6 miles east of the town of West Glacier.

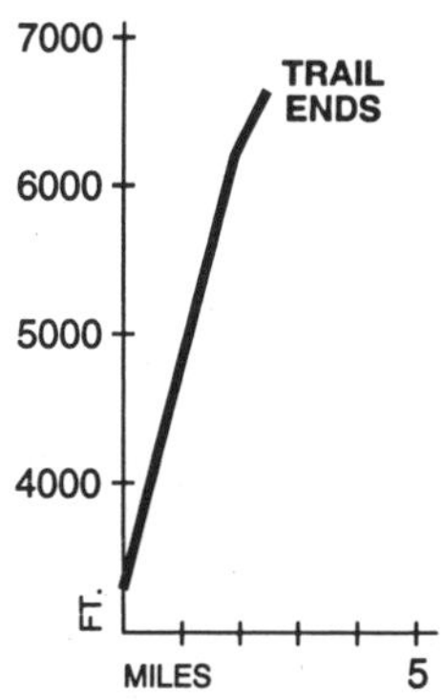

0.0 Trailhead on US 2
2.3 Trail peters out atop Ousel Peak

The trail: This hike follows a rather steep and little-used trail up Ousel Peak, which boasts views of the northern peaks of the Flathead Range and Glacier National Park on the far side of the Middle Fork of the Flathead. Travelers should expect to cross a few deadfalls and brushy spots; horse travel is not recommended here. There is a route across the summit of Ousel Peak to link up with Trail 388, which descends toward Hungry Horse Reservoir. This route is not marked and should be attempted only by experienced route finders.

From its beginning on the west side of the highway, the trail climbs rather steeply through the lodgepole pine forest that covers the north-facing slope of Ousel Peak.

After a brief ascent, the trail makes its way into a tiny dell occupied by a gurgling rivulet. The damp microclimate found here supports a lush growth of coastal vegetation, dominated by cedars and birches in the canopy, and featuring mosses and false Solomonseal in the understory. This moist depression soon gives way to well-drained slopes again, and lodgepole pine and an occasional larch block out the views as the trail resumes its climb. As the trail continues its ascent up the north side of the ridge, the understory of scattered thimbleberry bushes gives way to a dense undergrowth of false huckleberry, which collects water in wet weather and provides travelers with a thorough soaking for no extra charge. Along the upper part of the route, there are breaks in the forest canopy that allow glimpses across the river into Glacier National Park. Mounts Stanton, Vaught, and Heavens Peak can be seen across the low rise of Snyder Ridge, while the picturesque spires surrounding Gunsight Pass rise farther to the south.

TRAIL 1 *OUSEL PEAK*

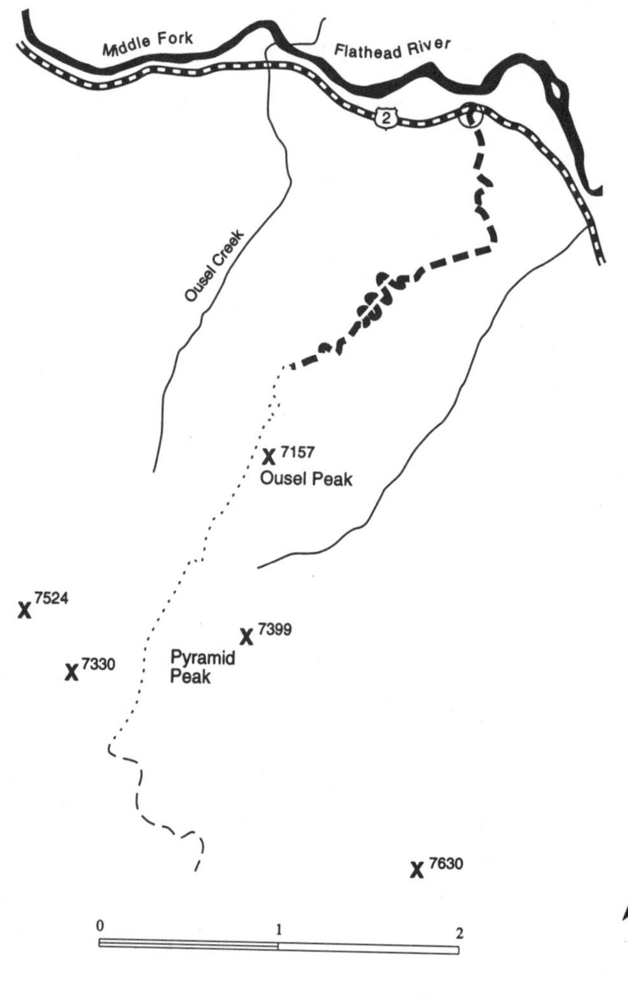

The trail continues to climb and leaves the lowland forest for spruce and fir above. After crossing several wooded benches, the route makes its way to the first false summit on the crest of the ridge. This high point boasts northward views of Harrison Lake, which lies nestled in the verdant forests below the glacier-clad slopes of Blackfoot Mountain. The trail runs southwest along the crest of the ridge, dropping into a low saddle before resuming its ascent up the next series of humps. After winding onto the eastern slope of the ridge, the trail climbs to the top of the next rise, where it enters the site of an old burn. The trail becomes tough to follow as it picks its way through the burned stumps left behind by the blaze; look for the route cutting across the face of the next rise to the southwest. The trail enters a pocket of subalpine fir untouched by the fire as it wanders out onto the eastern slope of the ridge. The route soon makes its way into open meadows that allow excellent views of Pyramid Peak, which rises just across a narrow valley to the south. Beyond it, the other summits of the Flathead Range trail away into the distance.

The trail continues to follow the ridgeline back into the old burn, finally petering out on the last rise before the summit of Ousel Peak. It is possible for a hiker with good wilderness skills to follow the ridgetop across the summit of Ousel Peak to link up with Trail 331 on the southern flank of the mountain. This trail is difficult to locate in its upper reaches and requires a lot of map-reading and patience to find. The Forest Service plans to mark the route with cairns, but as of this writing, the route remains unmarked.

Triangle Peak rears its head along the crest of the Flathead Range.

TRAIL 2 *GRANT RIDGE LOOP*

Trail 146, 339
General description: A day hike or short backpack, 9.0 mi. (14.5 km) round trip.
Difficulty: Moderately strenuous
Trail maintenance: Occasional
Traffic: Moderate
Elevation gain: 3,605 ft.
Elevation loss: 3,600 ft.
Maximum elevation: 6,850 ft.
Topo maps: Stanton Lake, Pinnacle.
Finding the trailhead: The trail begins at the Stanton Lake trailhead, at mile 169.9 on U.S. Highway 2, 16 miles east of the town of West Glacier. The terminus of the route is 0.5 mile to the south along the highway and is marked by a sign for the Grant Ridge trail. No parking is available here.

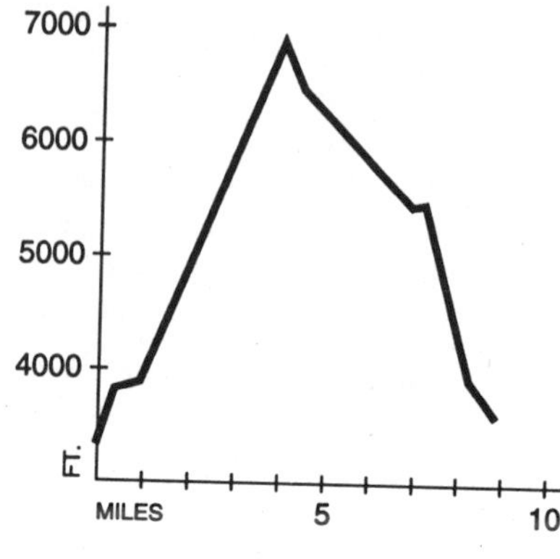

0.0 Trailhead
0.9 Junction with trail to Stanton Lake. Stay left for the Grant Ridge Loop.
4.0 Trail reaches saddle on Grant Ridge.
9.0 Trail reaches US 2, completing the loop.

The trail: The Grant Ridge Loop provides a long day trip to the high country at the foot of Great Northern Mountain. Along with excellent views of the glacier-clad crest of the Flathead Range, this trail offers an outstanding opportunity to view such wildlife as golden eagles and mountain goats. There is no water along the trail, so hikers should bring along their own supply. Climbers can use the trail as an approach route to Great Northern Mountain, although the southwestern approach is much shorter and thus more popular.

The hike begins as a gentle climb through a stand of scattered western larch, survivors of a low-intensity forest fire. While the thick bark of the larches protected them from the direct effects of the fire, the blaze altered the structure of the forest in a way that will spell doom for many of these stout giants. The open canopy created by the burn allows strong gusts of wind to enter the stand, catching the trees broadside and pitching them over during winter windstorms. The enormous boles of wind-thrown trees litter the forest here, a silent testimonial to the power of these winter storms. As the trail enters the valley of Stanton Creek, it follows along the hillside far above the rushing waters. The grade is quite level here, and the trail even descends a bit before reaching an unmarked fork. The trail to the right runs 0.25 mile to reach the northeastern shore of Stanton Lake, a glacier-carved expanse of water that is well worth the short side trip. This trail continues along the north shore of the lake through jungles of cow parsnip and bracken fern before petering out in the valley above the lake.

Meanwhile, the left fork is the Grant Ridge trail, which descends to a knee-deep

TRAIL 2 *GRANT RIDGE LOOP*

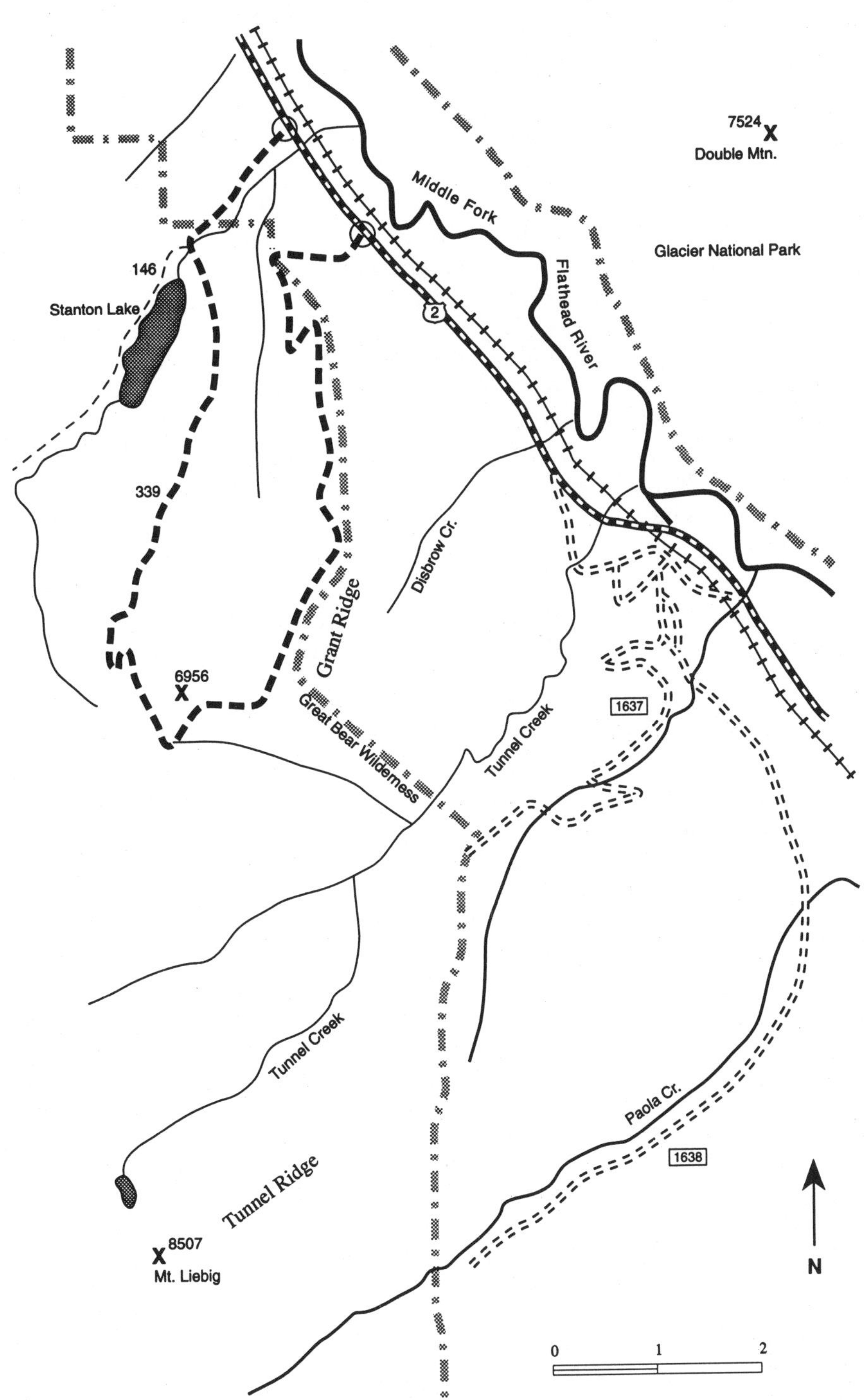

ford of Stanton Creek on its way to Grant Ridge. After crossing the stream, the trail climbs gradually up the side of the ridge, following the southward course of the valley. The lowland forest of larch gives way to lodgepole-dominated slopes and brushy couloirs. After a steady climb, the trail enters a sparse subalpine forest with a beargrass understory. A backward glance reveals the horn peaks at the head of Pinchot Creek in Glacier National Park, while across the Stanton Valley lie the rocky spur ridges that protrude from the south face of Nyack Mountain.

As the trail continues around the side of the ridge, Great Northern Mountain swings into view at the head of the valley. This loftiest peak of the Flathead Range dominates the lesser peaks surrounding it; its tilted strata resemble the carelessly-stacked volumes in an enormous and run-down library. As the trail continues to climb across beargrass-clad slopes, it rounds the western flank of the ridge to enter a rocky bowl crowned with ragged fir. The trail continues to climb as it runs southward toward a high col near the head of this basin. Upon reaching the saddle, the trail gets a bit sketchy; turn north and follow the ridgeline for a short distance to pick up the trail cutting across the southeast slope of the next high point along the ridge crest.

The route maintains a level gradient as it passes below this first summit, then swings eastward below the ridgeline. Looking southwest through a scattering of ancient whitebark pine, you'll see Mount Grant and its enormous glacier at the head of the Tunnel Creek valley, seemingly only a stone's throw away. Golden eagles cruise the thermals above this panorama of windswept snowfields and rugged outcrops, searching for tasty ground squirrels and marmots that take shelter among the boulder fields and alpine meadows. To the east, the Cloudcroft Peaks can be seen in the distance, rising above the Coal Creek country of Glacier National Park. The ridgetop descends to meet the trail, whereupon the route follows the crest of the ridge for a short distance. After crossing the next saddle, the trail swings onto the north slope of the ridge to pass below the next summit.

After reaching the ridgeline once more, the trail continues its descent along the spine of the ridge, as subalpine fir give way to a montane forest of lodgepole pines. The trail then departs the ridgeline to return to the northern slope of the ridge, where it makes a long descent with a number of switchbacks. Young western larch blankets this well-drained slope, turning a brilliant yellow in October before dropping their needles for the winter. The trail bottoms out on a series of moist, timbered benches, and runs eastward through Douglas-fir and older larch. Finally, as the trail nears the highway, it swings northward once more for the final descent to reach the highway, 0.5 mile south of the Stanton Lake trailhead.

TRAIL 3 *DICKEY LAKE*

Trail 149

General description: A day hike from the road to Dickey Lake, 2.4 mi. (3.9 km).

Difficulty: Moderate to head of valley, strenuous to lake.

Trail maintenance: Occasional.

Traffic: Light.

Elevation gain: 1,460 ft.

A lone boulder protrudes from Dickey Lake.

Maximum elevation: 6,040 ft.
Topo map: Pinnacle.
Finding the trailhead: Take the Dickey Creek Road from the north end of the settlement of Essex on U. S. Highway 2. This improved gravel road crosses the railroad tracks and forks; take the right fork for three miles up the Dickey Creek Valley to reach a sharp leftward curve in the road. At this point, an unimproved road climbs to the right for 25 yards to reach the unmarked trailhead parking lot beside Dickey Creek.

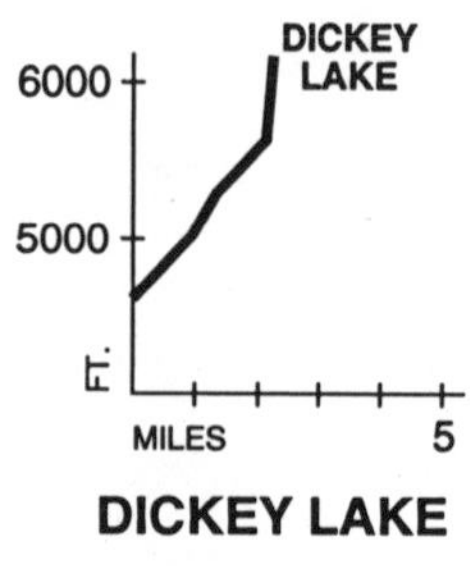

0.0 Trailhead.
0.9 End of old forest road.
2.2 Trail peters out.
2.4 Dickey Lake.

The trail: The Dickey Creek trail is a seldom-used route that follows an old access road up the rather open valley of Dickey Creek. The trail peters out at the foot of the headwall below the lake; a steep scramble is necessary to reach the shores of this scenic gem. This final pitch is far too steep for horses, and is a bit hazardous even for hikers who are unaccustomed to off-trail travel.

The trail begins by crossing a berm and making a frigid mid-calf-depth ford of Dickey Creek. The trail follows an old brush-choked jeep trail up the North Fork of

TRAIL 3 *DICKEY LAKE*
TRAIL 4 *MARION LAKE*

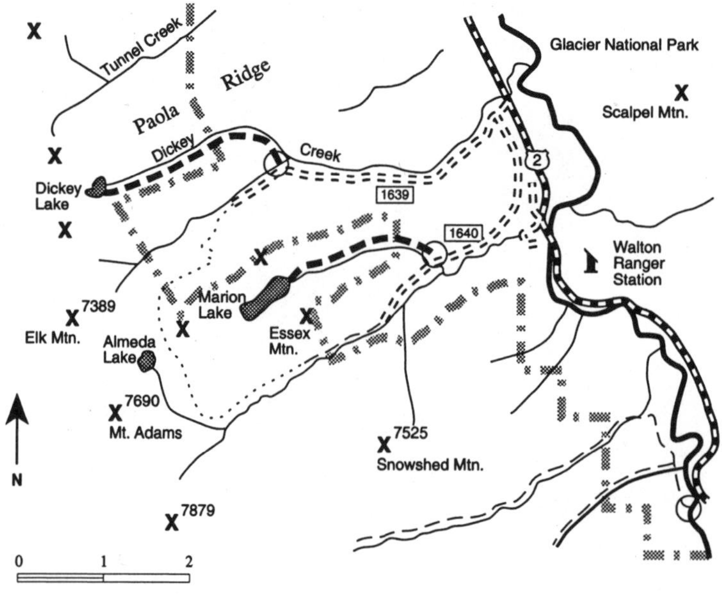

Dickey Creek, which climbs gently as it follows the curve of the valley around to the west. After a mile, the trail leaves the old road behind and continues its gradual ascent through brush fields of cow parsnip, elderberry, and alder. The lack of forest cover allows sweeping views of the steep, glacier-carved walls that crowd the narrow valley on both sides. The trail passes through a stand of gigantic old-growth subalpine fir, then wanders through the brush on its way to a willow-dominated floodplain. The path then continues its leisurely climb, crossing a spring with a deceptively boggy mud bottom before passing a first set of waterfalls. Frequent avalanches keep the surrounding slopes bare of trees, while the more flexible underbrush thrives in these openings.

As the trail approaches the head of the valley, it crosses a series of springs that bubble up among the debris left by perennial snow slides. The trail ends here, but a route can be found by crossing the boulder field that crowds the south bank of the stream and climbing up the headwall just to the left of an extensive brush field. About halfway up, the route swings northward into the brush, climbing even more steeply before it finally reaches the high shelf containing Dickey Lake. This high alpine tarn occupies a glacier-carved cirque at the foot of sheer cliffs which remain snow-clad well into July. Dark boulders rise from the eerie chalk-green waters of the lake, which is stocked aerially with trout from time to time by state fisheries personnel.

TRAIL 4 *MARION LAKE*

Trail 150
General description: A day hike from the road to Marion Lake, 1.7 mi. (2.7 km).
Difficulty: Moderately strenuous.
Trail maintenance: Yearly.
Traffic: Moderate.
Elevation gain: 1,810 ft.
Maximum elevation: 5,920 ft.
Topo map: Pinnacle.

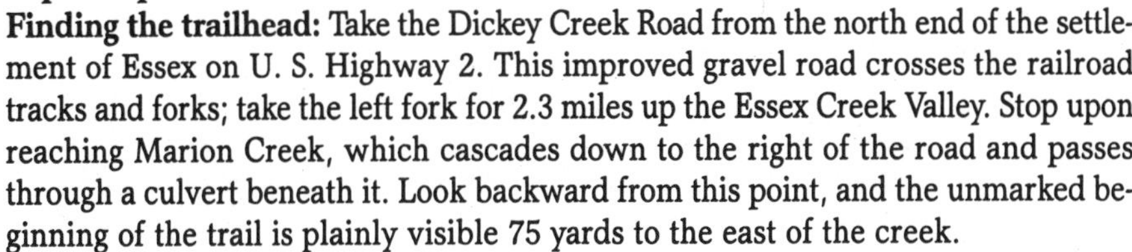

Finding the trailhead: Take the Dickey Creek Road from the north end of the settlement of Essex on U. S. Highway 2. This improved gravel road crosses the railroad tracks and forks; take the left fork for 2.3 miles up the Essex Creek Valley. Stop upon reaching Marion Creek, which cascades down to the right of the road and passes through a culvert beneath it. Look backward from this point, and the unmarked beginning of the trail is plainly visible 75 yards to the east of the creek.

0.0 Trailhead.
1.7 Marion Lake.

The trail: The Marion Lake trail is a short and rather popular hike that provides access to a montane lake surrounded by spruce forest and overlooked by a picturesque but nameless peak. The trail is suitable for both horses and hikers and is also a winter destination for adventuresome cross-country skiers.

The trail begins in a grove of young Douglas-fir, topped by a scattering of old larch.

Douglas-fir seedlings are superior competitors in the shady realm beneath the forest canopy and will ultimately take over the canopy if the forest remains undisturbed by fire and logging. The trail climbs steeply up the hill, then swings westward into the valley of Marion Creek. Openings in the forest allow views of the forest-clad hogback of Essex Mountain, which rims the southern side of the valley. The well-defined route makes its way through progressively larger and more brushy forest openings, interspersed with stands of old Douglas-fir. Thimbleberries grow thickly here, providing a late-summer feast for hikers and bears alike.

The grade of the trail steepens as it continues westward through the brush, and rushing falls can be glimpsed in the valley bottom far below. Shortly thereafter, the trail levels out as the creek valley flattens on its final approach to the lake. False huckleberries become quite dense in the understory, and scattered spruces rise overhead as the trail reaches the south shore of the lake. A thick boom of driftwood clogs the outlet of the lake, and the still waters beyond it reflect a nameless summit at the head of the glacier-carved valley.

TRAIL 5 *VINEGAR MOUNTAIN*

Trail 155, 260, 323

General description: A backpack from the Nimrod trailhead to Twentyfive Mile Creek, 14.4 mi. (23.2 km).

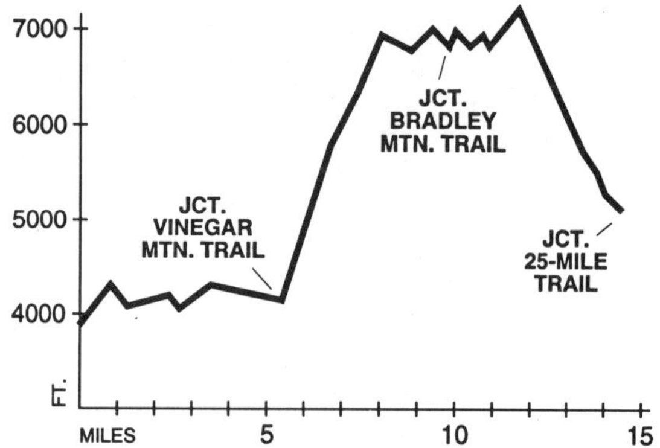

Difficulty: Moderately strenuous.

Trail maintenance: Yearly on Vinegar Mountain, occasional on Mount Bradley.

Traffic: Light (beyond Spruce Park).

Elevation gain: 4,103 ft.

Elevation loss: 2,893 ft.

Maximum elevation: 7,190 ft. (on the Mount Bradley Trail)

Topo maps: Nimrod, Mount Bradley.

Finding the trailhead: Start from the Nimrod trailhead, at mile 184.8 on U. S. Highway 2.

0.0 Nimrod Trailhead
0.1 Pack bridge over Bear Creek.
1.0 Trail crosses Edna Creek.
1.1 Junction with Tranquil Basin trail. Stay right for Vinegar Mountain.
2.6 Trail crosses Spruce Creek.
5.4 Spruce Park. Junction with Vinegar Mountain Trail. Turn left.
9.8 Junction with Mount Bradley Trail (323). Turn right for Mount Bradley.

11.8 High point of trail beyond the summit of Mount Bradley.
14.4 Junction with Twentyfive Mile Creek trail.

The trail: The Vinegar Mountain trail climbs high into the mountains that rise above the Middle Fork of the Flathead. Once on top, the trail crosses through open alpine country on its way across Mount Bradley before descending back into the river valley. Water sources are difficult to come by in late summer, and the Mount Bradley section of the trail receives a lower level of maintenance and may be hard to follow. The Vinegar Mountain trail also links up with the Devil Creek trail, offering the potential for extended loop trips.

From the Nimrod trailhead, turn east to cross the bridge over Bear Creek and embark upon the Big River Trail (155). This trail winds around through the timber for a mile or so before turning southwest and crossing Edna Creek. After passing the Edna Creek Trail (489), the Big River trail crosses openings that boast views of the river and the steep cutbanks surrounding it. Several miles further on, the trail descends rather steeply to reach a calf-deep ford of Spruce Creek before submerging itself into the forested lowlands that border the river. Wide puddles collect on the trail after summer rainstorms, making the going quite muddy in places. Views are limited for the next 2.5 miles; the trail finally emerges beside the river just before reaching Spruce Park.

From Spruce Park, the Vinegar Mountain trail departs the Big River trail at a marked intersection. This trail crosses a series of wooded benches and then runs northward as it climbs for almost a full mile before making a dogleg back to the east. Soon after, the dense Douglas-fir gives way to open groves of pine and spruce, revealing Spruce Point across the river. Beargrass and huckleberries dominate the understory as the trail climbs over the ridgeline and into the broad, horseshoe-shaped basin that represents the head of the Vinegar Creek valley. Some of the best views of the Flathead Range can be had from this point; Red Sky Mountain and Mount Baptiste are the most prominent of the peaks that line Charlie Creek on the far side of the Middle Fork valley.

The trail climb's more gently as it crosses the open fields of beargrass that line the bowl. The entire population of beargrass blooms synchronously every three to five years, unleashing a flowery spectacle of white bulbs on bloom years. After passing one saddle, the trail crosses a southern slope of Forster Mountain. About halfway across this slope is the old trailbed from a route that once climbed to the top of the mountain; stick to the lowermost trail to continue the trek. The trail then descends gradually to the pass beyond, where it reaches a junction with a trail that runs northward down the valley of Moose Creek. Meanwhile, the Mount Bradley trail climbs up the hillside beyond the pass and continues to follow the ridgetops southeast.

The Mount Bradley Option. The Mount Bradley trail receives a lower level of maintenance than the rest of the Vinegar Mountain trail, and may be difficult to follow in places. Nevertheless, it offers the loftiest traveling in the area, and boasts spectacular views as it follows the windswept ridgetops toward the valley of Twentyfive Mile Creek. Plan on using a detailed topographic map for this section of the trail.

TRAIL 5 *VINEGAR MOUNTAIN*

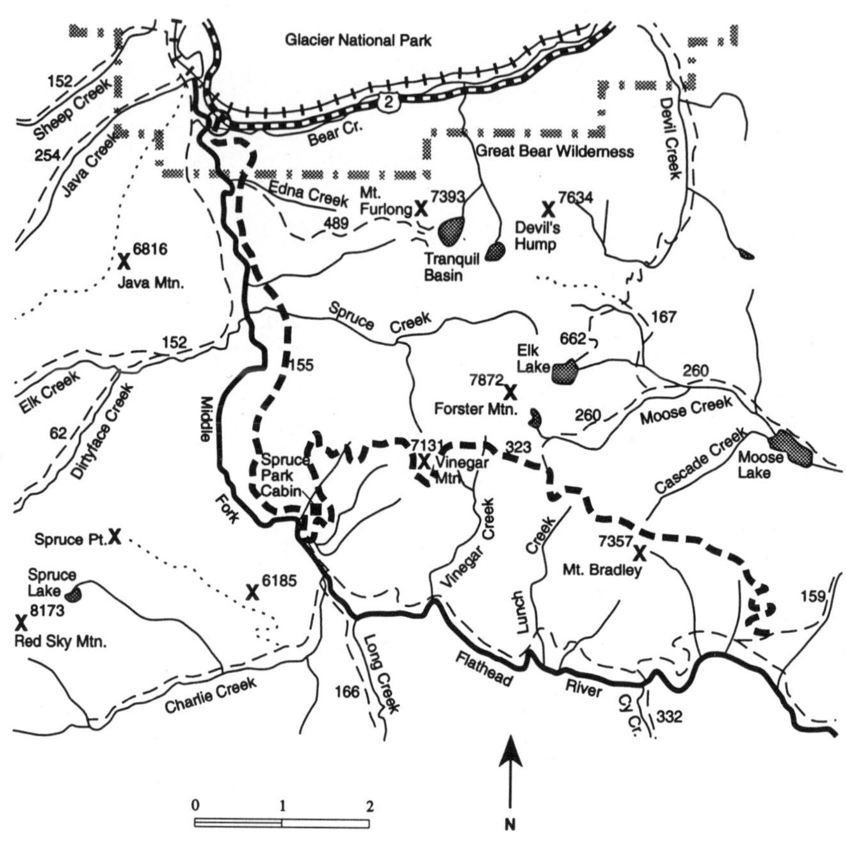

Beyond the junction, the Mount Bradley Trail climbs steadily southward to reach the edge of a spur ridge. Views from this point are highlighted by the rocky peaks of Twin Peak and Hematite Mountain across the valley of the Middle Fork. After rounding the ridgeline, the trail resumes an easterly course as it makes its way to the next saddle. Here, the path becomes quite faint; follow cairns up the west slope of Mount Bradley to find the trail as it cuts across the north face of the peak. Dwarfed subalpine fir cling to a precarious existence at this high altitude, and the tundra bursts into a profusion of blossoms during the brief alpine summer. Beyond Mount Bradley, the trail reaches the top of a rocky ridge that boasts fantastic views of the surrounding ranges. The snowy crest of Silvertip Mountain can be seen far to the south, beyond the closer summit of Horseshoe Peak. The spires of Glacier National Park crowd the northern horizon, and the Gable Peaks can be seen by looking up the valley of the Middle Fork.

The trail crowds the ridgeline as it continues eastward, reaching its high point on a rocky knob before beginning a gradual descent through an old burn. The trail becomes a bit faint as it drops onto the south side of the ridge. As the trail enters a shallow basin covered in lodgepole pines, the sweeping vistas disappear, and the trail curves off to the south as it continues to descend. Upon rounding the hillside onto the southeastern slope of the ridge, the gradient steepens to a steady, switchbacking descent to the east of a stream-bearing ravine. Gaps in the foliage above allow views of the cliffs of Patrol Ridge, which rises to the east across the valley of Twentyfive Mile Creek. The descent soon becomes rather monotonous, finally reaching the trail's end at a junction with the Twentyfive Mile Creek Trail (159) about a third of a mile east of its junction with the Big River trail.

TRAIL 6 *TRANQUIL BASIN OVERLOOK*

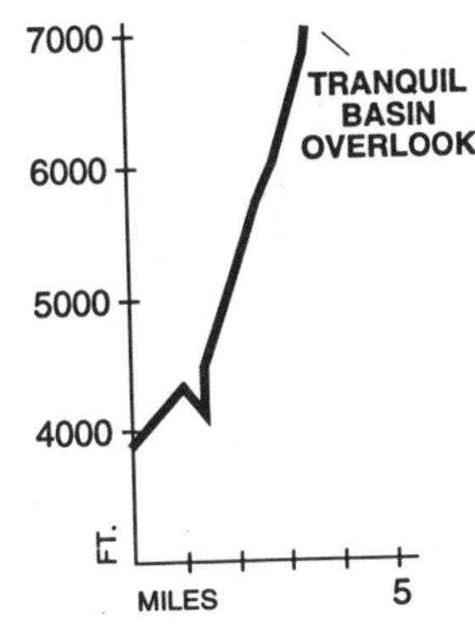

Trail 155, 489 (see map on p. 31)
General description: A day hike from the Nimrod trailhead to the Tranquil Basin Overlook, 3.5 mi. (5.6 km).
Difficulty: Strenuous.
Trail maintenance: Occasional.
Traffic: Moderate.
Elevation gain: 3,270 ft.
Elevation loss: 150 ft.
Maximum elevation: 7,010 ft.
Topo map: Nimrod.
Finding the trailhead: Start at the Nimrod trailhead, at mile 184.8 on U.S. Highway 2.

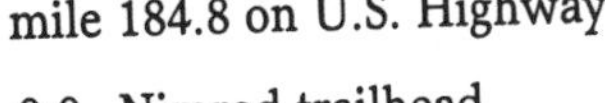

0.0 Nimrod trailhead.
0.1 Pack bridge over Bear Creek.
1.0 Trail crosses Edna Creek.
1.1 Junction with Edna Creek Trail. Turn left for the overlook.
3.5 Tranquil Basin Overlook.

The trail: This trail provides a rigorous day hike to the top of a high ridgeline, just behind the summit of Mount Furlong. The overlook boasts excellent views of the snowy peaks of the Flathead Range, the lakes of the Tranquil Basin, and the twisted spires that rise in the distance to the north of Marias Pass. From the overlook, it is possible to scramble down to reach the floor of the Tranquil Basin.

From the trailhead, cross the pack bridge over Bear Creek to reach the beginning of the Big River Trail (155). Follow this trail as it climbs around a series of low, forested hills before turning southwest to follow the course of the Middle Fork of the Flathead River. The trail descends for a short distance before reaching Edna Creek, a small but substantial tributary that courses downward from the slopes of Mount Furlong. Fifty yards beyond this stream lies the junction with the trail to the Tranquil Basin Overlook, which is marked "Edna Creek Trail 489."

This narrow track wastes no time in running uphill as steeply as possible. At first, the trail follows the low ridge directly above Edna Creek. Later, the trail leaves the

Mount Forster framed by the cliffs of the Tranquil Basin.

stream behind and bends around to the east as it climbs high onto a western spur of Mount Furlong. The trail climbs aggressively up the side of this ridge, through a forest of Douglas-fir underlain by an abundant growth of thimbleberry bushes. After the first mile, the ascent relents a bit, but the grueling climb resumes 0.5 mile later. As the route wanders onto the north slope of the ridge, alder-choked openings offer brief glimpses down the Middle Fork Valley.

The trail then runs through a saddle and onto the southern face of the ridge, still climbing eastward through open timber and huckleberries. Across the river valley, the snowy crest of the Flathead Range marches in an orderly procession across the western skyline. To the south lie the drier tundra-clad summits of Forster and Vinegar mountains. The views continue to improve as the trail wends its way into a steep-sided bowl covered in beargrass and studded with a few hardy subalpine fir. The trail climbs across the face of this bowl and passes into an almost identical cirque on its way to the high col behind Mount Furlong.

The views form this saddle are nothing less than inspiring, with the clear, cold pools of the Tranquil Basin resting just below in a subalpine parkland surrounded by low cliffs. A short jaunt to the south reveals distant views of Little Dog and Summit mountains rising to the north. Mount Cameahwait rises prominently among the stately summits of the Flathead Range, and Great Northern Mountain is the highest visible peak in the northern marches of the range. There is no trail descending to the lakes of the Tranquil Basin, although it is possible to follow the ridge crest south from the overlook to reach a relatively safe route of descent.

TRAIL 7 *DEVIL CREEK*

Trail 167, 602, 260

General description: A backpack from Devil Creek campground to Elk Lake, 5.9 mi.(9.5 km); to foot of Moose Lake, 8.2 mi. (13.2 km).

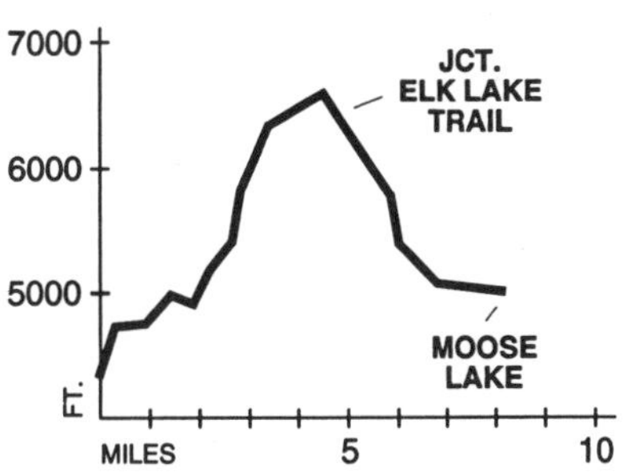

Difficulty: Moderate.
Trail maintenance: Yearly.
Traffic: Moderate.
Elevation gain: 2,106 ft.
Elevation loss: 1,556 ft.
Maximum elevation: 6,506 ft.
Topo maps: Blacktail, Mount Bradley.

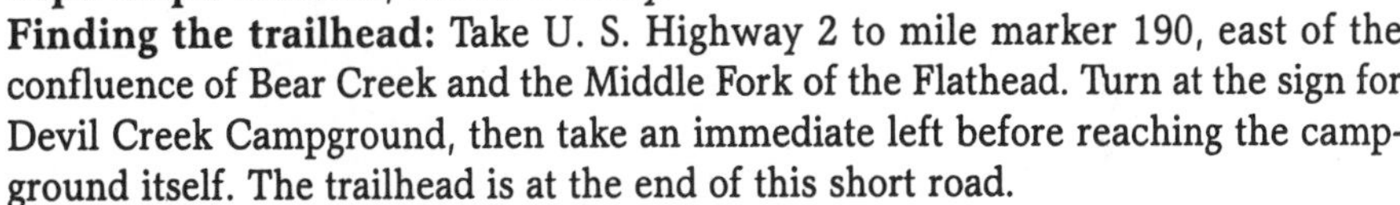

Finding the trailhead: Take U. S. Highway 2 to mile marker 190, east of the confluence of Bear Creek and the Middle Fork of the Flathead. Turn at the sign for Devil Creek Campground, then take an immediate left before reaching the campground itself. The trailhead is at the end of this short road.

- 0.0 Trailhead at Devil Creek Campground.
- 2.7 Trail fords Devil Creek to its west bank.
- 4.6 Trail reaches saddle into Moose Creek valley.
- 4.8 Junction with Elk Lake and Moose Creek trails; stay straight for Elk Lake; turn left for Moose Lake.
- 6.1 Junction with connector trail to Vinegar Mountain.
- 7.8 Head of Moose Lake.
- 8.2 Foot of Moose Lake.

The trail: This trail provides an access route for backpackers and stock parties bound for the Moose Creek basin. Elk and Moose lakes provide fishing potential, while the scenery is typified by steep but relatively small mountains and subalpine to alpine plant communities. This trail can be combined with the Vinegar Mountain trail in several ways to create loop trips of varying lengths.

From the Devil Creek campground, the trail climbs steadily southward through the narrow canyon of lower Devil Creek. The canyon soon opens out into a broad valley, and the gradient of the trail eases off into a series of flat benches interspersed with short bursts of climbing. Early on, openings in the forest allow pleasant views of the nameless peaks that surround the upper end of the valley.

The trail continues its gradual climb as it crosses a small tributary stream and makes its way across brushy avalanche fields. On the far side of the valley looms the bulky mass of Devil's Hump, with its low outcroppings of bedrock forming overhangs and shallow caves. As the trail continues to climb into the upper part of the valley, patches of timber alternate with brushy openings. This section of the trail can be quite a quagmire following a soaking rain. The trail descends to the creek bottom for a time, crossing gravel outwash before returning to the more stable footing of the hillside. As the valley bottom steepens, the trail maintains a moderate uphill grade until the trail nears the stream bank beside a series of dancing cascades. Shortly thereafter, the trail fords the creek to its west bank (the stream course is choked with fallen logs that offer *ad hoc* bridges for the adventurous hiker).

The trail then winds its way up the west side of the stream, among the enormous boles of old-growth spruce and fir trees. After a short distance, the trail departs from the valley floor to switchback high onto the western wall of the valley. The route resumes its southward course at the top of the grade, and passes through several mud bogs on its way to a second crossing of Devil Creek. After this crossing, the trail begins a workmanlike ascent up the headwall of the valley, working its way up through an old burn that occupies the broad pass into the Moose Creek valley. Looking west from this vantage point, the dual summits of Devils Hump rise at the head of an open bowl, while the multiple peaks of Mount Bradley rise across the valley to the south.

The trail descends southward from the pass into the Moose Creek drainage, reaching a junction on the bank of a small alpine stream. To the left, the trail to Moose Lake begins its long descent, while an unmaintained path climbs into a lofty bowl to the right. Meanwhile, the spur trail to Elk Lake lies straight ahead. This trail descends gradually as it continues southward, passing several small streams on its way through a subalpine basin. The trail rounds the corner of a major ridge and turns west, climbing gently to reach the head of the valley. Here, among picturesque stands of subalpine fir, Elk Lake is nestled at the foot of Forster Mountain. The lake offers good fishing for cutthroat trout. Travelers who camp here should locate their camps away from the lakeshore, which is quite fragile and has been damaged in the past by careless campers.

The Moose Lake Option. From the junction below the pass, a well-maintained trail runs eastward toward the floor of Moose Creek valley. The trail descends beside the eastern bank of the tiny rill for a distance before crossing the stream and turning south. This area abounds in huckleberry bushes, and beargrass clumps provide pleasant diversions when in bloom. The trail crosses two more rivulets in rapid succession before descending steeply beside the second one to reach a junction with a connecting trail to Vinegar Mountain. Thus reinforced, the trail turns east to cross the now united course of the three small streams. The route runs parallel to this tributary through open timber parklands as it descends toward the creek bottoms. As the trail loses altitude, scattered copses of trees give way to solid forest. The occasional break in the trees reveals a view to the south of a high waterfall that cascades downward from the folds of Mount Bradley.

The descent slows as the trail crosses an old avalanche scar, then flattens out altogether as the route wanders onto the level floodplain of Moose Creek. Here, age-old spruce and fir stand amid the wreckage of their fallen fellows, and the trail meanders back and forth through a lush growth of tall grasses and cow parsnip. There are several more substantial mudholes on the way to the upper end of Moose Lake. This shallow body of water is overlooked by the northern spurs of Mount Bradley, and willows crowd its head and foot. Waterfowl can often be spotted dabbling for aquatic vegetation and insects among the flooded clumps of brush at the lake's upper end. The trail follows the shoreline around the north side of the lake, climbing high onto the hillside about halfway. The lake is entirely lacking in favorable

TRAIL 6 *TRANQUIL BASIN OVERLOOK*
TRAIL 7 *DEVIL CREEK*

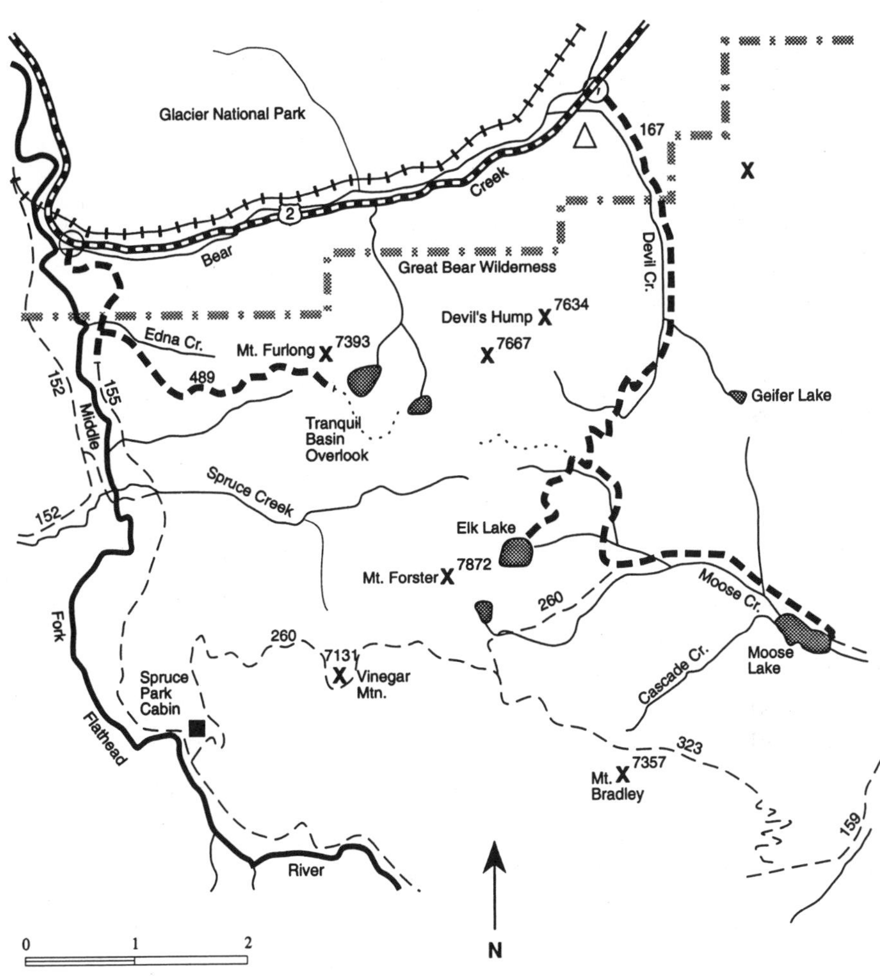

camping spots near its shores. Travelers who are making the long loop onto the Mount Bradley trail should continue east from the foot of the lake for 0.5 mile to reach the Twentyfive Mile Creek trail on the far side of a knee-deep ford.

TRAIL 8 *SNAKE LOOP*

Trail 165, 660

General description: A day trip over Snake Point, 4.4 mi. (7.1 km) round trip.
Difficulty: Moderately strenuous.
Trail maintenance: Occasional.
Traffic: Light.
Elevation gain: 1,540 ft.
Elevation loss: 1,540 ft.
Maximum elevation: 6,120 ft.
Topo maps: Blacktail, Mount Bradley.

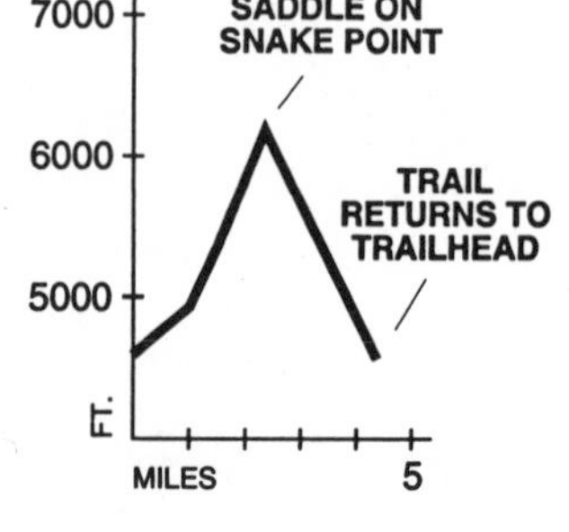

Finding the trailhead: Take U. S. Highway 2 to mile marker 191.8, then turn south onto the dirt road just west of the Bear Creek Bridge. The road forks; take the left fork and turn left again at the next fork to cross Giefer Creek. Follow this road south, taking the right fork at the next junction and staying on this road as it passes through an open metal gate. The road reaches its terminus at the Forest Service rental cabin on Mule Creek, which is the site of the Giefer Creek trailhead.

0.0 Giefer Creek trailhead. Trail crosses Mule Creek.
0.2 Great Bear Wilderness boundary.
0.9 Junction with Snake Loop Trail. Turn left.
2.2 Trail reaches saddle beneath Snake Point.
4.2 Trail rejoins Giefer Creek Trail.
4.4 Giefer Creek trailhead.

The trail: This trail provides a brief day hike to the high country of Snake Point, with views into the southern part of Glacier National Park. It begins by making a shallow ford of Mule Creek and immediately climbing up a steep skid road onto a clearcut bench. At the far edge of the clearcut, the trail crosses the wilderness boundary and meets the trail coming down from Snake Point. The easiest way to complete the loop is to keep going straight and attack it from a counterclockwise direction. This trail is the Giefer Creek Trail (165), and it follows the benches above Giefer Creek through a forest of lodgepole pine and Douglas-fir. After a mile of traveling, the trail crosses a small tributary stream and reaches a second junction with the Snake Point Loop.

Turn left onto the less-traveled path, which begins to ascend gradually across the back side of Snake Point. The trail climbs steadily, high above Snake Creek, and openings in the forest allow views of avalanche paths cut neatly into the forests of Baldhead Mountain across the valley. This mountain is quite lofty (7,794 ft.), but its gentle slopes and domed summit make it appear much less imposing. As the trail continues to climb, huckleberry bushes begin to populate the forest floor below the canopy of lodgepoles, and the bulbous blossoms of beargrass plants break up the monotony of the forest. The gradient steepens as the route swings westward into a dry ravine, then resumes its northward course as it ascends into a saddle behind the first summit of Snake Point.

Only the bulky mass of Baldhead Mountain can be seen from the saddle itself, but an old, unmaintained trail climbs across the open slope to the north to allow views of the sawtooth spires that crowd the headwaters of Grizzly Creek to the south. It is also possible to scramble to the top of the knob to the north for superior views of the craggy summits to the north of Marias Pass. Meanwhile, the loop trail continues through the pass and descends to an unmarked junction; turn left to complete the loop. This trail descends across the northeastern slope of the hillside, which is covered in a thick forest of Douglas-fir with a dense understory of false huckleberry. This slope retains moisture much better than the south-facing slopes crossed earlier in the hike, and the plants that grow here require more water than do the relatively drought-tolerant lodgepole pine and beargrass.

Lodgepole pine again dominates the canopy farther down the slope, and the underbrush becomes sparse again. Several large openings carpeted with wildflowers allow views of Glacier National Park's southern ranges. Mount Shields dominates the foreground to the west, while the rocky summit of Elk Mountain overlooks the Bear Creek valley to the east. The trail completes its descent via a series of switchbacks through the beargrass-lit forest and reaches the bottom of the hill at the edge of the clearcut. The trail runs southwest along the forest edge to cover the remaining distance to its junction with the Giefer Creek trail, just a few hundred yards from the trailhead.

TRAIL 8 *SNAKE LOOP*

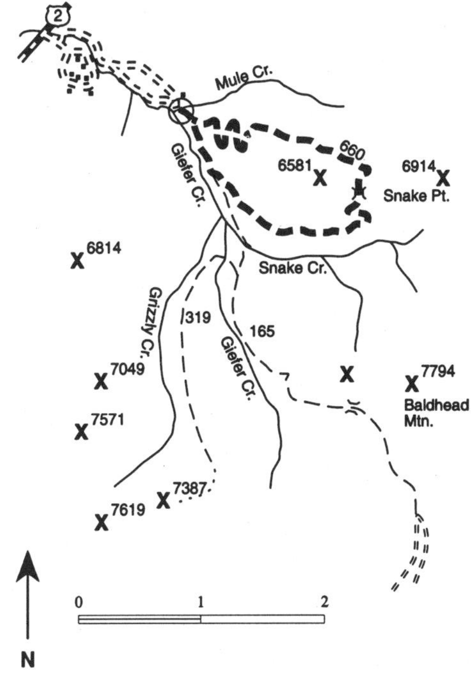

Nameless peaks rise above the head of Grizzly Peak.

TRAIL 9 *GRIZZLY CREEK*

Trail 165, 319

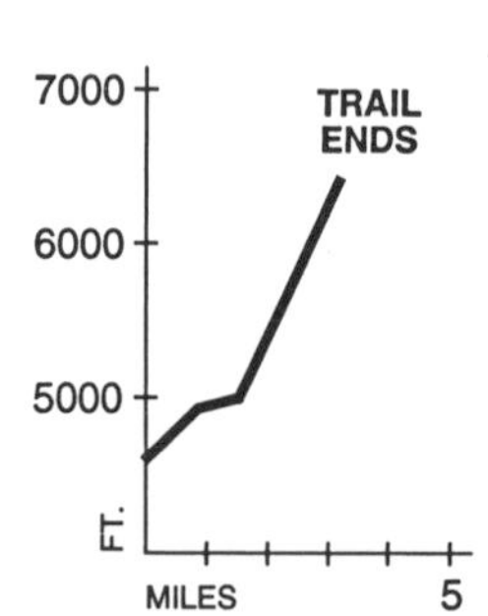

General description: A day hike from the Giefer Creek trailhead to the end of the Grizzly Creek Trail, 3.3 mi. (5.3 km).
Difficulty: Moderately strenuous.
Trail maintenance: Occasional.
Traffic: Light.
Elevation gain: 1,800 ft.
Elevation loss: 40 ft.
Maximum elevation: 6,340 ft.
Topo maps: Blacktail, Mount Bradley.
Finding the trailhead: Giefer Creek trailhead (see Snake Loop, p. 32).

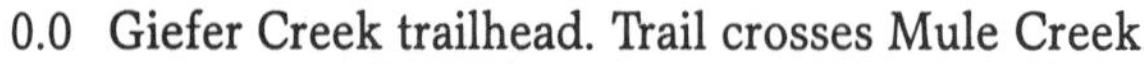

0.0 Giefer Creek trailhead. Trail crosses Mule Creek.
0.2 Great Bear Wilderness boundary.
0.9 Junction with Snake Loop Trail. Stay right for Grizzly Creek.
1.3 Trail fords Snake Creek.
1.4 Junction with Grizzly Creek trail. Turn right.
1.5 Trail fords Giefer Creek.
3.3 Trail peters out atop ridgeline.

The trail: This trail follows a low ridgetop to the headwaters of Grizzly Creek, which is surrounded by a series of low but imposing peaks. It also boasts good views into the southern part of Glacier National Park. From the trailhead follow the Giefer Creek Trail (165) as it makes a shallow ford of Mule Creek and climbs a steep tractor path onto a clearcut bluff above Giefer Creek. The trail runs southeast across the clearcut, reaching the boundary of the Great Bear Wilderness at the forest edge. Shortly thereafter, the trail passes the first unmarked junction with the Snake Loop trail; stay right for Grizzly Creek. The trail crosses wooded benches above Giefer Creek, crossing a tiny rivulet before reaching the second Snake Loop Junction. The trail continues southwest, reaching the sizable wash of Snake Creek, which it fords at an ankle-deep crossing. The trail continues to follow the east bank of Giefer Creek for several hundred yards, crossing a woodland spring before reaching the junction with the Grizzly Creek Trail.

This track cuts back to the west, quickly making a shallow ford of Giefer Creek and climbing onto the ridgetop that separates this stream from Grizzly Creek. Once atop the ridgeline, the trail climbs gently through lowland forest, then steepens as it passes onto the northwest slope of the ridge. With increasing altitude, subalpine fir come to dominate the overstory, and the forest gradually opens up to reveal the angular peaks and ridges surrounding the head of the valley. Avalanches have groomed neat paths across the forested ridges across the valley, and grizzly bears can sometimes be spotted foraging in these distant openings. The trail reaches the crest

TRAIL 9 GRIZZLY CREEK

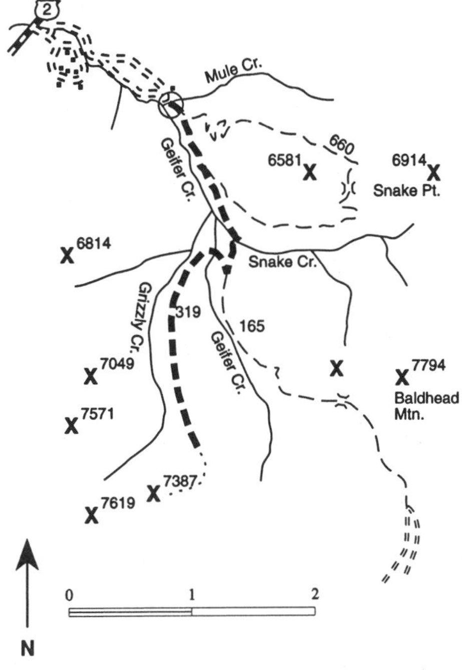

of the ridge amid a sparse forest of spindly fir and continues southward along the ridgeline.

The trail peters out atop a flat rise just before reaching the base of the nearest major peak. Verdant summits rise all around, providing suitable terrain for mountain goats and aeries for golden eagles. Look north to see the peaks of Glacier National Park that soar skyward in a stunning panorama: the needle-sharp pinnacle of Mount Saint Nicholas in the west, Eagle Ribs rising above a low ridge in the center, and the twin spires of Little Dog and Summit Mountain farther east. To the east rises the rocky dome of Baldhead Mountain, just two miles away as the crow flies. Beyond this point is a steep and arduous bushwhack through dense thickets of false huckleberries for travelers wishing to scramble to the top of this point.

TRAIL 10 *GRANITE CREEK- CASTLE LAKE*

Trail 156, 155, 209
General description: A backpack from the Granite Creek trailhead to Castle Lake, 8.6 mi. (13.8 km).
Difficulty: Moderate.
Trail maintenance: Yearly.
Traffic: Moderate.
Elevation gain: 1,375 ft.
Elevation loss: 1,375 ft.
Maximum elevation: 5,200 ft.

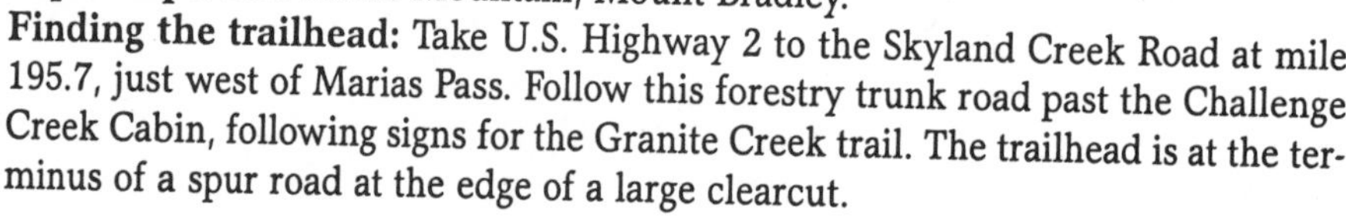

Topo maps: Red Plume Mountain, Mount Bradley.
Finding the trailhead: Take U.S. Highway 2 to the Skyland Creek Road at mile 195.7, just west of Marias Pass. Follow this forestry trunk road past the Challenge Creek Cabin, following signs for the Granite Creek trail. The trailhead is at the terminus of a spur road at the edge of a large clearcut.

0.0 Granite Creek trailhead.
1.1 Trail fords Granite Creek.
5.5 Junction with Granite Cabin cutoff trail. Turn right for Castle Lake.
5.7 Junction with Big River trail. Turn right for Castle Lake.
6.4 Granite Cabin.
7.3 Junction with Castle Creek trail. Turn left for Castle Lake.
7.5 Ford of Middle Fork River.
8.6 Castle Lake.

The trail: The Granite Creek trail is the route of choice for travelers bound for Schafer Meadows. In contrast to the Morrison Creek trail, this trail holds up well under high traffic, with few boggy spots to make traveling unpleasant. This route is a much shorter route to the Schafer Meadows area than the Big River trail. Castle Lake is one of the more popular destinations in the area, offering forage for horses and fishing opportunities for visitors. Heavy visitor use has resulted in negative impacts on the surrounding country; be especially careful to minimize wear and tear

The cliffs of Patrol Ridge rise above the mouth of Granite Creek.

on this popular lake basin.

The trail begins by crossing through a narrow band of timber and hopping a small stream on its way to a second large clearcut. Here, the trail joins a dirt road, which soon splits into two forks. Follow the right-hand fork, which bears toward the creek bottom below. A trail sign marks the spot where the Granite Creek trail departs from this road, slowly making its way down to a calf-deep crossing of Granite Creek. Once on the far bank, the trail enters undisturbed forest as it continues its descent above the western bank of the creek.

As the trail approaches the Middle Fork valley, open slopes afford the first views of the trek. The cliffs of Patrol Ridge rise from the slopes above the trail, and across the river valley rises the verdant mass of Trinity Mountain. Before reaching the Big River trail, the Granite Creek trail splits, with the left fork continuing down the valley and the right fork climbing across the hillside toward the Granite Cabin. Travelers bound for Castle Lake should take the right fork, which climbs through a low saddle before descending toward the Big River Trail (155). Turn west along this trail, which follows the Middle Fork River through a forest choked with berry bushes to reach Granite Cabin. Beyond the cabin, the trail wanders high above the river, crossing open avalanche slopes that allow views of the sparkling riffles and swirling emerald pools below. After a mile and a half on the Big River trail, the Castle Lake trail junction is reached.

This trail descends steeply through a dense forest of young Douglas-fir to reach

TRAIL 10 *GRANITE CREEK- CASTLE LAKE*

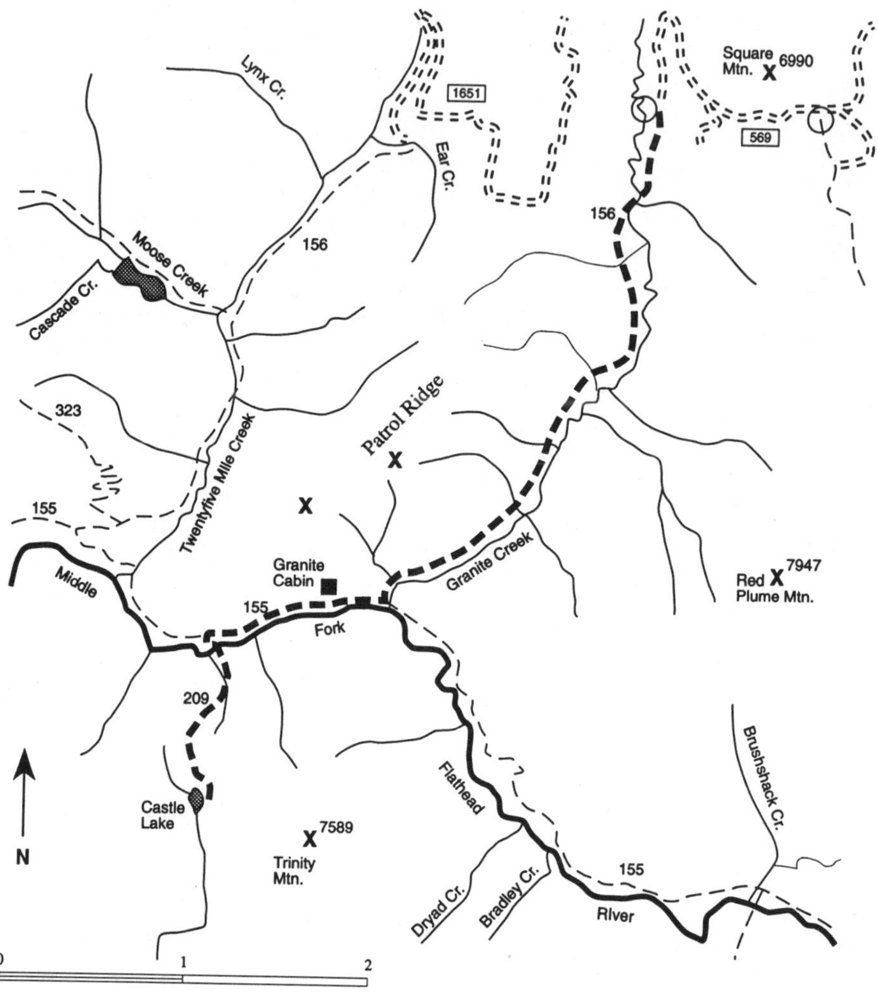

the river bank just below its confluence with tiny Castle Creek. After a difficult waist-deep ford of the river, the trail climbs onto the gravel spit that separates the two watercourses. From here, it is a challenging one-mile climb through damp forests to reach the basin of Castle Lake. The lake rests in a wide, grassy bowl surrounded by forested hillsides, with sheer cliffs rising to the south at the head of the valley. Keep an eye out for the mountain goats that can often be spotted clambering from ledge to ledge on these steep rock faces. The water level of the lake fluctuates greatly from year to year, and the emergent lake bottom is covered with grasses and white Indian paintbrush blossoms during low water years. A healthy population of cutthroat trout provide fair to good fishing for visitors with a penchant for angling.

TRAIL 11 *DOLLY VARDEN CREEK*

Trail 173 (see map on p. 42)
General description: An extended trip from Schafer Meadows to the Pentagon Creek divide, 10.4 mi. (16.7 km).
Difficulty: Moderate.
Trail maintenance: Yearly.
Traffic: Very light.
Elevation gain: 2,310 ft.
Maximum elevation: 7,150
Topo maps: Gable Peaks, Trilobite Peak.

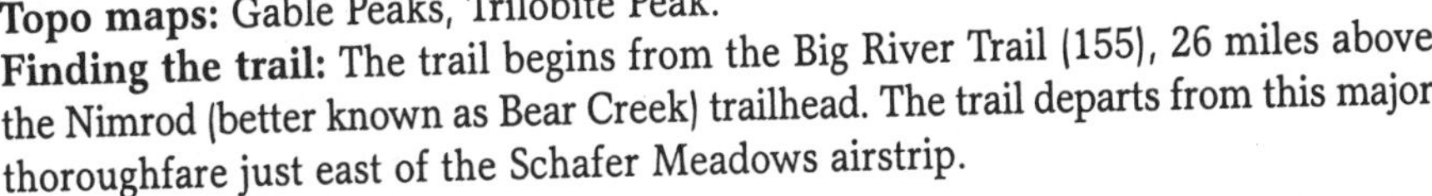

Finding the trail: The trail begins from the Big River Trail (155), 26 miles above the Nimrod (better known as Bear Creek) trailhead. The trail departs from this major thoroughfare just east of the Schafer Meadows airstrip.

0.0 Schafer Meadows
0.1 Ford of Middle Fork River.
0.6 Junction with Schafer Creek trail. Stay left for Dolly Varden Creek.
1.7 Junction with Trilobite Range (Chair Mountain) Trail (241). Stay right for Dolly Varden Creek.
5.9 Junction with Argosy Creek trail. Bear left for Dolly Varden Creek.
6.1 Junction with Chair Mountain cutoff Trail (686). Stay right for Dolly Varden Creek.
10.4 Pass into Pentagon Creek drainage.

The trail: This trail is a major valley-bottom route that connects Schafer Meadows with the Pentagon Creek trail. It can be reached from the northern end via the Granite or Morrison Creek trails, and from the south via the Pentagon Creek trail or the Elk Ridge route. This trail is often used by hikers accessing Argosy Creek and the Trilobite Range. Scenery is rather limited in the lower part of the valley, but improves beyond Argosy Creek, with craggy reefs of limestone looming to the west and the backbone of the Trilobite Range towering to the east of the valley. Dolly Varden Creek was named for the bull trout that spawn there; this trout was formerly known throughout the west as the Dolly Varden.

From the trail junction east of the Schafer airstrip, the Dolly Varden trail runs south, making a ford of the Middle Fork and crossing the flat bottomlands. Two-thirds of a mile down the trail, there is a fork; the Schafer Creek trail fords Dolly Varden Creek and runs to the southwest, while the left fork continues southward along Dolly Varden Creek. A mile farther on, the trail passes a junction with the Chair Mountain trail, which is discussed in detail on page 45, The Trilobite Range. As the trail continues to ascend gently up the valley floor, the mixed forest gives way to pure stands of lodgepole pine, which grow in abundance in the wake of a forest fire. The dense stands of trees are known locally as "doghair lodgepole," because the trees grow "as thick as the hair on a dog's back." The low level of plant diversity in these stands makes them unfavorable habitat for most species of wild animals. The peaks to the west can occasionally be glimpsed above the treetops; otherwise, this section of the trail is quite monotonous.

The miles of straight line travel are finally interrupted when the trail descends to the floodplain of the creek. At one point, a meandering channel of the stream takes over the trail bed, and travelers must choose between a lengthy knee-deep ford or a hundred-yard bushwhack to avoid the encroaching waters. For the next several miles, the creek swings near the trail at regular intervals, and the resulting openings in the forest allow views of the turreted peaks of Argosy Mountain across the valley. There are several ups and downs as the path climbs to avoid steep cutbanks, and after the last of these the trail descends to a fork. The right fork is the well-traveled Argosy Creek Trail, while the less beaten track to the left is the Dolly Varden trail.

Half a mile beyond the Argosy trail junction, the Dolly Varden trail reaches a second junction in a brushy forest clearing. From this point, the Chair Mountain cutoff trail climbs to meet the trail that follows the crest of the Trilobite Range. Meanwhile, the Dolly Varden trail plods onward and upward, passing through more viewless forests. The trail crosses numerous small tributary streams on its way to a series of beaver ponds that have been built in the main channel of Dolly Varden Creek. These ponds frame the sphinxlike peaks that line the western rim of the valley. The trail follows the east bank of the ever-shrinking stream, until the water finally disappears in a mossy spring.

Rugged peaks form the valley rim of upper Dolly Varden Creek.

The gradient of the valley steepens as the trail approaches its head, and stout subalpine fir replace the lodgepole that dominate the lower valley. The trail follows the dry valley bottom, beneath which the rushing waters of Dolly Varden Creek flow through channels in the porous bedrock. Reaching the head of the valley, the trail turns east and begins to climb rather steeply across brushy slopes dominated by false huckleberry. With increasing altitude, the brush gives way to subalpine meadows spangled with wildflowers. After rounding the base of a bald hill, the trail continues its ascent in a southwesterly direction, passing among sparse groves of stunted subalpine firs.

As the trail crosses the headwall of the valley, views open up of the rugged cliffs to the west and the broad back of Trilobite Mountain to the southeast. The trail climbs the final distance through rocky meadows to reach the pass into Pentagon Creek. From this point, Pentagon Mountain's imposing north face looms above the pass, and the lesser peaks of Pot and Shadow Mountains rim the eastern edge of the Pentagon Valley. A good-quality trail descends southward from the pass to meet up with the Spotted Bear River Trail (see p. 72) at Pentagon Cabin.

TRAIL 12 *TRILOBITE RANGE*

Trail 241

General description: An extended trip from Dolly Varden Creek to Switchback Pass, 16.7 mi. (26.9 km).

Difficulty: Moderately strenuous.

Trail maintenance: Frequent.

Traffic: Very light to Trilobite Lakes; light beyond the lakes.

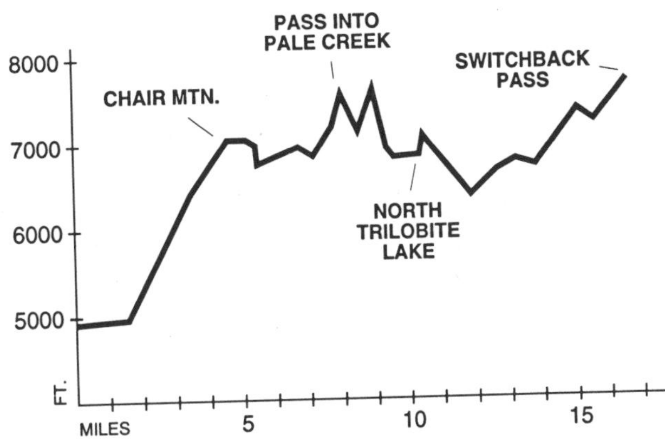

Elevation gain: 4,930 ft.

Elevation loss: 2,003 ft.

Maximum elevation: 7,767 ft.

Topo maps: Gable Peaks, Trilobite Peak, Pentagon Mountain.

Finding the trail: This trail begins from a junction marked "Chair Mountain Trail," on the Dolly Varden Creek Trail (173), 1.7 miles above its junction with the Big River Trail (155).

0.0 Schafer Meadows
0.1 Ford of Middle Fork River.
0.6 Junction with Schafer Creek trail. Stay left for Dolly Varden Creek.
1.7 Chair Mountain junction with Dolly Varden Creek Trail. Turn right for the

TRAIL 11 *DOLLY VARDEN CREEK*
TRAIL 12 *TRILOBITE RANGE*

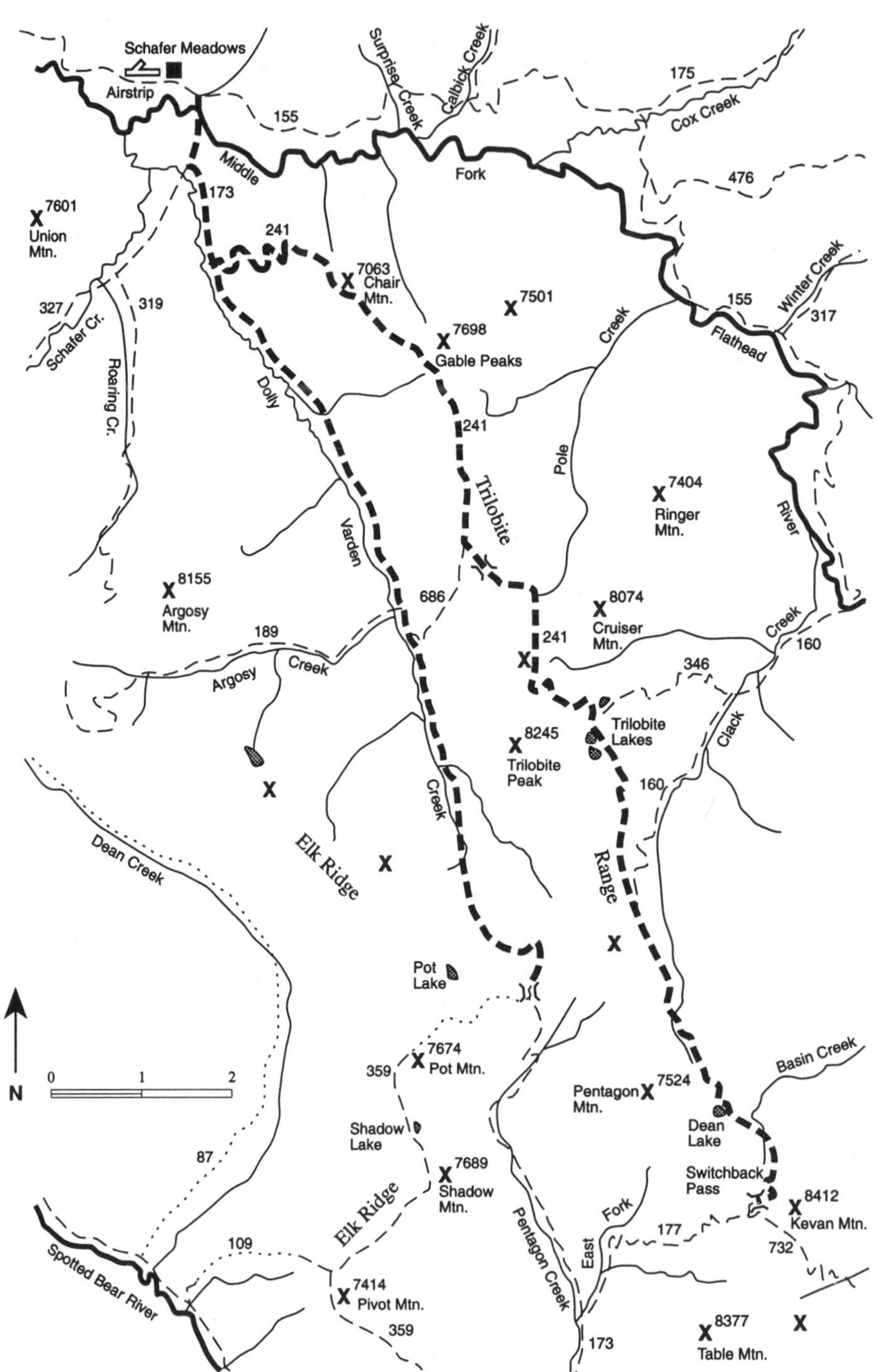

Trilobite Range trail.
4.6 Chair Mountain.
7.6 Junction with Chair Mountain cutoff trail. Turn left for the Trilobite Range.
8.1 Pass into the Pale Creek drainage.
10.4 North Trilobite Lake. Junction with Clack Creek cutoff trail. Turn left for the Trilobite trail.
10.7 Middle Trilobite Lake.
12.6 Junction with Clack Creek trail. Stay right for the Trilobite Trail.
15.1 Dean Lake.
16.7 Switchback Pass.

The trail: This remote trail runs along the crest of the rugged Trilobite Range for over twelve miles, linking the Schafer Meadows area with Switchback Pass. Despite its outstanding scenic value, the trail receives relatively little use and is an excellent choice for travelers seeking solitude on a long expedition. In addition to the routing discussed here, this trail can be accessed from the Dolly Varden valley via the Chair Mountain cutoff trail, as well as several routes running up from the Clack Creek Valley. The section crossing the divide between Dolly Varden and Pale Creek is extremely steep and narrow and is not recommended for horse parties.

From the Chair Mountain trail junction on the Dolly Varden Creek Trail, travelers bound for the Trilobite Range should take the uphill trail. This trail climbs steadily via a series of switchbacks up the lodgepole-covered slopes of Chair Mountain. The understory vegetation is dominated by delicate grouse whortleberry bushes, which produce a tiny but tasty fruit during late August. Brief glimpses of Argosy and Union mountains can be had by looking through the trees. Farther on, an opening in the lodgepole allows a full view up the Schafer Creek valley, with fortresslike peaks surrounding it on all sides. When the trail crests the ridgeline, views also open up to the north. The Middle Fork of the Flathead wanders through its forested valley far below, and the distant peaks of Glacier National Park to the north and the Lewis and Clark Range to the northeast can be seen on a clear day.

The trail continues to climb steadily as it follows the ridgeline eastward, steepening noticeably on its final approach to the summit of Chair Mountain. Instead of climbing to the top of the grassy peak, however, the trail turns south to cross the slope below the summit and runs out onto a grassy expanse of meadow. Argosy Mountain rises dramatically across the valley, its multi-colored cliffs draped with snowslips of the purest white. As the trail rounds the shoulder of Chair Mountain, the bulky massif of the Gable Peaks swings into view across the grassy saddle to the southeast. The trail follows the ridgetop in this direction, becoming a bit faint as it crosses the expanse of meadow, but soon gathering itself before entering a mixed subalpine forest of fir and lodgepole pine.

The trail winds to the east of a wooded hillock, then descends onto another grassy slope dotted with a multitude of wildflowers. To the south, the Dolly Varden valley stretches away like a hall of the gods, with towering peaks rising on either side. The trail then descends for several hundred feet into the trees below, where it continues southward beneath the massive cliffs of the Gable Peaks. It then begins to climb once more, working its way across a rocky slope devastated by forest fire. In early summer, the Rocky Mountain bluebirds that make their homes in the fire-killed snags can be seen flitting among the debris left by the blaze. The trail climbs up and down in small increments, rounding high rocky knobs and finding tiny spring creeks in the folds of the steep slope.

After several miles, the trail crests a knob sporting a copse of surviving subalpine fir, and the Trilobite Range trail reaches a junction with the cutoff trail (686) that returns to the valley floor. Travelers who are not paying close attention may miss this junction entirely, as the Trilobite Range trail takes a sharp, unexpected turn to the east and ascends straight up the hill, while the more well-worn cutoff trail continues straight ahead. The Trilobite trail climbs steeply toward a high pass on the crest of the rocky ridge; the final pitch is a real killer. Once atop the divide, the rather faint trail follows a series of cairns southward along the crest of the ridge for a short time. To the northeast rise the peaks of the Lewis and Clark Range, and in the foreground, Cruiser Mountain rises above the barren basin of Pale Creek. To the south, the dignified crest of Trilobite Mountain rises along the ridgeline.

The trail continues south until it reaches a flat, grassy shelf. Here, the route turns eastward across the trackless meadow, bearing toward Cruiser Mountain. The trail becomes distinct again as it descends down the hillside toward the headwaters of Pale Creek. Once it reaches the floor of this high valley, the trail climbs gently through hummocky parkland. The trail continues to run southeast, climbing steeply as it mounts the high saddle to the east of Trilobite Mountain. From this high vantage point, the flat-bottomed bowl of the Trilobite Basin stretches away to the south, with its picturesque groves and well-tended meadows providing an idyllic counterpoint to the menacing cliffs that tower to the west.

The trail switchbacks down into the basin and strikes a southward course, passing

Argosy Mountain viewed from the slopes of Chair Mountain.

through meadows of glacier lilies, beargrass, and buttercups where playful ground squirrels romp and frolic. As the trail nears the south side of the basin, a line of cairns runs south, while the trail bends to the east. Ignore the cairns and follow the trail to the shore of the northernmost of the shallow Trilobite Lakes, where it reaches a junction. To the left is a cutoff trail to Clack Creek, while the Trilobite trail turns south again, climbing into a low saddle between an outlying hillock and the main bulk of Trilobite Mountain. The trail then descends to reach the outlet of the middle lake, which lies at the foot of sheer cliffs. The trail then turns southeast, following the outlet stream for a time before returning to its southerly course and crossing a series of high benches below the southern lake.

The subalpine fir close ranks around the trail as it descends for a mile, finally emerging in an alpine meadow where glacier lilies nod their yellow heads. To the west, the cliffs of nameless peaks march rank on rank, culminating in the formidable spire of Pentagon Mountain to the south. The trail begins to climb again as it passes through the alpine parkland at the foot of the cliffs; look for mountain goats scrambling among the rock ledges high above. Just before reaching a junction with the Clack Creek trail, the Trilobite trail crosses an old filled-in pond where the path all but disappears. Fortunately, the trail is easy to spot as it cuts across the hillside on the far side of this young meadow. Once the marked trail junction has been reached, stay right for Switchback Pass.

Beyond the junction, the Trilobite trail becomes quite muddy as it ascends across open benches and through miniature forests. Across the valley, verdant forests crown the upturned strata of Bow Mountain. To the northeast, Mount Field reigns above the jagged peaks of the Lewis and Clark Range. The trail crosses a series of small streams and climbs up the low hillside that borders them to the east. Broad switchbacks carry the traveler up the hillside at the foot of Pentagon Mountain's ragged east face, and then the trail straightens out to pass an empty cirque on its way to Dean Lake. This clear, cold alpine tarn rests beneath the toe of an unnamed spur ridge that projects eastward from the crest of the Trilobite Range.

The trail rounds the eastern shore of the lake, passing beneath the stout boughs of an occasional whitebark pine before dropping into the upper drainage of Basin Creek. The trail crosses this stream, then follows it upward, while Kevan Mountain looms to the south. After climbing across a series of fir-clad hummocks, the trail makes its final ascent to Switchback Pass. At the pass, a faint track runs south to link up with the North Wall trail, while the more well-worn route runs west into the Pentagon Creek valley (see Switchback Pass, p. 79).

TRAIL 13 *ARGOSY CREEK*

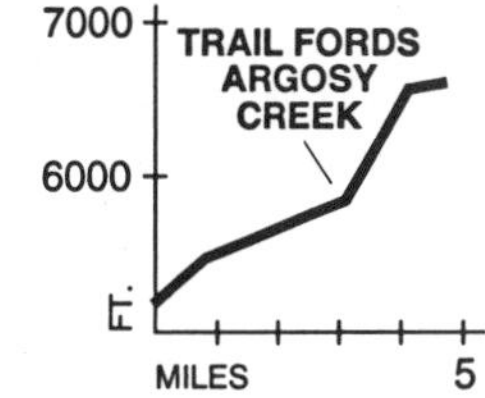

Trail 189
General description: An extended trip from Dolly Varden Creek to the end of the Argosy Creek trail, 4.7 mi. (7.6 km).
Difficulty: Moderately strenuous.
Trail maintenance: Occasionally.

Traffic: Very light.
Elevation gain: 1,400 ft.
Maximum elevation: 6,600 ft.
Topo maps: Trilobite Peak, Whitcomb Peak.
Finding the trail: This trail departs from a marked intersection at mile 5.9 on the Dolly Varden Creek Trail.

0.0 Junction with Dolly Varden Creek trail.
0.1 Trail fords Dolly Varden and Argosy Creeks.
3.0 Trail crosses Argosy Creek to south bank.
4.3 Trail reaches a fork in high basin. Stay right.
4.7 Trail peters out atop Dean Ridge.

The trail: This trail provides a spur trip for visitors to the Dolly Varden Creek valley. From its junction with the Dolly Varden Creek Trail, the trail running up Argosy Creek runs southwest to reach the bank of Dolly Varden Creek just above its confluence with Argosy Creek. The trail completes the knee-deep ford of both creeks before turning west along the north bank of Argosy Creek. After an initial start in a closed-canopy forest of lodgepole pine, the trail soon finds its way onto a high bluff overlooking the creek. Looking upstream, rocky foothills rise above the south bank of the creek. The trail climbs steadily as it wanders inland through a lodgepole forest interrupted by avalanche slopes that yield views of an unnamed spur of Argosy Mountain to the north. The trail finally levels out as it makes a beeline to the west through a forest of young lodgepole.

A bit farther on, the trail reaches an unmarked fork. The right fork, heavily blazed but rather faint, represents the main trail up Argosy Creek. The left fork is more well-traveled and descends toward the stream's side, where it branches into myriad channels and disappears in an outfitter's camping spot. A trail can be picked up again that returns from this area to reunite with the main trail, but it is difficult to follow, and through traffic should avoid this low-lying area entirely and choose the higher route instead. This trail, though faint, can be followed fairly readily as it continues west through forests and avalanche slopes. To the north, the red shale cliffs of Argosy Mountain rise above the valley. As the trail exits the final avalanche chute, it receives the trail rising from the creekside camping area and enters a riparian forest of fir. The trail crosses several minor tributaries and passes through boggy terrain before reaching a ford of Argosy Creek.

Once it reaches the far bank of the creek, the trail begins to climb steadily up a brushy hillside scattered with enormous Douglas-fir. Upon reaching a tributary stream, the trail makes a crossing and climbs steeply up its west banks before crossing once again. The trail makes its way through a dwarfed forest of subalpine fir as it switchbacks higher and higher onto the hillside, until it eventually reaches a high, flat shelf. The trail forks here; follow the right fork to climb onto a high shoulder of Dean Ridge. The trail peters out in the old burn on the ridgetop, which boasts views of both Argosy Mountain and the Trilobite Range far to the east.

TRAIL 13 *ARGOSY CREEK*

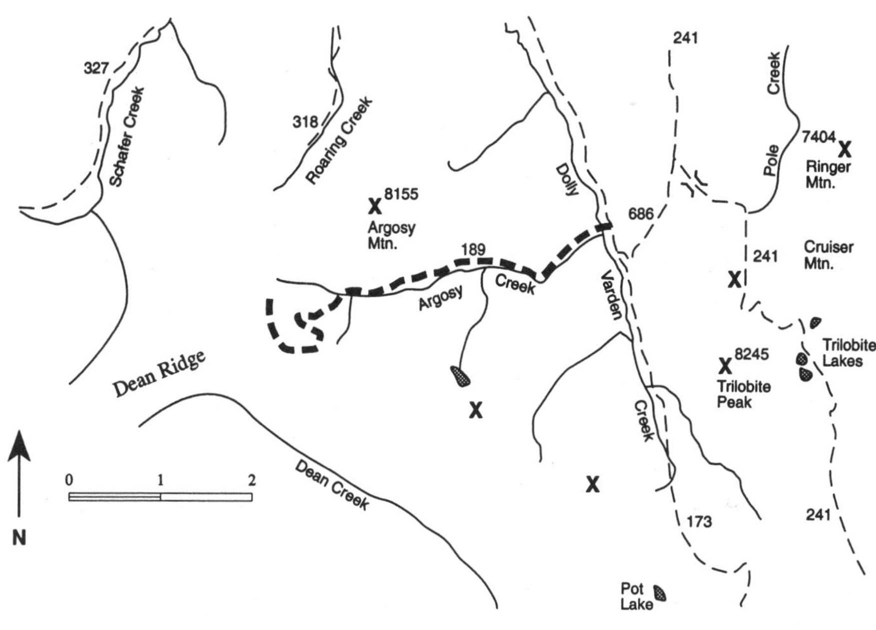

TRAIL 14 *GATEWAY GORGE*

Trail 322

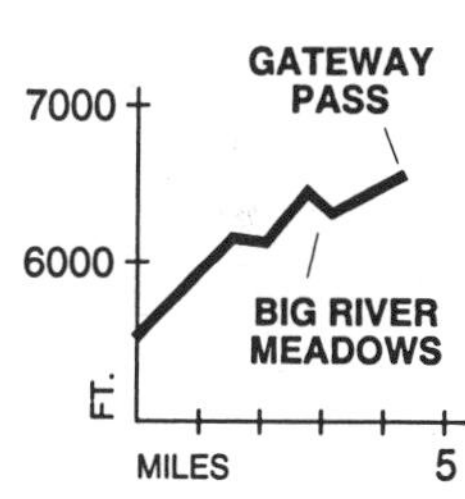

General description: An extended trip from Strawberry Creek to Gateway Pass, 4.3 mi. (6.9 km).
Difficulty: Moderate.
Trail maintenance: Yearly.
Traffic: Moderate.
Elevation gain: 980 ft.
Elevation loss: 70 ft.
Maximum elevation: 6,478 ft.
Topo maps: Gooseberry Park, Gateway Pass.
Finding the trail: This trail departs from a marked trail junction on the Strawberry Creek Trail (161), 4.1 miles east of Gooseberry Park.

0.0 Gateway Gorge junction on Strawberry Creek Trail.
1.4 Trail enters Gateway Gorge.
1.7 Trail exits Gateway Gorge.
2.0 Trail fords Gateway Creek.
2.2 Junction with East Fork Strawberry Creek Trail. Stay right for Gateway Pass.
3.1 Big River Meadows.
4.3 Gateway Pass.

Gateway Rock looms above Gateway Creek.

The trail: This trail provides access from the valley of the Middle Fork to the rugged Birch Creek country via a low pass over the Continental Divide. Along the way, it passes such scenic attractions as Gateway Gorge and Big River Meadows. Because of the relatively low elevation of Gateway Pass, this route is passable even in early summer, when the higher passes are still clogged with snow. However, rock slides in Gateway Gorge often make passage difficult for stock parties early in the season.

From the trail junction on Strawberry Creek, the Gateway Gorge trail climbs moderately for 1.5 mile through the trees, with occasional mud hazards during wet weather. After crossing a tributary stream, the trail breaks out abruptly onto a grassy slope, with the massive buttes flanking Gateway Gorge rising dead ahead. As the trail climbs into the gorge, take a few backward glances as the peaks of the Trilobite Range reveal themselves in succession through the window formed by Gateway Gorge. The towering cliffs that flank the creek dwarf trees and travelers alike, and their size and ancient age provide an instructive yardstick for measuring the importance of man's best efforts. Note also the intricate network of bighorn sheep trails in the talus below the far wall of the gorge. These cliffs have provided a home for mountain sheep for millennia. The trail climbs across slopes of loose talus as it passes through the gorge, then descends again as it approaches the far end.

The trail continues eastward beside the creek for a short distance before making a knee-deep ford to reach its south bank. Several hundred yards farther, the trail reaches a junction with the trail that runs north to Sabido Cabin and the East Fork

TRAIL 14 *GATEWAY GORGE*

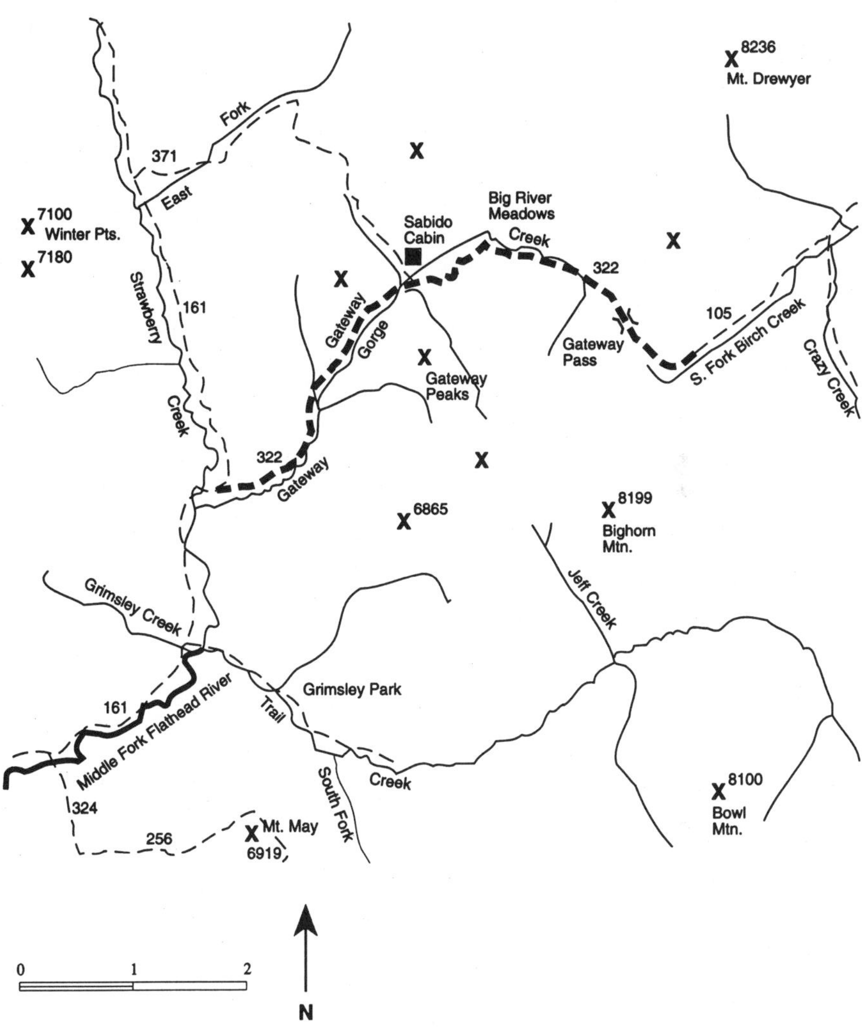

of Strawberry Creek. Stay right for Gateway Pass, as the trail climbs a wooded hillside that offers a few final glimpses of the mountains that surround the gorge. After a brief but steady ascent, the trail runs out into the western fringe of Big River Meadows, a broad expanse of grass dissected by tiny, willow-choked streamlets. To the north, an eroded tailbone of the Sawtooth Range stands guard over the valley, the multicolored bands of sediment showing in its washed-out slopes. The trail crosses the full 1.5-mile length of the meadows, braiding out into a number of channels as it does so. Subalpine fir begin to crowd in as the trail makes its final ascent to Gateway Pass. The pass itself has little scenic value, but the country beyond it contains some of the most awe-inspiring scenery in the Rockies.

ADDITIONAL TRAILS

Deerlick Creek (145), Great Bear Trail (328), Skiumah Creek (204), Rescue Creek (326), Cascadilla Creek (498), Tunnel Creek (498), Essex Creek (151), Java Creek (254), and **Java Mountain (158)** trails are rarely maintained, very brushy, and difficult to follow.

Giefer Creek Trail (165) is a well-maintained trail that provides access to the upper end of the **Twentyfive Mile Creek Trail (159).** This latter trail is washed out and overgrown in its upper reaches, but is in fairly good condition below Moose Lake.

Sheep Creek - Elk Creek (152) and **Dirtyface (62)** trails are washed out and overgrown in their upper reaches, but are passable in the lower parts of their respective valleys.

Spruce Lookout Trail (677) is not maintained frequently, but is reportedly easy to follow.

Charlie Creek (330) and **Bergsicker Creek (217)** trails are maintained only occasionally and are quite overgrown in their upper reaches.

Cy Creek (332) and **Long Creek (166)** trails are maintained frequently. A washout on the back side of Twin Peak makes the upper end of the Cy Creek trail impassable to stock parties.

Morrison Creek Trail (154) receives heavy horse traffic and is very muddy. Avoid it in early summer and early autumn.

Miner Creek Trail (81) is good as far as Scott Lake but is choked with brush and blowdowns above it. The access trail to **Flotilla Lake (215)** receives heavy use and is steep in spots.

Schafer Creek Trail (327) is a main access route to Schafer Meadows and is maintained annually. The spur trail up **Roaring Creek (318)** has lots of fords and disappears into the creek after several miles. The spur trail to **Capitol Mountain (522)** is rarely maintained and will only be found by determined wilderness travelers.

Lodgepole Creek Trail (179) is maintained frequently as far as its junction with the Calbick Creek trail. Beyond this point, the trail is narrow and muddy and is only maintained occasionally. The **Calbick Creek Trail (391)** is not maintained and has all but disappeared.

Lodgepole Mountain Trail (337) is maintained yearly and provides pleasant though unspectacular views.

Cox Creek Trail (176) is maintained yearly and receives heavy use.

Winter Creek Trail (317) is narrow and is maintained infrequently. **Trails 338** and **478** are steep with lots of brush. Once on the open ridgeline, the going gets easier. Expect lots of solitude.

Clack Creek (160) and **Trilobite Lake Cutoff (346)** trails are maintained frequently. The latter trail is quite steep and prone to blowdowns early in the season.

Strawberry Creek (161) and **East Fork Strawberry Creek (371)** trails are maintained frequently. The former receives lots of traffic, while the latter receives less use and is steep in places with a few brushy spots.

Bowl Creek Trail (324) is maintained annually and is legendary for its continuous string of mud bogs.

SPOTTED BEAR COUNTRY

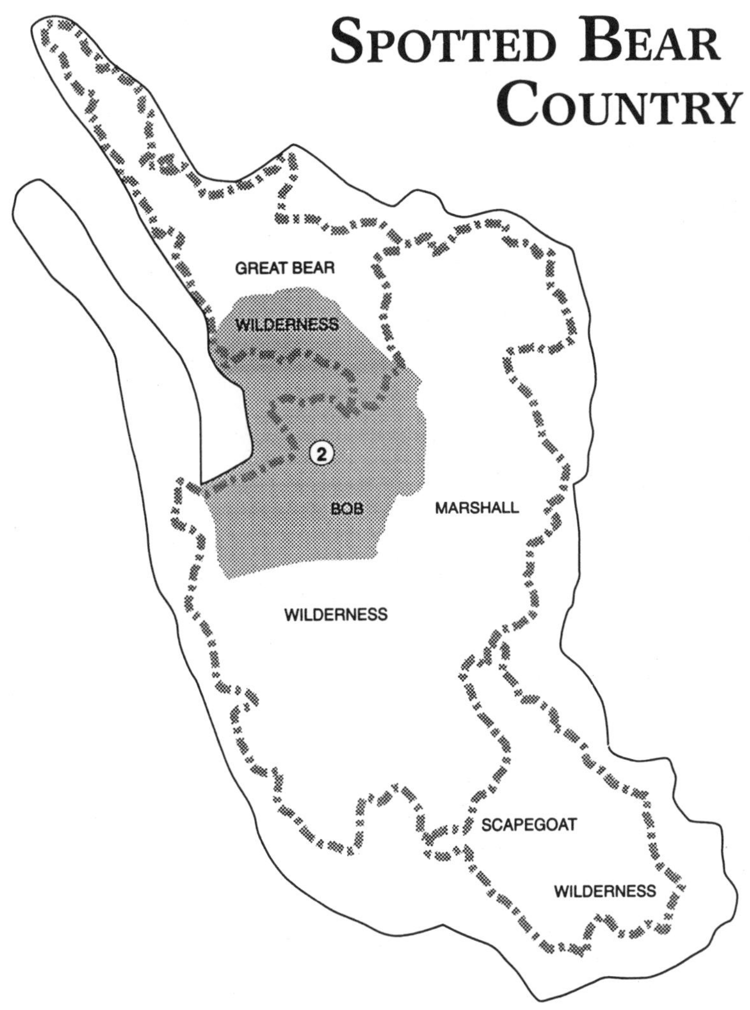

It takes more than fifty miles of dirt road to bypass Hungry Horse Reservoir and reach the Spotted Bear Ranger Station. This remote site is the headquarters for the largest ranger district in the USDA Forest Service system in the lower forty-eight states, and it administers the entire upper basin of the South Fork of the Flathead River. There are a few guest ranches scattered about, but the nearest gas stations and stores are in the town of Hungry Horse, fifty-five miles away. Spotted Bear is the gateway to the heart of the Bob Marshall Wilderness and offers excellent access to its remote ranges and silent basins.

Most of the wilderness complex is characterized by a series of overthrust strata of rock that tilt upward to the east, resulting in steep east-facing walls and gentle western slopes. In contrast, the Spotted Bear country is dominated by an upwarp of the Earth's crust known as the White River Syncline. As the rock masses of the overthrust moved eastward, the pressure on these rocks caused them to bend like an accordion, forming a rounded ridge of continuous rock called a *syncline.* Erosion ultimately wore away the center of the syncline, leaving the tilted cliffs that face each other on either side of the Flathead's South Fork. The mountain range from Sergeant Mountain in the north to Turtlehead Mountain in the south forms the eastern side of the syncline, while the tilted walls of Picture Ridge define its western side. The bending of the rock strata is particularly evident on the northern end of the syncline and can be viewed in cross-section in the twisted bands of rock that make up the backbone of Sergeant Mountain.

The valley floors of this area are covered with unbroken forest of lodgepole pine and Douglas-fir. White-tailed deer and black bear thrive here, in the company of a scattering of grizzly bears. Drier meadows along the ridgetops provide summer range for small bands of elk, and the loftier peaks are haunted by isolated groups of mountain goats. The streams and rivers here harbor excellent populations of trout; indeed, the South Fork of the Flathead and the lower reaches of the Spotted Bear River are considered to be blue-ribbon waters.

TRAIL 15 *SUNBURST LAKE*

Trail 218, 693

General description: Backpack from Gorge Creek trailhead to Sunburst Lake, 8.8 mi. (14.2 km).

Difficulty: Moderate.

Trail maintenance: Yearly.

Traffic: Moderate.

Elevation gain: 1,362 ft.

Elevation loss: 80 ft.

Maximum elevation: 5,322 ft.

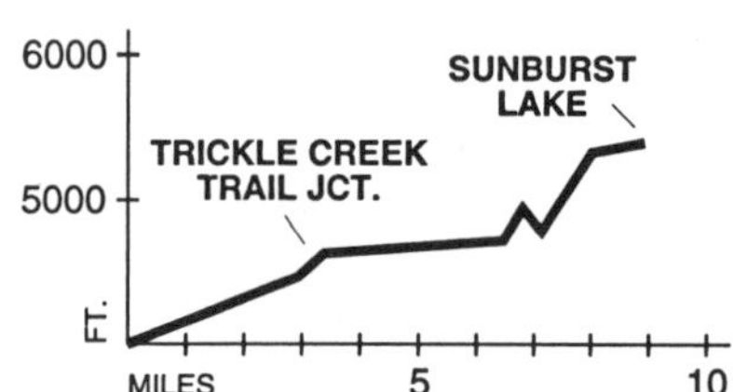

Topo maps: Meadow Creek, String Creek, Sunburst Lake.

Finding the trailhead: Follow the Bunker Creek Road (2826) about 6 miles past the Meadow Creek trailhead. Follow signs for Sunburst Lake. The trailhead is just beyond an extensive staging area for horse parties.

0.0 Gorge Creek trailhead.
1.8 Trail crosses Feather Creek.
2.4 Junction with the Picture Ridge Cutoff Trail (226). Keep going straight for Sunburst Lake.
3.1 Junction with the Stadium Creek Trail (115). Bear right.
7.7 Junction with the spur trail to Sunburst Lake (693). Turn left.
8.8 Sunburst Lake.

The trail: This trail provides an overnight trip of only moderate difficulty to spectacular Sunburst Lake, which is nestled at the foot of the north face of Swan Peak. In addition to its outstanding scenic views, Sunburst Lake provides high-quality fishing for native cutthroat trout. The lake can also be reached from the Napa Point

TRAIL 15 *SUNBURST LAKE*

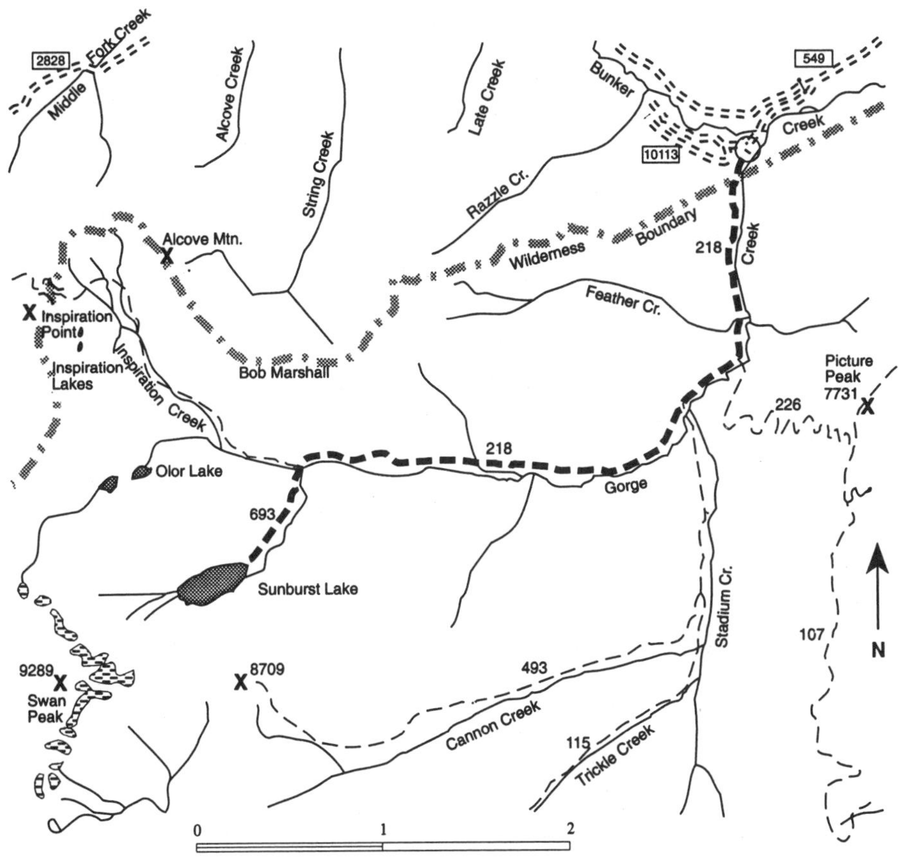

trailhead via an alternate route along Inspiration Creek; this route received maintenance in 1993 and is passable although steep, rough, and washed out in several places along the creek. Maintenance will continue on an occasional basis.

From the Gorge Creek trailhead, the trail begins by moving south along the bank of Gorge Creek. The trail wanders close to the stream from time to time, revealing a deep rift in the bedrock that bears the foaming waters of the creek far below. The trail continues through the mixed forest of lodgepole pine and Douglas-fir, crossing Feather Creek via a shallow ford. Shortly thereafter, the trail reaches a packer's camp, where an unmarked but heavily traveled ford of Gorge Creek leads to the Picture Ridge Cutoff Trail (226). The main trail climbs to avoid a cutbank, then descends to the creek bank again before reaching a series of open slopes.

The trail begins to climb across the slopes of grass and wildflowers, following the valley as it bends around to the west. Halfway around the curve, a faint track takes off to the left, bound for the Stadium Creek valley. The main trail sticks to the higher ground, passing several more unmarked spur paths that descend to the level of the creek. Forests alternate with brushy avalanche fields as the trail climbs gradually up the valley, and the forested foothills of the Swan Range rise on all sides. As the trail nears the Sunburst Lake trail junction, it passes through an old burn site. The mineral-rich soil of the burn supports a diverse profusion of plant life, from young conifers to shrubs and wildflowers. Note that a few old larch were able to survive the blaze. These fire-resistant trees possess a thick bark that flakes away from the trunk as it burns, sparing the living cambium underneath from damage. The trail passes through an island of unburned trees before entering the main part of the burn, which features a sneak preview of the glacier-clad north face of Swan Peak. After miles of forested foothills, it is quite a surprise to behold the craggy crest of this sheer peak rising from the low hills surrounding it.

At the far edge of the burn, the trail reaches a junction with the Sunburst Lake Trail (693). Turn left and follow the more well-worn path as it descends along the edge of the burn to reach the bank of Gorge Creek. Pack and saddle stock are not allowed around the shore of Sunburst Lake, and stock parties are asked to camp here and cover the short remaining distance to the lake on foot. The trail makes a knee-deep crossing of the rapid waters; thrill-seeking hikers can attempt a crossing on one of the many fallen logs that span the stream.

Once on the far side, the trail climbs southward through the moist forest to the west of Sunburst Lake's outlet stream. The trail wanders within sight of the water from time to time, revealing a crystal-clear brook that rushes over a bed of slanted bedrock. Tiny tributaries of this creek often overflow into the trail during wet weather, and extensive mud bogs exist on the flat benches above the initial grade. The final approach to the lake is guarded by enormous spruce trees, which rise

View of Black Bear Mountain from Picture Ridge.

toward the sky like the columns of a long-forgotten palace.

The lakeshore itself is surrounded by a thick growth of false huckleberry and is accessed by a network of deer trails. A thick log boom clogs the outlet of the lake, providing a dry passage to the eastern shore. Towering above the head of the lake is the dark face of Swan Peak. Its sheer cliffs are bedecked with small glaciers and permanent snowfields from which the brilliant threads of waterfalls cascade toward the valley floor. The lake itself is a brilliant sea green and is home to a thriving population of cutthroats. In the interest of preserving this outstanding fishing opportunity, anglers should keep only the fish that they intend to eat.

TRAIL 16 *PICTURE RIDGE*

Trail 107, 105

General description: Backpack from Meadow Creek trailhead to Black Bear Cabin, 15.1 mi. (24.3 km).

Difficulty: Strenuous.

Trail maintenance: Rare from Meadow Creek trailhead to Sarah Peak; frequent beyond.

Traffic: Light.

Elevation gain: 4,005 ft.

Elevation loss: 3,813 ft.

Maximum elevation: 7,720 ft.

Topo maps: Meadow Creek, Marmot Mountain, Pagoda Mountain.

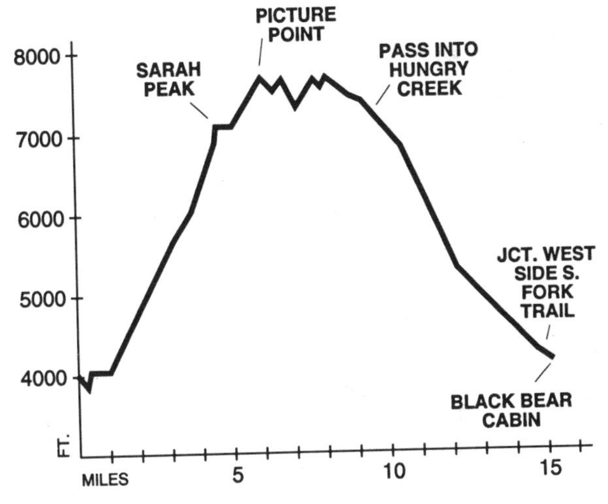

Finding the trailhead: The trail starts from the Meadow Creek trailhead, on the Bunker Creek Road (2826), which is reached at the end of the west side Hungry Horse Road (895). It is well marked with road signs.

0.0 Meadow Creek trailhead.
0.3 Trail fords Bunker Creek.
1.0 Picture Ridge Trail (107) splits off to the right.
4.6 Trail reaches the ridgeline behind Sarah Peak.
6.0 Picture Point.
6.2 Junction with the Picture Ridge Cutoff Trail (226). Stay left.
7.0 Spur trail descends to Picture Lake.
7.3 Heavily used spur trail descends to an outfitter's camp. Bear right.
9.5 Trail crosses the divide into the Hungry Creek drainage.
14.9 Junction with the west side South Fork Trail (263). Turn right.
15.1 Black Bear Cabin.

TRAIL 16 *PICTURE RIDGE*

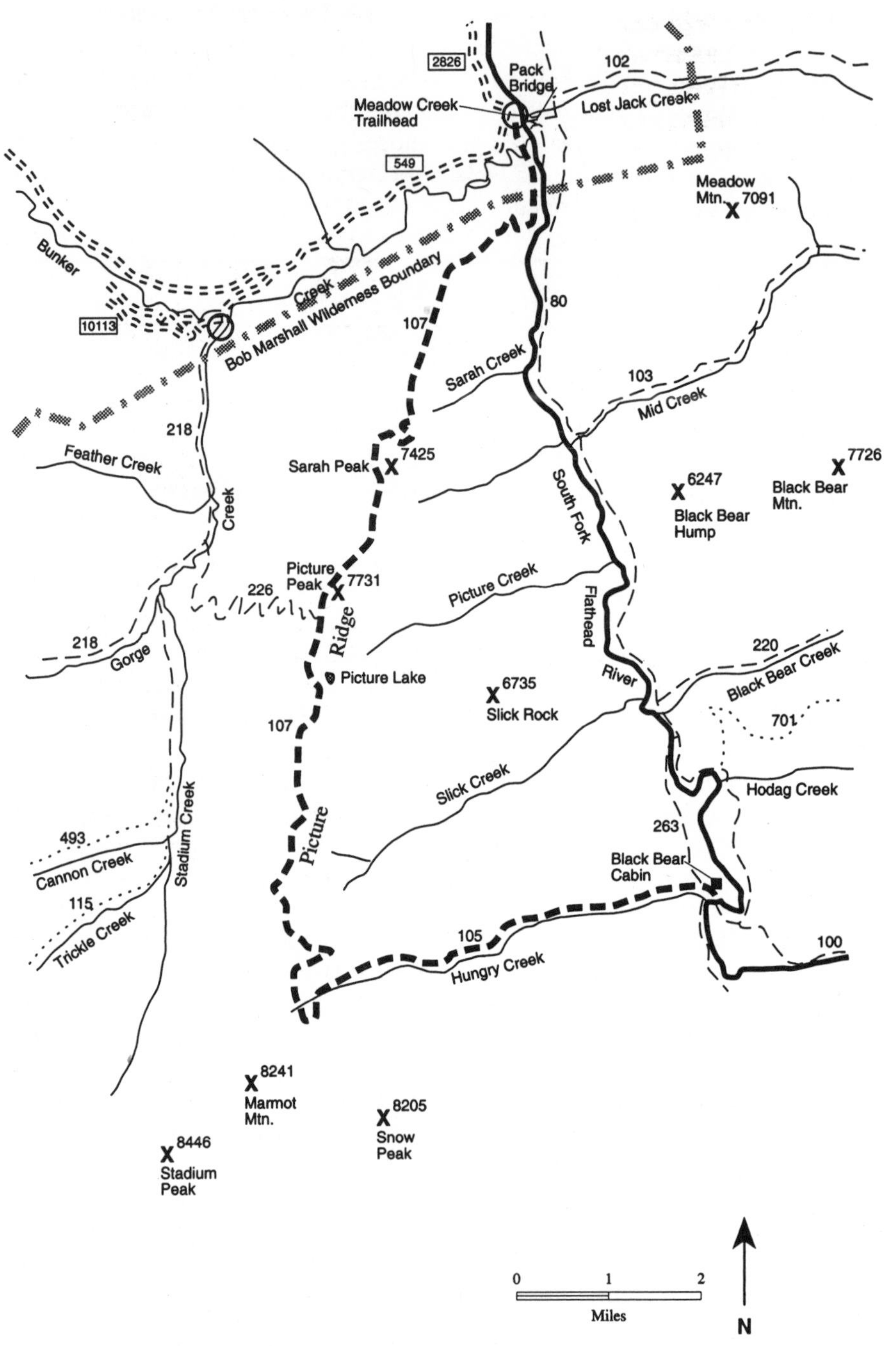

The trail: The Picture Ridge trail provides a ridgeline trek with outstanding views of Swan Peak to the west and the spires of the White River Overthrust to the east. The trail from the Meadow Creek trailhead to Sarah Peak is poorly maintained, with lots of downed timber and quite a few faint spots. Horse parties and inexperienced hikers should use the Picture Ridge Cutoff Trail (226) from Gorge Creek to access the ridge. This route is discussed briefly in the section on Sunburst Lake.

From the Meadow Creek trailhead, follow an unmarked trail southward along the west bank of the South Fork. This trail is soon joined by a spur trail from the outfitter's roost, and thus bolstered, the trail descends to Bunker Creek. After a waist-deep and fast-flowing ford, the trail climbs the bluff opposite the point of its approach to the creek. The trail is overgrown with brush here, but can be picked up easily on top of the hill. The trail travels the level top of the bench southward for a mile, passing the wilderness boundary to reach a trail sign that marks the spot where the Picture Ridge Trail begins its ascent.

Turn right at this junction, as the steep, overgrown path runs southward up the eastern slope of the ridge. From time to time, the trail breaks out onto open, grassy slopes that boast views of Meadow and Black Bear Mountains. The trail becomes quite faint as it crosses these slopes, forcing hikers to rely on scattered blazes and instinct to follow the trail. Eventually, the trail reaches subalpine forest, and soon afterward it switches back to the north to continue its ascent. The trail passes a small spring beneath the summit of Sarah Peak, then climbs to the west of this peak to reach the ridgeline. Through gaps in the lodgepole, the snowy crest of Swan Peak can be glimpsed to the west. To the east are unobstructed views of the limestone cliffs that tower above Mid and Black Bear creeks.

Views continue to improve as the trail moves south along the ridgetop. The route climbs and falls, passing below the summit of Picture Point before reaching a junction with the well-traveled cutoff trail to Gorge Creek (226). The trail, now splitting into several parallel paths, continues southward through a scattering of whitebark pine. Swan Peak rises like an enormous mirage to the west, providing a spectacular backdrop, and the rest of the jagged Swan Range trails away to the south of it. The trail passes above the tiny, greenish mirror of Picture Lake and soon reaches a spur trail that descends to its shores. The main trail then climbs through a meadowy glen dotted with the blossoms of glacier lilies.

After reaching a high point, a deceptively well-trodden spur trail descends to a packer's camp in the basin below, while the rather faint main trail continues to climb along the ridgeline. The route hugs the ridgetop as it passes above the headwaters of Slick Creek, with Silvertip and Pagoda Mountains crowning the skyline to the east. As the trail approaches the divide into Hungry Creek, it abandons the ridgeline and descends across the eastern slope of the ridge. Ahead lie the summits of Marmot Mountain and Snow Peak, which are the highest points on Picture Ridge. The trail descends through a saddle leading into the Hungry Creek valley, then turns west for a steady drop to the high basin below.

After reaching the floor of this alpine bowl, the trail continues southward to reach Hungry Creek. After crossing the creek, the trail begins its eastward descent of the valley. The trail soon returns to the north bank of the stream, passing through beargrass-studded meadows and subalpine forests overlooked by Mount Snow to the south. After several miles of steady descent, the trail reaches the dank spruce forests of the bottomland. The trail passes through a veritable rainforest of thimbleberry, and crosses muddy spots at regular intervals. Several miles later, the canyon narrows, and the trail passes beneath talus slopes, as an unnamed, cliffy promontory rises across the valley. The trail soon makes its way into the dry forests of the South Fork valley, reaching a junction with the West Side Trail (263) just north of the Black Bear Cabin.

TRAIL 17 *BLACK BEAR CREEK*

Trail 80, 220

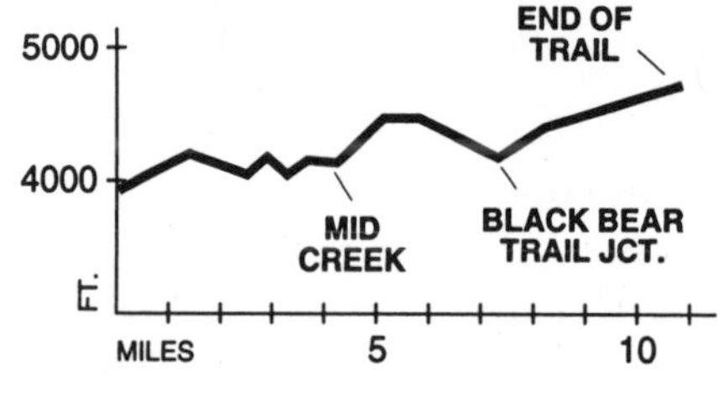

General description: Backpack from Meadow Creek trailhead to the end of the Black Bear trail, 10.8 mi. (17.4 km).
Difficulty: Moderate.
Trail maintenance: Yearly along the South Fork; occasional beyond.
Traffic: Heavy to Black Bear Creek; light beyond.
Elevation gain: 1,390 ft.
Elevation loss: 670 ft.
Maximum elevation: 4,680 ft.
Topo maps: Meadow Creek, Marmot Mountain, Cathedral Peak.
Finding the trailhead: Meadow Creek trailhead (see Picture Ridge).

- 0.0 Meadow Creek trailhead.
- 0.1 Trail crosses a pack bridge over the Meadow Creek Gorge.
- 0.3 Junction with the east side South Fork Trail (80). Turn right.
- 4.0 Junction with the Mid Creek Trail (103). Keep going straight for Black Bear Creek.
- 4.1 Trail fords Mid Creek.
- 7.2 Junction with the Black Bear Creek Trail (220). Turn left.
- 10.8 Trail peters out in the upper drainage of Black Bear Creek.

The trail: The Black Bear Creek trail provides a dead-end valley bottom journey that crosses excellent bear and elk habitat to reach the wild headwaters of Black Bear Creek. From the trailhead, cross the Meadow Creek pack bridge, which spans a deep, rocky gorge bearing the South Fork of the Flathead. Follow the road-sized trail to the east for several hundred yards to a marked junction with signs for Big Prairie. Turn right at this intersection, following the wide, muddy track southward across forested benches. The trail wanders up the low ridge separating Meadow Creek from the South Fork, through a morass of churned-up muck. After several miles of forest traveling, the trail reaches an overlook point high above the South Fork. Shortly afterward, the trail forks into two channels. The right fork is a narrow, cliff-hugging path that offers firm footing for hikers. It is by far the more scenic route as well,

TRAIL 17 *BLACK BEAR CREEK*
TRAIL 18 *MID CREEK*

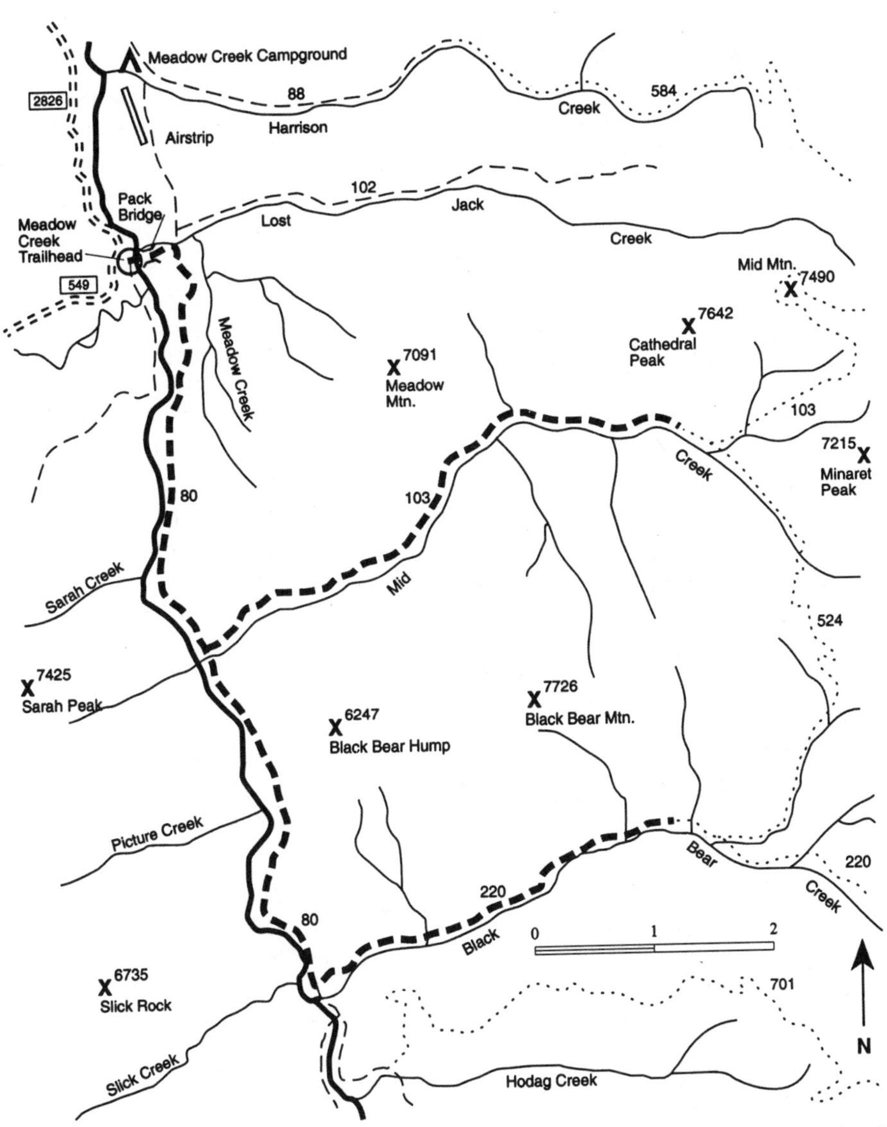

although it is too narrow for stock parties. Horsemen should use the higher inland route.

After these trails rejoin, they cross the flat, wooded benches above the river. Just before descending to Mid Creek, the trail passes an unmarked junction with the Mid Creek trail. The route then descends to the creek itself, which it crosses via a knee-deep ford. Enterprising hikers can probably find a log to cross and avoid getting their feet wet. The trail then climbs up the far side of the ravine beneath a gray rock face and then strikes off across the western slope of Black Bear Hump. As the trail makes its way upward, openings in the canopy allow good views of Picture Ridge, crowned by Sarah Peak to the north and Slick Rock to the south. The trail reaches a high point about halfway to Black Bear Creek and then begins a gentle descent to the benches overlooking the north bank of the creek. Here, the South Fork trail reaches a marked junction with the Black Bear Creek trail, which runs eastward up the side valley.

This trail climbs steadily across the north side of the Black Bear canyon, reaching a meadowy high point which boasts sweeping views up the valley of the South Fork. The peaks at the head of Black Bear Creek are also briefly visible, but are soon obscured by folds in the hillside. As the trail progresses eastward, open meadows on the south-facing slope yield only views of the forest-clad slopes across the creek. Tall snags stand above the vigorous growth of young trees, bearing mute testimony to the wildfire that once leveled the mighty forest. The trail winds onward, crossing a mossy feeder creek before traversing steep boulder fields and fragrant forests. After several miles of traveling, a meadowy slope allows a view of the sheer west face of Silvertip Mountain, by far the loftiest peak of the White River Syncline. The rocky cliffs of Black Bear Mountain rise high atop the slopes above the trail.

As the trail continues up the valley, Silvertip recedes behind a hillside, and is replaced by the high cliffs that form the headwall of the valley. The trail delves back into the forest, and occasional clumps of alder bar the way. The trail emerges from the forest onto an open bench above the creek, which it follows for a short time through a riparian forest of birch, cottonwood, and Douglas-fir. Upon approaching a series of cliffs that overshadow the north bank of the stream, the path descends onto the gravel bar. Here, the trail wanders east through luxuriant underbrush and occasional islands of trees. The trail peters out before reaching the next tributary stream, reaching its terminus beneath the yellow-and-gray mudstone cliffs.

TRAIL 18 *MID CREEK*

Trail 80, 103 (see map on p. 59)

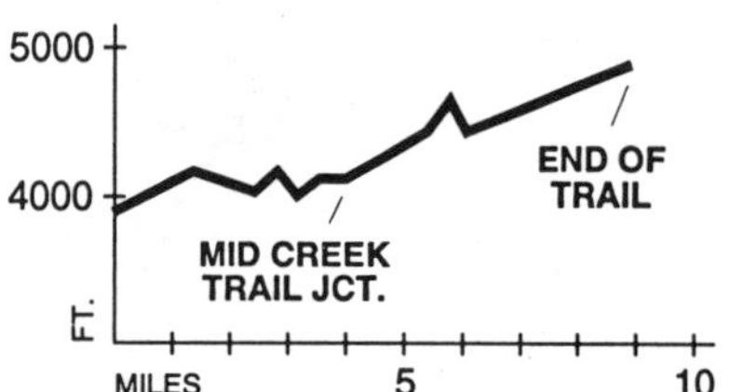

General description: A backpack from the Meadow Creek trailhead to the end of the Mid Creek trail, 9.0 mi. (14.5 km).
Difficulty: Moderate*
Trail maintenance: Yearly along the South Fork; rare beyond.
Traffic: Heavy to Mid Creek; light beyond.
Elevation gain: 1,200 ft.
Elevation loss: 280 ft.
Maximum elevation: 4,880 ft.
Topo maps: Meadow Creek, Cathedral Peak.
Finding the trailhead: Meadow Creek trailhead (see Picture Ridge, p. 55).

*Because of the difficulty involved in finding this trail, it is recommended for experienced hikers only.

0.0 Meadow Creek trailhead.
0.1 Trail crosses a pack bridge over the Meadow Creek Gorge.

0.3 Junction with the east side South Fork Trail (80). Turn right.
4.0 Unmarked junction with the Mid Creek Trail (103). Turn left.
9.0 Trail peters out in the upper drainage of Mid Creek.

The trail: The Mid Creek trail is a seldom-used route that follows a tributary of the South Fork of the Flathead. Downed timber and dense undergrowth make this trail impassable to horses in most years, but provides an excellent destination for hikers seeking wilderness solitude. The trail is reached via the East Side South Fork Trail (80), and the section of this trail leading to Mid Creek is discussed in detail in the section on Black Bear Creek.

From its junction with the South Fork trail, the Mid Creek trail runs northeastward, ascending across the slopes high above the north bank of the stream. Early on, openings reveal Black Bear Hump across the narrow valley, as well as Slick Rock on the far side of the South Fork. The vegetation alternates between a mixed forest, principally Douglas-fir and birch, and steep, rocky Douglas-fir savannah. In this latter plant community, yarrow and aster bloom in the dry meadows between the copses of trees. As the trail winds across the steep slope, the rock strata of Black Bear Mountain rise in sweeping curves across the valley. The trail makes occasional dips to the north as it crosses tiny feeder streams, passing through patches of brush as it does so.

The terrain becomes increasingly wet and brushy as the valley bends around to the east. Several small but substantial tributaries are crossed as the valley bottom rises to meet the trail. The trail descends into the tall brush of the valley bottom as it reaches a burned nub which rises across the creek. The rocky tooth of Silvertip Mountain reveals itself at the head of the valley as the trail crosses the flats before climbing onto a grassy bench above a dry channel of the creek. The trail enters a small park of tall grass, in which a rough-hewn table of split logs has been built. The trail has not been maintained beyond this park in recent memory and is all but impossible to pick out. The snags on the surrounding hillsides provide aeries for hawks and eagles, and hummingbirds are frequent visitors to the wildflowers that bloom here.

TRAIL 19 *SPOTTED BEAR LOOKOUT*

Trail 84

General description: A day hike from Spotted Bear Ranger Station to Spotted Bear Lookout, 5.9 mi. (9.5 km).

Difficulty: Moderately strenuous.

Trail maintenance: Yearly.

Traffic: Light.

Elevation gain: 3,940 ft.

Elevation loss: 260 ft.

Maximum elevation: 7,230 ft.

Topo maps: Tin Creek, Spotted Bear Mountain.

Finding the trailhead: The trail begins on the road just beyond the Spotted Bear

Ranger Station. The road forks, and the left fork is barred by a locked gate. The trail begins from this gate.

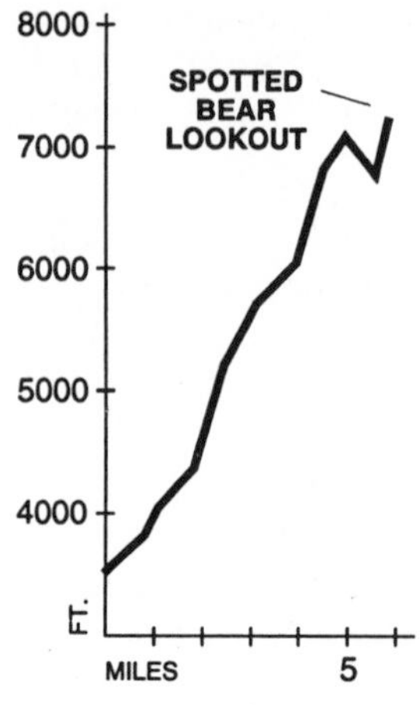

- 0.0 Trailhead near the Spotted Bear Ranger Station.
- 0.6 Trail crosses a dirt road.
- 1.2 Trail reaches a junction with the trail running to Spotted Bear Lake (88). Turn right for the lookout.
- 2.4 Trail reaches the ridgeline on Spotted Bear Mountain.
- 5.9 Spotted Bear Lookout.

The trail: This seldom-used but very accessible trail climbs to the top of Spotted Bear Mountain, which commands a sweeping view of the surrounding ranges. From the trailhead, the trail to the lookout climbs along a low sidehill, passing below a recent clearcut. The trail soon crosses a dirt road and fords two substantial streams as it winds through a lowland forest of Douglas-fir and occasional ponderosa pine. After crossing through the lowlands for a little over a mile, the trail forks into two paths. Travelers might not notice the junction until the trail sign for Spotted Bear Lake is reached, a point twenty yards beyond the junction. The left-hand trail is more heavily beaten, and it runs northeast to Spotted Bear Lake The less-traveled right fork is the sometimes muddy and rather overgrown Spotted Bear Lookout trail, and it crosses the remaining for-

Looking north to the lookout from the summit of Spotted Bear Mountain.

TRAIL 19 *SPOTTED BEAR LOOKOUT*

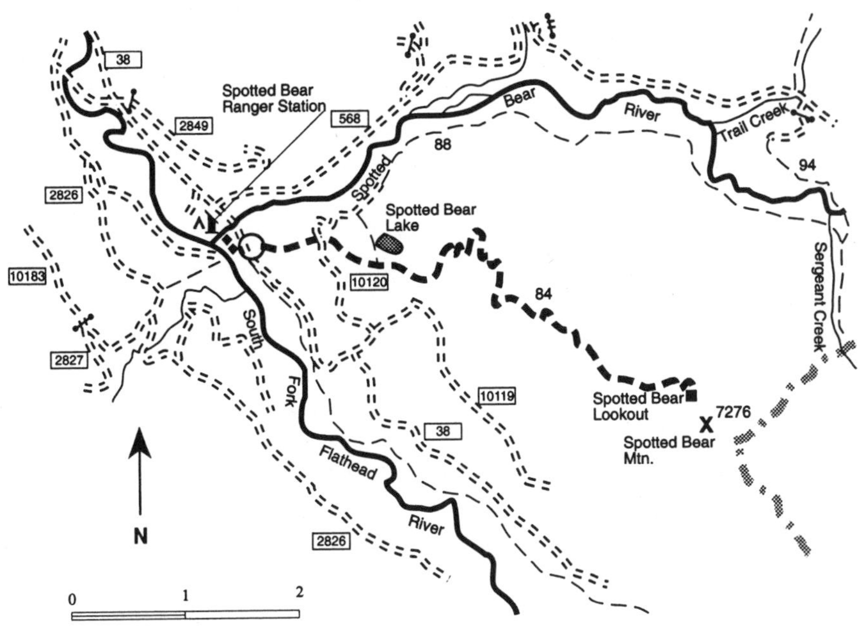

ested benches to reach the base of Spotted Bear Mountain.

The trail to the right begins its ascent at the foot of buff-colored cliffs streaked with gray and leaves the worst of the muck behind as it mounts the steeper slopes. The trail climbs through a sparse forest of Douglas-fir, which allows brief glimpses of Spotted Bear Lake and Bruce Ridge across the valley. The trail switchbacks steadily up the western slope of the mountain to reach an open bench containing a number of snow course markers mounted on posts. These markers are used by watershed managers to estimate the annual snow load, which helps them regulate the amount of water released from Hungry Horse Reservoir each year. The trail soon reaches the ridgeline, climbing through dense pockets of Douglas-fir. Views to the west continue to expand, allowing glimpses of the snowy peaks of the Swan Range to the west.

Upon reaching the foot of the next steep point, the trail climbs through a rock garden of wildflowers and moss on the spine of the ridge, and views to the north and northeast are finally revealed. The trail reaches the next crest of the ridge, then passes through alpine meadows dotted with clumps of subalpine fir. The trail climbs across a bald false summit, which allows sweeping views highlighted by the tilted strata of Meadow Mountain to the south, as well as Swan Peak to the west. Ahead, the lookout is perched atop the next point along the ridgeline. The trail descends into the saddle beyond, then climbs the final several hundred feet through a rocky dwarf forest of subalpine fir.

The lookout itself rises from the mountaintop like a lighthouse in a stormy sea of peaks and commands spectacular views in all directions. To the north, vistas extend all the way to Mount Saint Nicholas in Glacier National Park and also encompass Hungry Horse Reservoir and the spiny peaks of the Flathead Range. Argosy and

Pentagon mountains dominate the eastern skyline, while Silvertip Mountain rises above its lesser fellows to the south. The broad sweep of the Swan Range crowns the western horizon, with Swan Peak towering high above a continuous wall of serrated rock. The true summit of Spotted Bear Mountain lies a quarter mile to the south and can be reached easily by a short jaunt across the alpine tundra to the south.

TRAIL 20 *PAGODA MOUNTAIN*

Trail 100

General description: An extended trip from the South Fork of the Flathead to the White River, 9.6 mi. (15.5 km).

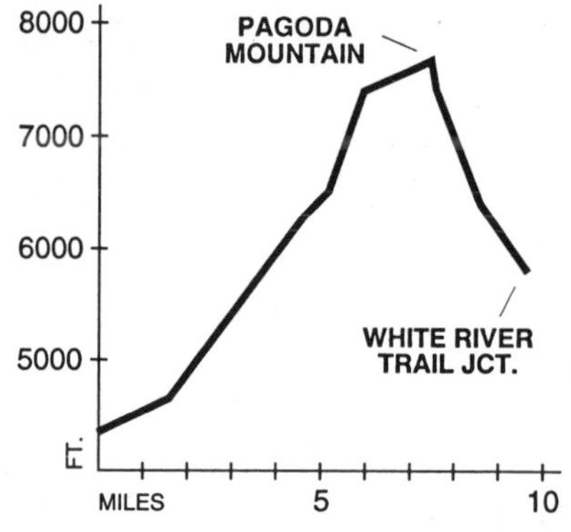

Difficulty: Moderately strenuous.
Trail maintenance: Yearly.
Traffic: Light.
Elevation gain: 3,250 ft.
Elevation loss: 1,860 ft.
Maximum elevation: 7,590 ft.
Topo maps: Pagoda Mountain, Amphitheatre Mountain.
Finding the trail: The trail begins from the east side South Fork trail at a junction about a mile south of the Black Bear pack bridge. The trail is marked "Helen Creek Trail" at its outset.

0.0 Junction of east side South Fork (80) and Pagoda Mountain (100) trails.
1.7 Trail fords the North Fork of Helen Creek.
6.1 Trail passes high above the headwaters of Damnation Creek.
7.4 Trail crosses the divide into the White River drainage.
9.6 Trail reaches a junction with the White River Trail (112).

The trail: This trail links the South Fork and White River valleys via a high route that features outstanding vistas of the surrounding country. The trail begins by ascending the valley of Helen Creek, a steep, wooded canyon with very limited views. After several miles, a pointed hill rises above the valley, signifying the confluence of the two forks of Helen Creek. Upon reaching this spot, the trail fords the North Fork and continues its eastward progress beside the main body of Helen Creek. The trail continues its steady and monotonous ascent through spruce and Douglas-fir forest, passing a falls in the creek below that can only be seen after a steep downhill bushwhack. Shortly thereafter, a beehive-shaped cliff reveals itself across the valley, and the trail passes above a rocky, moss-lined gorge.

After the trail crosses a broad boulder field, the valley begins a slow arc to the south. Subalpine fir appear among the lowland trees, and avalanche slopes filled with beargrass blossoms interrupt the forest. Soon, the trail crosses Helen Creek and climbs into a shallow basin filled with old whitebark pine. These trees are festooned with a hanging lichen known as "old man's beard," which is a favorite winter food of mule deer. This lichen is really a symbiotic community consisting of a primitive fungus, which supplies structural support, and an algae, which supplies energy through photosynthesis.

After switchbacking upward for some distance, the trail takes a long, climbing dogleg to the west to reach the ridgeline. Once atop the crest of the ridge, the entire length of the Swan Range can be seen stretching across the western skyline. The trail drops onto the southern face of the ridge, passing high above the headwaters of Damnation Creek. The foot of Big Salmon Lake can be seen on the far side of the South Fork Valley, with Charlotte Peak rising above it. Farther south, Spire Peak and Scarface Mountain rise prominently in a sea of lower mountains. The trail passes beneath the flat crown of Pagoda Mountain and heads into a pass at the foot of a much more impressive (though nameless) peak that rises to the southeast.

The trail crosses a badly eroded area and then descends through a high basin dotted with scrubby subalpine fir. To the east, the bedrock rises in a broad swell that represents the back side of the Chinese Wall. As the trail descends steadily through a riot of wildflowers, the rugged spires of Amphitheatre Mountain, Moccasin Butte, and Gladiator Mountain soar skyward to the south along the Continental Divide. The trail descends past a boulder-strewn talus slope, then passes into the forest that cloaks the White River valley. One last grassy meadow allows views of the peaks surrounding Moccasin Butte before the trail disappears into the trees for good. The descent eases as the trail makes its way toward the White River, and the trail crosses a dry wash just before reaching its junction with the White River Trail (112).

A ridge of the White River syncline as seen from the eastern slope of Pagoda Mountain.

TRAIL 20 *PAGODA MOUNTAIN*

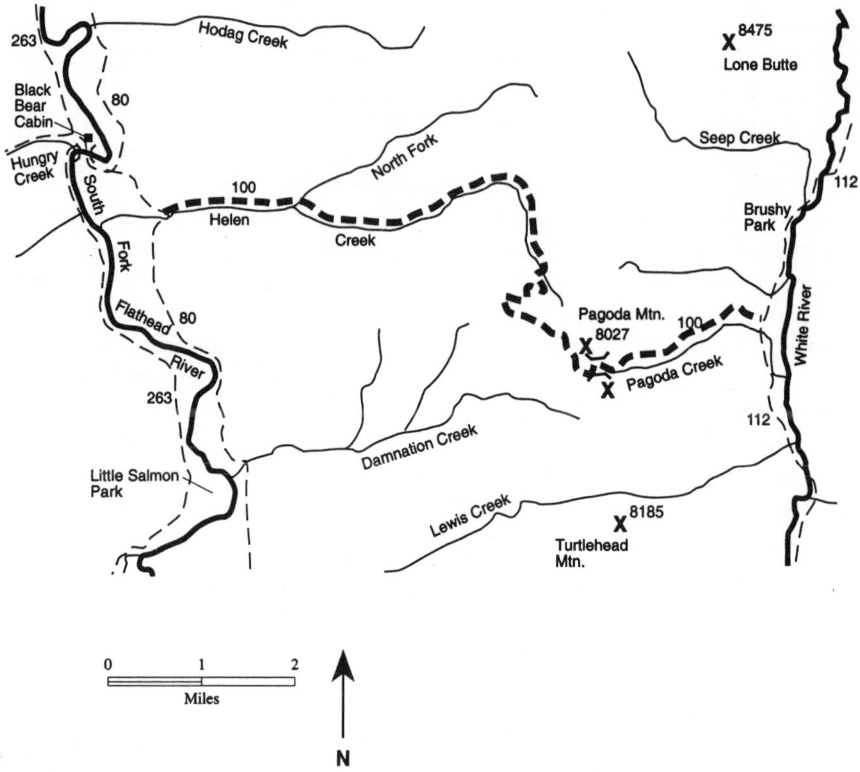

TRAIL 21 *TWIN PEAK*

Trail 237, 230, 200

General description: A backpack from the Upper Twin Creek trailhead to the base of Twin Peak, 10.8 mi. (17.4 km).

Difficulty: Moderately strenuous.

Trail maintenance: Occasional.

Traffic: Very light.

Elevation gain: 3,860 ft.

Elevation loss: 1,064 ft.

Maximum elevation: 6,640 ft.

Topo maps: Tin Creek, Spotted Bear Mountain, Horseshoe Peak.

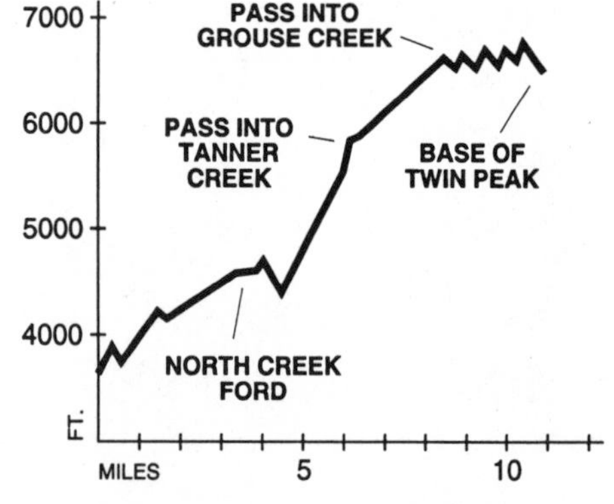

Finding the trailhead: The trail begins about 100 yards north of Upper Twin Creek, at a marked trailhead on the east side Hungry Horse Reservoir Road. Parking is available at a lot beside the creek.

0.0 Upper Twin Creek trailhead.
1.6 Trail turns into the valley of North Creek.
2.8 Trail fords North Creek.
4.5 Junction with the Twin Creek Trail (237). Turn left for Twin Peak.
6.2 Trail crosses the divide into the Tanner Creek drainage.
8.6 Trail passes into the Grouse Creek drainage.
9.6 Junction with the Long Creek Trail (200). Turn right for Twin Peak.
10.8 Trail reaches the base of Twin Peak.

The trail: This trail accesses the alpine ridges at the headwaters of Long Creek, after a long passage through the lowlands of the Upper Twin Creek drainage. The trail receives relatively light use, making it an ideal destination for those who seek solitude. From the trail's beginning beside the Hungry Horse Reservoir East Side Road, the trail crosses a flat bench to reach the base of a steep hillside. The trail climbs across this grassy west-facing slope, then turns east to follow the valley of Upper Twin Creek. The trail passes in and out of a mixed forest, staying high above the level of the creek. The cliffs of Beacon Mountain rise above the trail to the northeast. The trail ascends gradually, crossing a wooded tableland at the foot of this peak, then continues eastward to reach a high overlook point above the creek. From this vantage point, the distant peaks along the Continental Divide can be seen along the horizon.

After passing this observation point, the trail turns north into the valley of North Creek, climbing gradually through a sparse stand of Douglas-fir. The trail maintains its position high above this creek for a mile, then allows the creek bottom to rise toward it. After passing a side valley, the trail reaches an ankle-deep ford of North Creek and then climbs through a low saddle to the east. The route then strikes off across a bewildering flatland of dense forest to reach the bank of a tiny stream that flows westward. The trail follows the marshy bank of this brook past several substantial ponds, where waterfowl can be spotted dabbling among flooded treetrunks. Beyond the second and largest pond, the route is tricky to follow; the trail grows faint as it crosses a marshy meadow on a northeasterly bearing but becomes apparent again as it climbs onto the higher ground of the forest.

After a shallow uphill grade, the trail descends rather steeply, making a number of crossings of a small stream on its way to a trail junction. To the right, a trail descends back toward the Upper Twin Valley, which it follows for several miles before becoming hard to find. Turn left for the Twin Peak trail, which begins a steady ascent across a hillside covered in lodgepole pine and huckleberry bushes. As the trail runs to the northwest, the formless hills gradually coalesce into a steep ridge. Avalanche slopes interrupt the forest as the trail gains altitude, allowing views of Spy Mountain and Vulture Peak to the east. The lowland forest is soon replaced by subalpine fir, and the trail climbs the final pitch through clumps of alder to reach the pass into the Tanner Creek drainage.

The country takes on a distinctly alpine character as the trail makes its way northeastward toward the headwaters of Tanner Creek. The brushy subalpine forest gives way to open slopes of beargrass, and views open up toward the Flathead Range. The trail continues its steady ascent until it reaches the high col that leads

TRAIL 21 *TWIN PEAK*

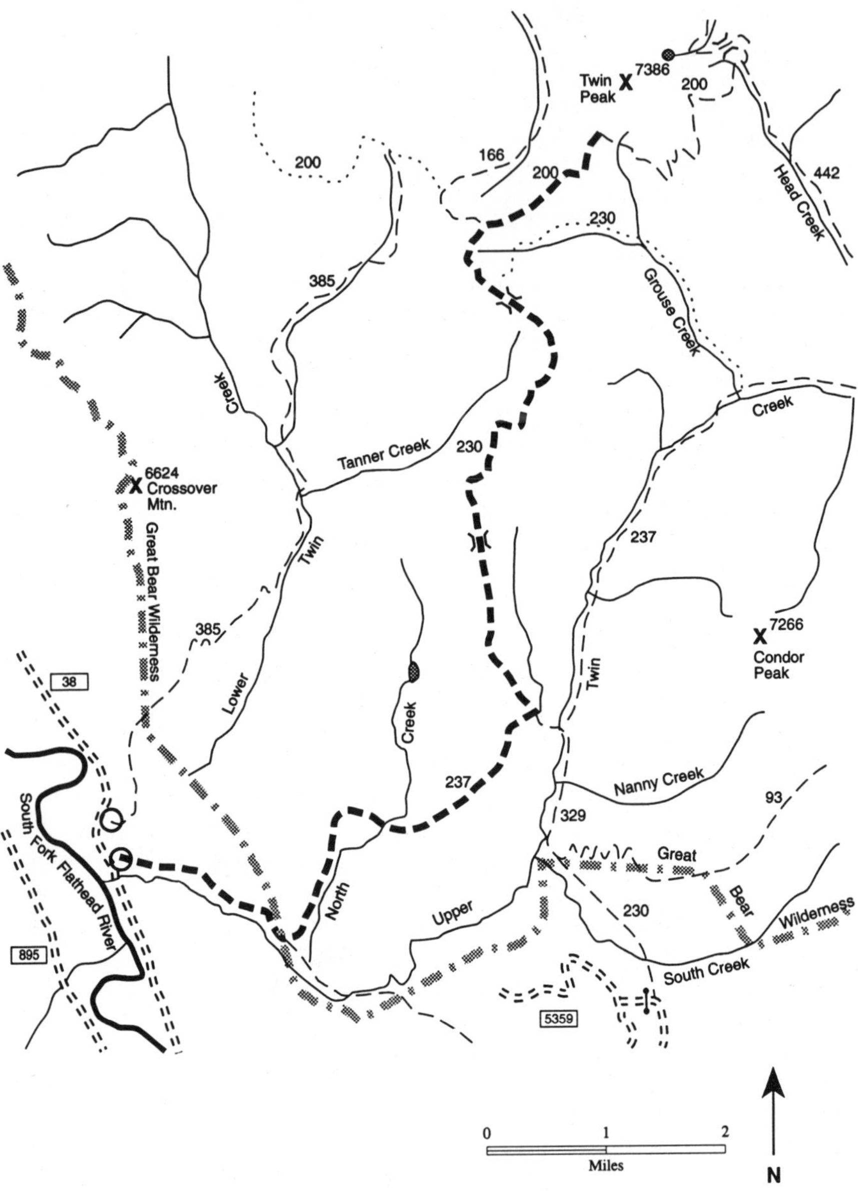

into the Grouse Creek Valley. After dipping into the alpine basin beyond, travelers will pass several shallow tarns, overlooked by talus slopes that are home to the playful ground squirrel as well as the elusive pika. This latter creature is a tiny denizen of the boulder fields and is not a rodent but a miniature, short-eared member of the rabbit family. The trail soon crosses the headwaters of Grouse Creek, passing the spot where an old abandoned trail once descended to the valley floor. The trail then climbs around the head of the valley to reach a high saddle in the ridge to the north.

At this saddle, the trail reaches a marked junction. The trail descending into the valley straight ahead becomes the Long Creek Trail (166). Turn right to complete the trek to the base of Twin Peak. The trail rises and falls as it sticks to the tundra-covered ridgeline on its northeastward course. Golden eagles soar along these high ridges, seeking to surprise an unwary marmot or pika. After cresting the final rise along the ridge, the trail drops into the forested saddle at the base of Twin Peak. The Cy Creek Trail (332) runs east from this point, climbing steadily to a high col above the Head Creek valley and then through another pass to the Cy Creek drainage. There is an extensive washout on this section of trail, making it challenging for foot travel and impassable for horses.

TRAIL 22 *GUNSIGHT LAKE*

Trail 327, 43

General description: A long day hike or backpack from the Big Bill trailhead to Gunsight Lake, 6.6 mi. (10.6 km).

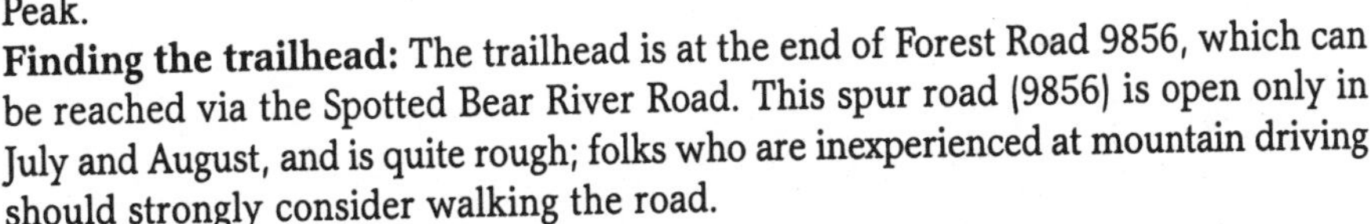

Difficulty: Moderate.
Trail maintenance: Yearly.
Traffic: Moderate.
Elevation gain: 1,390 ft.
Elevation loss: 570 ft.
Maximum elevation: 6,990 ft.
Topo maps: Spotted Bear Mountain, Whitcomb Peak.

Finding the trailhead: The trailhead is at the end of Forest Road 9856, which can be reached via the Spotted Bear River Road. This spur road (9856) is open only in July and August, and is quite rough; folks who are inexperienced at mountain driving should strongly consider walking the road.

0.0 Big Bill trailhead.
1.0 Trail crosses Big Bill Creek.
2.0 Saddle into the Whitcomb Creek drainage. Junction with the Spy Mountain Trail (75). Bear right for Gunsight Lake.
4.9 Whitcomb Peak.
5.3 Junction with the Upper Twin Creek Trail (237). Stay right.
5.4 Junction with the Miner Creek Trail (81). Bear right for Gunsight Lake.
6.0 Schafer Creek Trail (327) drops away to the left. Keep going straight ahead for Gunsight Lake.
6.3 Unmarked junction with the spur trail to Gunsight Rock. Stay left for the lake.
6.6 Gunsight Lake.

The trail: This trail accesses the high country surrounding Whitcomb Peak, passing some fascinating rock formations on its way to a subalpine pond. The high altitude of the trailhead makes this route one of the easiest routes to the timberline, but the road to the trailhead does not open until the first of July. The trail to Gunsight Lake can also be used as a travel corridor into the Miner and Schafer Creek drainages for travelers who are looking for an extended journey.

From the trailhead, the path runs northeast, climbing gently as it wanders into the upper end of the Big Bill Creek drainage. The trail makes its way through a diverse forest of lodgepole, larch, and subalpine fir, and openings in the forest allow views of the peaks surrounding the Sergeant Creek Valley. From the west, Meadow, Cathedral, and Mid mountains rise along the leading edge of the White River Syncline. As the trail makes its way around the headwaters of Big Bill Creek, Gildart Peak and Thunderbolt Mountain of the Swan Range rear their snow-clad summits along the western horizon. Upon reaching the eastern edge of the valley, the trail turns north and climbs moderately into rounded hills draped with grassy slopes and dotted with the blossoms of lupine, paintbrush, and sego lily. This area is a favorite summer range for elk and mule deer. After passing through these high meadows, the trail resumes its easterly course and mounts the high pass into the Whitcomb Creek valley.

At this saddle, there is a marked junction with the Spy Mountain Trail (238), a rarely-maintained track that follows the ridgelines to the northwest. The trail to Gunsight Lake continues through the pass and runs onto the western slope of the valley beyond. Bearing north, the route climbs gently across slopes of beargrass and scattered subalpine fir. At the head of the valley, the tilted capstone of Whitcomb Peak rises above the ridgetop, while farther east are the twin pillars of Gunsight Rock.

Whitcomb Peak from the Gunsight Lake Trail.

TRAIL 22 *GUNSIGHT LAKE*

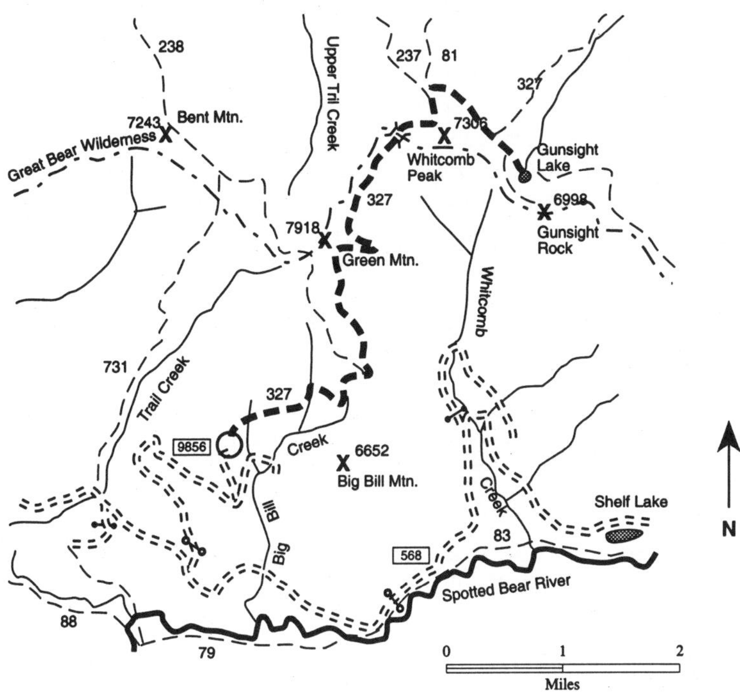

As the trail continues its approach toward Whitcomb Peak, the rocky tooth of Pentagon Mountain becomes visible on the eastern horizon. The old snags at the head of the drainage provide nest holes for the Rocky Mountain bluebird, which forages for insects in these high alpine meadows. A look back to the south reveals the curving bands of rock that make up Sergeant Mountain, providing a natural lesson in geology. The force of colliding continental plates placed enormous pressure on the rock strata along the fault zone. The rock had enough plasticity to bend without shattering, so it became folded like the bellows of an accordion. Over time, erosion has worn away at the folded rock, but this exposed layer still remains intact to tell the story of the enormous forces that shaped the continent. The lofty peak that is visible beyond Sergeant's crest is Silvertip Mountain, the tallest peak of the White River Syncline.

At the head of the valley, the trail crosses a pass below the western face of Whitcomb Peak, which stands above the trail like a haunted dolmen from neolithic times. Snow lingers into July on the cool northwest face of this peak, and drifts across the trail should be expected here. Expansive views to the northwest feature the Flathead Range, with Horseshoe Peak dominating the scene. The trail soon winds out onto a northern finger ridge of Whitcomb, passing the faint trail (237) that descends into the Upper Twin drainage. Once the trail reaches a saddle in the ridgeline, the trail for Miner Creek (81) takes off to the north, while the trail to Gunsight Lake rounds the ridgecrest and turns southeast. Soakem Mountain is the peak looming across the valley to the north, while the summit of Argosy Mountain can be seen above the buttresses of Dean Ridge to the east.

The trail descends across hummocky country to reach yet another trail junction on the bank of a small creek. To the left, the Schafer Creek Trail (327) descends toward the Middle Fork of the Flathead, while the Gunsight Trail (43) crosses the stream and continues straight ahead. This trail crosses marshy terrain and continues eastward, and Gunsight Rock soon looms into sight above it. The twin chimneys of Gunsight Rock are separated by a deep notch, like the peep sight once used on rifles. After a short distance, the trail forks, with the right fork climbing to the rock itself and the left fork descending gradually to Gunsight Lake. This lake is a shallow, weedy affair that provides an ideal breeding ground for mosquitoes (so bring repellant). Towering above the water is the enormous rock formation that gives the lake its name.

TRAIL 23 *SPOTTED BEAR RIVER*

Trail 83

General description: A backpack from the Spotted Bear River trailhead to Spotted Bear Pass, 18.5 mi. (29.8 km).

Difficulty: Moderate.

Trail maintenance: Yearly.

Traffic: Moderate.

Elevation gain: 2,657 ft.

Elevation loss: 372 ft.

Maximum elevation: 6,725 ft.

Topo maps: Whitcomb Peak, Trilobite Peak, Bungalow Mountain, Three Sisters, Slategoat Mountain.

Finding the trailhead: The trail begins at the Spotted Bear River trailhead, at the end of the Spotted Bear River Road (568). The last five miles of this road are closed from September through June; the trail can also be reached from a trailhead at the Beaver Creek campground.

0.0 Spotted Bear River trailhead.
0.1 Junction with the Spotted Bear River Trail (83). Turn left.

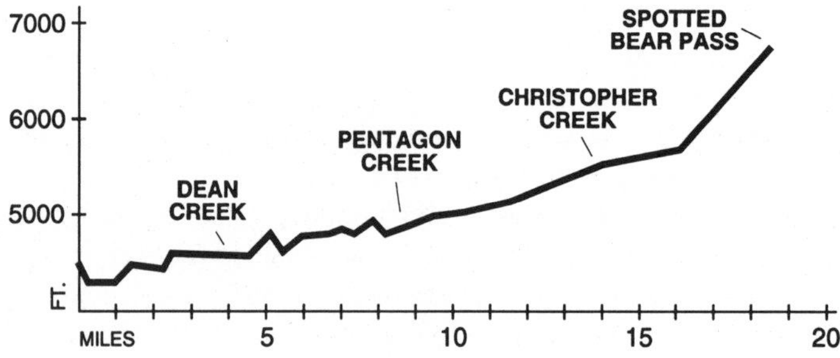

0.6 Dean Ridge Trail (43) descends to meet the Spotted Bear River trail .
1.0 Junction with the Silvertip Creek Trail (89). Bear left.
1.1 Silvertip Cabin.
1.4 Blue Lakes.
4.0 Trail enters the Great Bear Wilderness.
4.1 Trail fords Dean Creek.
4.6 Boundary of the Bob Marshall Wilderness. Junction with the Elk Ridge Trail (109). Keep going straight for Spotted Bear Pass.
5.9 Dean Falls.
8.8 Pentagon Cabin. Pentagon Creek-Switchback Pass Trail (173) enters from the left.
8.9 Trail fords Pentagon Creek.
9.0 Junction with the Hart Lake-Table Hill trail. Keep going straight.
9.4 Trail fords Hart Creek.
9.9 Wall Creek - Bungalow Mountain Trail (90) takes off to the right.
12.6 Trail fords the Spotted Bear River.
14.0 Trail crosses Christopher Creek.
16.0 Trail crosses the Spotted Bear River to reach its east bank.
18.5 Spotted Bear Pass.

The trail: The Spotted Bear River trail is a major access corridor for travelers bound for the Trilobite Range, the Chinese Wall, and Bungalow Mountain. In addition, the trail is used by anglers whose destination is the river itself. Despite its fairly high level of traffic, this trail is very resilient and does not get terribly muddy even in the wettest weather. The trail actually begins at the Beaver Creek Campground and follows the river to reach the upper trailhead; this trail description will begin from this latter point.

The hike along the Spotted Bear River begins with a short descent on a spur trail that links the trailhead with the main river trail. Turn left at the junction and head eastward, as the trail runs level across forested slopes high above the water. After crossing a small stream choked with thimbleberry bushes, the trail passes an unmarked junction with the Dean Ridge Trail (43). (At the time this book was written, the junction was masked by blowdowns and was hard to identify.) After the unmarked junction, the well-traveled Silvertip Trail (89) curves away to the right on its way to a ford of the Spotted Bear River. The main trail passes the Silvertip Cabin in its small woodland meadow and then glides between the aquamarine pools of the Blue Lakes. These woodland ponds are situated on the valley floor within a forest of Douglas-fir, and the larger of the two contains a sparse population of trout which provides rather poor fishing.

As the trail continues eastward, the cliffs of Limestone Peak to the south are the only reliable gauge of progress; the forested slopes north of the river are unbroken by terrain features. The route emerges from the forest at Dean Creek, where a knee-deep ford or a hazardous log crossing lead to the opposite shore. Once the trail reaches the far bank, it begins to climb steadily on its easterly course. Atop a high bench just east of Dean Creek, the trail reaches the Bob Marshall Wilderness boundary, at which point a trail sign marks the route ascending Elk Ridge. The river trail

TRAIL 23 *SPOTTED BEAR RIVER*

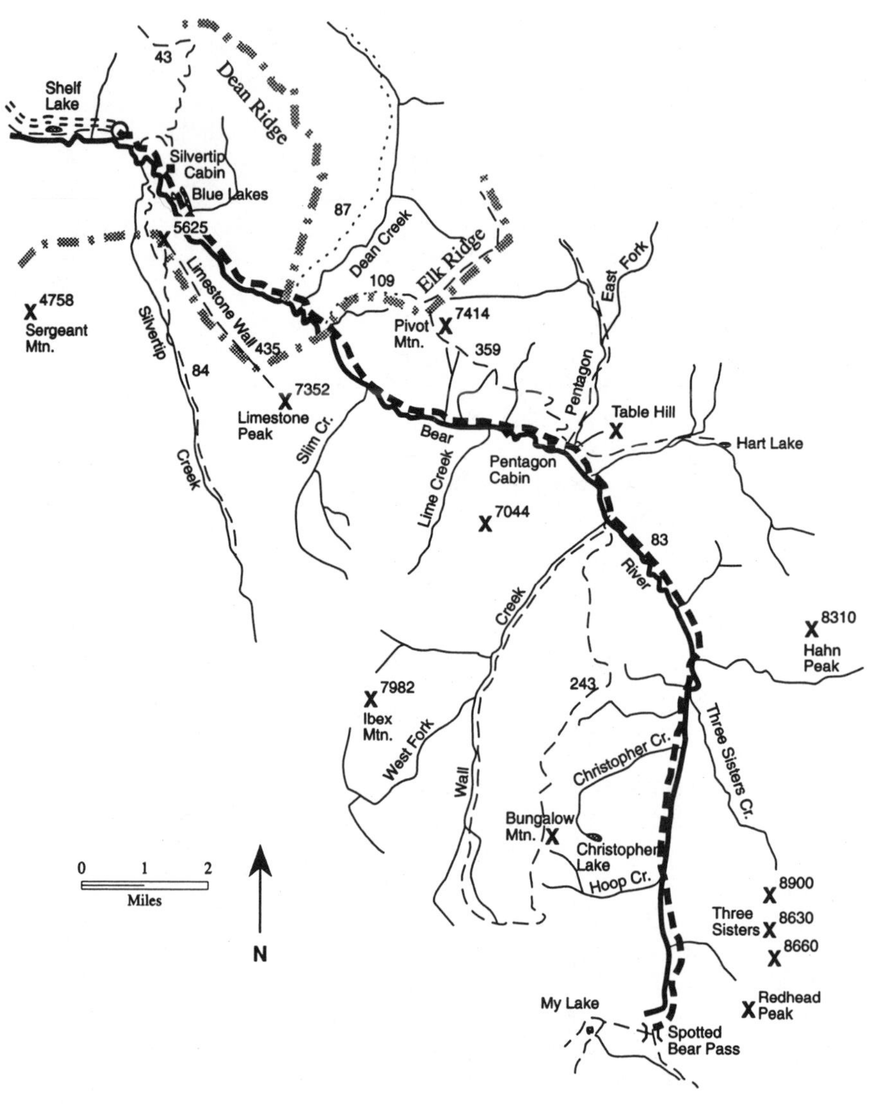

immediately descends to cross a small feeder stream before resuming its climb along the river.

A mile and a half later, the trail passes an overlook of Dean Falls, the foaming cataract which plunges almost a hundred feet through a steep-walled, mossy canyon. This is a barrier to the upstream movement of trout; these fish are not present above the falls, according to Forest Service personnel. The trail climbs a bit farther, then descends to the level of the river, where a backward glance reveals the summit of Limestone Peak. The trail alternates between spruce bottomland and pine-clad hills for the balance of the distance to Pentagon Cabin. The trail up Pentagon Creek (173) that runs toward Switchback Pass departs from the Spotted Bear River trail opposite this structure.

After a knee-deep ford of Pentagon Creek, the trail passes the route to Table Hill and Hart Lake before crossing more bottomland to reach Hart Creek. A knee-deep crossing of Hart Creek is necessary to continue along the trail, which soon passes the Wall Creek Trail (90) junction. The trail then continues eastward for 2.7 miles of unbroken forest travel. The canopy occasionally thins out enough to reveal the northern ribs of Bungalow Mountain to the south. As the valley takes a sharp bend to the south, the trail makes an ankle-deep crossing of the river, well below its confluence with Three Sisters Creek. The trail clings to the sidehill above the river as it charts its new southward course and works its way through clumps of alder and across several small streams.

The valley bottom gradually broadens, and the Spotted Bear River becomes reduced to a quiet woodland creek. The trail hopscotches across Christopher Creek and makes its way through the level forest, which is underlain by grouse whortleberry and false huckleberry. After a time, the trail leaves the valley floor in favor of the gentle slopes to the west and passes beneath the striated cliffs of Bungalow Mountain. After returning to the viewless forest, the trail passes at the foot of a second series of cliffs. It then descends into swampy bottomland, where it remains until the next crossing of the "river." This ford is located beneath its confluence with Hoop Creek and is an easy crossing that never exceeds ankle depth.

The trail then begins its gradual but steady ascent up the east wall of the valley. A sparse overstory of spruce and fir allows a luxuriant growth of false huckleberries in the understory, and these bushes provide travelers with a real soaking in wet weather. Bungalow Mountain can occasionally be seen through openings in the forest as the trail ascends. The route passes below a stairstep waterfall on a tributary stream before making the final westward turn toward Spotted Bear Pass. The final approach to this divide provides the best of the trail's rather limited scenery: The ragged peaks surrounding Switchback Pass can be viewed by looking down the river valley to the north. Spotted Bear Pass is a low, wooded defile, and offers no views of its own. At the pass, the main trail (111) runs straight ahead into the valley of Rock Creek, while to the right, the northern end of the Chinese Wall Trail (194) ascends the ridgeline on its way to My Lake.

TRAIL 24 ELK RIDGE

Trail 83, 109, 359

General description: A wilderness route from the Spotted Bear River to Pentagon Pass,10.4 mi. (16.7 km).

Difficulty: Strenuous.*

Trail maintenance: Yearly along the Spotted Bear River; rare beyond.

Traffic: Moderate to Elk Ridge trail; very light beyond.

Elevation gain: 4,378 ft.

Elevation loss: 1,658 ft

Maximum elevation: 7,720 ft.
Topo maps: Whitcomb Peak, Trilobite Peak.
Finding the trailhead: The trip begins at the Spotted Bear River trailhead. See the Spotted Bear River.

*Some difficult off-trail scrambling will be required.

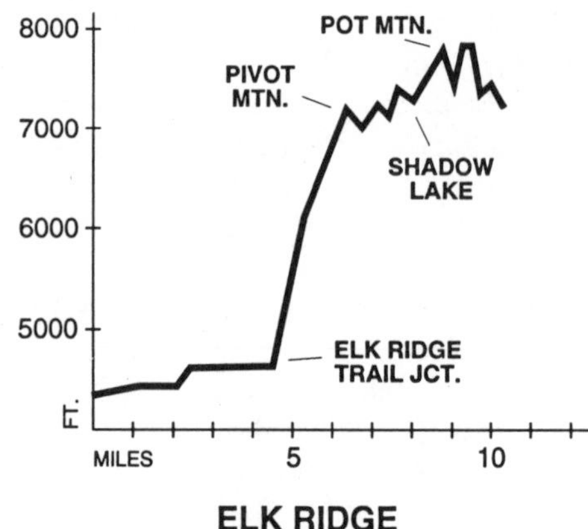

ELK RIDGE

0.0 Spotted Bear River trailhead.
0.1 Junction with the Spotted Bear River Trail (83). Turn left.
0.6 Dean Ridge Trail (43) descends to meet the Spotted Bear River trail.
1.0 Junction with the Silvertip Creek Trail (89). Bear left.
1.1 Silvertip Cabin.
1.4 Blue Lakes.
4.0 Trail enters the Great Bear Wilderness.
4.1 Trail fords Dean Creek.
4.6 Boundary of the Bob Marshall Wilderness. Junction with the Elk Ridge Trail (109). Turn left.
6.5 Junction with the Pivot Mountain Trail. Bear left to continue the hike.
7.5 Shadow Mountain.
8.2 Shadow Lake.
9.0 Summit of Pot Mountain. All traces of a trail end here.
10.4 Route reaches the Pentagon Creek-Dolly Varden Creek Trail (173).

The trail: This route is very primitive indeed. It follows the bed of an old trail, no longer maintained, to a former fire lookout on Pot Mountain. Contrary to some maps, no trail ever existed beyond this point, and it is a tough scramble over some extremely steep pitches to reach the pass into Dolly Varden Creek. This latter part of the route is quite dangerous and should be attempted only by experts that possess some rock climbing skills. The scenery along this ridgeline route is breathtaking, featuring excellent views of Silvertip and Pentagon Mountains, as well as seldom-seen Pot and Shadow lakes.

This trek begins at the Spotted Bear River trailhead and follows the river trail for 4.6 miles. This part of the trip is discussed on page 72. This trail reaches the Elk Ridge trail junction just beyond the crossing of Dean Creek, at a large sign proclaiming the boundary of the Bob Marshall Wilderness. A smaller sign points the way to the old Elk Ridge trail, which runs westward as it begins to climb the slope above. After a short distance, the trail begins to switchback up the ridgeline to the west of a small stream and undergoes a sharp increase in gradient. The track is ultimately obscured by competing elk and hunter trails, and it is necessary to bushwhack the steep ridgetop as it ascends toward the summit of Pivot Mountain. After a time, the grade eases off a bit, and grassy glades allow views of Silvertip Mountain to the south. Stick

TRAIL 24 *ELK RIDGE*

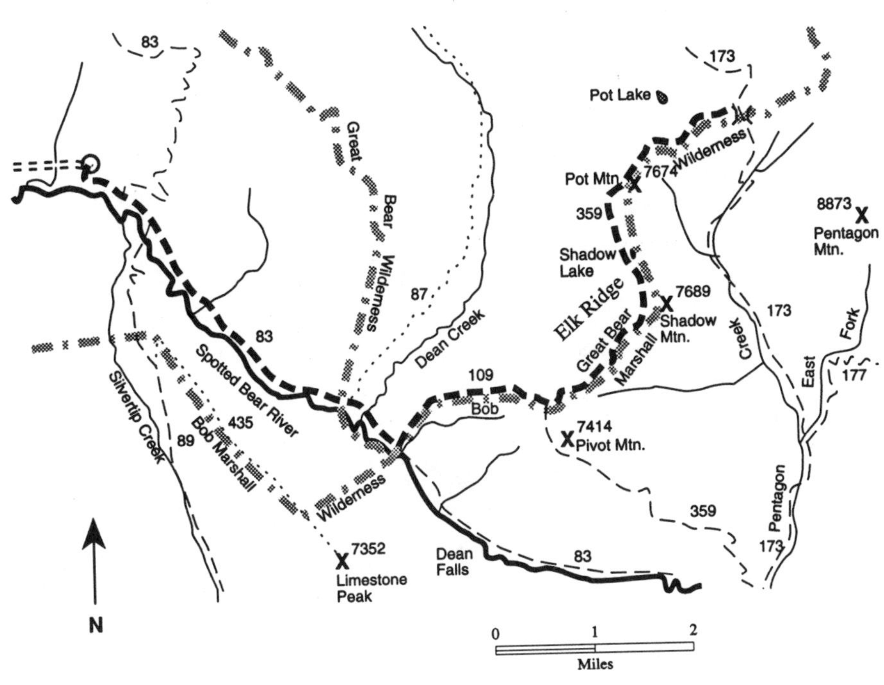

to the ridgeline, avoiding the false trails that run eastward onto a steep and grassy slope. Ultimately, the old trail gathers itself just to the west of the ridge crest as the grassy glades turn to subalpine forest.

The trail continues its climb up the ridgeline, dropping onto the western side of the slope to pass below the summit of Pivot Mountain. The trail is joined by the Pivot Mountain Trail (359) before plotting a northeasterly course through an open forest of subalpine fir with virtually no understory vegetation. The trail reaches the ridgeline behind Pivot Mountain and follows it into saddles and over small knobs on the ridge. To the east, Pentagon, Kevan, and Table mountains loom in a spectacular tableau of sheer cliff faces. The trail drops into a final low saddle at the base of Shadow Mountain, then heads due north to climb the slope below the west side of its summit. The trail crosses several talus slopes, allowing views of Dean Ridge and distant peaks farther to the northwest.

Once beyond Shadow Mountain, the trail abandons the ridgeline and instead follows a bald rise downhill to the northwest. The trail becomes a bit sketchy in spots as it crosses rocky meadows, but gathers itself again as it passes the western shores of tiny Shadow Lake. This high-elevation pool is a good spot to find waterfowl; great blue herons have even been spotted at this lofty watering hole. The trail crosses the outlet stream and once again becomes extremely faint. Watch for blazes and sawed

Pot Lake and the Dolly Varden Valley.

logs as the old trail bed climbs across the slope beyond the lake. The trail climbs steadily, reaching an old lookout site atop Pot Mountain. From this point, the sheer west face of Pentagon Mountain seems but a stone's throw away, and the peaks of the Trilobite Range can be seen trailing away to the north. The old lookout tower still stands amid the barren rubble at the summit of the ridge, marking the end of the old trail. Hikers traveling beyond this point must make their own way across difficult terrain to reach the pass above Pentagon Creek.

Hikers continuing onward to must now descend across the low cliffs that interrupt the ridgeline to the north. Once this obstacle has been crossed, the going gets a bit safer. The route crosses the next two high points along the ridge, which provide calf-burning ascents and tricky traversing across steep slopes. Once the final summit is reached, a long and steep descent through young subalpine fir brings hikers to more level ground. During the descent, look for Pot Lake in its grassy depression to the north. This lake is seldom seen and even more rarely visited by humans. Once the base of the ridge has been reached, the route runs east across grassy meadows dotted with low outcrops of chalky rock. A final, low hill must be surmounted before the route descends to meet the trail crossing the Pentagon-Dolly Varden divide, with a developed trail (173) coming up to the pass from both south and north.

TRAIL 25 *SWITCHBACK PASS*

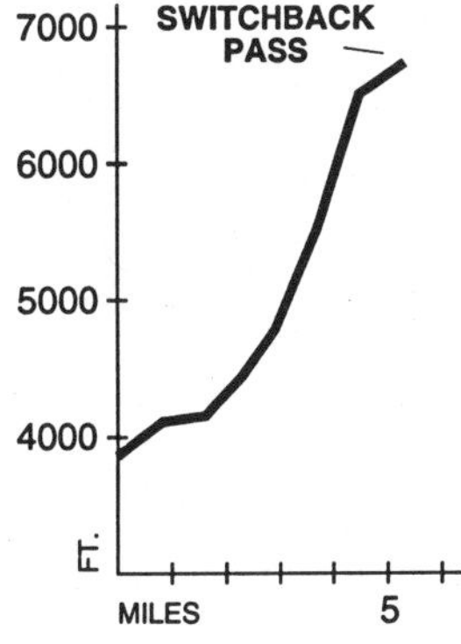

Trail 173, 177
General description: An extended trip from Pentagon Cabin to Switchback Pass, 5.3 mi. (8.5 km).
Difficulty: Moderately strenuous.
Trail maintenance: Yearly.
Traffic: Light.
Elevation gain: 2,947 ft.
Elevation loss: 40 ft.
Maximum elevation: 7,767 ft.
Topo maps: Bungalow Mountain, Trilobite Peak, Pentagon Mountain.
Finding the trail: This trail begins at the Pentagon Cabin on the Spotted Bear River Trail.

- 0.0 Pentagon Cabin. Turn north on the Pentagon Creek Trail (173).
- 0.1 Junction with the Pivot Mountain Trail (359). Bear right.
- 1.2 Trail fords Pentagon Creek.
- 1.7 Junction with the Switchback Pass Trail (177). Turn right.
- 2.3 Trail fords a major tributary of the East Fork of Pentagon Creek and begins climbing.
- 5.3 Switchback Pass.

The trail: This trail runs from Pentagon Cabin on the Spotted Bear River trail to the high pass at the southern terminus of the Trilobite Range trail. The current trail does not have a particular abundance of switchbacks, so it is hard to see how the pass got its name. It does provide access to the very foot of some of the most spectacular peaks in the area, and the pass itself is a side trip for many travelers visiting the Spotted Bear valley.

The trail begins opposite the Pentagon Cabin complex and soon passes the trail climbing westward toward Pivot Mountain (359). It climbs across the wooded slopes for several hundred vertical feet before leveling off high above Pentagon Creek and turning north. The trail remains relatively level for a mile or so as it passes through the forested valley, with limited views of the tree-cloaked hillsides along the way. The trail then descends to the creek and makes a calf-deep crossing, to continue northward on its east bank. Shortly thereafter, the trail reaches the confluence of the East Fork with the main body of Pentagon Creek. At this point, the more well-traveled Switchback Pass route (177) splits away to the right, while the fainter Pentagon Creek Trail (173) continues northward along Pentagon Creek.

The Switchback Pass trail crosses several small tributaries before reaching an ankle-deep ford of a much larger stream. After this crossing, the trail continues to follow the east bank of the East Fork for a short distance. It then turns east and mounts a spur ridge of Table Mountain, ascending quite steeply as it makes its way back and forth across the ridgeline. The trail can be quite muddy in the early going, but it dries out as it passes an enormous pile of loose rubble and works its way

TRAIL 25 *SWITCHBACK PASS*

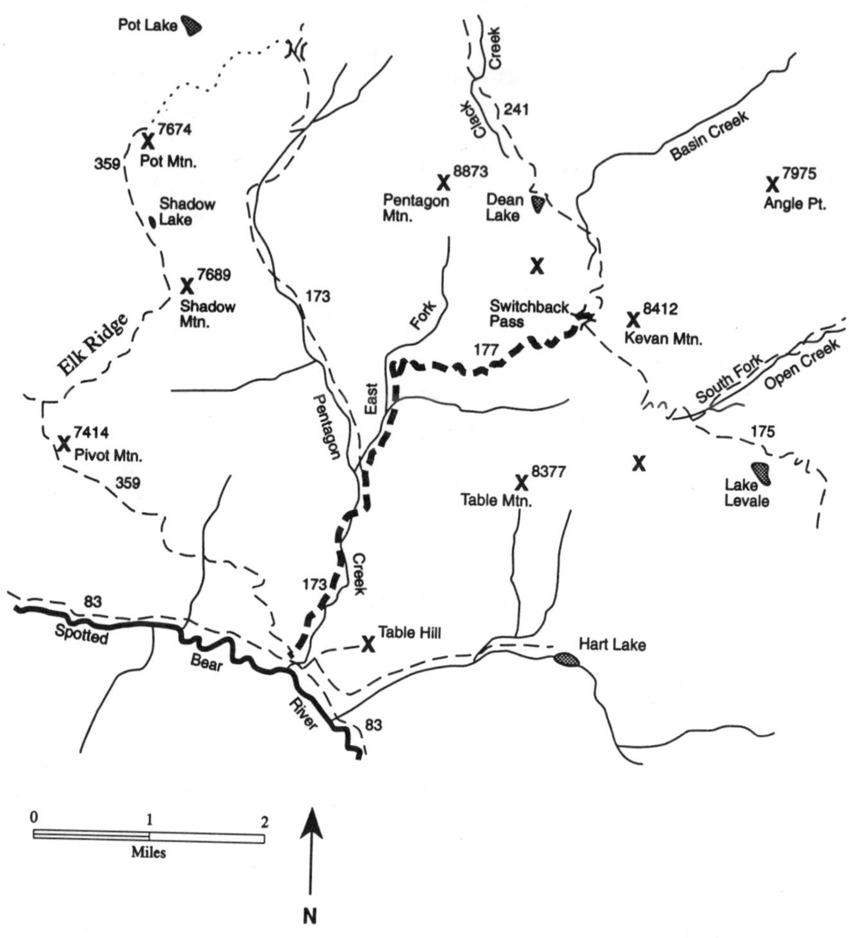

onto a south-facing slope. Here, openings in the forest reveal the looming crest of Table Mountain high above the trail, and the Wall Creek Cliffs can be seen along the southern skyline.

As the trail works its way back to the northern side of the ridge, a nameless spur of Pentagon Mountain rises above, and the sheer walls of Pentagon itself loom to the northeast. The trail ascends to reach the flattened top of the ridge, and becomes a more gentle climb as it meanders through groves of subalpine fir. A high plateau just below the pass contains flowery expanses of meadow, where glacier lilies bloom beneath the silent gaze of the sheer peaks surrounding the pass. Once the rocky saddle of Switchback Pass is reached, a trail junction offers a faint route to the south toward the North Wall (742) and the southern end of the Trilobite Range Trail (241).

TRAIL 26 *HART LAKE*

Trail 83, unnumbered trail

General description: A backpack from the Spotted Bear River trailhead to Hart Lake, 11.2 mi. (18.0 km).

Difficulty: Moderate.

Trail maintenance: Yearly along the Spotted Bear River; occasional beyond.

Traffic: Moderate to Pentagon Creek; very light beyond.

Elevation gain: 1,632 ft.

Elevation loss: 372 ft.

Maximum elevation: 5,700 ft.

Topo maps: Whitcomb Peak, Trilobite Peak, Bungalow Mountain, Three Sisters.

Finding the trailhead: This trip begins at the Spotted Bear River trailhead (see the Spotted Bear River Trail).

0.0 Spotted Bear River trailhead.
0.1 Junction with the Spotted Bear River Trail (83). Turn left.
0.6 Dean Ridge Trail (43) descends to meet the Spotted Bear River trail
1.0 Junction with the Silvertip Creek Trail (89). Bear left.
1.1 Silvertip Cabin.
1.4 Blue Lakes.
4.0 Trail enters the Great Bear Wilderness.
4.1 Trail fords Dean Creek.
4.6 Boundary of the Bob Marshall Wilderness. Junction with the Elk Ridge Trail (109). Keep going straight for Spotted Bear Pass.
5.9 Dean Falls.
8.8 Pentagon Cabin. Pentagon Creek-Switchback Pass Trail (173) enters from the left.
8.9 Trail fords Pentagon Creek.
9.0 Junction with the Hart Lake-Table Hill trail. Turn left.
9.1 Junction with the Table Hill trail. Turn right here.
9.4 Trail enters the Hart Creek valley.
10.6 Trail crosses a tributary of Hart Creek.
11.2 Hart Lake.

The trail: Hart Lake is most often visited as a side trip from the Spotted Bear River trail. However, for travelers seeking a secluded spot away from the heavier traffic of the valley bottoms, this lake has possibilities. Detailed coverage of the initial section of this trip, along the Spotted Bear River trail, can be found in an earlier section of the guide (p. 72).

The Hart Lake Trail splits away from the Spotted Bear River Trail from a marked intersection just beyond the ford of Pentagon Creek. The trail initially runs north-

TRAIL 26 *HART LAKE*

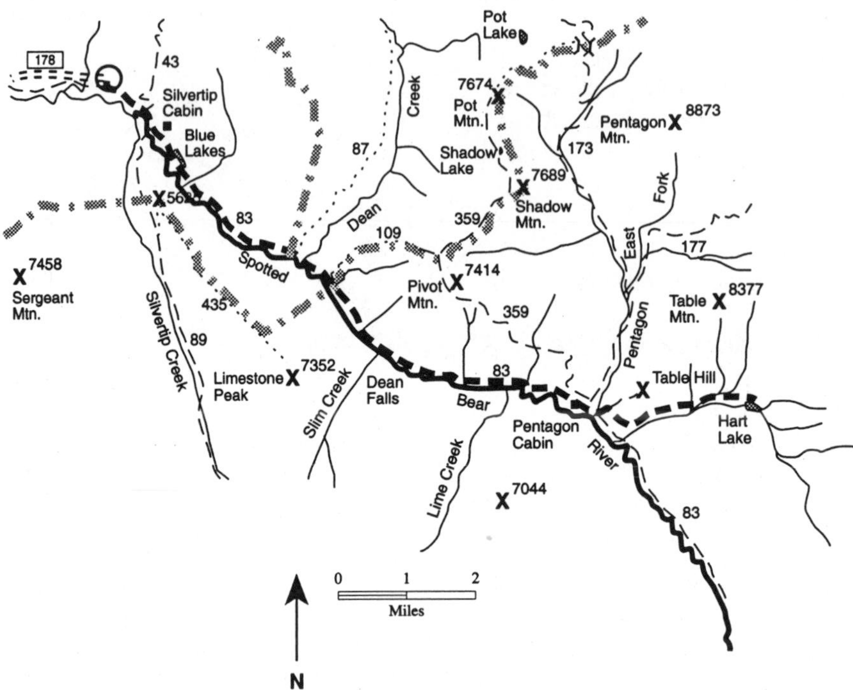

ward along the bank of this stream, but soon finds itself climbing the south slope of Table Hill. The trail soon reaches a junction with a trail that climbs steeply to the top of this point; this trail does not appear on some maps. At the junction, turn right for Hart Lake and follow the trail southeast as it climbs gently across the south-facing slope. The trail reaches the edge of the hill in a grassy glade, which affords one last look up the Spotted Bear valley, a view that highlights the rocky crest of the southernmost of the Three Sisters.

The trail then turns northeast up the forested valley of Hart Creek. It rises and falls, but gains altitude overall as it approaches a crossing of a small tributary. Once on the far side, the route crosses one more dry wash before climbing rather steeply on its final ascent to the lake. The lake itself is a turquoise gem, with old cottonwood trees leaning out over its western shores. Looking east, a velvet carpet of Douglas-fir stretches away toward the buff-colored outcrop of Hahn Peak.

TRAIL 27 *BUNGALOW MOUNTAIN*

Trail 90, 243

General description: An extended trip from the Spotted Bear River to Wall Creek Pass, 8.2 mi. (13.2 km).

Difficulty: Moderately strenuous.

Trail maintenance: Occasional.
Traffic: Light.
Elevation gain: 3,330 ft.
Elevation loss: 1,430 ft.
Maximum elevation: 7,900 ft.
Topo map: Bungalow Mountain.
Finding the trail: The trip begins at the Wall Creek Trail junction on the Spotted Bear River Trail, 1.1 miles east of the Pentagon Cabin.

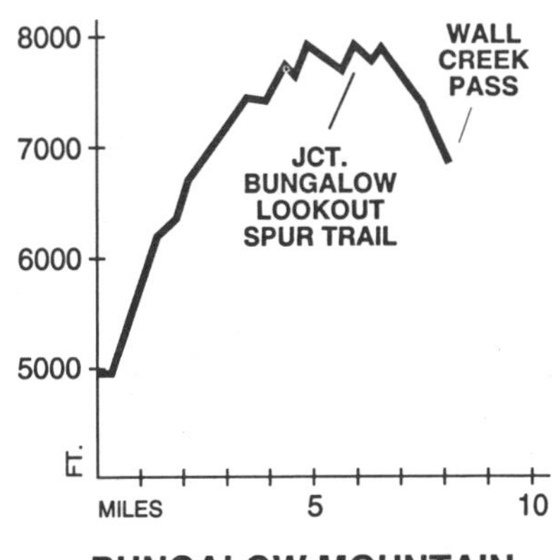

0.0 Junction of the Spotted Bear River (83) and Wall Creek (90) trails. Turn south on the Wall Creek Trail.

0.2 Trail fords the Spotted Bear River.
0.5 Junction with the Bungalow Mountain Trail (243). Turn left and begin climbing.
3.4 Trail crests the first hump on the ridgeline of Bungalow Mountain.
6.0 Junction with the spur trail to the old lookout site. Through traffic should keep going straight.
7.5 Junction with unmarked track that runs to the headwaters of Hoop Creek. Bear right for Wall Creek Pass.
8.2 Wall Creek Pass.

Silvertip Mountain rises beyond the Wall Creek Cliffs.

TRAIL 27 *BUNGALOW MOUNTAIN*

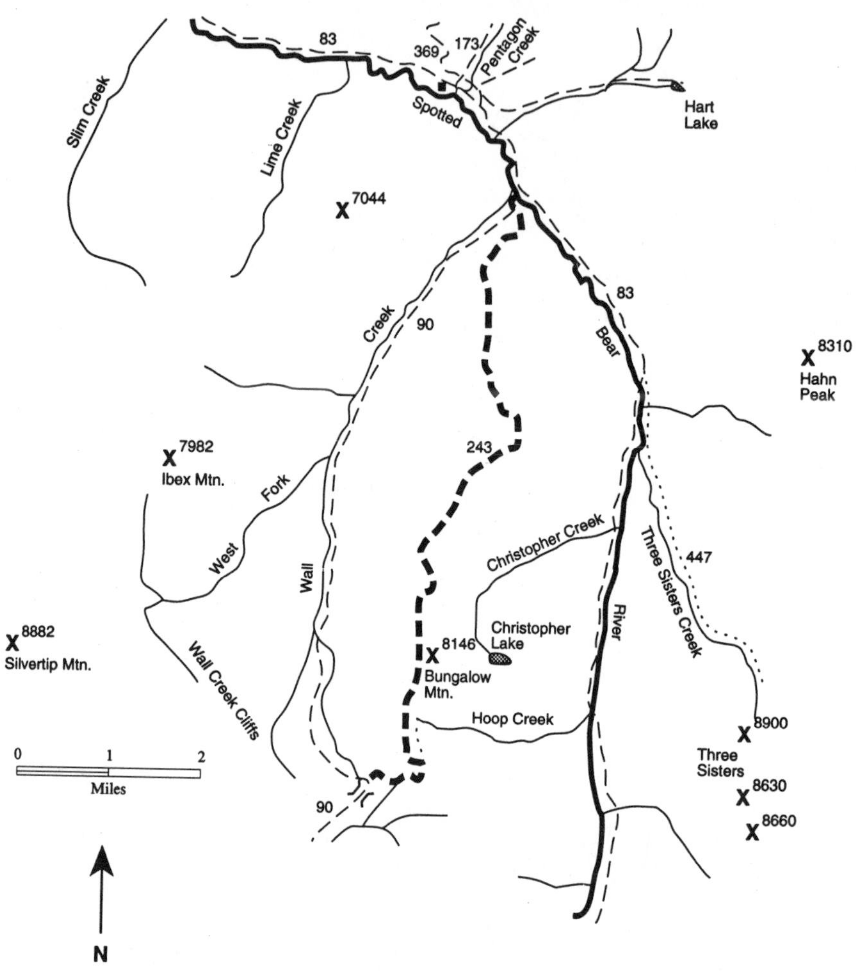

The trail: The Bungalow Mountain trail offers a high and dry alternative to the muddy Wall Creek trail for travelers connecting the Spotted Bear River with the White River basin. This trail offers outstanding mountain vistas from its lofty crest. There are several problem spots where the trail tends to wash out; it is always passable for hikers but may pose a real danger to horses. For the sake of safety, parties using stock should choose an alternate route such as Wall Creek or Spotted Bear Pass.

From the Spotted Bear trail follow the Wall Creek Trail (90) down to its ford of the Spotted Bear River. After a swift knee-deep crossing, the trail starts up the Wall Creek valley, then climbs to the top of a bluff that overlooks the river. The trail runs east for a short distance then turns inland once again to reach a junction with the Bungalow Mountain Trail (243). Turn left onto this trail, which ascends steeply through a dense lowland forest. As the trail switchbacks upward, it fights its way through clumps of alder before reaching a dry forest of lodgepole pine. Following a workmanlike ascent, the trail reaches the crest of the ridge, where a clearing at the edge of the north-facing slope allows views of the Pentagon, Table, and Kevan mountains.

The ascent then becomes gentler, climbing across an extensive series of dry benches. Pure stands of lodgepole pine cover the well-drained slopes, while small patches of subalpine fir and false huckleberry thrive in the moister seeps and ravines. The trail passes close to a seasonal stream that represents the only surface water on the entire trail, then continues its steady ascent of the ridge. Emerging on a sandy shelf, the trail offers its first glimpse of Silvertip Mountain and the Wall Creek Cliffs below it. The trail then begins a steep ascent to the southeast, finally reaching the bald top of the first point along the ridgeline. This point looks out on the peaks of the Continental Divide, from Hahn Peak in the south to Redhead Peak in the north, as well as the mountains surrounding Switchback Pass.

After dropping into the saddle beyond, the trail climbs through the last of the young pines before entering a sun-dappled forest of mature subalpine fir. A mile later, the trail emerges on the rim of an alpine bowl containing numerous alpine larch. These specialized trees grow only on moist, north-facing slopes near timberline. Views from this point are dominated by the Three Sisters and Redhead Peak immediately to the north of them. Beyond these peaks, Old Baldy and Rocky Mountain rise in the distance. The trail sags onto the slopes above the bowl as it makes its way around the southern rim, then turns south again to follow the ridgeline once more. Upon reaching the next saddle, Silvertip Mountain asserts its massive presence across the narrow Wall Creek valley.

The trail becomes quite faint as it crosses the bare soil of this saddle; it crosses over the ridgeline and drops onto the western side at about the midpoint of the depression. The route then traverses a steep, eroded slope of loose dirt, which drops away toward the forest below. The trail bed is often washed out on this section, so travelers should proceed with extreme caution. After crossing a short stretch of forest, the trail wanders out onto a second bare slope, and this time, sheer cliffs lurk below to discourage any misstep. This slope is a hundred yards across, and on the far side the trail returns to stable footing for the rest of the trek.

Soon afterward, the main trail reaches the junction with a spur trail that covers the short distance to the summit of Bungalow Mountain. Travelers who fail to take this side trip in fair weather are truly robbing themselves of some of the most spectacular scenery in the Spotted Bear Country. From the old lookout site, Silvertip Mountain seems only a stone's throw away to the west. Far beyond (and just to the south) this magnificent pinnacle, the snow-marbled summit of Swan Peak rises on the far horizon. To the south, the tombstone summit of Lone Butte rises above the twisted spires of the White Rive Syncline. The peaks of the Great Divide loom ito the east, from the Chinese Wall in the south to Kevan Mountain in the north. The northern horizon is crowded with the distant peaks of Glacier National Park.

Once beyond the summit of Bungalow Mountain, the main trail descends to a grassy saddle to the south, where it becomes faint again. Not to worry; the trail follows the ridgetop rather strictly for the next mile or so and becomes distinct again once on the far side of the saddle. As it descends, the trail begins to curve to the southeast, until it reaches the edge of the basin containing the headwaters of Hoop Creek. An unmarked route runs northward into this basin, while the main trail doglegs back to the southwest. An old burn allows excellent views of Lone Butte as the trail descends a south-facing slope before angling west to reach the low saddle containing the Wall Creek trail.

ADDITIONAL TRAILS

Lower Twin Creek Trail (385) is sketchy and difficult to find, especially in its upper reaches. It is slated for reconstruction in the near future.

Grouse Creek (236) and **Head Creek (442)** trails have long been abandoned and are almost impossible to find.

Upper Twin Creek Trail (237) is fairly passable for the lower two miles, but its upper end is choked with brush and requires numerous fords.

Dean Creek Trail (43) is maintained infrequently and is difficult to follow in places.

Silvertip Creek Trail (88) is quite muddy, and offers no views. It is primarily used to access outfitter camps.

Dean Creek (87) and **Limestone Peak (435)** trails no longer exist.

Pivot Mountain Trail (436) is maintained on an occasional basis and provides an alternate route to Elk Ridge.

Pentagon Creek Trail (173) is maintained frequently and provides access to the Dolly Varden Creek drainage from the Spotted Bear Valley.

Wall Creek Trail (90) is a valley-bottom mudbath used heavily by stock parties. It offers views of the Wall Creek Cliffs.

Harrison-Sergeant Creek Trail (88) is maintained frequently and is generally passable, though unspectacular.

Harrison (584), **Mid (103)**, and **Black Bear (220, 524) Creek**, as well as the trail above **Hodag Creek (701)**, have been abandoned and are extremely difficult to find.

Lost Jack Trail (102) is cleared annually, but its beginning is poorly marked and difficult to tell from the numerous game trails on the valley bottoms of the South Fork.

Picture Ridge Cutoff Trail (226) is maintained yearly and provides a long, switchbacking climb to reach the Picture Ridge trail.

Trickle Creek (115) and **Cannon Creek (493)** trails are maintained for the first several miles beyond the Gorge Creek trail and then fade out entirely.

SWAN RANGE

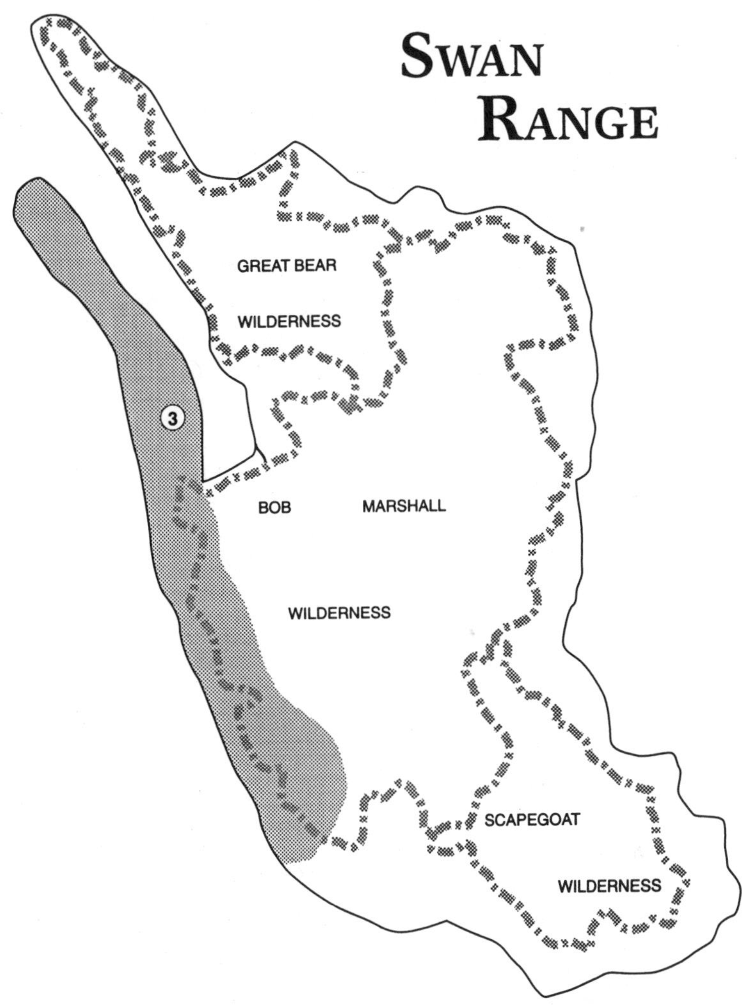

This steep and snow-capped range of mountains looms above the western rim of the Bob Marshall Wilderness and provides a daunting obstacle to travelers bound for its remote interior. A number of trails thread their way through the lofty peaks to reach the drainages beyond. In addition, the verdant meadows and gem-like lakes that are nestled among the crags make popular destinations in themselves. The trails of the Jewel Basin hiking area in the north and Holland Lake in the south lie outside the wilderness boundary, but provide excellent day-hiking opportunities.

The western slopes of the Swan Range receive a great deal of precipitation throughout the year and this supports a lush growth of forest vegetation. West-facing valley bottoms harbor stands of ancient larch and cedar, which are typical of the damp coastal climate of the Cascade Ranges in western Washington and Oregon. The well-drained slopes above them support a diverse forest Douglas-fir, birch, hemlock, and lodgepole pine. Alpine areas are typified by late-lingering snows, and lush meadows, dominated by glacier lilies and other wildflowers, are dotted with ragged copses of subalpine fir. Burns and avalanche slopes regenerate quickly here and are typically choked with cow parsnip and thimbleberry, as well as a variety of woody shrubs. The Swan Range harbors a relatively dense population of grizzly bears that thrive on lush plant growth in the spring and switch to berries later in the summer.

The Swan Mountains themselves stretch unbroken for over one hundred miles, from the town of Columbia Falls in the north to Monture Mountain, which rises above the Blackfoot River Valley far to the south. The northern half of the range is not yet protected by wilderness status, but does feature the Jewel Basin hiking area and the wild and remote Swan Crest trail. The range is crowned by Swan Peak (9,289 ft.) and Holland Peak (9,356 ft.), two of the most stunning pinnacles of the entire wilderness system. A few small glaciers are perched on the eastern faces of the range, the largest of which adorn Swan Peak. These are the only glaciers in the Bob Marshall Wilderness complex.

To the west of the range, the Swan and Clearwater valleys provide excellent access. Montana Highway 83 runs down the center of the valley, and a network of logging roads extends to the trailheads at the foot of the range. The settlements of Swan Lake, Condon, Holland Lake, and Seeley Lake offer most services required by backcountry travelers. The bulk of the Swan Range is administered by the Swan Lake Ranger District of the Flathead National Forest (located in Bigfork, MT), while the country south of Holland Lake is under the jurisdiction of the Seeley Lake District of the Lolo National Forest.

TRAIL 28 *PYRAMID PASS*

Trail 416

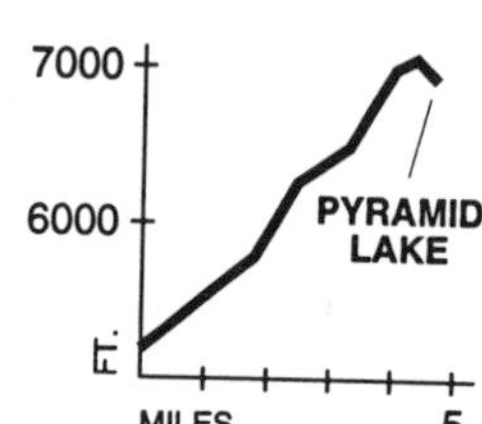

General description: A long day hike or backpack from the Pyramid Pass trailhead to Pyramid Lake, 4.6 mi. (7.4 km).

Difficulty: Moderately strenuous.

Trail maintenance: Yearly.

Traffic: Moderate.

Elevation gain: 1,790 ft.

Elevation loss: 100 ft.

Maximum elevation: 7,000 ft.

Topo maps: Morrell Lake, Crimson Peak.

Finding the trailhead: From the town of Seeley Lake, take the Cottonwood Creek Road (477). Turn left on the Morrell Creek Road (4353) and follow it for about 6 miles. Take the first road to the right, and follow the signs to the heavily developed Pyramid Pass trailhead.

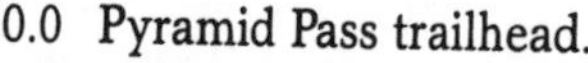

0.0 Pyramid Pass trailhead.

0.8 Old logging road ends as trail enters from the north. Turn right for Pyramid Pass.

3.2 First crossing of Trail Creek.

Pyramid Peak and Pyramid Lake.

3.8 Trail passes an unnamed lake.
4.2 Pyramid Pass. Trail enters the Bob Marshall Wilderness.
4.4 Junction with the Blackfoot Divide Trail (278). Keep going straight.
4.5 Junction with spur trail to Pyramid Lake. Turn left.
4.6 Pyramid Lake.

The trail: The Pyramid Pass trail follows old logging roads to the high country and visits several trout-filled lakes on its way into the Bob Marshall Wilderness. This trail is an excellent choice for hikers seeking a challenging day trip, which might include fishing or a bushwhack up nearby Pyramid Peak. In addition, the trail is a major route for stock traffic traveling into the Youngs Creek valley. This trail sticks primarily to high, well drained slopes. As a result, it remains in good condition even after heavy rains.

From the trailhead, the trail meanders south, following an overgrown logging road. Trails from outfitters' camps join the trail as it bends back to the northeast, swinging around a dry ravine then climbing through old seed-tree cuts. The wounds left by logging activity have been covered by a vigorous growth of kinnickinnick and aromatic ceanothus bushes. As the trail wanders upward on a generally easterly course, it is joined by several more hunter trails. The trail finally receives a rather well-beaten trail from the north and then turns south to climb gently across the forested hillside.

The trail soon rounds a bend in the hill and turns east into a meadowy valley.

TRAIL 28 *PYRAMID PASS*

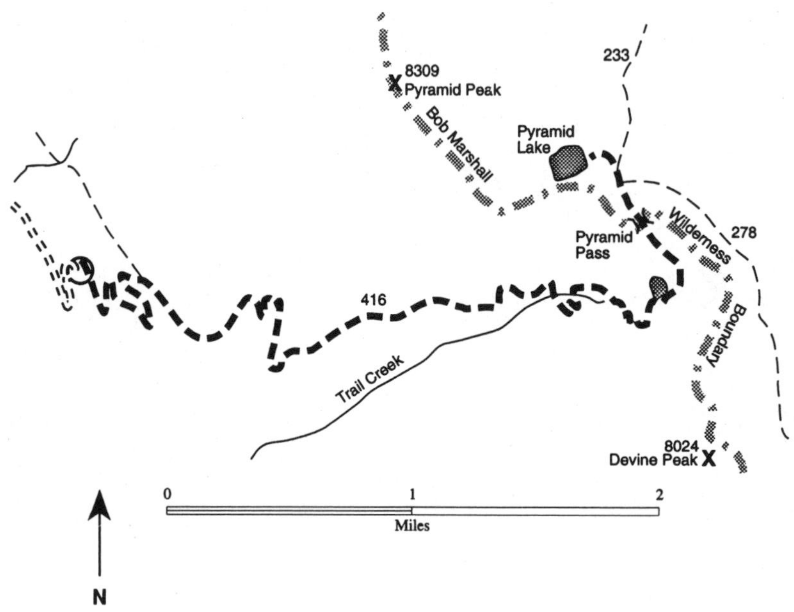

Above this opening rise the rounded summits of several imposing points, including Pyramid Peak to the north. Orderly avalanche slopes roll down from the summits to merge into the meadows below. After passing the midpoint of this tiny valley, the trail begins to climb amid second-growth timber and assorted undergrowth. The trail soon turns south again to return to the forest, where it climbs to reach the crest of the next ridge. Amid sweeping views to the south and west, the trail turns up the ridgeline and climbs steeply, following an old skid road. These tracks are built by bulldozers to skid cut logs down to developed roads, where they are loaded onto logging trucks. Soon, the trail abandons the ridgeline and turns east once more, crossing the south-facing slope above Trail Creek valley.

The old road bed gives way to true trail as the route runs eastward, crossing several grassy avalanche slopes on its way to the hanging upper basin of Trail Creek. Once the trail reaches the gladed forests of this high shelf, it crosses Trail Creek in the first of a series of shallow fords. The going can be a bit muddy here as the trail climbs through a brushy subalpine forest. After 0.5 mile of steady ascent and several more stream crossings, the trail turns north to make the final approach to the unnamed tarn below Pyramid Pass. This small pool is filled with trout, and boulder fields sweep down from the hilltop above to reach its eastern shoreline. The trail picks its way through the loose rocks and then winds its way up the rocky shelves on the far side of this lake.

Pyramid Pass lies just a quarter mile beyond the lake and serves as the boundary of the Bob Marshall Wilderness. The pass is a low, wooded defile between rounded hills and does not allow panoramic views of the surrounding country. As the trail begins to descend from the pass, it passes a junction with the Blackfoot Divide trail, which descends to the east. A short distance farther, the spur trail to Pyramid Lake takes off to the west. Follow it for a tenth of a mile across marshy meadows to reach the shoreline of this large, round body of water. The lake is surrounded by an open forest of subalpine fir and is guarded by the bulky mass of Pyramid Peak, which looms to the west. From the western shore of the lake, it is a relatively brush-free (though strenuous) scramble to the summit of this mountain.

TRAIL 29 *MORRELL FALLS*

Trail 30

General description: A short day hike from the Morrell Creek trailhead to Morrell Falls, 2.6 mi. (4.2 km).

Difficulty: Easy.

Trail maintenance: Yearly.

Traffic: Heavy.

Elevation gain: 170 ft.

Elevation loss: 50 ft.

Maximum elevation: 4,880 ft.

Topo map: Morrell Lake.

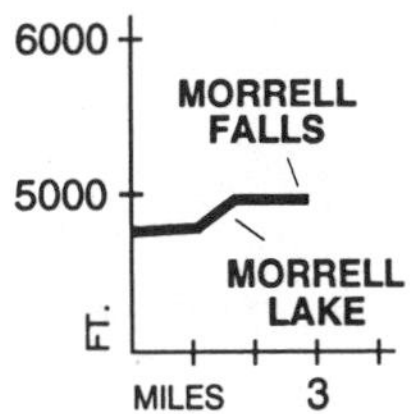

Finding the trailhead: From the town of Seeley Lake take the Cottonwood Creek Road (477). Turn left on the Morrell Creek Road (4353), and follow it for about 6

Morrell Falls.

TRAIL 29 *MORRELL FALLS*

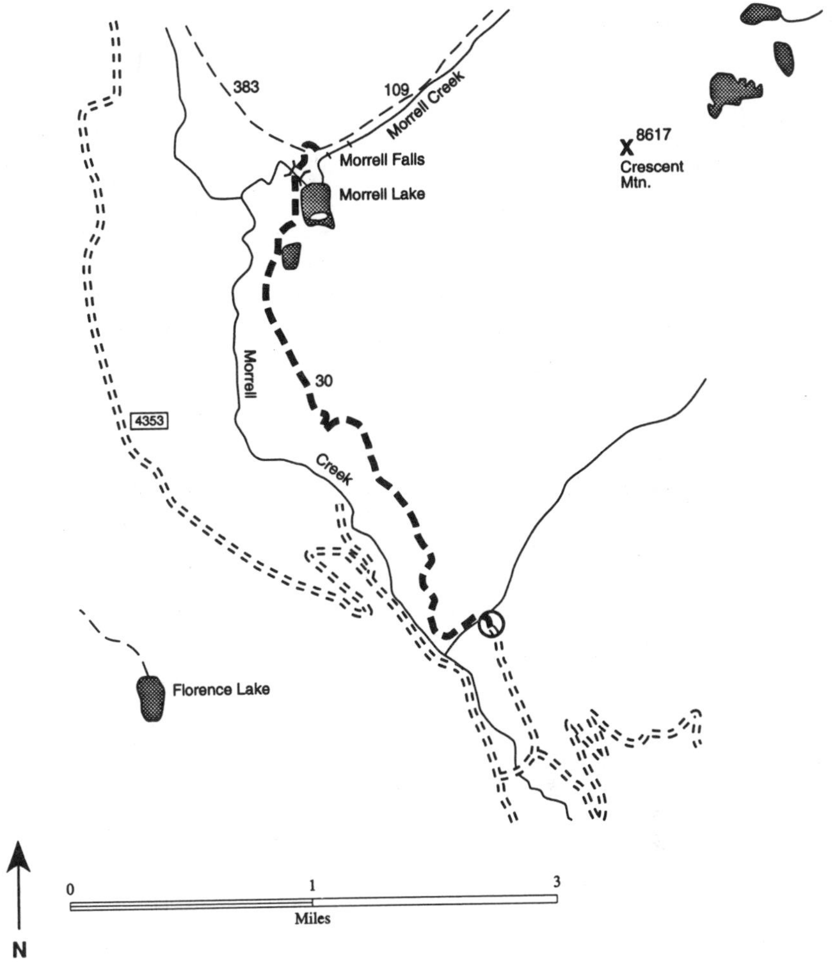

miles. Take the first road to the right, which crosses Morrell Creek and reaches another junction. Turn left here and follow signs for Morrell Falls.

0.0 Morrell Creek trailhead.
2.2 Morrell Lake.
2.4 Trail crosses bridge over Morrell Creek.
2.5 Junction with the trail to the Upper Falls and Grizzly Basin (409). Bear right for Morrell Falls.
2.6 Morrell Falls.

The trail: This trail provides an easy stroll through forested bottomland to reach a spectacular waterfall on Morrell Creek. The route is especially popular with families and can also be enjoyed by beginner and out-of-shape hikers. Due to the large numbers of visitors to this area in summer months, it is the wrong choice for solitude seekers. The best time to view the falls is early summer, when snowmelt causes enormous quantities of water to thunder over the lip.

The trail begins by following an old roadbed across a small stream and then striking northward through the lodgepole pine. The trail is wide and well-beaten as it makes its way through the level forest. Lodgepole pines are dependent on fires and other disturbances to reproduce. The heat of a forest fire melts the resin that seals the cones shut, allowing the seeds inside to be released after the fire, even if the tree bearing them dies in the blaze. Young lodgepole seedlings require full sunlight to grow and flourish in the openings provided by forest fires. A bit farther down the trail is one such opening, populated by a dense growth of lodgepole saplings. Beyond the opening lies a second stand of mature lodgepoles, but with a difference: Here, the saplings of Douglas-fir and spruce abound in the understory. Because these trees can tolerate a lot of shade, they tend to replace lodgepole in the forest canopy over a period of centuries if the forest is undisturbed by fire.

Farther on, stately larch rise above the trail as it begins a series of small climbs. A climax forest of Douglas-fir dominates the low ridges that rise toward Crescent Mountain in the east. The trail passes a shallow woodland pond and reaches a marked junction with the Morrell Creek Trail (383). Stay right, as the trail reaches the shores of Morrell Lake, with its tiny wooded island punctuating the still waters. Waterfowl can often be spotted at this woodland pond, which lies below the gray cliffs that gird the lower half of Crescent Mountain.

The trail departs from the northern shore of the lake and soon crosses Morrell Creek via a sturdy footbridge. The trail then bends around to the east, passing the point where a rather steep trail ascends toward the upper falls and the Grizzly Basin beyond. Fifty yards farther on, the trail runs out onto a gravel spit below the thundering falls. This foaming cataract plunges across a sheer cliff the size of a five-story building and dwarfs even the trees that crowd it on either side. There are a number of driftwood logs strewn about that serve as handy perches for visitors who wish to sit and contemplate the raw power and beauty of this magnificent cascade.

TRAIL 30 *UPPER HOLLAND LOOP*

Trail 415, 35, 110, 42

General description: A long day hike loop to Upper Holland and Sapphire Lakes, 13.3 mi. (21.4 km) round trip.

Difficulty: Moderately strenuous if hiked counterclockwise; strenuous if hiked clockwise.

Trail maintenance: Yearly.

Traffic: Heavy.

Elevation gain: 3,630 ft.

Elevation loss: 3,630 ft.

Maximum elevation: 7,460 ft.

Topo map: Holland Lake.

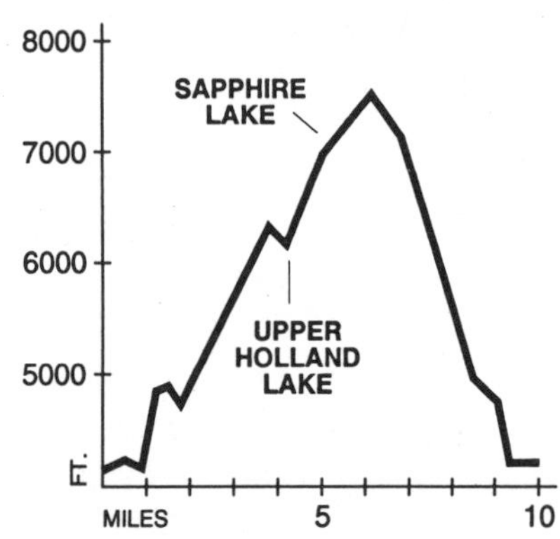

Finding the trailhead: Follow the Holland Lake Road eastward from Montana Highway 83, following signs for Holland Lake Lodge on the north side of the lake. The North Holland Lake trailhead is at the end of the north shore road, just beyond the lodge.

- 0.0 Holland Lake north trailhead.
- 0.1 Junction with the Holland Falls Trail (416). Bear left for Upper Holland Lake.
- 1.2 Junction with the Foothills Trail (192). Keep right.
- 1.3 Junction with the Necklace Lakes Trail (42). Bear right.
- 2.0 Trail crosses first footbridge over Holland Creek.
- 2.1 Junction with the Owl Creek Trail (35). Bear left for Upper Holland Lake.
- 3.2 Trail returns to the north bank of Holland Creek via a footbridge.
- 6.5 Foot of Upper Holland Lake.
- 6.8 Junction with the trail to Sapphire Lake (110). Turn left and begin climbing.

TRAIL 30 *UPPER HOLLAND LOOP*

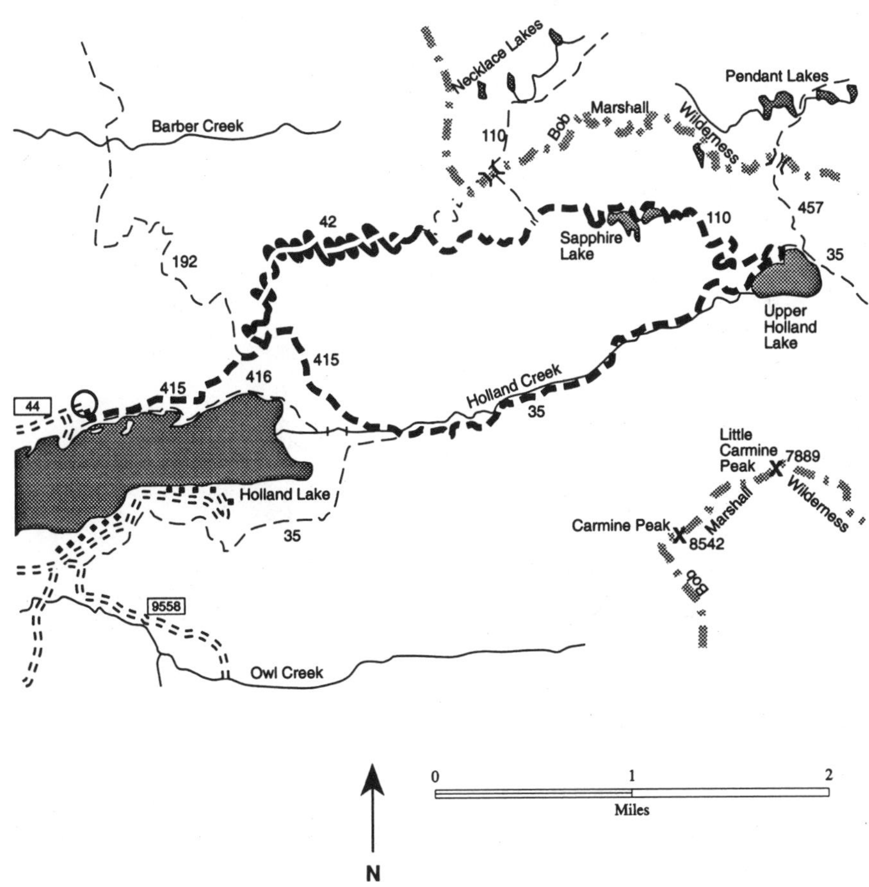

7.9 Little Sapphire Lake.
8.1 Sapphire Lake.
8.8 Junction with old Holland Lookout Trail (42). Turn left to complete the loop.
9.4 Junction with the Holland Lookout spur trail. Bear left.
12.0 Trail returns to the Holland Lake Trail (415). Turn right for the trailhead.
12.1 Trail passes the junction with the foothills Trail (192). Stay left.
13.2 Junction with the Holland Falls Trail (416).
13.3 Trail returns to the Holland Lake north trailhead.

The trail: This trail provides a long day hike visiting several high lakes that lie west of the Continental Divide. The trail receives heavy traffic both from hikers and from horse parties originating at Holland Lake Lodge. This route also connects with several of the major passes into the Bob Marshall Wilderness.

The trail starts off on the north shore of Holland Lake and soon reaches an old roadbed that runs through the forest along the lakeshore. At this point, turn left, following signs for Upper Holland Lake as the trail climbs onto a low hilltop that overlooks the water. The going is fairly level as the trail crosses the bluffs above the lakeshore, then begins a steady ascent of the hillside near the head of the lake. The trail passes junctions for the Foothills and old Holland Lookout trails, then turns south to climb onto the steep western wall of the Swan Valley. From its junction with the Foothills Trail, the Holland Lake Trail 415 and Holland Gordon Trail 35 are closed to bicycles in order to eliminate the potential safety hazard caused by mixing bicycles

Carmine Peak is framed by the smallest of the Sapphire Lakes.

and heavy stock use. The path then levels out and breaks out of the trees as it passes high above the head of Holland Lake and reveals a sparkling panorama of the snow-clad Mission Mountains to the west.

Holland Creek cuts a wide cleft into the wall of the Swan Valley, and the trail turns into this valley on its way to Upper Holland Lake. A footbridge soon affords a crossing of the creek, and the path runs east along the banks of the stream, passing numerous woodland cascades. The trail soon reaches a junction with the Owl Creek trail, and from this point, twin trails run in tandem to Upper Holland Lake. The streamside trail is more scenic, with frequent views of waterfalls, where water ousels do pushups on the streamside boulders. These tiny birds dive fearlessly into the foaming waters and scuttle along the bottom, searching for aquatic insects. After a mile of gentle climbing through Douglas-fir forest and sunny aspen stands, the trail reaches a second footlog across the stream.

The trail then crosses a section of boardwalk and passes through some trees on its way to the open slopes beyond. Across the valley, the tip of Carmine Peak can barely be seen above a long avalanche chute. The trail continues a moderate climb up the valley, punctuated with numerous switchbacks, until it reaches an overlook point. This spot offers a final westward glimpse of the Mission Mountains. The trail then continues upward along the north bank of the stream, passing a final waterfall as it crosses open slopes that offer ever-expanding views of Carmine Peak's jagged crest. The valley then levels off and begins to widen, and the trail skirts northward, below the mossy outcrops that line the edge of the valley. Six and a half miles from the trailhead, the trail reaches the foot of Upper Holland Lake. This large, valley bottom pool is a popular picnic and fishing spot and is overlooked by the wooded ziggurat of Waldbillig Mountain.

To complete the loop, follow the trail around the north shore of the lake to reach a junction with the Sapphire Lake trail, which climbs to the west of an extensive boulder field. After a rather steep and switchbacking ascent, the trail climbs onto a series of high shelves defined by flat sheaves of bedrock protruding through the soil. The trail climbs gently through the open forest covering this rocky landscape for the next 0.25 mile to reach the smaller of the Sapphire Lakes. These lakes are bordered by tongues of bedrock that stick out into the water and support miniature subalpine forests. Carmine Peak provides a stunning backdrop for these attractive tarns, and several smaller summits rise immediately west of the lakes.

The trail continues to climb after passing the larger of the two lakes and reaches a trail junction in the last copse of trees in the alpine valley above. This junction is difficult to spot from below, but is marked with a trail sign. Turn left here and climb through the high saddle to the north of the last knob on the ridgeline. From this pass, the trail descends steeply for a short distance, then levels off as it turns northwest and crosses the grassy slopes several thousand feet above the floor of the Swan Valley. After rounding a corner on the hill and reaching the Holland Lookout trail, the loop route begins a foot-pounding descent as it zigzags down the slope toward Holland Lake. The open forests of the higher elevations close in to shut out the views as the trail descends. The trail finally runs out onto a low spur ridge before meeting the trail to Upper Holland Lake and thus closing the loop. Remember always to take the left fork at trail junctions, until the path returns to the marked spur trail for the trailhead.

TRAIL 31 GORDON PASS - KOESSLER LAKE

Trail 415, 35, 291, unnumbered
General description: A backpack from Holland Lake to Koessler Lake, 15.0 mi. (24.1 km).
Difficulty: Moderate.
Trail maintenance: Yearly to the Doctor Lake Trail junction; occasional beyond.
Traffic: Heavy to Doctor Lake Trail; light beyond.
Elevation gain: 3,680 ft.
Elevation loss: 1,700 ft.
Maximum elevation: 6,790 ft.
Topo maps: Holland Lake, Shaw Creek.
Finding the trailhead: North Holland Lake trailhead (see The Upper Holland Loop).

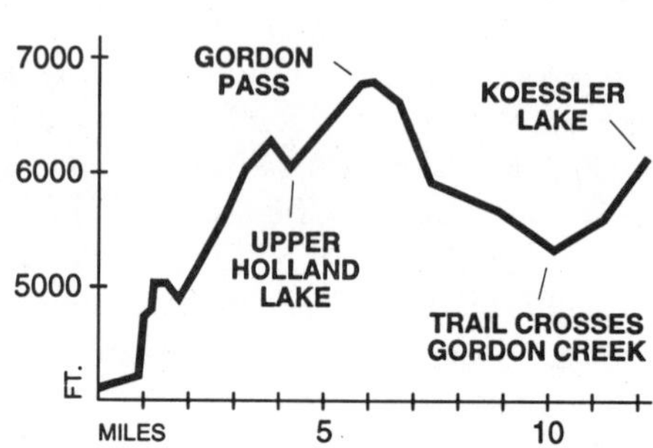

- 0.0 Holland Lake north trailhead.
- 0.1 Junction with the Holland Falls Trail (416). Bear left for Upper Holland Lake.
- 1.2 Junction with the Foothills Trail (192). Keep right.
- 1.3 Junction with the Necklace Lakes Trail (42). Bear right.
- 2.0 Trail crosses first footbridge over Holland Creek.
- 2.1 Junction with the Owl Creek Trail (35). Bear left for Upper Holland Lake.
- 3.2 Trail returns to the north bank of Holland Creek via a footbridge.
- 6.5 Foot of Upper Holland Lake.
- 6.8 Junction with the trail to Sapphire Lake (110). Bear right for Gordon Pass.
- 7.0 Junction withe the Pendant Pass Trail (457). Stay right.
- 8.7 Gordon Pass. Trail enters the Bob Marshall Wilderness.
- 11.2 Trail crosses Gordon Creek.
- 12.6 Junction with the Doctor Lake Trail (291). Turn right for Koessler Lake.
- 12.9 Trail fords Gordon Creek.
- 14.0 Unmarked junction with the Koessler Lake Trail. Turn right and begin climbing.
- 15.0 Koessler Lake.

The trail: Gordon Pass is one of the easiest routes over the Swan Range and into the wilderness beyond. The pass itself also has outstanding scenic value, and leads to several lakes that provide excellent fishing. The most accessible of these is Koessler Lake, which rests in a glacier-carved cirque at the foot of the imposing cliff walls of Ptarmigan Peak.

The trail begins on the north shore of Holland Lake and follows the Upper Holland Loop trail as its climbs the wall above Holland Lake and runs up the Holland Creek valley to reach Upper Holland Lake. This part of the trip is discussed under the Upper Holland Loop. From Upper Holland Lake follow the trail around the north

Ptarmigan Peak overshadows the cirque containing Lick Lake.

shore. This trail passes junctions with the Sapphire Lake and Pendant Pass trails before leaving the head of the lake to cross the meadows above it. Waldbillig Mountain rises to the north as a faint trail takes off to the left; this is the old Gordon Pass trail which is no longer maintained. Stick to the well-beaten right fork, which soon fords Holland Creek. This route climbs gently across the hillsides as the valley turns south and passes through a pleasant subalpine forest of scattered trees and vigorous underbrush.

A mile and a half beyond the head of the lake, the trail passes through the low trough of Gordon Pass and enters the Bob Marshall Wilderness. As the trail runs down a shallow grade across rocky shelves, views open up in spectacular fashion. To the west, the red and green shales of Carmine and Wolverine Peaks rise to jagged points, while the sheer faces of Ptarmigan and Ptarmiganet rise farther to the south. The trail runs southeast for 0.5 mile, then begins to switchback its way down into the Lick Creek valley. The trail turns onto an eastward course while still several hundred feet above the valley and eases its descent as it passes through several burned spots. This fire had sufficient intensity to kill the trees, but was never able to reach the forest canopy, or "crown out." As a result, the dead snags still retain their limbs and smaller branches, an unusual state of affairs following a hot forest fire.

As the trail reaches the valley floor, it crosses Gordon Creek, which flows into the main valley from the north. The trail follows the valley bottom as it runs eastward, crossing several avalanche slopes that allow brief views of the forested ridges to the south. The trail crosses several small streams before reaching a third open slope. Here, a rough track descends to meet up with the Doctor Lake Trail, but this trail is easier to find by continuing eastward along the Gordon Creek Trail for another quarter mile to reach a marked trail junction. Travelers bound for Koessler Lake should turn right onto the Doctor Lake Trail (291), which descends westward toward a ford of Gordon Creek.

After an ankle-deep ford (or a log crossing for daring hikers), the trail follows the western bank of Doctor Creek as it works its way southward. The trail soon passes inland, crossing a number of quagmires on its way onto the drier slopes above. Upon reaching a narrow, open ravine, the trail arrives at an unmarked junction. The official trail runs along the creek to Doctor Lake, but this path has been swallowed up by the forest in the absence of maintenance. To the right, a rough but well-trodden trail climbs the hillside, then continues southwest into the hanging valley that contains Koessler Lake. The north shore of the lake is bordered by pleasant subalpine parkland, with beargrass dominating the openings. The sheer east wall of Ptarmigan Peak rises above the head of the lake and is festooned with snowslips that never melt. The lake itself harbors a healthy population of rainbow and cutthroat trout. Please camp in the meadows a quarter below the lake to reduce impacts to this fragile site.

TRAIL 31 *GORDON PASS - KOESSLER LAKE*

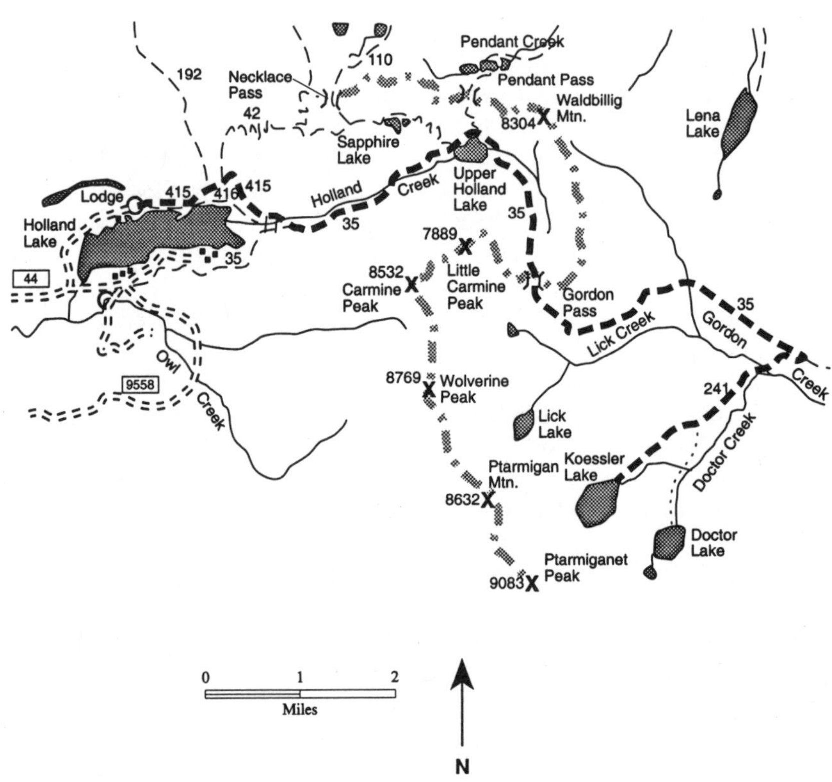

TRAIL 32 *PENDANT PASS - LENA LAKE*

Trail 415, 35, 457, 212, unnumbered
General description: A backpack from Holland Lake to Lena Lake, 13.9 mi. (22.4 km).
Difficulty: Moderately strenuous.
Trail maintenance: Yearly.
Traffic: Heavy to Pendant Cabin; light beyond.
Elevation gain: 3,835 ft.
Elevation loss: 1,135 ft.
Maximum elevation: 6,740 ft.
Topo maps: Holland Lake, Shaw Creek, Holland Peak, Big Salmon Lake West.
Finding the trailhead: North Holland Lake trailhead (see The Upper Holland Loop, p. 94).

- 0.0 Holland Lake north trailhead.
- 0.1 Junction with the Holland Falls Trail (416). Bear left for Upper Holland Lake.
- 1.2 Junction with the Foothills Trail (192). Keep right.
- 1.3 Junction with the Necklace Lakes Trail (42). Bear right.
- 2.0 Trail crosses first footbridge over Holland Creek.
- 2.1 Junction with the Owl Creek Trail (35). Bear left for Upper Holland Lake.
- 3.2 Trail returns to the north bank of Holland Creek via a footbridge.
- 6.5 Foot of Upper Holland Lake.
- 6.8 Junction with the trail to Sapphire Lake (110). Bear right for Pendant Pass.
- 7.0 Junction with the Pendant Pass Trail (457). Turn left.
- 7.4 Pendant Pass. Trail enters the Bob Marshall Wilderness.
- 7.6 Trail crosses the outlet stream of the uppermost Pendant Lake.
- 8.0 Trail fords creek below the lowermost Pendant Lake.
- 9.2 Trail fords creek to reach its southern bank.
- 10.5 Trail fords Big Salmon Creek.
- 10.6 Pendant Cabin. Junction with the Shaw Creek Trail (212). Turn right for Lena Lake.
- 12.6 Junction with the Holbrook-Bartlett-Burnt Creek Trail (131). Stay right for Lena Lake.
- 13.1 Junction with the Lena Creek Trail. Turn right.
- 13.9 Foot of Lena Lake.

The trail: This trail provides access to the Big Salmon valley via a rather low pass in the Swan Range. Along the way, it passes the Pendant Lakes, a series of small, shallow lakes that sit at the bottom of a high, forested basin. The ultimate destination of the trip is Lena Lake, a large body of water that occupies an out-of-the-way side valley beneath the wooded slopes of Shaw Peak. The trail to Upper Holland Lake is discussed in the section covering the Upper Holland Loop.

The trip follows the Upper Holland Loop Trail to Upper Holland Lake, where the Pendant Pass Trail (457) begins its climb from the northern side of the lake. After a

TRAIL 32 *PENDANT PASS - LENA LAKE*

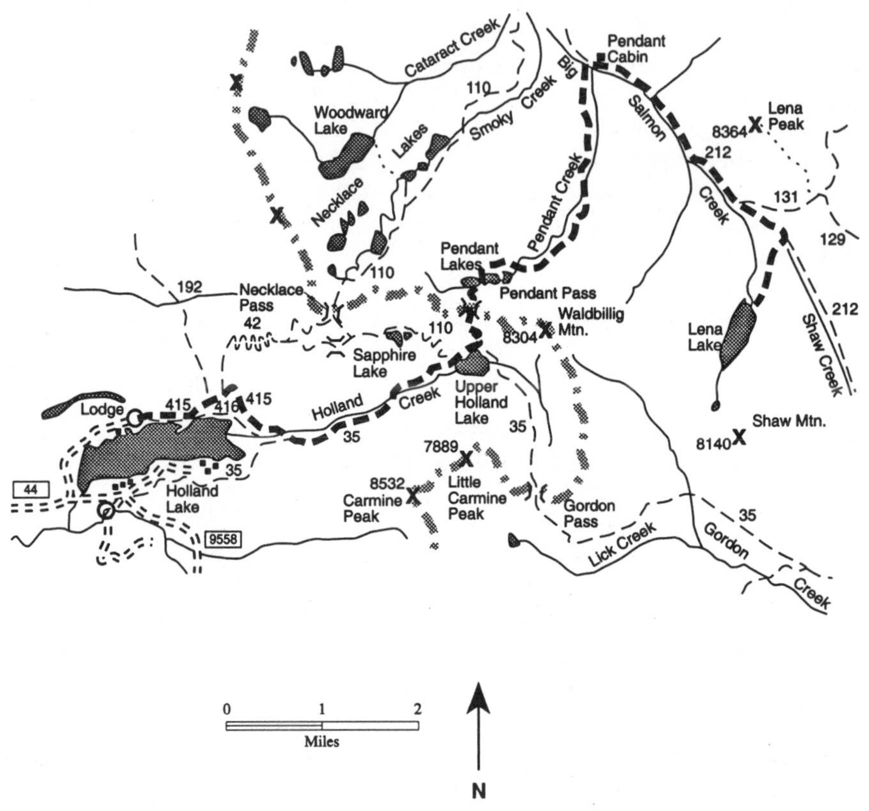

brief but vigorous ascent, the gradient becomes rather flat and the trail runs across open subalpine forest to reach the low pass. This point marks the boundary of the Bob Marshall Wilderness and allows views of Carmine and Little Carmine Peaks to the south. The trail then descends a short distance through an increasingly brushy forest to reach the uppermost of the Pendant Lakes. This round, weedy pool is surrounded by forested hills and provides habitat for passing waterfowl.

The trail crosses the outlet of the upper lake and wanders across the wooded valley floor, passing the much smaller middle lake. Sedges and marsh grasses have almost completely taken over this pond, demonstrating the dynamic nature of mountain watercourses. Lakes are constantly being filled in by sediment from the streams that feed them, and over time, the surrounding vegetation can encroach into the former lake bed. This lake will probably become a grassy meadow some day, and later the surrounding forest may take over the meadow. This natural progression of a site through various stages of vegetation is called *forest succession*. The same principle can be imagined for the slopes above, with bedrock becoming encrusted with lichens. As a thin soil begins to form, hardy grasses and weeds might take root in the cracks of the rock, further breaking it up and forming a deeper soil that might one day support trees and shrubs.

Beyond the second pond, the trail continues eastward to cross the outlet of the third pond. The trail then climbs gently up the slope of Waldbillig Mountain before beginning a steady descent across avalanche slopes populated by cow parsnip and corn lilies. A smattering of spindly forget-me-nots and hardy mountain asters provide splashes of color along the edge of the path. At the foot of these avalanche fields, the trail slows its descent and passes into a copse of large spruce trees. It then crosses Pendant Creek at a shallow ford and travels gently down the valley through open parklands bursting with beargrass blossoms and bordered by stately stands of silent spruce trees. Upon reaching Big Salmon Creek, the trail makes an ankle-deep crossing (the falls shown on some maps are actually about a mile downstream of this ford). On the far bank is a junction with the Big Salmon Trail (212).

The route to Lena Lake runs straight ahead, while the left-hand trail runs toward Big Salmon Lake and a rather faint footpath runs upstream to the Pendant Cabin. The trail swings around to the southeast as it rounds the Pendant Cabin compound, and climbs vigorously along the edge of the Big Salmon Creek valley. The trail then levels out and crosses a major tributary stream that enters the valley from the northeast. The next two miles alternate between soggy spruce bottomland and drier slopes covered in an open forest of subalpine fir. At one point, the trail climbs above a creekside meadow into the open timber. A backward glance at this point reveals the twin pinnacles of Holland Peak far to the north. After another stretch of boggy forest, the trail passes the junction with a suite of trails (131, 195, and 129) that run eastward to meet the South Fork of the Flathead.

Travelers bound for Lena Lake should stick to the valley-bottom trail, which continues southeast to reach a low, marshy pass into the Shaw Creek drainage. At this point, turn southwest onto the well-marked Lena Creek trail. This wide track crosses some mudholes of Olympic proportions before climbing onto the firmer ground to the west. It climbs steadily as it follows a sparsely forested bluff for a mile to reach the foot of Lena Lake. Lena Lake is over a mile long and occupies a forested depression between Shaw Mountain and an unnamed foothill. The rocky crag that can be seen far to the west is Ptarmigan Mountain.

TRAIL 33 *NECKLACE LAKES*

Trail 415, 42, 110

General description: A backpack from Holland Lake to the Big Salmon trail, 9.4mi. (15.1 km).

Difficulty: Strenuous (west to east), moderately strenuous (east to west).

Trail maintenance: Yearly.

Traffic: Heavy.

Elevation gain: 3,640 ft.

Elevation loss: 2,180 ft.

Maximum elevation: 7,540 ft.

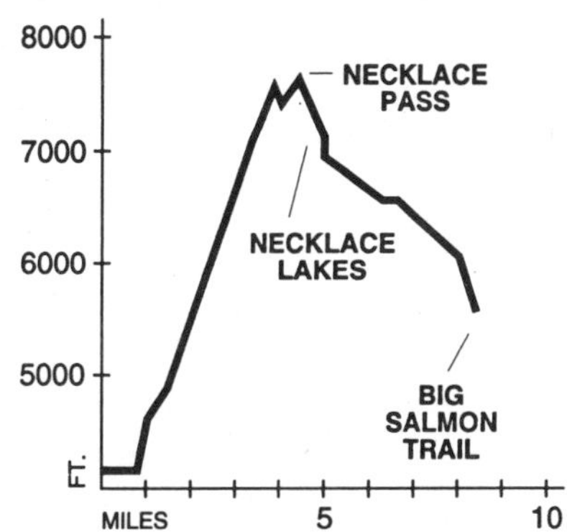

TRAIL 33 *NECKLACE LAKES*

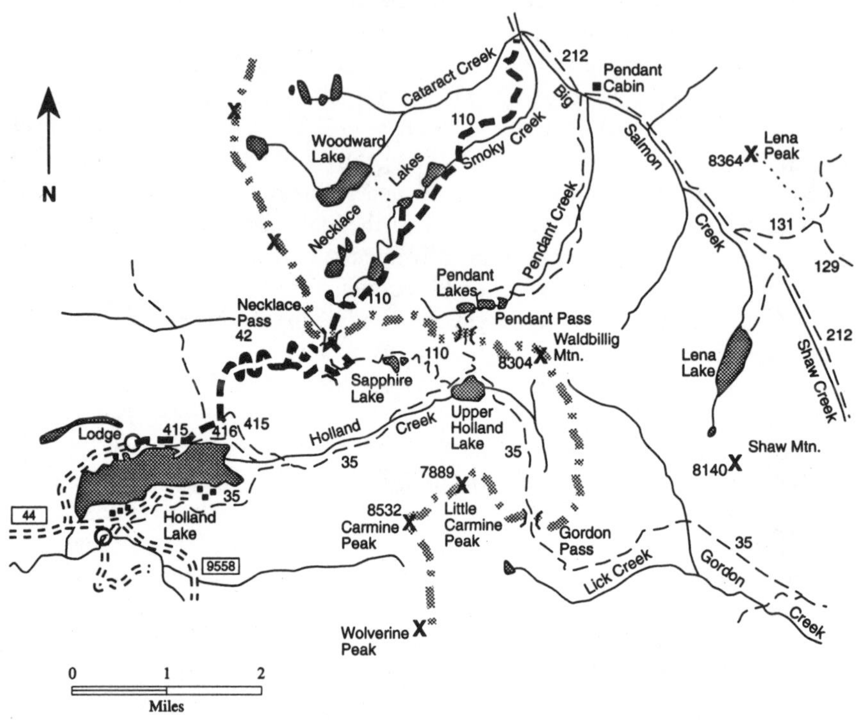

Topo maps: Holland Lake, Holland Peak.
Finding the trailhead: North Holland Lake trailhead (see The Upper Holland Loop, p. 94).

- 0.0 Holland Lake north trailhead.
- 0.1 Junction with the Holland Falls Trail (416). Bear left for Upper Holland Lake.
- 1.2 Junction with the Foothills Trail (192). Keep right.
- 1.3 Junction with the old Holland Lookout Trail (42). Turn left, start climbing.
- 4.1 Junction with the Holland Lookout Trail. Bear right.
- 4.8 Junction with the Sapphire Lake Trail (110). Turn left for Necklace Pass.
- 5.2 Necklace Pass. Trail enters the Bob Marshall Wilderness Area.
- 5.6 Trail passes the uppermost of the Necklace Lakes.
- 6.9 Unmarked junction with the trail to Woodward Lake. Turn right for the Big Salmon trail.
- 7.4 Trail passes the lowermost of the Necklace Lakes.
- 7.7 Trail fords Smoky Creek.
- 9.4 Trail reaches its junction with the Big Salmon Trail (110).

The peaks of the Swan Range rise beyond one of the Necklace Lakes.

The trail: The Necklace Lakes are a series of subalpine tarns that lie in a wide, rocky basin, surrounded by the peaks of the Swan Range. The direct trail to Necklace Pass, discussed here, is extremely steep and offers no water along the way. This route is best used for return trips from the Big Salmon valley. Travelers bound for the Necklace Lakes from the Holland Lake side would be better advised to follow the Upper Holland Loop and connect with the Necklace Lakes trail just beyond Sapphire Lake.

From the north Holland Lake trailhead, take the trail east for seventy-five yards to the first junction, which is the Holland Falls Trail (416). Turn left here, following signs for Upper Holland Lake, as the trail climbs onto a low bluff above the lake. As the trail nears the head of the lake, it passes the Foothills Trail (197), then reaches a junction with the trail to old Holland Lookout Trail (42). Turn left on this trail, which climbs onto the western wall of the Swan Valley and begins a grueling, zigzagging ascent through the forest. As the trail gains altitude, it passes out of the lowland forest of Douglas-fir and into a more open stand of subalpine fir. Views to the west include Holland Lake far below and the snowy Mission Mountains on the far side of the Swan Valley. After an ascent of 2,400 feet, the trail reaches a marked junction with the Holland Lookout trail, which continues to the summit of the mountain. The Necklace Pass trail turns southeast, traversing along steep, grassy slopes with excellent views in all directions. Half a mile farther on, the trail makes a final climb into a rocky saddle before dropping into the high valley containing Sapphire Lake.

At the floor of this valley, the trail reaches a trail junction. The trail to the south descends a short distance to reach Sapphire Lake, while the trail to the north climbs toward Necklace Pass. This trail leaves a scattering of firs behind and climbs up the rocky valley to reach the pass. Along the way, look for marmots and ground squirrels on the flowery meadows below the boulder fields. Upon reaching the pass, the trail enters the Bob Marshall Wilderness and begins its descent into the valley beyond. Alpine larch and subalpine fir are scattered about the trail as it crosses meadowy glens on its way to the Necklace Lakes.

The trail passes within sight of the uppermost lake, and a short spur trail runs northward to reach its shore. The main trail bends northeast, wandering beside the shores of a much larger lake. This beautiful tarn is surrounded by a rocky shoreline and frames the southern spur of Holland Peak to the north. A glance to the west reveals another spectacular but nameless summit. Beyond this second lake, the trail descends through rounded shelves of bedrock that harbor subalpine parkland in their interstices. After almost a mile of gentle descent, the trail forks. The well-beaten left fork runs to the shores of a shallow middle lake and beyond as an unmarked route to Woodward Lake (discussed later). The right fork constitutes the main trail, and it climbs for a bit before dropping into the woods beside the lowermost lake. Beyond this lake, the trail crosses Smoky Creek and descends gently onto the flat ridgetop separating Smoky and Cataract Creeks. The grade of the trail then steepens as it plummets for the final 1.5 mile to reach its junction with the Big Salmon trail.

Woodward Lake Option. From the trail junction below the upper Necklace Lakes, turn left to descend through a meadowy dale to reach the shallow, weedy middle lake. The path crosses Smoky Creek to reach a camping spot at the head of this pond. Bear northwest from the campsite across a muddy flats to pick up the faint track to Woodward Lake. This path works its way westward through hummocky country to reach an isolated pond that sits above a steep slope. The path works its way around the eastern shore of the pond, then descends the slope beyond to reach the foot of Woodward Lake. This large lake sits at the base of a tall, nameless peak, and boasts good fishing for rainbow and cutthroat trout.

TRAIL 34 *HOLLAND FALLS*

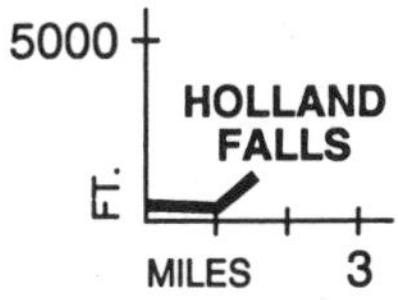

5000
HOLLAND FALLS
FT.
MILES 3

Trail 416
General description: A short day hike from the Holland Lake trailhead to Holland Falls, 1.7 mi. (2.7 km).
Difficulty: Easy.
Trail maintenance: Yearly.
Traffic: Heavy.
Elevation gain: 240 ft.
Maximum elevation: 4,280 ft.
Topo map: Holland Lake.
Finding the trailhead: North Holland Lake trailhead (see The Upper Holland Loop, p. 94).

- 0.0 Holland Lake north trailhead.
- 0.1 Junction with the Upper Holland Lake Trail (415). Bear right for Holland Falls.
- 1.7 Holland Falls.

The trail: This short trail, running from the Holland Lake Lodge to the falls at the head of the lake, provides a pleasant stroll for hikers who have a limited time to explore the area. This route has National Recreation Trail status and is closed to bicycles, horses, and motorized vehicles in order to enhance the recreational experience of hikers. However, motorboat traffic is heavy on the lake during the summer months, especially on weekends. Perhaps the best time of year to hike this trail is early autumn, when the larch and hardwoods surrounding the lake burst into bright yellows and oranges.

The trail begins at the North Holland trailhead and soon reaches a junction with trails to Upper Holland Lake and the Holland Lake Lodge. The falls trail, marked with trail signs, runs eastward along the shoreline toward the Swan Range. The lake has a moderating effect on the microclimate of the surrounding valley, and the result is a forest of outstanding diversity. Douglas-fir dominates the canopy, but western larch, ponderosa pine, spruce, and paper birch are also present in appreciable numbers. The trail passes forested islands and quiet bays where water lilies bloom. Listen for the lonely call of the loon, a frequent visitor to these waters.

Nearing the head of the lake, the trail crosses several small streams, then begins a modest ascent across the head of the valley. As the trail climbs, it meets a spur trail that descends to a motorboat landing at the head of the lake; stay left for the falls. The trail crosses talus slopes made up of huge boulders broken from the cliffs above by the power of "frost cracking." During winter, water seeps into crevices in the bedrock. The water expands as it freezes, wedging the cracks open and splitting

Holland Falls.

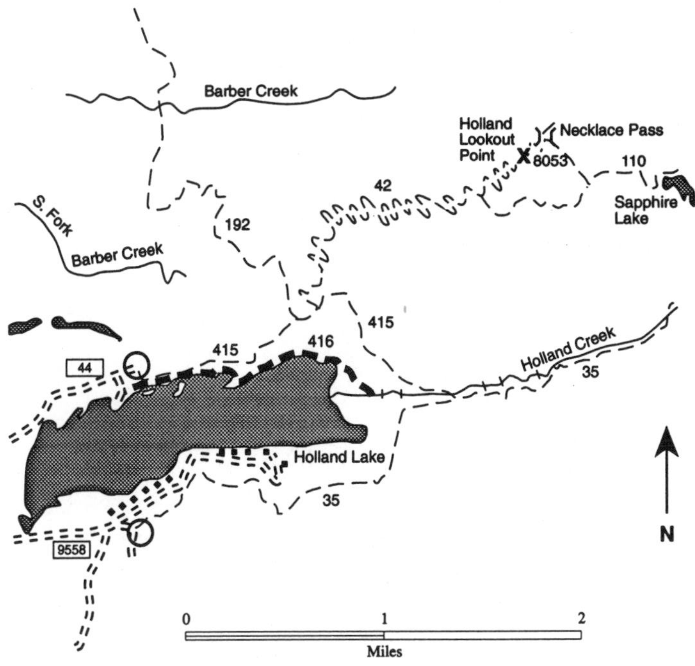

chunks of rock away from the cliff face. These rocks accumulate in broad aprons on the slopes below the cliffs. The openings created by the talus slopes allow excellent views of the Mission Mountains, which rise beyond the lake on the western horizon.

As the trail approaches its terminus, it passes through a copse of ivory-barked aspen trees, then makes its way onto the rocky promontory of bedrock below the falls. The going here is quite uneven and care must be taken to avoid a misstep that might end up in injury. Holland Falls tumbles about forty feet across a jumbled headwall of bedrock, then makes its way down a series of mossy cascades to the alluvial delta at the head of the lake.

TRAIL 35 *SMITH CREEK PASS*

Trail 29

General description: A long day hike or backpack from the Smith Creek trailhead to the Little Salmon overlook, 5.7 mi. (9.2 km).

Difficulty: Moderately strenuous.

Trail maintenance: Frequent.

Traffic: Moderate.
Elevation gain: 3,730 ft.
Elevation loss: 630 ft.
Maximum elevation: 7,950 ft.
Topo maps: Condon, Holland Peak.
Finding the trailhead: Depart Montana Highway 83 just south of the Condon airstrip, at the Falls Creek Road (901). This road passes a junction with Forest Road 9550; stay left and follow the signs for Trail 29. After crossing Smith and Falls Creeks, the road reaches a fork. Turn right on Forest Road 9762 for the last 1.5 miles to the trailhead.

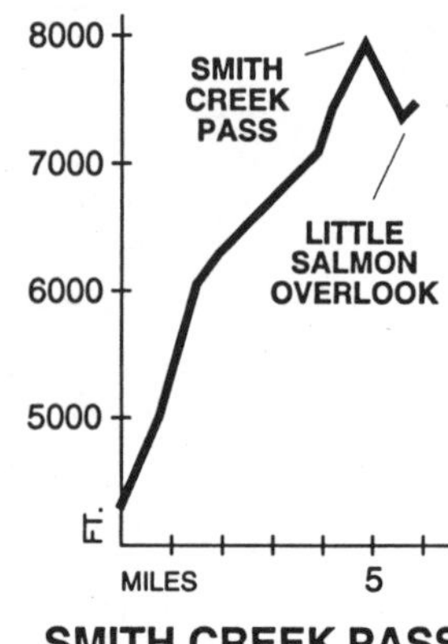

SMITH CREEK PASS

0.0 Smith Creek trailhead.
0.7 Trail crosses closed logging road.
3.0 Trail rounds hillside into the Smith Creek valley.
4.5 Trail crosses divide into the Condon Creek drainage.
4.9 Smith Creek Pass. Trail enters the Bob Marshall Wilderness.
5.7 Little Salmon Overlook.

The trail: This trail offers a long day trip over the Swan Range and into the western edge of the Bob Marshall Wilderness. This trail description ends at Little Salmon Overlook, a scenic point offering outstanding views of the jagged peaks that rim the Little Salmon valley. The Little Salmon trail continues beyond this point for a long distance, finally reaching the South Fork of the Flathead.

The trail begins its initial climb through the wooded bottomland of Smith Creek. After 0.5 mile, the trail doglegs to the north and climbs the hillside, passing along the edge of an old seed-tree cut. This logging practice leaves a scattering of desirable trees in the clearcut to serve as the breeding stock for the next generation of seedlings. The trail soon reaches a closed logging road, which it crosses at an oblique angle before resuming its ascent in a northerly direction. The trail enters the virgin forest, passing back and forth across the slope as it ascends. The grade becomes gentler as the trail approaches the top of the ridge, and the lowland forest of Douglas-fir and lodgepole pine gives way to a forest of subalpine fir.

The trail soon winds around onto the eastern slope of the hill, entering the Smith Creek valley once again. As the trail passes a tiny spring, a grassy meadow allows sweeping views of the Swan Valley, with the snow-capped Mission Mountains bordering its western side. The trail then descends for a while, then resumes its moderate ascent through a closed-canopy forest of subalpine fir. The forest begins to open up as the trail turns northward into a meadowy gulch. The grade then steepens, as the path climbs across an open slope covered in beargrass. To the south, Cooney Mountain and the taller, more impressive summit beyond it rise above the headwaters of Smith Creek. At the top of the slope, the trail reaches the high col separating Smith and Condon creeks.

From this lofty vantage point, the tooth-shaped pinnacles that crowd the Swan Divide rise across the high basin, and to the northwest lies the outlying spur of Condon Peak. The trail moves through alpine meadows and dwarfed fir as it con-

TRAIL 35 *SMITH CREEK PASS*

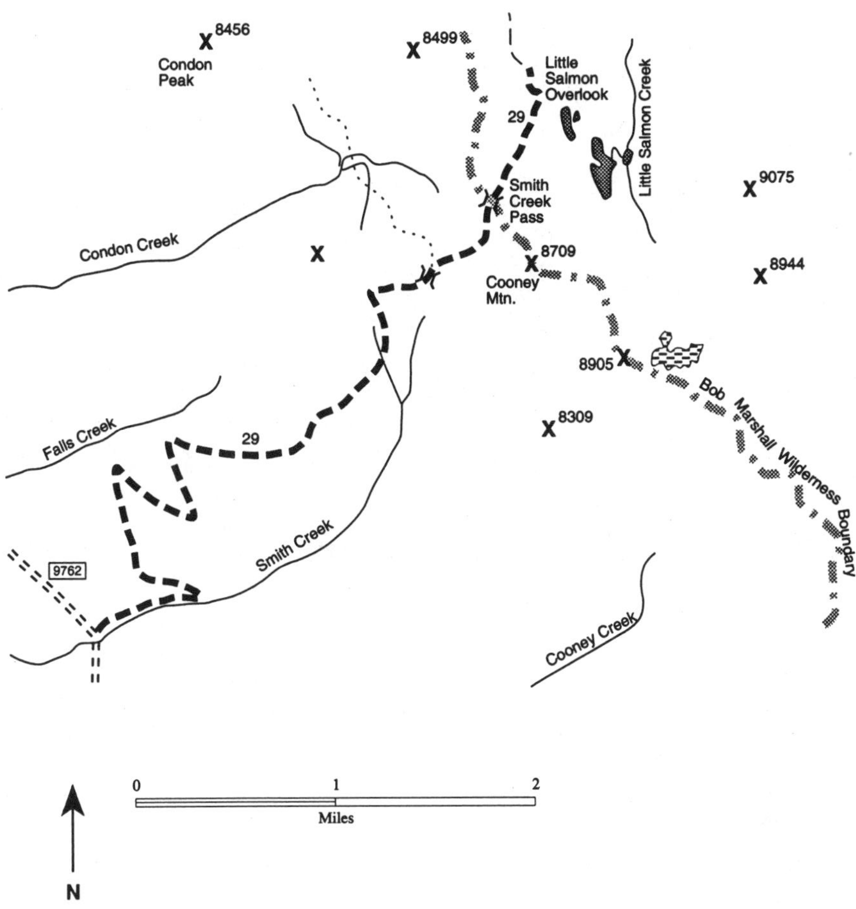

tinues eastward beneath the brow of Cooney Mountain. After a shallow ford of an alpine stream, the trail passes a high snowmelt tarn before bending northward around the head of the valley. The trail continues a moderate ascent through a high-altitude forest, then slips across a rock face to enter the deep notch of Smith Creek Pass. This pass reveals a lonely, glacier-carved valley far below, with nameless summits around its head and several turquoise tarns on its forested floor. Above the head of the valley, ridges of glacial debris known as *moraines* bear testament to recent glacial activity on the slopes above the valley.

Travelers who turn around at the pass are missing the most outstanding scenery of the entire trip. Follow the trail down into the basin below, crossing alpine fell fields dotted with subalpine larch and fir. The trail runs high above the shallow ponds that occupy the floor of the hanging valley, then climbs briefly to reach the rocky knob of the Little Salmon Overlook. This spot has been worn bare by pack and saddle

The crags of the Swan Range unveiled at the Little Salmon Overlook.

stock; take care to minimize any further impacts on this sensitive site. From the overlook, the jagged east face of the Swan Range soars skyward, with views extending as far north as Owl Peak. The trail to the South Fork of the Flathead continues beyond the overlook, descending to the floor of the Little Salmon valley.

TRAIL 36 *LION CREEK PASS*

Trail 25

General description: A backpack from the Lion Creek trailhead to Palisade Lake, 10.0 mi. (16.1 km).
Difficulty: Moderately strenuous.
Trail maintenance: Frequent.
Traffic: Light.
Elevation gain: 3,840 ft.
Elevation loss: 1,300 ft.
Maximum elevation: 6,990 ft.
Topo maps: Salmon Prairie, Swan Peak, Sunburst Lake.
Finding the trailhead: From Montana

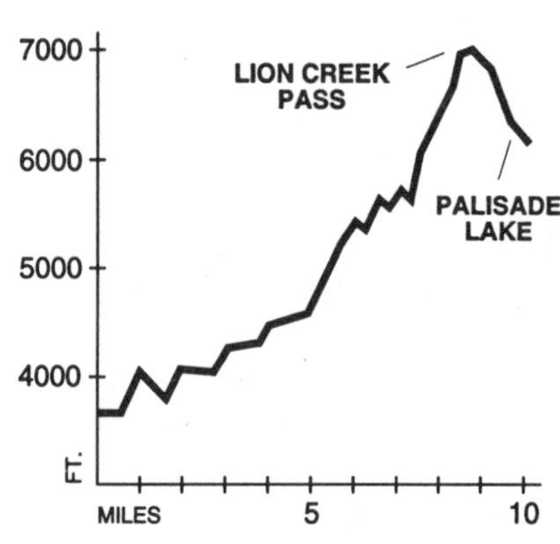

Highway 83, follow the Lion Creek Road, turning left onto Forest Road 5383 at the sign for Trail 25. This road is marked as unimproved on the maps, but is passable to two-wheel drive vehicles. The trailhead is located at the end of this road.

0.0 Lion Creek trailhead.
0.1 Footlog over Lion Creek.
0.2 Spur trail from road 9883 joins the Lion Creek trail.
1.6 Outfitter's trail from the end of road 5383 joins the main trail.
5.6 Falls on Lion Creek.
7.0 Trail fords Lion Creek as the valley bends northward.
7.3 Unmarked trail junction. Turn right for Lion Creek Pass.
8.8 Lion Creek Pass. Trail enters the Bob Marshall Wilderness.
9.0 Trail passes an unnamed tarn.
9.8 Junction with the spur trail to Palisade Lake. Turn left.
10.0 Palisade Lake.

The trail: This trail features a long valley-bottom hike through a forest of enormous cedar trees, followed by a brisk climb over a high pass in the Swan Range. At the end of the trip is Palisade Lake, which offers fishing opportunities to passing anglers. The trail connecting Palisade Lake with the Little Salmon trail is difficult to follow, with numerous blowdowns. It is not passable to horse parties and makes for a difficult passage for hikers bound for the heart of the Bob Marshall Wilderness.

The trail departs from the parking area above the south bank of Lion Creek, and immediately descends into the forested bottoms. Towering cedar and larch loom above the crystal waters of the creek, which flow languidly through deep pools

TRAIL 36 *LION CREEK PASS*

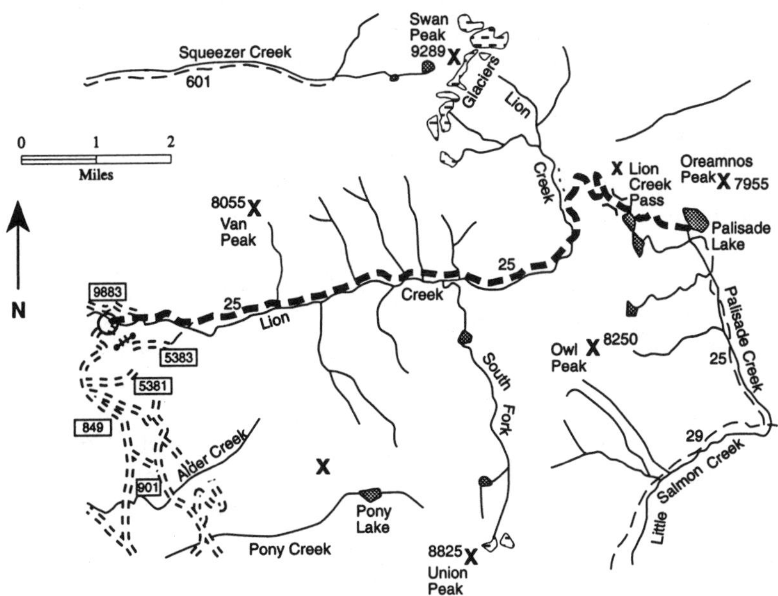

Unnamed tarn near Lion Creek Pass.

choked with fallen trees. The trail fords the deep but slow-moving stream; a footlog has been prepared just upstream of the ford for the benefit of hikers. The trail then climbs into the drier forest above the bottoms, which is characterized by scattered Douglas-fir and an understory of snowberry bushes. The trail soon receives a faint track coming from the Van Lake Road and continues to follow the valley into the Swan Mountains. The trail is joined by an outfitter's trail that comes in from the the end of a closed logging road to the south.

After climbing in brief spurts across level forest and open platforms of mossy bedrock, the trail passes beneath the rubble-strewn slopes of Van Peak. Below this mountain, the trail passes through an enchanting rainforest of cedar, fern, and moss-covered boulders. It then leaves the forest behind, climbing across a brushy avalanche chute choked with thimbleberry and occasional raspberry bushes. Once it reaches the forest beyond, the trail begins a stiff climb around a rocky point, then descends to the valley floor. The trail continues eastward through the trees to reach a crossing of a major tributary. This stream may be crossed via a shallow ford or the slippery logs that have fallen across the stream can be used. The trail then climbs gradually among the enormous boles of old-growth cedar and larch; some of these magnificent trees were alive when Europeans first set foot in North America.

The trail crosses another avalanche slope before returning to the forest and climbing aggressively beside a series of thundering falls. As the trail climbs briefly out of the forest, Union Peak becomes visible above the head of the South Fork of Lion

Creek. The trail begins to climb more insistently for the next several miles, as the cedar gives way to Douglas-fir and the understory of the forest gets brushier. Expect muddy traveling conditions on this part of the trail if it has rained recently. As the valley bends around to the north, the trail climbs a low hillock and then descends to cross the creek. A knee deep and slow-moving ford or a treacherous log walk are the options for crossing.

Once across the creek, the trail runs northward along the stream to reach an unmarked trail junction. The right fork is the Lion Creek Pass trail, which turns northeast and begins to climb. As the trail ascends steadily beneath the rocky face of a nameless mountain, openings in the subalpine forest reveal the south face of Swan Peak in all its glory. Permanent snowfields adorn its tilting strata of multicolored shale, which rise toward the heavens. As the trail continues to climb, open slopes of beargrass yield ever-improving views of this stunning peak. The trail doglegs to the southeast after 0.5 mile, climbing more gradually toward Lion Creek Pass. Nearing the top of the grade, the trail turns straight uphill in strenuous final effort. It then passes through a steep bowl of talus and climbs through a steep series of hairpin turns to reach the wooded pass.

Once atop the divide, the trail turns south, passing through an open parkland that allows views of Union Peak straight ahead. Upon reaching another unmarked trail junction, the trail veers to the left and descends to the northernmost of two high tarns. These unnamed lakes, blue-green and shallow, sport picturesque rocky shorelines and are surrounded by subalpine forest. The trail makes its way around the north end of the tarn, then continues eastward to descend steadily for 1.5 mile through brushy subalpine forest.

Just above the north end of Palisade Lake, the trail reaches yet another unmarked junction. The trail to the right continues down Palisade Creek toward the Little Salmon valley, while the left-hand trail descends to the swampy north shore of Palisade Lake. This broad lake sits at the base of Oreamnos Peak, an unimposing mound of short cliffs and grassy terraces. This combination makes for ideal mountain goat habitat, which explains why the peak bears the Latin name for goats. To the south, the more impressive peaks rising above the foot of the lake do not have names. Palisade Lake is home to a healthy population of native cutthroats. The lake is a poor choice for a camping spot, however, due to the marshiness of the surrounding country.

TRAIL 37 *INSPIRATION POINT*

Trail 31, 218

General description: A day hike from Napa Point trailhead to Inspiration Point, 5.0 mi. (8.0 km).

Difficulty: Moderately strenuous.

Trail maintenance: Yearly to Trail 7 junction; frequent between this junction and the Gorge Creek trail junction; occasional beyond.

Traffic: Moderate.

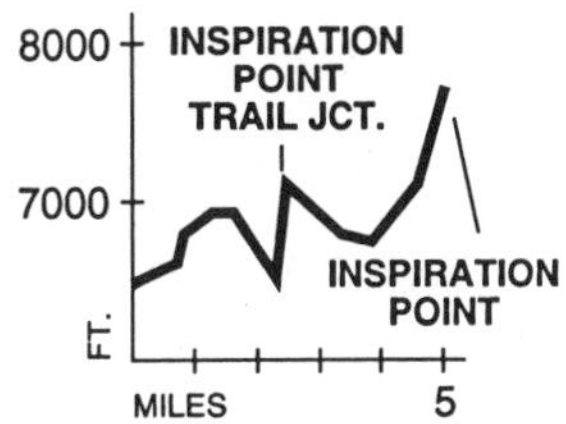

The north face of Swan Peak as seen from Inspiration Point.

Elevation gain: 2,015 ft.
Elevation loss: 910 ft.
Maximum elevation: 7,628 ft.
Topo maps: Thunderbolt Mountain.
Finding the trailhead: From Montana Highway 83 at the Goat Creek work station take the Goat Creek Road eastward. Bear to the left at the first fork, following signs for Napa Point trailhead. The 3-mile-long road to the trailhead is unimproved, but can be reached with two-wheel drive and careful navigation of the bumps and ruts.

0.0 Napa Point trailhead.
2.2 Junction with the Soap Creek trail. Keep going straight.
2.5 Junction with the trail to Inspiration Point (218). Turn right.
3.8 Trail crosses the headwaters of Swift Creek.
4.3 Junction with the Gorge Creek Trail (218). Turn right.
5.0 Summit of Inspiration Point.

The trail: This trail offers a day hiking opportunity for travelers wishing to visit the high country of the Swan Range without having to climb all the way up from the valley floor. The trail offers stunning views of Swan Peak at various points along its length and looks out over the western part of the Bob Marshall Wilderness at its

TRAIL 37 *INSPIRATION POINT*
TRAIL 38 *SWAN CREST TRAIL (SOUTHERN HALF)*

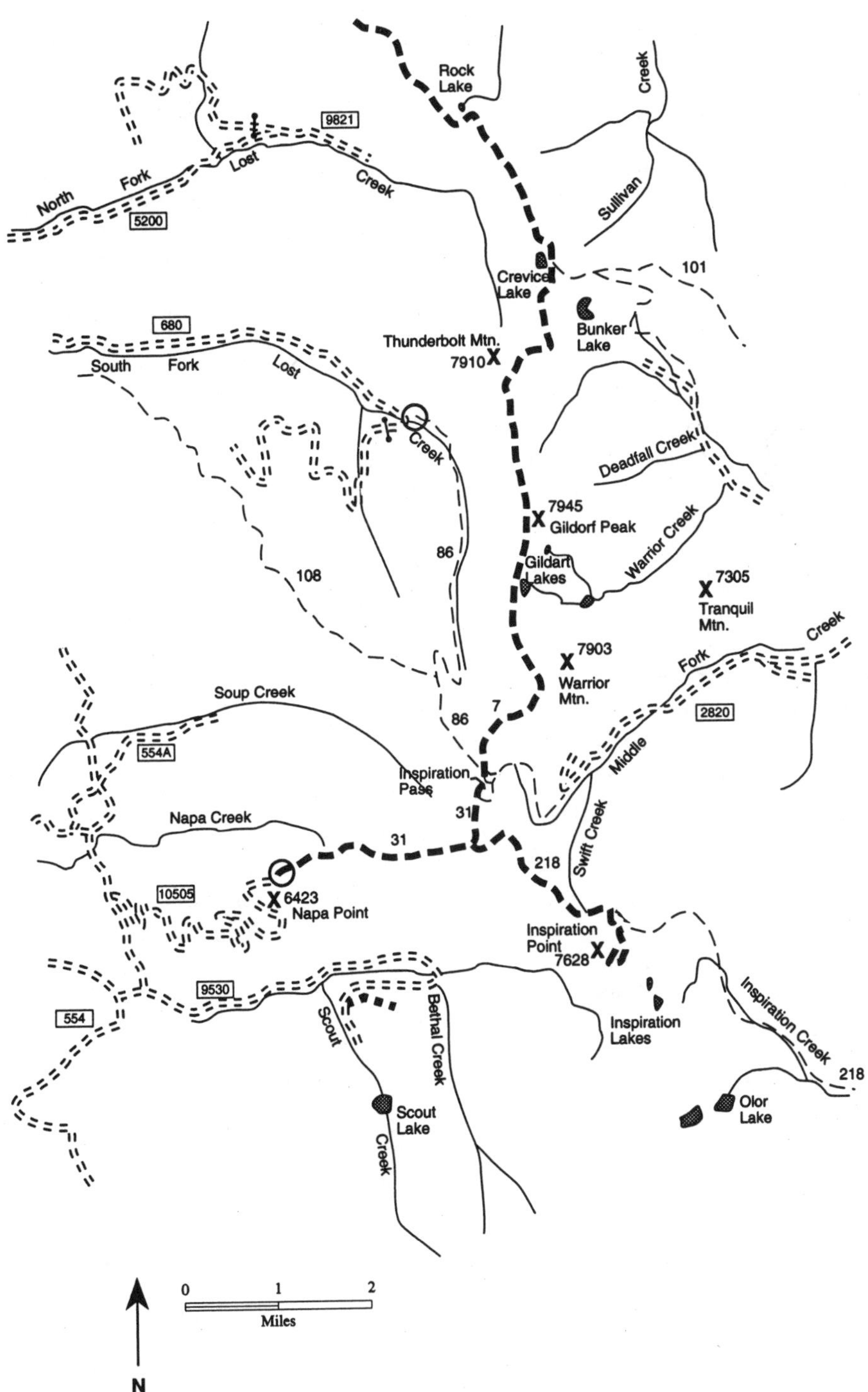

terminus on Inspiration Point. The last part of this hike is not shown on some maps; nevertheless, the trail up Inspiration Point is marked by a trail sign and is quite passable. However, this last portion of trail is probably not wide enough to allow the passage of horses.

The trail begins atop Napa Point, with a stunning view of Swan Peak rising above some unfortunately-placed clearcuts. The trail soon enters a charming alpine forest of subalpine fir and lodgepole pine, through which it travels for the next 0.25 mile. The trail then emerges onto alpine tundra spangled with sego lilies, wild peavine, and Indian paintbrush. After a vigorous climb to the ridgeline, the trail reaches a low saddle and then climbs the point beyond it. This low summit overlooks the upper drainage of Soup Creek. The trail then traverses below the next rise, and the sharp tooth of Swan Peak's eastern promontory becomes visible above the lesser mountains.

The trail continues to rise and fall fairly steeply for the next mile before dropping into the brushy saddle containing a junction with the Soup Creek trail (which does not appear on some maps). The Inspiration Point trail continues along the ridgeline, climbing steeply around the shoulder of the next point. After rounding its east face and climbing onto a high, flat bench, the trail descends into a series of low hummocks carpeted with glacier lilies and fir trees. Here it reaches a junction with the Swan Crest Trail (7), which enters from the left. Take the right-hand trail for Inspiration Point.

This trail turns south down a ridgeline of parkland hummocks, then drops into the upper basin of Swift Creek. The trail descends through a steep, rocky meadow with lots of loose stones—watch your footing. As the trail approaches Swift Creek, it passes into a scattering of old-growth spruce. The trail then begins climbing again, crossing lots of downed timber as it vaults the headwaters of the creek and passes below the cliffs of Inspiration Point. Upon reaching a series of flat benches, the trail arrives at a marked trail junction.

A rather sketchy-looking trail to Gorge Creek takes off to the left, while the Inspiration Point trail turns south and ascends to a wooded saddle abounding in glacier lilies. The trail then works its way out onto the steep talus slopes that make up the northeast face of Inspiration Point. As the trail rounds the corner of the point, it passes among old snags that serve as homes for cavity-dwelling pairs of Rocky Mountain bluebirds. To the south, the sheer face of Swan Peak towers above the surrounding mountains. The trail becomes overgrown by weeds as it switchbacks up the south face of the point and then returns to the eastern slope of the hill to continue its ascent. The trail pauses on a flat bench dotted with large boulders before making the final ascent to the summit of Inspiration Point. Here, an old lookout site commands a sweeping view of the surrounding mountains, from the Mission Mountains in the west to the White River Syncline in the east. To the north, the Inspiration Lakes lie like jewels amid the velvet forest of the valley floor.

TRAIL 38 *SWAN CREST TRAIL*

Trail 31, 7 (see map on p. 117 and p. 125)

General description: A backpack from the Napa Point trailhead to Sixmile Mountain, 23.5 mi. (37.8 km).

Difficulty: Moderately strenuous.

Trail maintenance: Yearly.

Traffic: Light between Inspiration Pass and Hall Peak; otherwise moderate.

Elevation gain: 6,338 ft.

Elevation loss: 5,355 ft.

Maximum elevation: 7,630 ft.

Topo maps: Thunderbolt Mountain, Connor Creek, Swan Lake.

Finding the trailhead: The trail begins at the Napa Point trailhead (see Inspiration Point, p. 115).

0.0 Napa Point trailhead.
2.2 Junction with the Soap Creek trail. Keep going straight.
2.5 Junction with the trail to Inspiration Point (218). Turn left for the Swan Crest Trail (7).
2.7 Junction with the Middle Fork Bunker Creek Trail (91). Bear left.
2.8 Inspiration Pass. Junction with the South Fork Lost Creek Trail (86). Turn right for the Swan Crest trail.
4.6 Warrior Mountain.
5.6 Junction with the spur trail to Gildart Lakes. Keep going straight.
8.8 Crevice Lakes shelter cabin (unsafe to use).
9.0 Upper Crevice Lake.
9.3 Lower Crevice Lake. Junction with the Bunker Creek Trail (101). Bear left.
10.6 Trail passes a small pond near Rock Lake.
13.0 Junction with the trail to Connor Creek (396). Turn left for the Swan Crest trail.
13.6 Junction with the Spring Slide Mountain Trail (78). Turn right.
14.9 Wire Trail to Connor Creek. Keep going straight ahead.
16.3 Trinkus Lake. Junction with the Bond Creek Trail (21). Turn right.
17.9 Trail crosses the headwaters of Branch Creek.
19.6 Trail passes a series of ponds behind Hall Peak.
20.7 Junction with the Posy Creek Trail (74). Turn left.

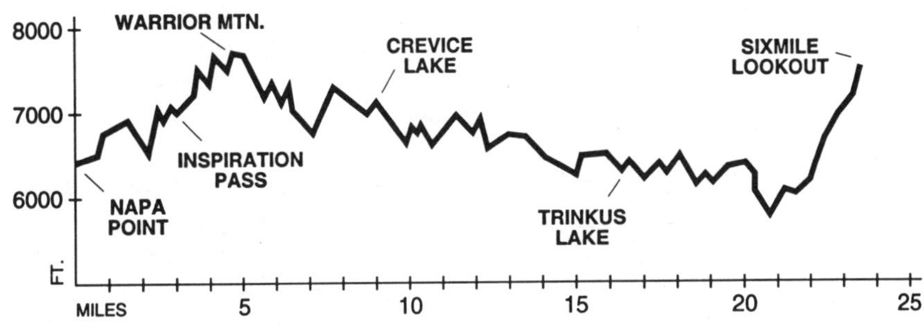

20.8 Junction with the Hall Lake Trail (61). Turn right for Sixmile Mountain.
22.2 Junction with the Sixmile Lookout Trail (10). Turn right.
23.5 Old lookout site, summit of Sixmile Mountain.

The trail: The Swan Crest trail runs the length of the northern Swan Range, from Inspiration Point in the south to Sixmile Mountain in the north. It remains in alpine and subalpine habitats above 6,000 feet for most of its length. Although the overall change in altitude along the trail is never great, the trail is constantly climbing or descending, sometimes quite steeply. Primary trails that access this lofty route from the Swan Valley are the Sixmile Mountain Trail (10), the Hall Lake Trail (61), the Bond Creek Trail (21), the Spring Slide Mountain Trail (78), the South Fork Lost Creek Trail (86), and the Inspiration Point Trail (31). This last route offers the most direct path to the Swan Crest trail, and so will be discussed in detail. There are also several trails rising to the crest of the Swan Range from the east, but these routes are maintained less frequently and are consequently harder to follow. Snow lingers through June in some of the higher saddles along the trail, and the route is faint in spots between Inspiration Pass and the Gildart Lakes.

From Napa Point, follow the Inspiration trail eastward as it dips and falls along the crest of the ridgeline. Travelers will enjoy excellent views of Swan Peak from a number of points along this trail. After 2.5 miles, this trail reaches a junction with the Swan Crest trail itself; the trail sign will indicate this as "Alpine Trail 7." Turn left and follow this trail northward as it gently rises and falls through fir copses and flowery meadows populated by numerous ground squirrels. The trail makes its way around the east side of a high point, then descends into Inspiration Pass, where it reaches a complex trail junction. First of all, the trail passes the rather faint Bunker Creek Trail (91), which drops away to the east. A few yards farther on, the trail reaches an intersection with the South Fork Lost Creek Trail (86). Travelers following the Swan Crest trail will have to make a right turn here and follow the smaller trail as it climbs gently toward the next point on the ridgeline.

The gradient soon steepens as the trail climbs several calf-burning pitches. A backward glance reveals a final view of Swan Peak's north face. Nearing the summit of the hill, the trail turns eastward to drop into a steep, open bowl that boasts views of Pentagon and Silvertip Mountains on the eastern horizon. Closer at hand, the lower summits of Inspiration Point and Alcove Mountain rise above the headwaters of Bunker Creek. As the trail begins to climb once more, it passes into a loose-knit stand of gnarled white-bark pines. The route soon rounds the next hillside into the open basin beyond. As the trail climbs into the open, it reveals the rocky summit of Warrior Mountain jutting into the Bunker Creek valley.

The trail then climbs to reach a broad, meadowy pass filled with glacier lilies and mountain avens. The trail peters out amid this profusion of tundra greenery, and it becomes necessary to follow the cairns northward as the trail climbs onto the next hump. Snowdrifts linger late into the summer in this area. The trail becomes distinct again as it mounts the high col behind Warrior Mountain. Looking northward from this aerie, Gildart Peak and Thunderbolt Mountain loom above the grassy meadows of an open bowl. From the saddle, the trail switches back to the southwest, rounding a rocky knob before commencing a spectacular cliff-hanging descent down the ridgeline to the north.

The trail becomes faint as it crosses the next saddle, picking up again as it rounds the eastern side of the next hillock. Look for cairns and scan ahead for distinct sections of the trail as it continues north along the ridgeline. Upon reaching the saddle at the base of Gildart Peak, the trail passes above the uppermost of the Gildart Lakes. A faint spur trail descends from the saddle to the north shore of this shallow turquoise gem. Looking back to the south, Warrior Mountain displays its sheer north face, while Tranquil Mountain rises farther east along the same ridge. The trail continues northward through a grassy dell, then without warning begins an uphill surge to the northeast. The route then levels off as it passes through a scruffy pine-fir forest on the western slopes of Gildart, high above the South Fork of Lost Creek.

The trail then descends through narrow meadows of corn lily to reach the broad saddle beyond. Ahead lies the ragged cockscomb of Thunderbolt Mountain, while farther east is the striated hump of Bruce Point. The trail continues along the ridgeline for a brief time, then dips into the headwaters of Bunker Creek while passing beneath the eastern face of Thunderbolt. The trail crosses several small streams before leaving the ragged timber behind and climbing across open slopes corrugated with bands of bedrock. As it ascends, the trail crosses meadows splashed with buttercups, shooting stars, and glacier lilies, with icy rills dissecting the tundra. Crossing a hilltop, the trail passes through a narrow notch in the rock and enters a strange wonderland of tilted reddish stone.

The trail continues to climb into the next saddle, then works its way to the east of the next point through a maze of rock bands. To the southeast, the barren peaks of Picture Ridge rise toward the sky, while the quiet waters of Bunker Lake glitter in the rocky basin below. The horn peak of Pentagon Mountain again can be seen

Looking north at Gildart Peak from Warrior Mountain.

far to the east, while farther south, Silvertip Mountain rises above lesser peaks of the White River Syncline. As the trail reaches the divide between Bunker and Sullivan creeks, it passes a rickety, clapboard shelter cabin, which is unuseable as a shelter. It then wanders the shoreline of Upper Crevice Lake, passing eerie pools dissected by fingerlike projections of bedrock. Just before reaching Lower Crevice Lake in the shallow saddle below, the trail receives several fainter routes which arrive from the east. The trail follows the eastern shoreline of Lower Crevice Lake and continues northward along its outlet stream.

When this stream drops into the valley to the west, the trail strikes off across the western slope of the next point. A series of high benches crowned with beargrass allow excellent views of Thunderbolt Mountain looming to the south in all its glory. The trail climbs gradually as it works its way to the ridgeline, where it is greeted by views of the Flathead Range to the northeast. As the trail levels off, it passes a tiny pond that reflects the north face of Thunderbolt Mountain. It then descends into an old burn where it picks up the old roadbed of and abandoned logging route. Shortly thereafter, the trail wanders beside a small lake that is a southern outlier of Rock Lake, which lies out of sight to the north.

The trail then runs northwest, crossing a blasted moonscape leveled by a forest fire. Upon reaching the crest of the ridge, the trail enters a pleasant subalpine forest spared by the blaze. The trail descends into the next saddle, and reaching the base of a rather substantial hill, turns west to continue along the crest of the Swan Range. The old roadbed bends around to the north again as it crosses another burned section on its way to the eastern slope of the next mountain along the ridge. To the east, the sawtooth peaks of the Flathead Range rise along the skyline. The nearest tall peak in this range is Mount Baptiste, while the loftier pinkish summits of Great Northern Mountain and Grant Peak rise far to the north.

After passing high above a pleasant basin, the trail reaches a junction marked by a huge rock cairn. The roadbed descends into the Connor Creek valley as Trail 396, while the Swan Crest Trail takes off to the left, following a westerly course. The trail remains level as it passes across the northern slope of the point, then crosses a flat pass covered in subalpine parkland. The trail then drops into a wooded glen sprinkled liberally with old snags, where it reaches a junction with the Spring Slide Mountain Trail (78). Turn right to stay on the Swan Crest Trail, which leaves Spring Slide Mountain behind to climb the ridge to the north. Atop the ridge, distant vistas to the north reveal the peaks of Glacier National Park crowding the horizon. To the northwest, the tawny summit of ConKelley Mountain rises in the foreground.

After a brief level stretch, the trail drops steeply through a lush meadow to reach the saddle below. Here it reaches a junction with the Wire Trail (396), which runs down into the Connor Creek valley. The Swan Crest trail works its way around the eastern side of the next rise, then pops through a narrow pass to cross the slopes above Trinkus Lake. As the trail descends across an opening in the trees, the lake and Spring Slide Mountain beyond it can be clearly seen. After descending almost to lake level, the trail reaches a junction with the Bond Creek Trail (21), which runs past the lake. The Swan Crest trail then turns north again, climbing up a shallow valley in the shadow of ConKelley Mountain.

The trail passes over the ridgeline and onto the eastern slope of the range, where it drops into an open bowl filled with brushy subalpine forest. The trail crosses several small streams as it passes below the impressive summit of ConKelley, then climbs around a spur ridge to the north. Descending into a second basin, the trail reaches a shallow, aquamarine pond at the base of a nameless rock outcrop. Enormous boulders have tumbled down from the summit, suggesting that the insidious power of frost cracking is at work on the cliffs during the winter.

The trail then mounts the pass separating Branch and Ball creeks, where travellers are immediately greeted by the awesome vista of Hall Peak's craggy summit rising to the northwest like a solitary tooth. The trail descends to a pass at the foot of the peak, then climbs moderately through the brushy forest that covers its eastern slopes. As the trail approaches the next saddle, it crosses a series of streams via well-built footbridges and makes its way onto the high plateau beyond. The trail passes the shorelines of three woodland ponds, set in the deep forest and providing a breeding ground for frogs and mosquitoes. A quarter mile farther, the trail turns westward, entering a high defile that leads to a long and steady descent into the Hall Creek valley.

The trail makes its way downward beside an intermittent stream, then works its way north, descending through tall brush to reach the low saddle separating Hall and Posey creeks. Here, a faint track (74) descends into Posey Creek, while the Swan Crest trail climbs twenty yards to reach a junction with the Hall Lake Trail (61). Stay right for Sixmile Mountain, as the trail climbs steeply up a rocky hillock above Hall Lake. At the ridgeline, the trail turns northeast, passing through a narrow ravine strewn with monolithic boulders. The trail continues its climb as it crosses the northern slope of a rocky hill, then turns southward through another boulder garden to reach the marshy meadows beyond. The trail leaves the brush behind as it picks its way westward, climbing gradually across shelves of bedrock to reach the Sixmile trail junction. From this point, Swan and Holland peaks are visible in the hazy distance to the southeast. The snow-capped Mission Range occupies the southwestern horizon.

The final leg to Sixmile Lookout takes off to the northwest, setting a moderate pace as it ascends across the talus slopes of a nameless mountain. On its way to the ridgetop, the trail passes through subalpine forests and below an extensive boulder field; look for pikas and marmots among the rocks. Upon reaching the crest of the ridge, the trail turns north and continues its steady ascent. Views open up all around as the trail approaches the final pitch to the summit. The trail zigzags upward through boulders punctuated by a few twisted limber pines on its final ascent to the old lookout site.

From this point, the entire length of Swan Lake can be seen in the valley below, as well as the northern half of Flathead Lake farther to the west. The verdant fields of the Flathead Valley stretch away to the northwest like a patchwork quilt, bounded to the east by the northern marches of the Swan Range. The rounded summit of Mount Orvis Evans lies to the north along the crest of the range, and the pointed horn to the northeast of it is Big Hawk Mountain. In the distance, Great Northern Mountain and Grant Peak crown the Flathead Range, while beyond them lie the peaks of Glacier National Park. Look southeast to see the Bob Marshall Wilderness; Pentagon and Silvertip mountains can be seen plainly on a clear day.

TRAIL 39 *HALL LAKE*

Trail 61

General description: A day hike or short backpack from the trailhead to Hall Lake, 4.4 mi. (7.1 km).

Difficulty: Moderately strenuous.

Trail maintenance: Frequent.

Traffic: Moderate.

Elevation gain: 2,180 ft.

Elevation loss: 80 ft.

Maximum elevation: 5,380 ft.

Topo map: Swan Lake.

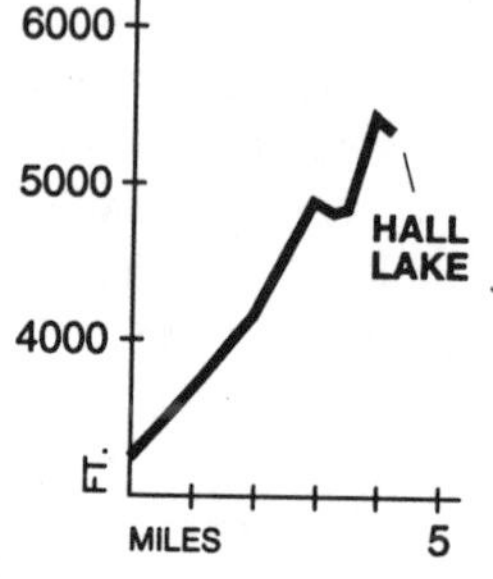

Finding the trailhead: From the town of Swan Lake head east on the unmarked gravel road that departs Montana Highway 83 beside the Alpine Chalet motel. This road passes through a residential area and past several ranches before forking. Take the right-hand fork and follow it eastward until it turns southward. At this point, the trailhead is marked by a square orange marker with a black "x" on it, as well as a trail mileage sign.

- 0.0 Hall Lake trailhead.
- 1.4 Trail crosses Groom Creek.
- 4.2 Junction with spur trail to Hall Lake. Turn left.
- 4.4 Foot of Hall Lake.

The trail: The Hall Lake trail provides a trip toward the crest of the Swan Range, to a high subalpine lake known for its fishing potential. From the trailhead, the route runs westward across the lowlands of the Swan Valley, passing among noble fir and paper birch on its way to the Swan Range. After a gradual climb of 1.5 miles, the trail reaches the mountains and passes into the wooded Groom Creek canyon. The trail runs upstream for a short distance before crossing the creek and turning northwest. It climbs steadily through an open forest of Douglas-fir; a backward glance reveals the tall summit of ConKelley Mountain. Reaching the end of the ridge, the trail climbs into the Hall Creek drainage.

The trail continues to climb steadily through a sun-dappled forest of larch and Douglas-fir, with huckleberry bushes growing in the understory. The trail crosses a broad talus slope, allowing views of Swan Lake to the west, then enters another open stand of Douglas-fir. The southern spur of Sixmile Mountain rises to the northwest as the trail reaches a long switchback to the south. After several hundred yards, the trail resumes its northerly course and climbs past scattered outcrops of mossy bedrock. Nearing the lake, the trail reaches a fork. The right fork climbs for one mile to reach the pass above the head of the lake; here, it joins the Swan Crest Trail (7). The left fork descends for 0.25 mile through the brushy valley of Hall Creek to reach the foot of the lake. This deep, blue-green pool provides excellent fishing. Hall Peak cannot be seen from the foot of the lake, but can be viewed from its brushy western shore.

TRAIL 38 *SWAN CREST TRAIL (NORTHERN HALF)*
TRAIL 39 *HALL LAKE*

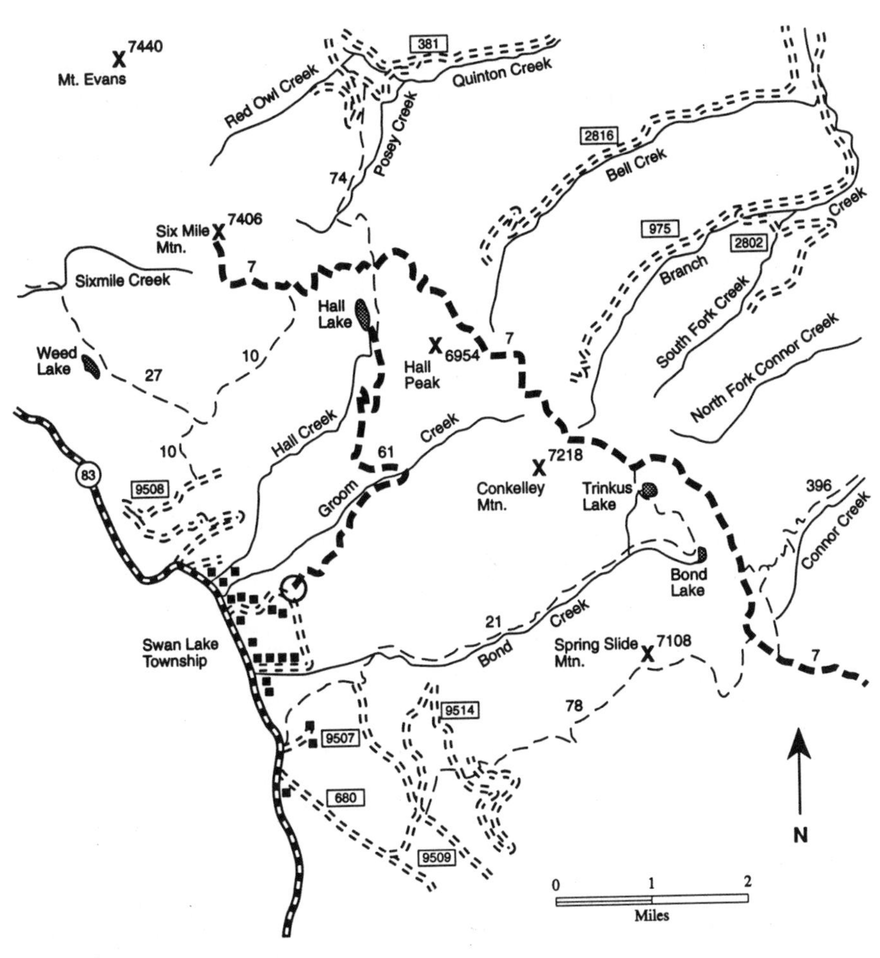

TRAIL 40 *JEWEL BASIN COMPLEX*

*Trail numbers are given at the beginning of individual trail descriptions.
General description: A collection of day hikes and short backpacks.
Trail maintenance: Yearly.
Traffic: Heavy.
Topo maps: Jewel Basin, Crater Lake.
Finding the trailhead: From Bigfork head east on Montana Highway 83 to the community of Echo Lake. Turn left here on the Echo Lake Road and follow it past the western shore of Echo Lake. Follow the brown signs for the Jewel Basin. The pavement ends and the road becomes narrow as it climbs the mountainside. After

about 5 miles of travel, the road reaches its end at the Noisy Creek trailhead, the most popular entry point for the Jewel Basin.

The trails: The Jewel Basin Hiking Area is widely known for its numerous small lakes set among charming alpine meadows and miniature fir forests. The trailhead is at 5,760 feet elevation, providing one of the few high-altitude access points to the Swan Range. Most of the hikes in the area are of moderate difficulty and offer day hiking opportunities for young and old alike. Overnight users should camp in designated areas to minimize their impacts on this fragile alpine basin. Horses, mountain bikes, and motorized vehicles are prohibited from using these popular trails. As a result, the trails hold up well even during rainstorms and are rarely muddy. The lakes south of Mount Aeneas on Trail 7 are discussed in a separate section, titled Big Hawk Lakes (trail 41).

TWIN LAKES

Trail #8

This trail runs 2.1 miles up a moderate slope to reach the Twin Lakes, a pair of crystal-clear pools set among tall subalpine fir. Beginning at the trailhead, this route runs northward, climbing moderately through a scattering of subalpine firs underlain by a dense growth of false huckleberries. After passing a junction with the Jewel Lakes trail (marked "Camp Misery Trail 68"), the trail continues north, passing high above the Noisy Creek valley. As the trail crosses steeper, well-drained slopes, beargrass carpets the ground. This member of the lily family blooms only every three to five years. Because most of the beargrass on a given slope usually come from the same genetic stock, they all bloom at one time when they reach the end of their flowering cycle.

Looking south at Twin Lakes.

TRAIL 40 *JEWEL BASIN COMPLEX*

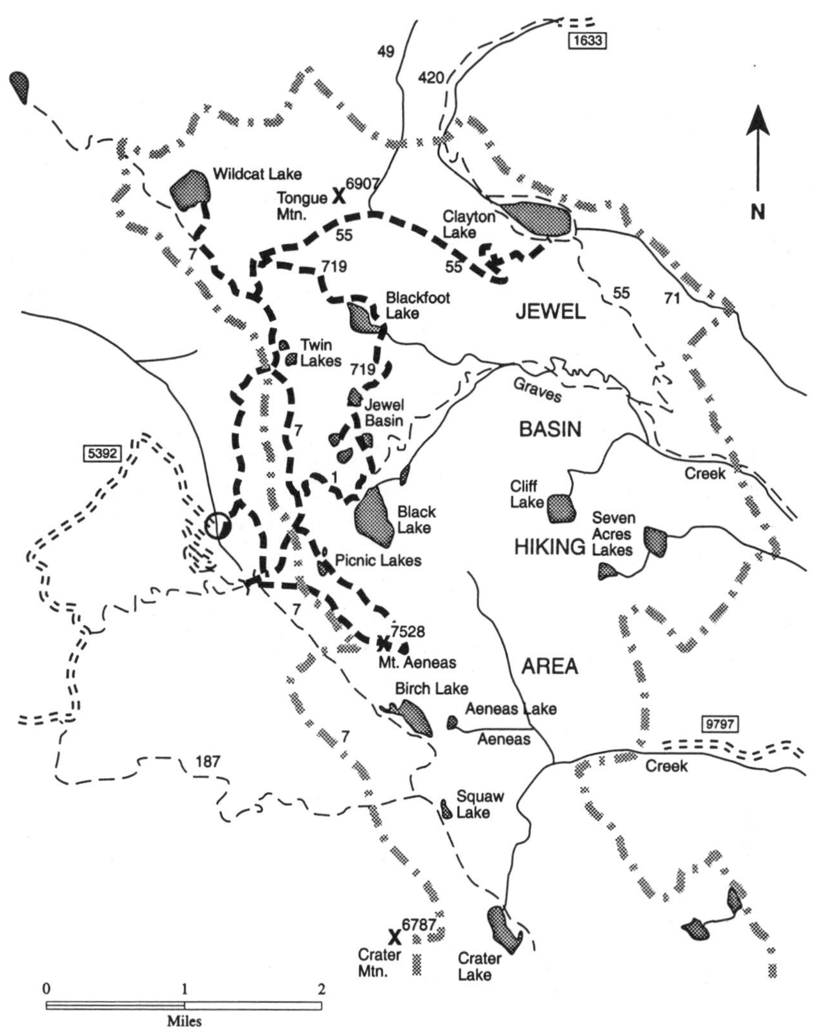

As the trail approaches an eastward bend in the slope, it offers broad vistas of the northern Flathead Valley, featuring Flathead and Echo lakes. Rounding a rocky knob, the trail passes among the skeletons of old white pine killed by an epidemic of white pine blister rust. This fungus virtually wiped out Montana's entire population of white pine. The path bends northeast and crosses a steep slope of loose scree on its way to the Noisy Creek Notch, a narrow gateway into the Graves Creek drainage on the east side of the Swan Divide. After passing through the notch turn left onto trail 7, then take an immediate right onto the spur trail descending to the Twin Lakes. These two turquoise gems, separated by a narrow isthmus, are set in an open subalpine forest and make an excellent spot for a picnic.

WILDCAT LAKE

Trail 7, 723

This trail runs northward from Noisy Creek Notch, following the crest of the Swan Range for 1.8 miles to reach the south shore of Wildcat Lake. From the Notch, follow Trail 7 north, as it passes above the beautiful Twin Lakes. The Flathead Range can be seen far to the east, and as the trail curls around the northern edge of the lake basin, Mount Aeneas becomes visible to the south. The trail soon rounds a hillside and climbs into a shallow, meadowy pass lit by the yellow blossoms of glacier lilies. These meadows harbor snowbanks late into the summer months, and the glacier lilies begin their spring growth beneath the snow, using reserves of energy stored in underground bulbs. Thus, in early summer, the narrow leaves of these hardy alpine flowers can be seen protruding through the snow toward the warmth of the summer sun.

Beyond this saddle, the trail passes between a shallow tundra pond and the rocky cliffs of a nameless peak. It then reaches a junction with the trail to Clayton Lake (55). Turn left up the hill to the northwest, as the trail tops a low pass that separates the Graves and Wildcat Creek drainages. The trail then descends steadily across ridges of rocky debris that support a sparse growth of dwarfed firs. Upon reaching the flat meadow at the bottom of the grade, the trail reaches a junction with the spur trail to Wildcat Lake (723). Turn right onto this trail which winds past the shorelines of several shallow ponds before dropping steeply into a narrow ravine at the foot of Tongue Mountain. The trail then runs north for the final distance to reach the south shore of Wildcat Lake. This large lake occupies the entire valley floor and offers fishing for native west-slope cutthroat trout.

CLAYTON LAKE

Trail 55

This trail runs eastward for 2.8 miles, connecting the Wildcat Lake Trail (7) with Clayton Lake. From its junction with Trail 7, the trail to Clayton Lake runs north for a brief stretch through flat, alpine meadows. At the junction with the Blackfoot Lake Trail (719), take the left-hand (and less-traveled) fork, which winds eastward across the open slopes of Tongue Mountain. The trail offers outstanding views to the south, featuring Mount Aeneas and its jagged eastern spur, as well as the shimmering waters of Blackfoot Lake in the valley below. The trail dips and climbs as it passes across a series of rocky knobs and then stays level as it crosses beargrass-covered slopes. As the trail rounds the eastern end of Tongue Mountain, it climbs steadily to reach the ridgeline.

Once atop the ridge, the trail offers outstanding vistas of the Flathead Range, crowned by Great Northern Mountain and Grant Peak. The spires of Glacier National Park crowd the horizon beyond. The trail continues in its easterly course, passing through ridgetop meadows that are splashed with wildflowers of all colors and descriptions. As the ridgeline begins to drop away, the deep blue mirror of Clayton Lake appears in the basin to the east. The trail drops into subalpine forest as the ridge continues its descent. As the ridge begins to peter out, the trail turns northeast across flat, forested benches on its way to the south shore of the lake. Clayton Lake harbors a population of cutthroat trout that provide angling opportunities for hikers that have brought their fishing gear. A trail rings the shoreline of the lake, and fire grates have been placed in designated camping spots scattered around the lakeshore. Trails radiate from the lake in all directions, bound for the logging roads that rise from Hungry Horse Reservoir.

JEWEL LAKES

Trail 8, 68, 7, 1, 719

This hike runs for 2.8 miles over a high saddle in the Swan Range to reach the Jewel Lakes. From the trailhead, follow the trail to Twin Lakes as it curls around to the north, then turn right onto the trail marked "Camp Misery Trail 68." This trail climbs through the brushy forest in a southeasterly direction for 0.4 miles to reach yet another trail junction, this time with Trail 7. Turn left on this trail, which climbs into a high saddle to the east. Here, amid alpine meadows, the trail forks; the right fork runs to the Picnic Lakes, while the left fork runs toward the Jewel Lakes. This trail passes through a parkland of alpine meadows and stunted firs to reach a junction with the Graves Creek Trail (1).

Turn right onto this trail, which descends steeply into the basin to the east. After passing a cutoff trail to the Picnic Lakes, the trail runs above Black Lake, which can be seen through the scattering of firs that surround the trail. This lake is arguably the most stunning of the twenty-two lakes in the Jewel Basin hiking area; its glassy surface reflects the craggy eastern buttresses of Mount Aeneas. The trail descends the parkland slope to the north of this large lake, reaching a spur trail to Black Lake about a mile below the pass. The trail to Jewel Lakes continues to descend to the east, reaching a rather faint trail junction. The weedy and overgrown trail down Graves Creek (1) cuts off to the right, while the much more well-defined trail to the Jewel Lakes bends northward.

This trail descends gently to he weedy shoreline of East Jewel. From here, a spur trail runs west to reach the shores of South Jewel. The main trail continues northward across the wooded flats, reaching a camping spot just to the south of North Jewel Lake. Both North and South Jewel support populations of rainbow trout, while the other two lakes are barren. This basin is a good place to give blood to the local hordes of blackflies; be sure to bring some insect repellant. The trail continues beyond North Jewel and is described in the following section.

BLACKFOOT LAKE

Trail 719

This trail runs for 2.3 miles between North Jewel Lake and the Clayton Lake Trail (55), passing marshy Blackfoot Lake along the way. From North Jewel, the trail crosses the outlet stream and passes beside a marshy pond. After climbing for a short distance, the trail descends eastward across a brushy slope covered in bracken fern and thimbleberry. Across the valley, a jagged ridge rises westward toward the summit of Mount Aeneas. After a moderate descent, the trail turns northward, following the hillside for a brief but steep descent to the south shore of Blackfoot Lake. This lake is a mud-bottomed, weedy affair that offers only mediocre fishing for rainbow and cutthroat trout. A family of beavers has built its lodge here, and these animals can sometimes be spotted as they paddle about on the lake.

After crossing the outlet stream, the trail runs inland, passing well to the east of the lakeshore. A short distance further on, the trail passes a spur route that runs to a designated camping spot on the eastern shore of the lake. The trail then begins a meandering climb through the brushy forest, mounting the south slope of Tongue Mountain. As the trail steadily gains altitude, it passes across open slopes lit up by a profusion of beargrass flowers. After a rather steep pitch of switchbacks that follow the bed of an intermittent stream, the trail reaches its terminus at a junction with the Clayton Lake Trail (55), just a few hundred yards northeast of Trail 7.

THE MOUNT AENEAS LOOP

Trail 8, 68, 7, 717

This moderately strenuous trail provides a 4.6-mile loop that visits the summit of Mount Aeneas as well as the charming alpine waters of the Picnic Lakes. From the Noisy Creek trailhead, take the trail running east toward the Twin Lakes. At the junction marked "Camp Misery Trail 68," turn right and climb for half a mile in a southeasterly direction, passing through brushy forests on the way to a junction with Trail 7. At this intersection, turn right, following the trail as it traverses along to reach a saddle that overlooks the Birch Creek drainage. This saddle is home to a complex trail junction. The Mount Aeneas Loop Trail (717) climbs straight up the ridgeline to the east.

As the trail makes its way up the ridge, it affords sweeping views of the northern Swan Valley, as well as Flathead Lake, which lies beyond the Mission Range. The trail drops onto the southern slope of the ridge as it continues to climb through dwarfed subalpine fir. Upon reaching a steep bowl, the trail begins to switchback up to the top of the ridge. The trail crests the ridgeline beside a microwave relay station, then turns east again to follow the narrow ridgetop toward the summit of Mount Aeneas. Look for mountain goats as the trail passes above the pretty basin containing the Picnic Lakes. The gradient steepens a bit as the trail makes its final assault on the summit of Mount Aeneas, which commands sweeping views in all directions. The Jewel Lakes and Black Lake can be seen in the basin to the north, while the peaks of Glacier National Park and the Flathead Range hover in the distance like a mirage. To the south, Three Eagles Mountain looms above Birch, Squaw, and Crater lakes.

Beyond the summit of Mount Aeneas, the trail descends rather steeply down the ridgeline to the east. Upon reaching a high, rubble-filled basin, the trail turns north to reach a high pass into the Graves Creek drainage. The trail continues to descend steeply as it runs northwest through alpine meadows and copses of dwarfed fir to reach the shores of the Picnic Lakes. These lakes have been provided with developed camping spots and an outhouse in an effort to reduce wear and tear on this fragile alpine landscape. The microwave relay station sits atop the cliffs that overlook the lake, providing an unwelcome intrusion in this alpine setting. The trail runs between the two lakes and continues northward across level alpine parkland to reach the windswept saddle where it joins the trail to Jewel Lakes. To complete the loop hike west through this pass and follow the trail signs that point the way to the trailhead below.

TRAIL 41 *BIG HAWK LAKES*

Trail 8, 68, 7

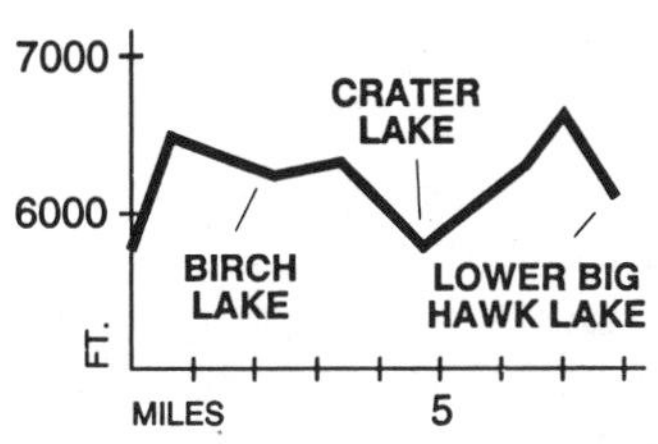

General description: A backpack from the Noisy Creek trailhead to Lower Big Hawk Lake, 7.8 mi. (12.6 km).
Difficulty: Moderate.
Trail maintenance: Yearly to Crater Lake; frequent beyond.
Traffic: Heavy to Crater Lake; light beyond.
Elevation gain: 1,430 ft.
Elevation loss: 1,190 ft.
Maximum elevation: 6,560 ft.
Topo maps: Jewel Basin, Crater Lake, Big Hawk Mountain.
Finding the trailhead: The trail begins at the Noisy Creek trailhead (see The Jewel Basin Complex, p. 125).

0.0 Noisy Creek trailhead.
0.2 Junction with the Camp Misery Trail (68). Turn right.
0.6 Junction with Alpine Trail 7. Turn right for Big Hawk Lakes.
0.8 Junction with the Mount Aeneas Trail (717). Take the lowermost trail heading east.
2.3 Foot of Birch Lake.
3.3 Junction with Trail 187. Stay left.
3.8 Spur trail descends to Squaw Lake. Keep going straight for Big Hawk Lakes.
4.7 Crater Lake. Trail crosses the outlet stream.
6.7 Junction with spur trail to Big Hawk Lakes. Turn Left.
7.0 Upper Big Hawk Lake.
7.8 Lower Big Hawk Lake.

The trail: This Jewel Basin trail offers the only long route for backpackers who are trying to get away from the crowds that throng the shorter trails. It passes Birch, Squaw, and Crater lakes on its way to the Big Hawk Lakes, offering a number of possibilities for an overnight stay. The trail is always in good condition and is closed to horse and mountain bike traffic.

From the Noisy Creek trailhead, there are two possible routes. The fastest way is to follow the closed dirt road on the south side of the parking lot. This road works its way around to the west, crossing over the far side of a nameless ridge before turning south and west to reach a high saddle. This pass can also be reached by hiking trails, by taking the trail to Twin Lakes up to Trail 68 and climbing southeast on this route to intersect Trail 7. This trail runs south a short distance to reach the same pass.

This saddle is the site of a rather complicated trail junction; hikers bound for Big Hawk Lakes should take the trail that descends gradually to the southeast. This trail traverses far above the valley of Birch Creek, passing above the rockbound waters of Martha Lake in its basin far below. The trail continues its gradual descent, finally reaching the broad, rocky shelf occupied by Birch Lake. Just before reaching the lakeshore, an unmarked trail splits off to the left toward a camping spot on the north shore. The main trail veers right, crossing the outlet stream and making its way along the south shore of the lake. Birch Lake is surrounded by picturesque subalpine fir, and the moist, low-lying areas around the shore harbor the delicate shooting star, which blooms in late June. The rugged summit of Mount Aeneas dominates the northern side of the lake.

The trail passes a second camping spot at the head of the lake before turning southward through the forest. The trail passes a marked junction with trail 187, then passes to the west of Squaw Lake, which can be glimpsed through the trees. The trail crests a rise just beyond the lake, where a spur trail runs northeast to reach a camping spot on the lakeshore. The main trail then climbs gently southward across bands of bare bedrock, with firs and tiny meadows occupying the interstices between the outcrops. The route soon begins to descend, working its way through a maze of white bedrock on its way to the shores of Crater Lake. This azure beauty is nestled in a basin of tilted bedrock and enormous boulders. A scattering of slender subalpine fir grows in the clefts between the rocks and on the fingerlike peninsulas that jut out into the lake. A healthy population of rainbow trout cruise the depths of the lake providing excellent fishing for the enterprising angler.

The trail leaves the lakeshore after crossing the outlet stream and climbs through the exposed ribs of rock above the eastern shore of the lake. After passing through several narrow, wooded draws, the trail emerges from the forest and climbs through the jumbled boulders at the foot of Three Eagles Mountain. The trail then turns

Angling at Crater Lake, which is beneath Three Eagles Mountain.

TRAIL 41 *BIG HAWK LAKES*

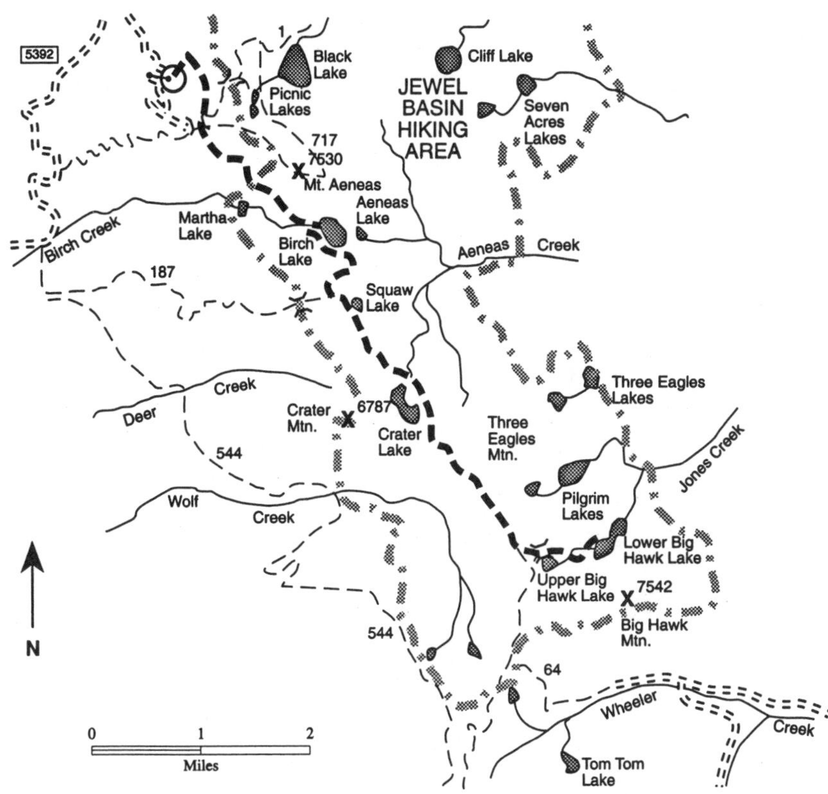

southward again, running level across open, arid slopes. Flathead Lake can be seen in the flat valley to the west of the Mission Range, and the fissured face of Broken Leg Mountain rises in the south. The trail begins to climb again as it crosses the slopes high above the Wolf Creek valley, and thick brush crowds the trail as it approaches a fork. Straight ahead, Trail 7 continues to a pass into the Wheeler Creek valley, while the trail to Big Hawk Lakes (722) takes off up the hill to the left.

This trail climbs steadily up the slope, then turns east to enter a wide pass. The stony prow of Big Hawk Mountain rises ahead as the trail approaches an unmarked junction. To the right, the spur trail crosses a small hump to reach the shores of Upper Big Hawk Lake, which harbors a population of large, cagey west-slope cutthroat that are all but impossible to catch. The main trail swings north to cross a low, wooded saddle before making its descent to the lower lake. The trail curls across the head of the valley as it descends, crossing an open slope that reveals views of Felix Peak and Unawah Mountain in the Flathead Range far to the east. The trail makes its way down to the north shore of the hourglass-shaped Lower Big Hawk Lake, reaching a camping spot at the narrows that splits the lake in two. Lower Big Hawk is home to a booming population of Yellowstone cutthroat that provides excellent fishing for the few anglers that reach the lake.

Upper Basin of the South Fork

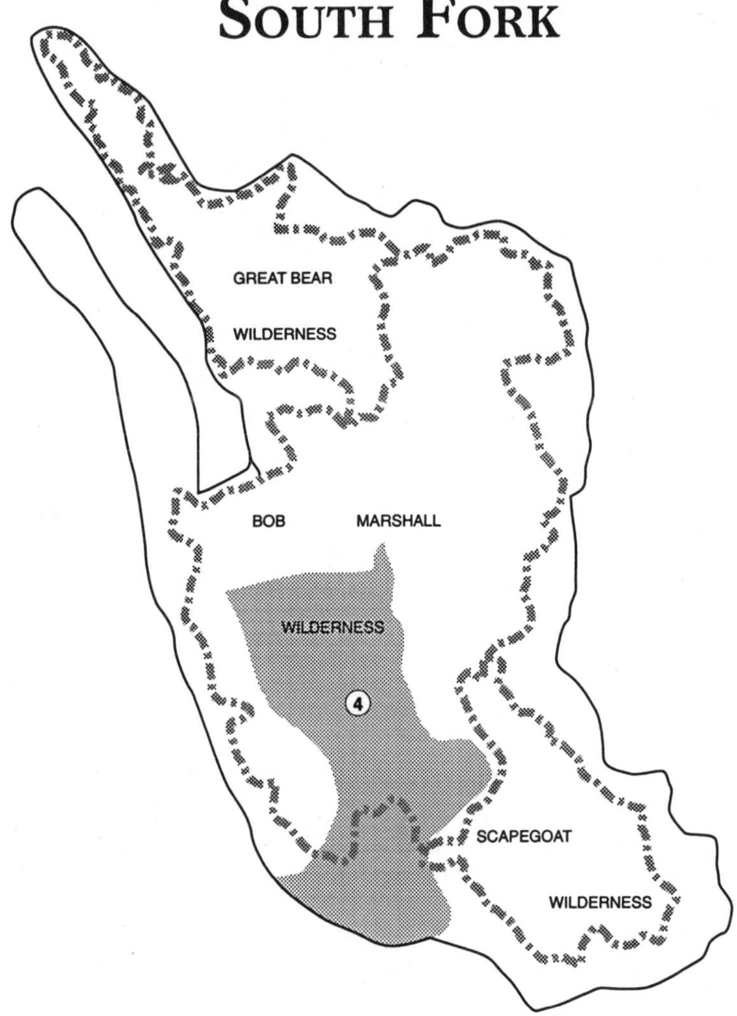

This area is the most remote section of the Bob Marshall Wilderness and can only be reached by traveling through the passes in the high mountains that surround its rim or via a long and muddy trip from Spotted Bear. The easiest and most popular pass is the Dry Fork Divide, which can be reached via the North Fork of the Blackfoot River (see The Scapegoat Massif). The relatively dry and open country of the South Fork, Danaher Creek, and Youngs Creek valleys attracts large numbers of hunters during early fall; travelers who are here to see the country would do well to avoid this area after mid-September.

The western part of the drainage is typified by narrow, wooded valleys that have an east-west orientation, while the eastern side of the basin is dominated by broad, flat-bottomed valleys dotted with wide, grassy meadows. These openings provide an

Scarface Peak provides a scenic backdrop for Bartlett Meadows.

important winter range for the South Fork elk herd, which is the only herd that remains in the wilderness complex year-round. The ponderosa pine and lodgepole savannahs of the valley bottoms give way to solid forests on the surrounding slopes. High ridges are dominated by the whitebark pine, which bears tasty pine nuts that are a favorite autumn food of grizzly bears. The tallest peaks receive little rainfall, and thus are home to a hardscrabble community of alpine desert plants.

The upper drainage of the South Fork has a long history of human presence. The Flathead Indians traveled through the basin frequently on their way to hunt the bison on the high plains to the east of the Rockies. Occasionally, early snows would block the passes surrounding the basin and trap hunting parties for the winter. These resourceful nomads survived on the inner bark of ponderosa pine. Some old trees still bear large, circular scars from the foraging activity of these people. The Blackfeet Indians also sallied into this drainage to fish and gather herbs and berries. The Flatheads and Blackfeet were bitter enemies, and bloody skirmishes developed whenever parties of the two tribes met. At the beginning of the twentieth century, the Danaher Valley was the site of several unsuccessful homesteading efforts. The most tenacious of these settlers was the Danaher family, which established a ranch on Bar Creek in the Danaher Valley. Ultimately, the ranch proved to be too isolated from markets to be profitable and was abandoned.

TRAIL 42 *BIG SALMON TRAIL*

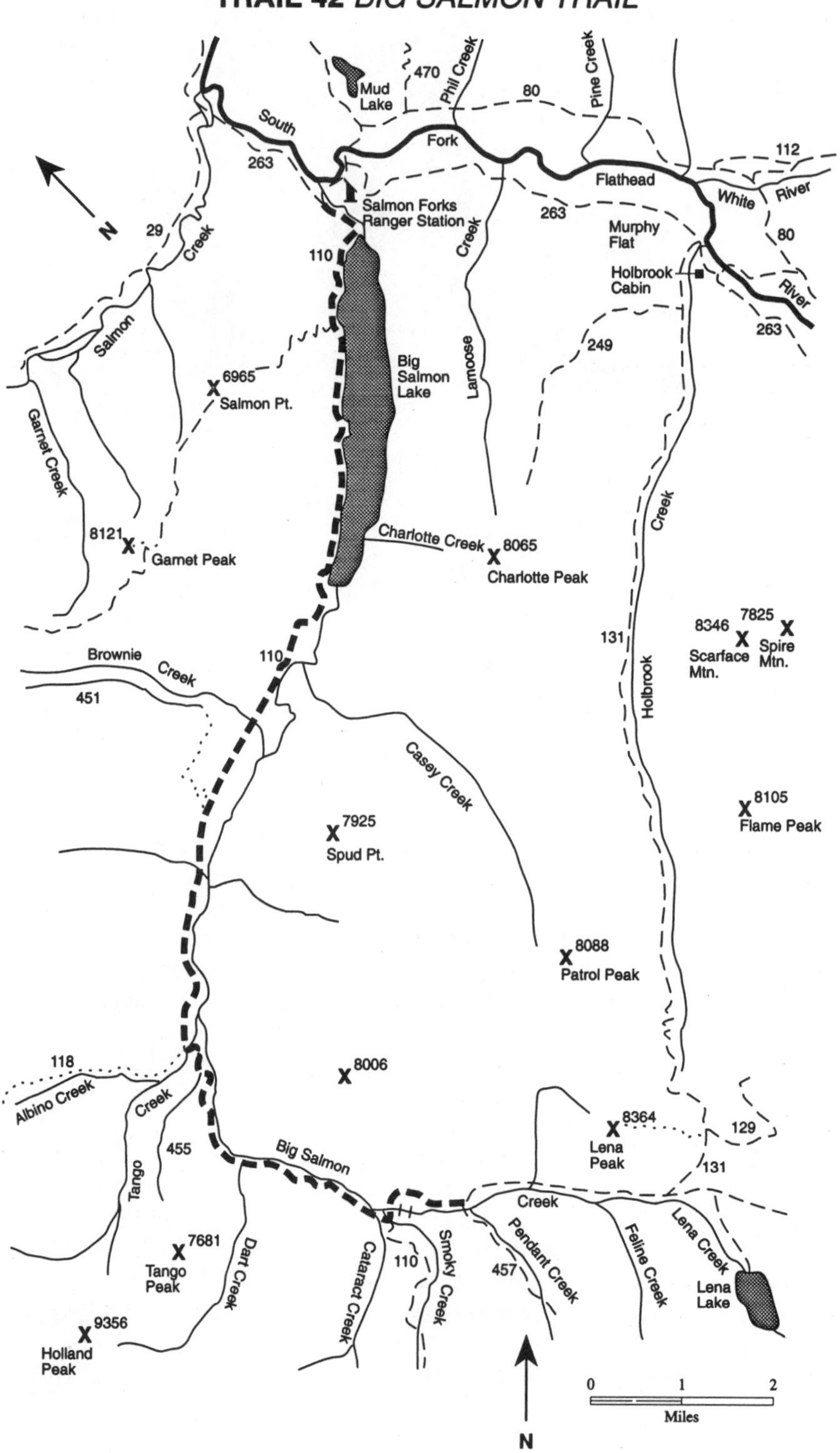

TRAIL 42 *BIG SALMON TRAIL*

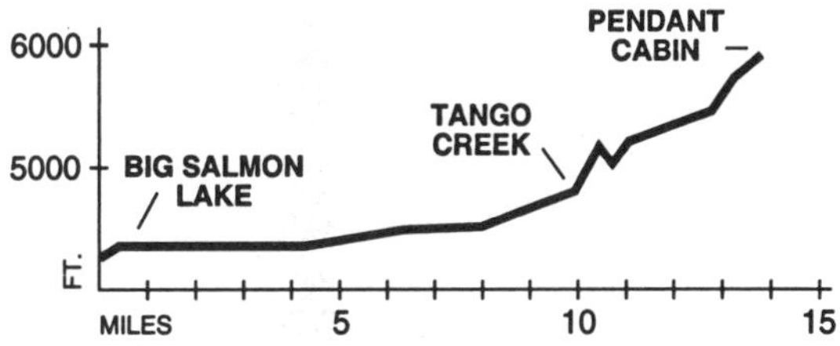

Trail 110

General description: An extended trip from the South Fork of the Flathead to Pendant Cabin, 13.8 mi. (22.2 km).

Difficulty: Moderate.

Trail maintenance: Yearly.

Traffic: Heavy.

Elevation gain: 1,707 ft.

Elevation loss: 150 ft.

Maximum elevation: 5,840 ft.

Topo maps: Pagoda Mountain, Big Salmon Lake East, Big Salmon Lake West.

Finding the trail: This trail begins at a junction on the west side South Fork Trail (263), just north of the Salmon Forks ranger station.

0.0 Junction of the west side South Fork (263) and Big Salmon trails.
0.4 Foot of Big Salmon Lake.
1.3 Junction with the Garnet Peak Trail (111). Keep going straight.
4.3 Head of Big Salmon Lake.
7.3 Unmarked junction with Brownie Creek route (451).
7.9 Trail fords Sappho Creek.
9.8 Trail crosses Tango Creek.
11.1 Ford of Dart Creek.
12.7 Trail fords Cataract Creek.
12.9 Junction with the Necklace Pass Trail (110). Bear left.
13.0 Trail crosses Smoky Creek. Big Salmon Falls.
13.3 Trail crosses Big Salmon Creek.
13.8 Pendant Cabin. Junction with Pendant Pass Trail (457).

The trail: This trail is a major route from the South Fork to the Holland Lake passes over the Swan Range. It is heavily traveled by stock parties and tends to be messy following wet weather. The trail is largely devoid of scenic value, with the exception of a stunning falls near its headwaters and Big Salmon Lake, the largest lake in the Bob Marshall complex.

From Salmon Forks, the trail climbs gently along the north bank of Big Salmon Creek. Soon, the lowland forests open up to reveal the watery expanse of Big Salmon Lake, four miles long and half a mile wide. The lake is a haven for a diverse assemblage of wildlife. Large numbers of waterfowl patrol its productive waters, while osprey hunt their fishy prey from the skies above. The lake harbors a healthy population of trout that provide good fishing. The dramatic cliffs of Charlotte Peak rise above the southern shore of the lake and can be seen off and on while the trail wanders the shore of the lake. The trail runs fairly level as it makes its way along the northern rim of the lake. After a mile of lakeshore travel, the trail passes a marked junction with the Garnet Mountain Trail (111). Beyond this trail junction, the trail wanders in and out of lowland larch and Douglas-fir, allowing frequent views of the lake for the next three miles.

Upon leaving the head of the lake, the trail continues southwest, climbing through the closed canopy of lowland forests. Three miles up the valley from the head of the lake is the first interruption in the forest: a narrow but tidy avalanche chute descending from the mountain to the north to the banks of Big Salmon Creek. The Brownie Creek Trail (151) starts from this opening, but don't bother looking, because it is almost impossible to find. After another mile of forest travel, the trail reaches Sappho Creek, which can be negotiated via a boulder-hop with a tricky mid-stream gate. The country becomes wetter as the trail continues westward, and soon the roar of Barrier Falls can be heard far off through the trees. The trail makes its way through an assortment of mud pits beneath towering spruce and Douglas-fir to reach an old burn site.

The forest in the burn has begun a vigorous regeneration, with healthy young trees and shrubs crowding the opening made by the fire. A few old larch trees were able to survive the fire by virtue of their thick, protective bark. The trail soon reaches a clearing beside Tango Creek, which is the site where the old, defunct trails to Tango Point and the Albino Basin once departed the main trail. There are downed logs across the creek upstream of the knee-deep ford for hikers who want to keep their feet dry. The trail climbs more briskly as it reaches an unusual set of waterfalls. Here,

Charlotte Peak rises gracefully above the still waters of Big Salmon Lake.

the strata of rock making up the creek bed are tilted at a forty-five degree angle. The creek has worn its way through a weaker rock layer that is sandwiched between two resistant ones, and the result is a sort of lean-to roof of rock over the rushing flume.

The trail next crosses an ankle-deep ford of Dart Creek as the valley bends around to the south. The sparse forest of old-growth spruce allows views of the western ramparts of Gyp Mountain, which rises across the valley. The trail makes a ford of Cataract Creek to reach the junction with the Necklace Pass trail. It then turns east to ford Big Salmon Creek just below an imposing waterfall. This cascade makes a sheer drop of some twenty-five feet across a cliff of darkened bedrock into the sheltered pool below. The trail climbs vigorously inland, up a series of switchbacks leading up the slopes of Gyp Mountain. After passing at the foot of reddish cliffs, the trail turns south for the gentle descent to the Pendant Cabin. The trail beyond this point is discussed in the section on Lena Lake, page 101.

TRAIL 43 *GARNET PEAK*

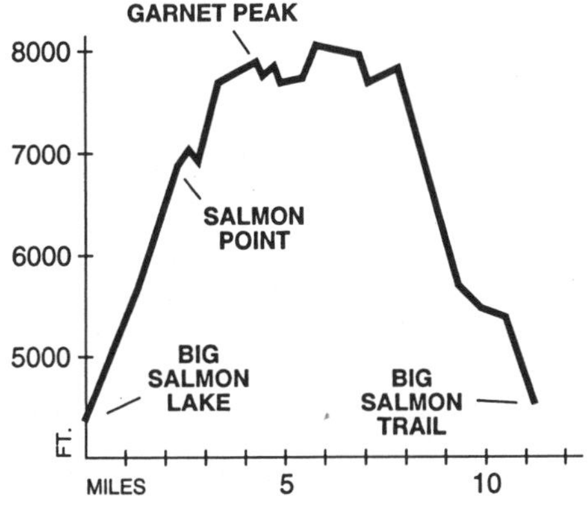

Trail 111, 451
General description: A wilderness route along the ridgeline between the Big and Little Salmon Creek drainages, 11.3 mi. (18.2 km).
Difficulty: Strenuous.
Trail maintenance: Occasional to Salmon Point; rare beyond.
Traffic: Very light.
Elevation gain: 4,006 ft.
Elevation loss: 3,829 ft.
Maximum elevation: 8,020 ft.
Topo maps: Big Salmon Lake East, Big Salmon Lake West.
Finding the trail: This trail begins at a junction on the Big Salmon Trail (110), about a mile west of the foot of Big Salmon Lake.

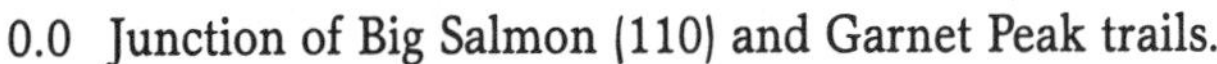

- 0.0 Junction of Big Salmon (110) and Garnet Peak trails.
- 2.4 Trail reaches the ridgeline behind Salmon Point.
- 4.4 Unmarked spur trail to old Garnet Peak lookout site. Bear left.
- 7.2 Trail descends into the upper basin of Brownie Creek.
- 9.7 Trail enters the Big Salmon valley.
- 11.3 Junction with the Big Salmon Trail.

The trail: This primitive route follows the ridgeline above the Big Salmon valley from a point near the foot of Big Salmon Lake to Brownie Creek. The trail becomes difficult to follow after reaching Salmon Point, and large sections of the route beyond Garnet Peak exist only as blazes on trees. The trail is especially difficult to follow during its descent into the Big Salmon valley from Brownie Creek. For this reason, the trail should only be attempted from the east to west. This route is recommended

TRAIL 43 *GARNET PEAK*

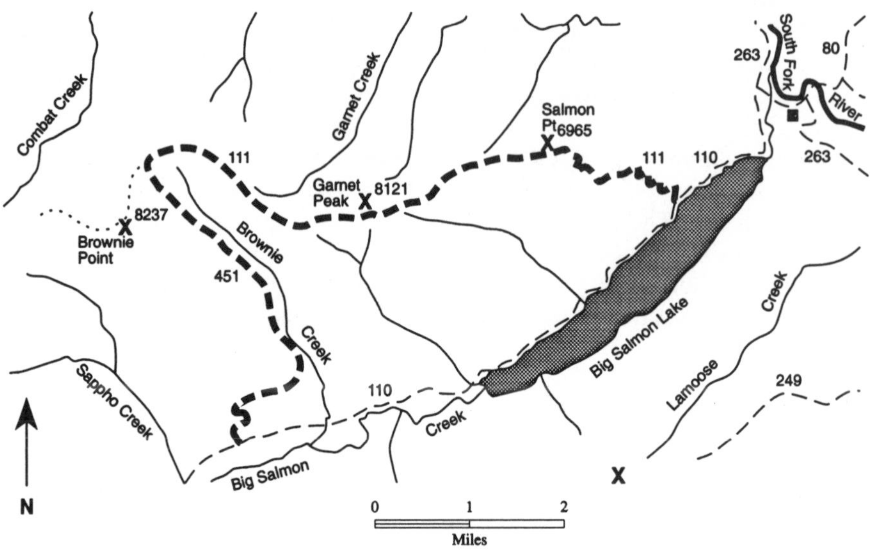

only for seasoned backpackers who are looking for a route-finding challenge.

From the shores of Big Salmon Lake, the trail climbs steadily through tall Douglas-fir and western larch, which block out views of the lake. About halfway to the top of Salmon Point, two openings in the forest allow views of Charlotte Peak to the south as well as the low summits overlooking the South Fork of the Flathead. The route then begins to steepen its ascent as it passes through a sparse growth of mature Douglas-fir, finally reaching a large open slope that offers sweeping vistas of the peaks along the Continental Divide. After passing through this opening, the trail enters a ridgetop hunting camp. The trail departs this camp in a westerly direction, crossing a marshy spring as it does so. This spring offers the last surface water east of the Brownie Creek valley.

The trail climbs more gently as it works its way westward. As the trail nears a sandy ravine, the trail switches back to the east to begin a zigzagging ascent. The trail finally crosses the sandy ravine to reach a miniature, sparsely wooded spur ridge. After a brief ascent, the trail returns to the forest to the east, completing its ascent beneath the caprock that guards the southern approaches to Salmon Point. The trail reaches the ridgetop to the west of the point, and an easy jog to the northeast leads to the summit. From this lofty perch, views feature Big Salmon Lake on the valley floor and the low peaks to the north of Little Salmon Creek, as well as broad vistas to the east and south.

The Garnet Peak trail rides the top of the ridge as it makes its way westward, crossing the next low summit before mounting the eastern slope of Garnet Peak. As the trail climbs up a narrow ravine that splits the ridgetop, it becomes progressively fainter, and there is a lot of downed timber across the path. After passing onto the south slope of the ridge for a gentler climb, the trail reaches the ridgetop once again. Look northward through the whitebark pine for excellent views of Stadium Peak and the more distant and glacier-clad Swan Peak can be had. The trail continues to follow the ridgetop to a point just east of the final summit of Garnet Peak, where it meets an abandoned trail leading to the old lookout site atop the peak.

The main route crosses a spur ridge that descends to the south and openings in the whitebark pine allow a spectacular view of Holland Peak to the west. The path drops into a series of high basins, becoming fainter and fainter. Use blazes and saw-work as your guide. After crossing a washout, the route begins to climb again and soon works its way back to the wooded ridgeline. The route stays strictly on the ridgetop as it works its way southwest for the next several miles. The next high point offers a grassy opening on its crest; Silvertip Mountain rises in the distance to the northeast, with Pentagon Mountain just to the left of it; Turtlehead Mountain rears its crown farther south of these two.

After passing through an old burn, the route scoots down a rocky series of switchbacks and returns quickly to the ridgetop. The next point overlooks a low basin rimmed all around with reddish cliffs. The path makes its way over cliffy knobs, and subalpine larch come to dominate the increasingly sparse vegetation. Swan Peak looms to the west, as seen through the window of Lion Creek Pass. The path reaches the saddle before the next high peak, then begins to descend southward into the upper basin of Brownie Creek. A trail once ran west from here to reach the sum-

Holland Peak as seen from the slopes below the old Garnet Lookout.

mit of Brownie Peak, but this trail is no longer worth looking for. After a series of switchbacks, the trail reaches the grassy floor of the bowl, spangled with flowers of all descriptions.

The route disappears entirely amid the lush growth of the meadow. To continue the journey, hike to the large spring at the head of the bowl and turn south, following the west bank of its outlet stream. As the valley falls away into hummocky country covered in a loose subalpine forest, the trail once again becomes distinct. The path runs downhill through copses of fir, crossing several rivulets as it works its way toward the cliffy ridge that guards the north rim of the valley. After crossing a substantial tributary stream, the trail climbs onto the western wall of the valley. It maintains a level pitch as the valley floor falls away, and soon the trail finds itself several hundred feet above the level of the creek. The forest becomes thicker as the trail rounds ridges and dips into gullies, finally emerging onto the slopes above Big Salmon Creek after two miles of traversing.

Rather than descending directly to the valley floor, the trail turns west and maintains its altitude for almost a full mile as it passes across an open slope choked with alder, ceanothus, serviceberry, and thimbleberry. The path is so faint and overgrown here that it will require the full attention of a seasoned trail-finder to stay on it. Look up during a pause in the bushwhacking to behold the inspiring heights of Holland Peak rising sheer at the head of the valley. After a time, the trail descends via some incredibly steep and gullied out switchbacks before turning west again to cross a small stream. The trail then continues its steep descent, angling its way westward across the slope to cross a second rivulet. The trail enters a sparse forest of Douglas-fir before reaching its terminus among confused camp trails on the eastern edge of a long avalanche slope. Follow the edge of the trees straight downhill to find the Big Salmon trail.

TRAIL 44 *BURNT CREEK*

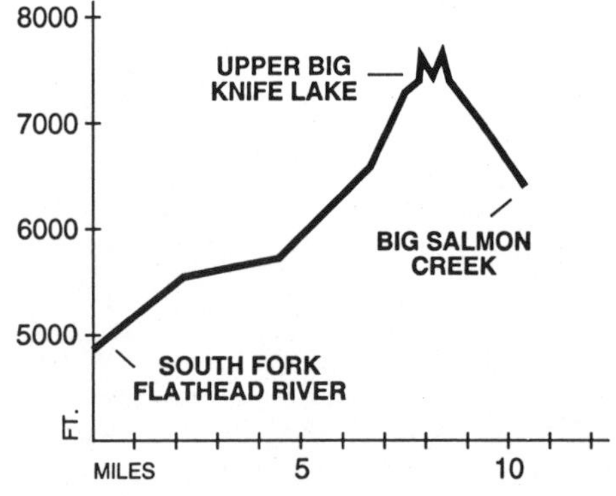

Trail 195, 129, 131
General description: An extended trip from the South Fork of the Flathead to the Shaw Creek Trail, 10.4 mi. (16.7 km).
Difficulty: Moderate (west to east); moderately strenuous (east to west).
Trail maintenance: Occasional.
Traffic: Light.
Elevation gain: 2,860 ft.
Elevation loss: 1,310 ft.
Maximum elevation: 7,580 ft.
Topo maps: Big Salmon Lake East, Big Salmon Lake West, Shaw Creek.
Finding the trail: The trail begins from a junction on the west side South Fork Trail (263), 0.25 mile north of its crossing of Burnt Creek.

0.0 Junction of west side South Fork (263) and Burnt Creek trails.
4.4 Trail makes two fords of Burnt Creek.
6.6 Trail fords Burnt Creek to reach its south bank.
7.8 Trail passes Upper Big Knife Lake.
8.1 Junction with the Bartlett Creek Trail (129). Turn right.
8.3 Trail crosses the divide into the Shaw Creek valley.
9.2 Junction with the Holbrook Creek Trail (131). Turn left.
10.4 Junction with the Shaw Creek Trail (212) south of Pendant Cabin.

The trail: This trail links the South Fork of the Flathead with the passes in the Swan Range above Holland Lake. It is less heavily traveled than either the Bartlett Creek or Holbrook Creek trails, and can be a bit faint in places. However, nowhere is the trail so indistinct that it poses a route-finding problem. The lower level of traffic here results in a firmer trail bed during wet weather as well as more solitude for visitors. The Big Knife Lakes at the head of the valley provide the only real scenic attraction along the route.

The trail begins on a high bluff, 0.25 mile north of the Burnt Creek ford on the West Side South Fork Trail (263). The route runs westward, atop the forested benches high above Burnt Creek. After crossing an open slope at the foot of Spire Mountain, the trail descends above a rocky canyon and makes its way down to the north bank of the creek. From this point, the cliffs of Bartlett Mountain rise sheer above the south bank of the stream and arc away westward toward the summit. Rather than crossing the creek, the trail follows its bed for ten yards and then climbs back onto the

TRAIL 44 *BURNT CREEK*

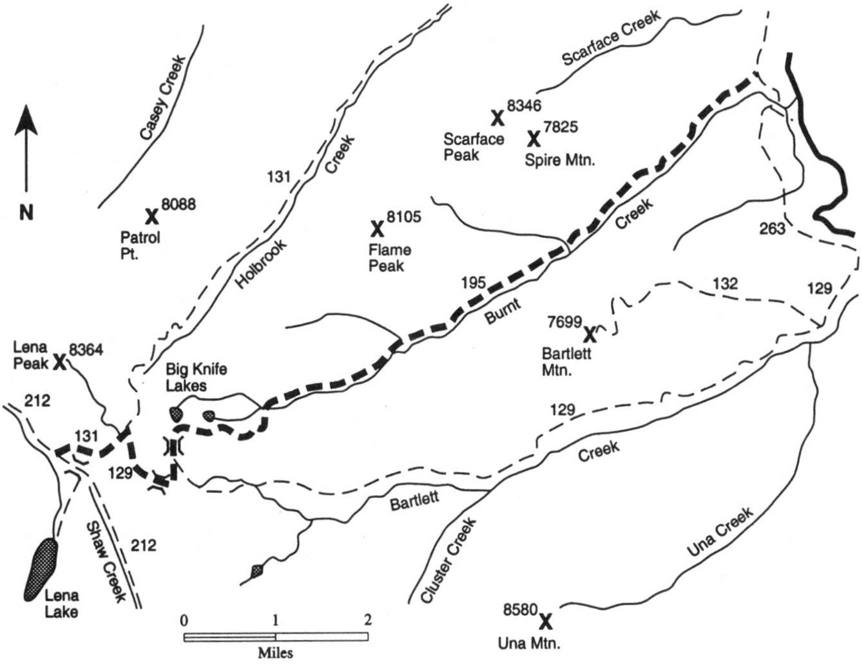

north bank. The trail alternates between brushy bottomland and wooded benches for the next mile or so, then climbs moderately as it works its way inland. The trail rises and falls as it crosses rolling country, and occasional openings in the forest permit fine views of Bartlett Mountain's northwest face.

The trail then makes its way into a flat basin, where it passes through an open meadow choked with willow at its western end. Amid the willows, the trail makes a ford to the south bank of the creek and runs west for one hundred yards through the dark spruce forest. It then re-crosses the stream, returning to the north bank and running westward through damp spruce bottomland. Leaving the flat basin behind, the trail begins to ascend moderately through a lodgepole pine forest underlain by abundant huckleberry bushes. After crossing a small tributary, the route becomes quite muddy as it passes through a low-lying area dotted with springs. The trail runs for the next several miles at the foot of Flame Peak, which is invisible above the forest canopy. It then begins to climb more vigorously, crossing open avalanche slopes dotted with beargrass blossoms. Upon re-entering the forest, the trail turns south to make a shallow ford of Burnt Creek.

Once on the far side of the creek, the trail passes through a series of muddy springs and turns west again. It then crosses a second stream and climbs steeply through a rocky subalpine forest. The trail passes out of sight of Lower Big Knife Lake, then passes into a high, flat basin forest with subalpine larch and fir and dotted with clear pools of standing water. The trail makes its way through muddy country to the south of Upper Big Knife Lake,which can be reached by a short hike to the north. This lake sits at the head of the valley, bounded on the west by steep boulder fields and on the east by picturesque wet meadows dotted with rocky pools. These ponds provide excellent habitat for frogs and mosquitoes, which flourish in this high basin.

Leaving the lake, the trail makes a brief but steep ascent to the pass into the Bartlett Creek drainage. It crosses a shallow basin as it works its way southward, through meadows that often harbor snowdrifts into late summer. The trail passes a junction with the Bartlett Creek Trail (129), then bends southwest as it climbs across an open hillside above the headwaters of the Bartlett Creek drainage. Una and Bulletnose mountains hulk far to the east, while in the forest at the foot of the hill lies a tiny lake that is the source of Bartlett Creek. The trail soon reaches a second pass, which looks westward toward the Swan Range.

The trail turns northwest and begins its descent through a sparse forest of subalpine firs. First Wolverine and Carmine peaks are visible to the southwest, and later the regal spire of Holland Peak can be seen along the northwestern horizon. A sliver of Lena Lake can be glimpsed as the trail drops off toward its junction with the Holbrook Trail (131). At this junction, the trail turns left and continues to descend beside a nameless stream. Ahead, Ptarmigan Mountain is nicely framed by Shaw Mountain and an unnamed ridge to the north of it. As the trail winds around the lower slopes of Lena Peak, it descends through patches of alder and occasional mudholes on its final approach to the upper section of the Big Salmon trail. This section is discussed in the description of the trail to Lena Lake, page 101.

TRAIL 45 *BARTLETT MOUNTAIN*

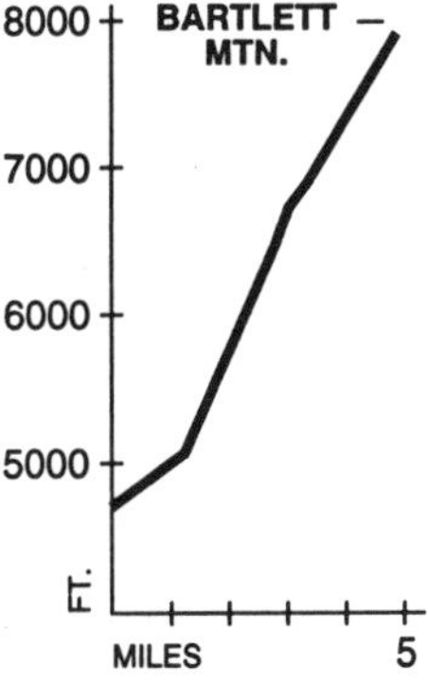

Trail 129, 132

General description: A spur trip from the South Fork of the Flathead to the summit of Bartlett Mountain, 4.7 mi. (7.6 km).

Difficulty: Moderately strenuous.

Trail maintenance: Occasional.

Traffic: Light.

Elevation gain: 3,069 ft.

Maximum elevation: 7,699 ft.

Topo map: Big Salmon Lake East.

Finding the trail: Begin at the Bartlett Creek Trail (129) junction on the west side South Fork Trail (263). This junction is located on the north bank of Bartlett Creek.

- 0.0 Junction of west side South Fork (263) and Bartlett Creek (129) trails.
- 0.1 Trail crosses Bartlett Meadows.
- 1.0 Unmarked junction with the Bartlett Mountain Trail (132). Turn right and begin climbing.
- 3.1 Trail reaches the base of Bartlett Mountain.
- 4.7 Summit of Bartlett Mountain.

The trail: The Bartlett Mountain trail provides a side trip to a lofty overlook for travelers in the South Fork valley. The trip begins on the Bartlett Creek Trail (129), which departs from the West Side South Fork Trail (263) on the north bank of Bartlett Creek. This trail runs northwest, climbing gently onto the high bluff that contains the grassy expanse of Bartlett Meadows. This wide opening offers excellent views of Spire Mountain and Scarface Peak, which loom to the north of Burnt Creek. The trail turns west as it passes through the meadows to enter a forest of tall larch. The trail climbs gently across the forested benches far above Bartlett Creek for 0.5 mile to reach the junction with the Bartlett Mountain Trail (132). This faint junction was not marked by a trail sign at the time of this writing, but heavily blazed trees flank the trail on either side.

At first the trail is a bit overgrown, but it becomes distinct as it climbs northward toward the ridgeline through open stands of Douglas-fir. Upon reaching the crest of the ridge, the trail turns westward to climb along the gently rising ridgetop. After a quarter mile or so, the trail reaches a south-facing meadow that permits views of Bulletnose and Una mountains across the Bartlett Creek valley. The trail then continues to follow the ridge through a scattering of mature Douglas-fir. After passing through a second, more closed meadow, the trail enters a forest of subalpine fir. Numerous blowdowns make traveling difficult as the trail approaches the base of Bartlett Mountain itself.

Here, the trail turns northwest along the base of a grassy east-facing slope of the mountain. The trail climbs steadily as it traverses the slope all the way to its abrupt edge, where grassy meadows reveal the rocky faces of Spire Mountain and Scarface

TRAIL 45 *BARTLETT MOUNTAIN*

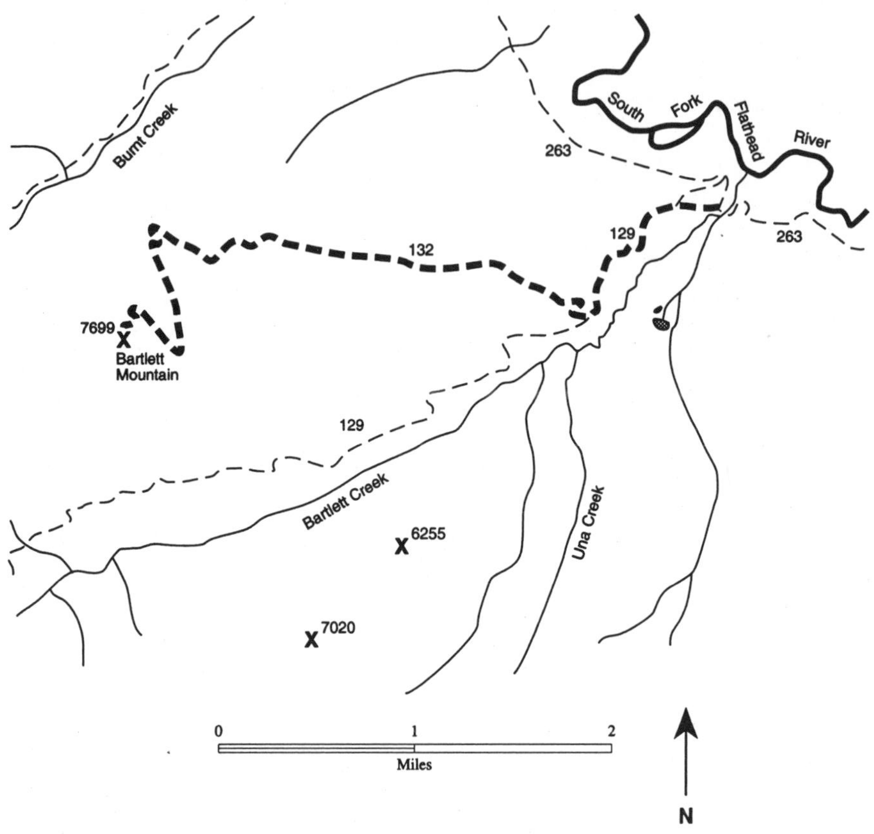

Peak to the north. The trail switchbacks up the narrowing meadow, and upon reaching its terminus, turns west to climb steadily through subalpine forests. The trail runs south all the way to the far edge of the slope, where it becomes quite faint upon entering a grassy meadow. The cliffy brow of Una Mountain rises from the verdant hills to the south. At this point, the trail climbs along the northern edge of the meadow and soon passes back into a ragged growth of whitebark pine. Once again the trail approaches the northern rim of the slope, along which it climbs the remaining distance to the summit of the mountain.

Looking westward from the edge of sheer cliffs, the snowy slopes of Fisher Mountain in the south and Holland Peak in the north dominate the skyline. To the northeast, the peaks looming above the Chinese Wall crowd the horizon, while farther south the Flathead Alps cluster around White River Pass. Spire Mountain and Scarface Peak loom to the north, across the gulf formed by the valley of Burnt Creek.

TRAIL 46 *CARDINAL PEAK - FOSSIL MOUNTAIN*

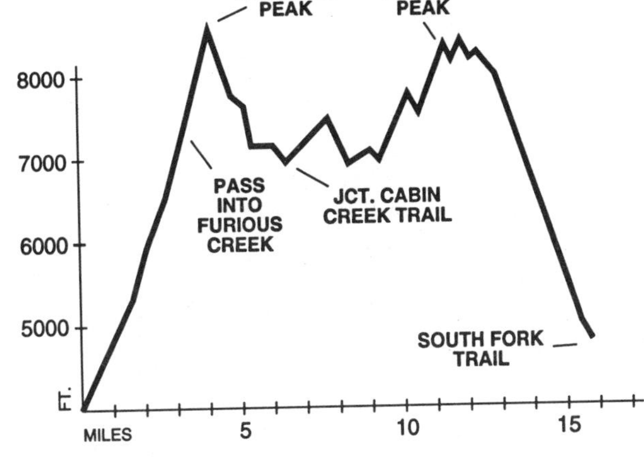

Trail 506, 136, 128

General description: A wilderness route along the divide between the Gordon Creek and Babcock Creek drainages, 15.8 mi. (25.4 km).

Difficulty: Strenuous.

Trail maintenance: Occasional from Gordon Creek to the Cabin Creek trail junction; rare from this point to Pilot Peak; frequent beyond.

Traffic: Very light.

Elevation gain: 7,039 ft.

Elevation loss: 7,234 ft.

Maximum elevation: 8,470 ft.

Topo maps: Shaw Creek, Morrell Lake, Una Mountain, Pilot Peak.

Finding the trail: This trail begins as the Cardinal Creek trail, which departs from the Gordon Creek trail about four miles east of the Shaw Creek cabin. The Gordon Creek trail approaches the creek just west of the junction, which is marked by a sign indicating the way to Big Prairie. From the east, a cutoff trail to the Cardinal Creek trail is marked by a blaze in the shape of a grinning jack-o-lantern face.

- 0.0 Junction of Gordon Creek (35) and Cardinal Creek (506) trails.
- 0.2 Trail fords Gordon Creek and enters the Cardinal Creek valley.
- 3.3 Trail crosses the divide into the Furious Creek drainage.
- 4.2 Unmarked junction with the spur trail to the summit of Cardinal Peak. Through traffic should bear north.
- 6.5 Junction with the Cabin Creek Trail (205). Turn left.
- 9.4 Trail crosses Kid Creek and fades out.
- 11.8 Summit of Gordon Mountain.
- 12.4 Fossil Mountain.
- 12.8 Saddle at the base of Pilot Peak. Trail drops from the ridgeline.
- 15.8 Junction with the west side South Fork Trail (263).

The trail: This faint track runs along the ridgetop to the the south of Gordon Creek. It sticks to the high, open country of the ridgeline, and although the trail is often faint and sometimes even nonexistent, the route is easy to follow for hikers that are comfortable with cross-country travel. The trail is easiest to find from west to east; it peters out entirely between Kid and Fossil mountains and may be difficult to pick

Looking south from Cardinal Peak toward the rugged north face of Goat Mountain.

up again for travelers coming westward from Gordon Peak. The trail is quite distinct between its western end and the Cabin Creek Trail (206), and thus the western half of it easily can be accessed by hikers and horse parties.

From the Gordon Creek Trail (35), two cutoff trails to Cardinal Peak run south to join in a grassy meadow. This opening is a popular camping spot and contains a trail down to the water's edge, which might be mistaken for the ford of Gordon Creek. The true ford lies twenty-five yards west of the meadow on a faint track that originates in the inland corner of the grassy opening. After a knee-deep crossing of Gordon Creek, the trail turns southwest, passing through a rather swampy bottomland forest. After a short distance, the trail begins to climb vigorously, surmounting the low ridgetop that overlooks the east bank of Cardinal Creek.

With this rushing stream within earshot, the trail turns southward, following the course of the valley through a montane forest of Douglas-fir. The trail alternates between steep climbs and level stretches as it climbs into a narrow canyon, where it crosses several avalanche paths choked with dense brush. As it approaches a sharp westward bend in the valley, the trail crosses an extensive brushfield that offers views of the nameless, rocky summits that crowd the southwestern rim of the drainage. The trail then leaves the valley floor and begins to climb in a southeasterly direction, repeatedly crossing small tributary streams. Montane forest soon gives way to subalpine fir and tall spruce as the trail gains altitude. As the path emerges in an alpine meadow dotted with columbines and mountain asters, the reddish crest of

TRAIL 46 *CARDINAL PEAK - FOSSIL MOUNTAIN*

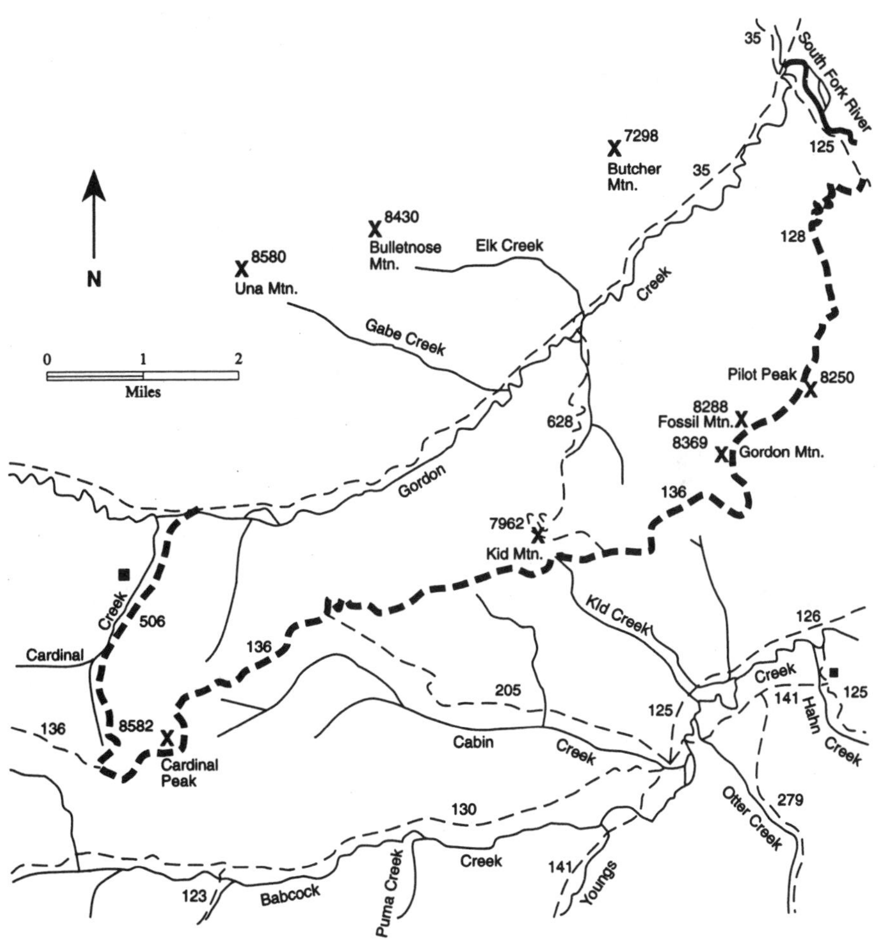

Cardinal Peak towers imperiously to the east, still over a thousand feet above the trail.

The trail then climbs through more open subalpine forest on its way to a low saddle overlooking the valley of tiny Furious Creek. At this point, a spur trail splits off to the west, following the crest of the ridge for several miles before petering out. The main trail bends eastward and begins the final ascent toward the summit of Cardinal Peak. As the trail winds toward the southern slope of the ridge, vistas of the surrounding peaks reveal themselves with each advancing step. To the east, a pair of lofty but unnamed summits rise along the ridgeline, while due south are the towering spires of Count Peak. Goat Mountain rises prominently to the west of it. The trail strikes out steeply up the ridgeline, then turns eastward to cross the southern slope of the peak. The trail reaches a ridgeline that descends southeast from the summit of Cardinal, where the trail bed has been obliterated by the passage of inconsiderate travelers who opted to trek straight up the ridgeline instead of following the switchbacks.

From this point, there are actually two ancestral trails: a spur route that switchbacks to the summit of Cardinal Peak and the main trail, which runs level across the eastern slope of the mountain. The summit trail makes its way upward through the twisted *krummholz* forms of subalpine fir; wind-blown snow scours the living buds that grow above the protection of snowbanks during wintertime, pruning these trees into a low-growing, shrublike form. At the summit, the trail reaches the site of an old fire lookout, where a scattering of glass and woody debris poses a hazard for the unwary traveler. From this high perch, impressive views stretch out in all directions. Holland Peak dominates the Swan Range in the west, while the low mass of Una Mountain hulks to the north. Look eastward past Fossil and Gordon mountains to see the twisted strata of Gust Mountain.

The main trail is initially difficult to spot as it runs northward, about two hundred vertical feet below the summit. The trail becomes distinct again as it passes among a scattering of subalpine larch. Rounding a steep-sided bowl, the trail turns eastward, following a ridgeline clothed in whitebark pine. The trail soon drops steeply into a wooded saddle, where a seasonal spring may offer water to the passing traveler during wet summers. The trail then swings south of the next high point, descending steadily across a wooded slope to reach a broad pass. Here, it reaches a junction with the Cabin Creek Trail (206). The well-beaten trail descending to the southeast is actually this latter trail, while the Cardinal—Fossil trail climbs straight up the ridgeline for fifty yards before swinging northward. The trail soon switchbacks up a stony meadow, then runs out onto the south slope of the ridge as it continues to climb. After crossing a wooded col, the trail turns onto the north slope of the ridge, where it completes the traverse to the next saddle.

The trail descends into this shallow pass, then climbs aggressively up the slope on the far side of it. After a short climb, the trail turns eastward, remaining fairly level as it rounds a spur ridge and then descends gently to reach Kid Creek. This gullied-out stream runs along the border of a meadowy slope below the crown of Kid Mountain. Beyond the stream, the trail becomes so faint as to be practically nonexistent as it climbs across the open slope toward the high pass to the east of Kid Mountain. From here, vestiges of the trail run eastward to the top of the next point, then descend onto a level, meadowy hilltop. Here, all traces of the trail disappear, and travelers must pick their own route across the flowery glades of this high plateau. Steer for Gordon Mountain, which can be reached by a narrow isthmus of land that connects the high plateau with its steep mountainsides.

A steep climb of Gordon Mountain ensues, after which the route turns north toward the summit of Fossil Mountain. After dropping into the grassy saddle between the two peaks, the trail climbs into the talus of Fossil Mountain, then turns east again on its way to the next saddle along the ridgeline. The trail makes its way around a final rocky point before making a gradual ascent across the south slope of the hillside to reach the pass that lies below the west face of Pilot Peak. A final view from the ridgecrest reveals Una and Bulletnose mountains to the north, as well as Gust Mountain rising above Hahn Creek in the south. Here, the trail drops off of the ridgetop and begins its long and steady descent toward the valley of the South Fork.

The trail then descends onto the north slope of Pilot Peak, staying level until it reaches a long spur ridge that drops away steeply to the northeast. The trail bed is in fine shape as it descends steadily through subalpine forests. After a quarter mile or so, the trail reaches the first of a series of steep, stony meadows spangled with wild pea, sego lily and arrowleaf balsamroot. To the east, a glance across the valley of the South Fork reveals the rugged peaks of Junction Mountain and the rest of the Flathead Alps. The trail descends past several notches in the ridgetop that allow westward views and finally reaches a rocky knob with a spur path leading up to it; this observation point offers the last open vistas on the trail. The trail then drops into the sparse, old-growth Douglas-fir forest on the lower slopes, and begins a long and tedious descent toward the valley floor. When the path finally makes it out onto flat benches forested in lodgepole pine, it reaches a junction with the West Side South Fork Trail (263).

TRAIL 47 *MONTURE CREEK - HAHN PASS*

Trail 27, 125
General description: A backpack from the Monture Creek trailhead to Youngs Creek, 21.4 mi. (34.4 km).
Difficulty: Moderate.
Trail maintenance: Yearly.
Traffic: Moderate.
Elevation gain: 2,600 ft.
Elevation loss: 1,870 ft.
Maximum elevation: 6,630 ft.
Topo maps: Dunham Point, Hahn Creek Pass, Pilot Peak.
Finding the trailhead: From Montana Highway 200 take the Monture Road, which departs from the highway near the town of Ovando. Follow this road to the base of the mountains, where it reaches a bridge over Monture Creek. Just before the bridge is a road to the right, with a sign for the O.S. Camp and Monture trail. Turn right on this road, which runs for 1 mile through the campground to reach the trailhead.

0.0 Monture Creek trailhead.
0.2 Trail crosses Spread Creek.
0.3 Junction with the Spread Mountain Trail (166). Keep going straight.

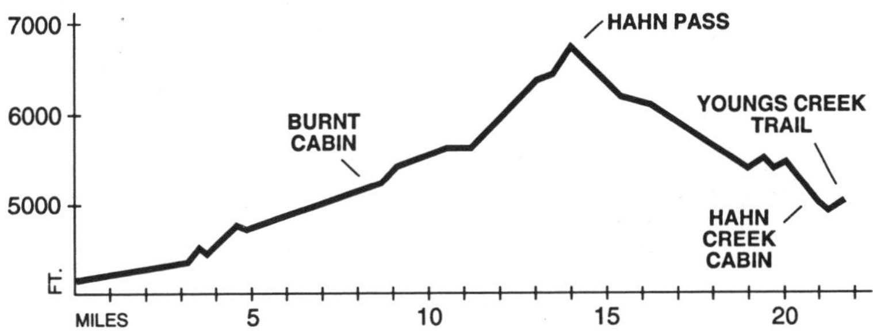

TRAIL 47 *MONTURE CREEK - HAHN PASS*

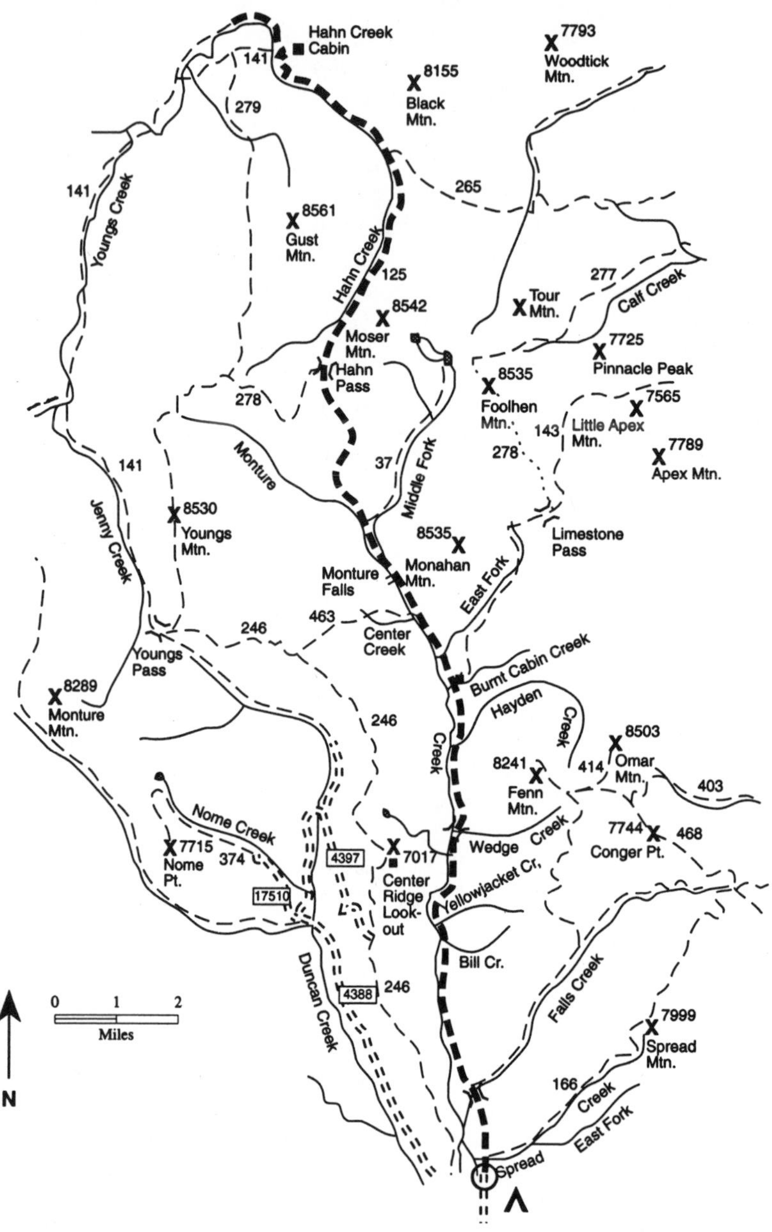

1.2 Junction with cutoff trail from Monture Cabin. Bridge over Falls Creek.
1.3 Junction with the Camp Pass Trail (16). Keep going straight for Hahn Pass.
6.2 Bridge over Wedge Creek.
7.3 Trail fords Hayden Creek.
8.2 Burnt Cabin. Junction with Limestone Pass Trail (402).

8.7 Bridge over the East Fork of Monture Creek.
9.2 Junction with the Center Creek Trail (483). Keep going straight.
10.2 Monture Falls.
10.4 Bridge over the Middle Fork of Monture Creek.
11.1 Unmarked junction with the Middle Fork Trail (37).
13.9 Hahn Pass. Trail enters the Bob Marshall Wilderness.
15.4 Bear Park.
17.8 Unmarked junction with the Foolhen Creek route (265).
20.8 Hahn Creek Cabin. Junction with the Youngs Creek Cutoff Trail (141). Bear north for the Youngs Creek Trail (125).
21.3 Trail fords Youngs Creek.
21.4 Junction with the Youngs Creek trail.

The trail: This trail provides a lengthy journey up Monture Creek, which heads at Hahn Pass. It is one of the lengthier trails running into the South Fork basin, but remains quite popular with stock parties because of its moderate grade and lack of mud, even in wet weather. From the trailhead, the trail follows the eastern edge of the flat Monture Creek valley. It soon passes a junction with the Spread Mountain trail, and runs among the Douglas-fir and larch to the banks of Falls Creek. On the south banks of the stream, a side trail from the Monture Cabin joins the main trail, while just beyond the bridge is a junction with the Camp Pass Trail (16). The Monture Creek trail continues northward, climbing imperceptibly through relatively viewless forests. Lodgepole pine dominate ridges of sandy soil, while the moister soils surrounding feeder streams support lofty western larch.

After crossing Bill Creek, the rate of ascent increases to a moderate pace as the trail wanders inland among low hillocks. Emerging between Fenn Mountain and the high point of Center Ridge, the trail follows the rim of a rock-walled gorge, carved deep into the bedrock by millennia of erosion. The gorge runs as far upstream as Wedge Creek, where a pack bridge leads to a level, valley-bottom trek through the lodgepole. After several miles, a rock-walled rift enters from the east, bearing the laughing waters of Hayden Creek. This substantial stream is difficult to cross without getting wet feet. Another mile of steady climbing lands the traveler at Burnt Cabin on the bank of the tiny stream of the same name. The Limestone Pass Trail (402) takes off to the east in the shadow of the cabin's northern side.

Beyond this landmark, the Monture Creek trail continues northward through grassy glades before returning to forest of lodgepole just before reaching the East Fork pack bridge. There is little to see for next several miles, as the trail continues north to reach the Center Creek Trail (463) in the midst of a mixed forest. Soon after, the trail climbs a sidehill above the creek and passes above Monture Falls; a short but steep off-trail descent yields a better view of this twenty-foot cascade. The trail then follows the rim of the sunny canyon above the falls to reach a pack bridge over the Middle Fork of Monture Creek. Half a mile beyond the Middle Fork bridge, the trail reaches a hilltop where an unmarked but discernible side trail departs eastward to ascend along the Middle Fork.

After two more miles of arrow-straight traveling through an unbroken forest of lodgepole pine, the trail climbs out of the bottomlands to begin its ascent of Hahn

Pass. The trail follows a northeasterly bend in the valley, then emerges on arid, open slopes laid bare by a forest fire some years ago. Above the head of the valley, the rugged cliffs of Moser Mountain are resplendent with reds and chalky greens. The trail climbs into several high depressions as it follows the dry watercourse. The lush wet meadows of the valley floor contrast sharply with the parched slopes surrounding them. The final climb to Hahn Pass crosses slopes of brittle talus and barren, rocky soil. Although Hahn Pass is clear of obstructing trees, there is little in the way of scenery here: only the low, stark cliffs of Moser Mountain above the pass and the rolling foothills stretching off in all directions.

As the trail descends into the burn of upper Hahn Creek, the views shut down for good, and the remainder of the trek passes in the company of closed forest canopies on forested hillsides. On its way downward, the trail passes through a broad avalanche slope known as Bear Park, then sinks into a deep forest of old-growth spruce. The valley bends northwest, passing the spot where the Foolhen Creek Trail (265) comes in from the east. The trail continues to descend as the spruce give way to lodgepole pine, and the route eventually runs out onto a grassy slope as the creek drops away to the west of it. Upon reaching the edge of the Youngs Creek valley, the trail begins to switchback down the ridgeline.

Nearing the valley floor, the trail turns east in its final approach to the Hahn Creek Cabin. In front of the cabin, the trail reaches a complex junction. To the left, a major Trail (141) runs westward to cut off the Youngs Creek Trail (141) near Cabin Creek, while an unmarked footpath runs past the cabin to the right. The main trail lies

Rugged country near Hahn Pass.

straight ahead, and it descends gently across wooded benches on its way to a ford of Youngs Creek. Just before reaching the main stream bed, the trail crosses some low-lying fens that have been flooded by enterprising beavers. These pools are far deeper than the ankle deep ford of Youngs Creek itself, which lies just beyond them. After making its crossing, the trail climbs moderately up the hillside to reach its junction with the Youngs Creek Trail (125).

TRAIL 48 *LIMESTONE PASS*

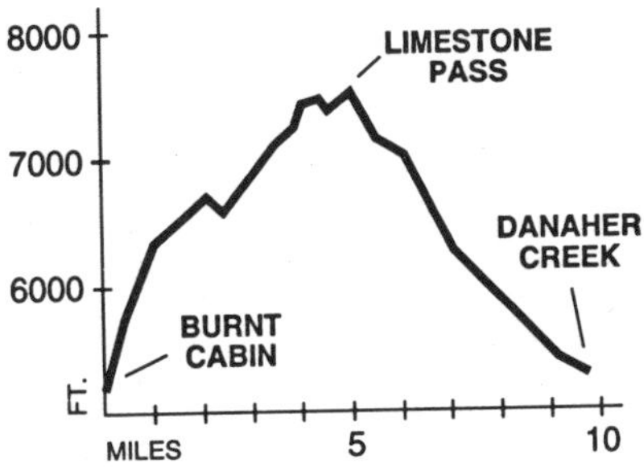

Trail 402, 143
General description: An extended trip from the Burnt Cabin to Danaher Creek, 9.7 mi. (15.6 km).
Difficulty: Moderately strenuous.
Trail maintenance: Yearly to the pass; frequent beyond.
Traffic: Light.
Elevation gain: 2,445 ft.
Elevation loss: 2,415 ft.
Maximum elevation: 7,460 ft.
Topo maps: Dunham Point, Hahn Creek Pass, Danaher Mountain.
Finding the trail: This trail begins at the Burnt Cabin, 8.2 miles up the Monture Creek trail.

- 0.0 Burnt Cabin.
- 2.4 Trail makes its first crossing of the East Fork of Monture Creek.
- 3.8 Limestone Pass. Trail enters the Bob Marshall Wilderness.
- 4.3 Trail crosses pass behind Apex Mountain.
- 4.9 Trail crosses pass behind Little Apex Mountain.
- 9.4 Trail reaches the Danaher Creek bottoms. Bear east.
- 9.5 Crossing of Limestone Creek.
- 9.7 Trail fords Danaher Creek to reach a junction with the Danaher Valley Trail (126).

The trail: This trail links the Monture and Danaher valleys over the high pass that sits at the base of Foolhen Mountain. From its beginnings at the Burnt Cabin, the trail runs east for a brief time before climbing northward across a pine-covered slope. The trail soon emerges into an arid slope of open Douglas-fir savannah. All around are the swells of forested foothills, with Fenn Mountain rising above them all to the south. The trail passes through another stand of lodgepole before climbing onto a sparsely-wooded plateau, where it resumes its eastward trek. The path soon enters the valley of Monture Creek's East Fork, where it bends to the northeast. The trail climbs gradually across forested slopes far above the valley floor, with occasional openings that allow vistas of Monahan Mountain on the far side of the valley.

Upon reaching the upper basin of this stream, the trail turns north again, crossing the creek a number of times as it follows the water upstream. To the east, the

TRAIL 48 *LIMESTONE PASS*

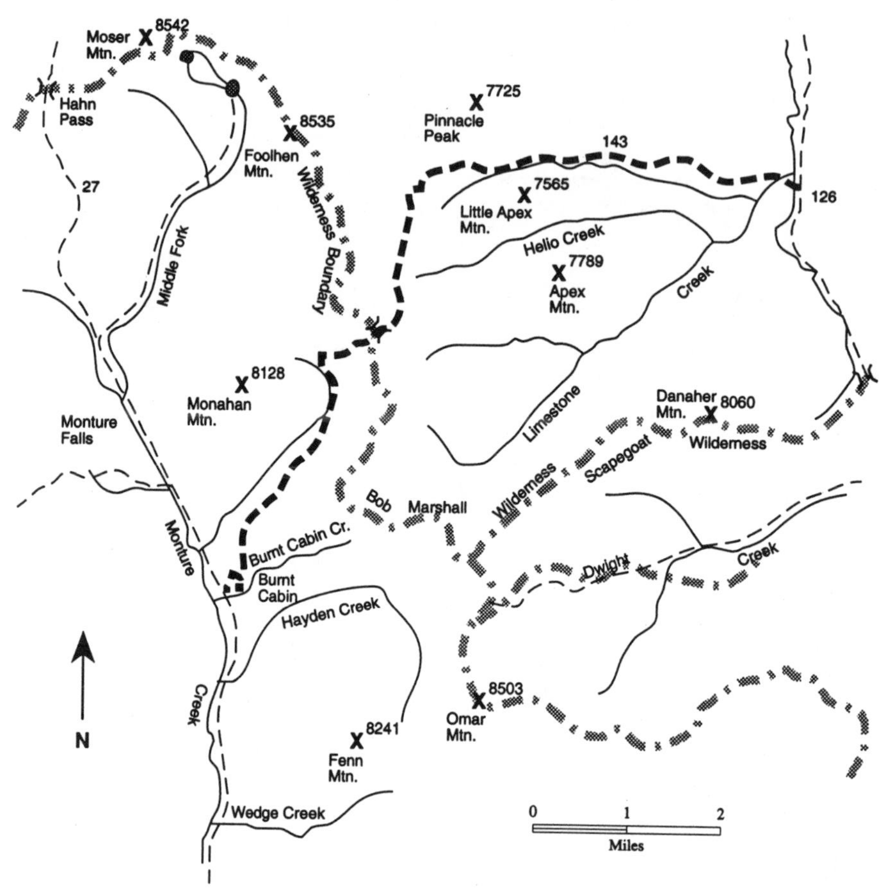

bare rock of the eroded mountainsides are suffused with reds and pale greens. Eventually, the copses of lodgepole pine and subalpine fir give way to sweeping meadows of beargrass, and the trail makes its way up a low ridge separating two branches of the stream. Upon reaching steeper slopes, the trail turns east, climbing steadily toward Limestone Pass. The trail passes into a series of tiny, rolling hills covered in beargrass and studded with old snags. Hidden in the folds of the hillocks lie protected vales filled with wet meadows. The trail wanders through this miniature landscape, making its gradual final ascent to reach the pass. From this vantage point, Evans Peak rises prominently to the east, beyond the dome of Danaher Mountain. Farther south, the low mass of Red Mountain occupies the horizon.

A faint track runs northward from the pass, climbing gently toward Foolhen Mountain before petering out in the tundra. The Limestone Pass trail is the more distinct trail that descends as it continues eastward for a short distance. The trail then turns northward through the rolling country of an old burn. Dropping into the headwaters of Helio Creek, travelers can view the ramparts of the Scapegoat Massif

Looking east from Limestone Pass toward Danaher Mountain (foreground) and Mount Evans (in the distance).

through a natural window framed by Apex and Little Apex mountains. From this viewpoint, the left-hand summit is Flint Mountain, while the slightly more distant peak to the right is Scapegoat Mountain.

The trail crosses numerous boggy rivulets before climbing through the saddle behind Little Apex. This ridge was left untouched by the blaze that razed the surrounding forests. The trail then drops into the next drainage to the north. Mudholes are common as the path descends to cross the stream and turn eastward. Pinnacle Peak dominates the northern rim of this valley, while the sheer faces of Scapegoat can be seen far off to the east. The trail runs through an open meadow near the base of Pinnacle's southern wall, then descends quite steeply into a dense forest of subalpine fir. As the forest begins to open up a bit, Little Apex rises imposingly to the south, and Apex Mountain looms beyond the saddle to the west of it. Mountain goats make their home on both of these rocky peaks, which rise like islands from the rolling hills all around.

As the trail sheds altitude, the subalpine forest gives way to a loose-knit stand of old Douglas-fir. The path slows its descent markedly as it continues eastward, leaving Little Apex far behind. As the sidehill gives way to a flat ridgetop, forest openings reveal the massive bulk of Danaher Mountain. This marks the final descent toward the Danaher Creek bottoms. In the forest atop a flat bluff, the trail reaches a junction with an unmarked hunter's route that runs north along the Danaher Valley; stay right for the Danaher Valley Trail (126). Meadows soon replace the woods atop the bluff, and the trail makes its way down a steep hillside to reach the valley floor. A number of unmarked trails radiate from this point; avoid the trails running north and south and take the trail that runs due east, crossing sagebrush flats and crossing a small tributary on its way to Danaher Creek. Here, a deep ford (or beaver dam walk) awaits travelers who wish to connect with the Danaher Valley trail, which follows the far bank of the creek.

TRAIL 49 *DANAHER VALLEY*

Trail 126

General description: An extended trip from the end of the east side South Fork trail to the Dry Fork Divide, 16.8 mi. (27.0 km).

Difficulty: Moderate.

Trail maintenance: Yearly.

Traffic: Heavy.

Elevation gain: 870 ft.

Elevation loss: 260 ft.

Maximum elevation: 5,370 ft.

Topo maps: Pilot Peak, Trap Mountain, Danaher Mountain.

Finding the trail: This trail begins at the terminus of the east side South Fork Trail (80), where its reaches the junction with the Youngs Creek Ford Trail junction.

0.0 Junction of east side South Fork (80), Youngs Ford (125), and Danaher Valley (126) trails.
1.9 Junction with the Catchem Creek Trail (269). Bear right.
2.0 Trail makes two crossings of a Danaher Creek side channel.
3.6 Trail fords Camp Creek and enters the Basin. Junction with the Camp Creek Pass Trail (233).
3.7 Unmarked junction with the Jumbo Mountain Lookout Trail (589). Bear left.
4.4 First junction with the Hoadley Pass Trail (271). Bear right.
5.0 Basin Creek Cabin. Second junction with the Hoadley Pass Trail. Danaher Valley trail fords Basin Creek.
7.0 Junctions with the Foolhen Creek (142) and Sentinel Mountain trails. Main trail leaves the Basin.
8.6 Trail fords Rapid Creek.
8.7 Junction with the Observation Pass Trail (139). Keep going straight.

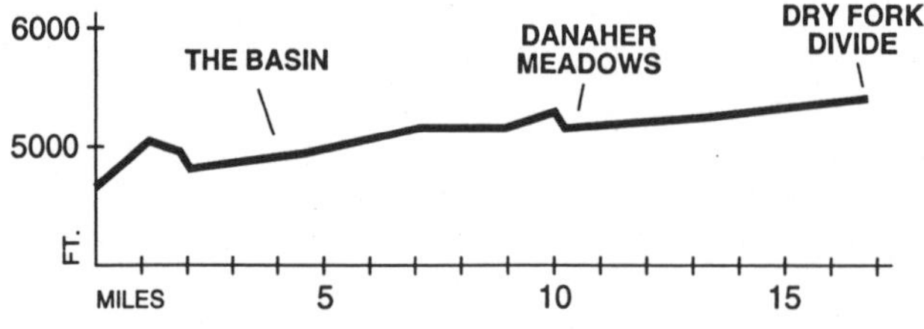

Woodtick and Jumbo mountains rise beyond the meadows of the Danaher Valley.

10.1 Trail enters Danaher Meadows.
10.6 Junction with the Alloy Creek Trail (265). Keep going straight.
11.0 Spur trail to Danaher Cabin.
11.2 Trail crosses Spring Creek.
11.6 Trail crosses Bar Creek.
12.0 Junction with the Triple Divide Trail (140). Bear right.
12.1 Trail crosses Antoine Creek.
14.4 Junction with the Limestone Pass Trail (143).
14.6 Trail leaves Danaher Meadows.
16.8 Dry Fork Divide. Scapegoat Wilderness boundary.

The trail: The Danaher Valley is known for its expanses of grassy meadows that allow sweeping views of the surrounding mountains. Flathead Indians often passed through this country on their way to hunt the buffalo on the high plains. Later, this valley was the site of the only homesteading activity on the western side of the wilderness, a small ranch established by the Danaher family near Bar Creek. This early attempt at ranching withered because of its long distance from markets. Today, the Danaher Valley is a popular haven for elk hunters, and spike camps spring up like weeds from mid September through October. But there is always a special magic here found in in the lonely wail of the coyote on the moonlit prairies and in the autumn bugles of elk in the surrounding hills.

TRAIL 49 *DANAHER VALLEY*

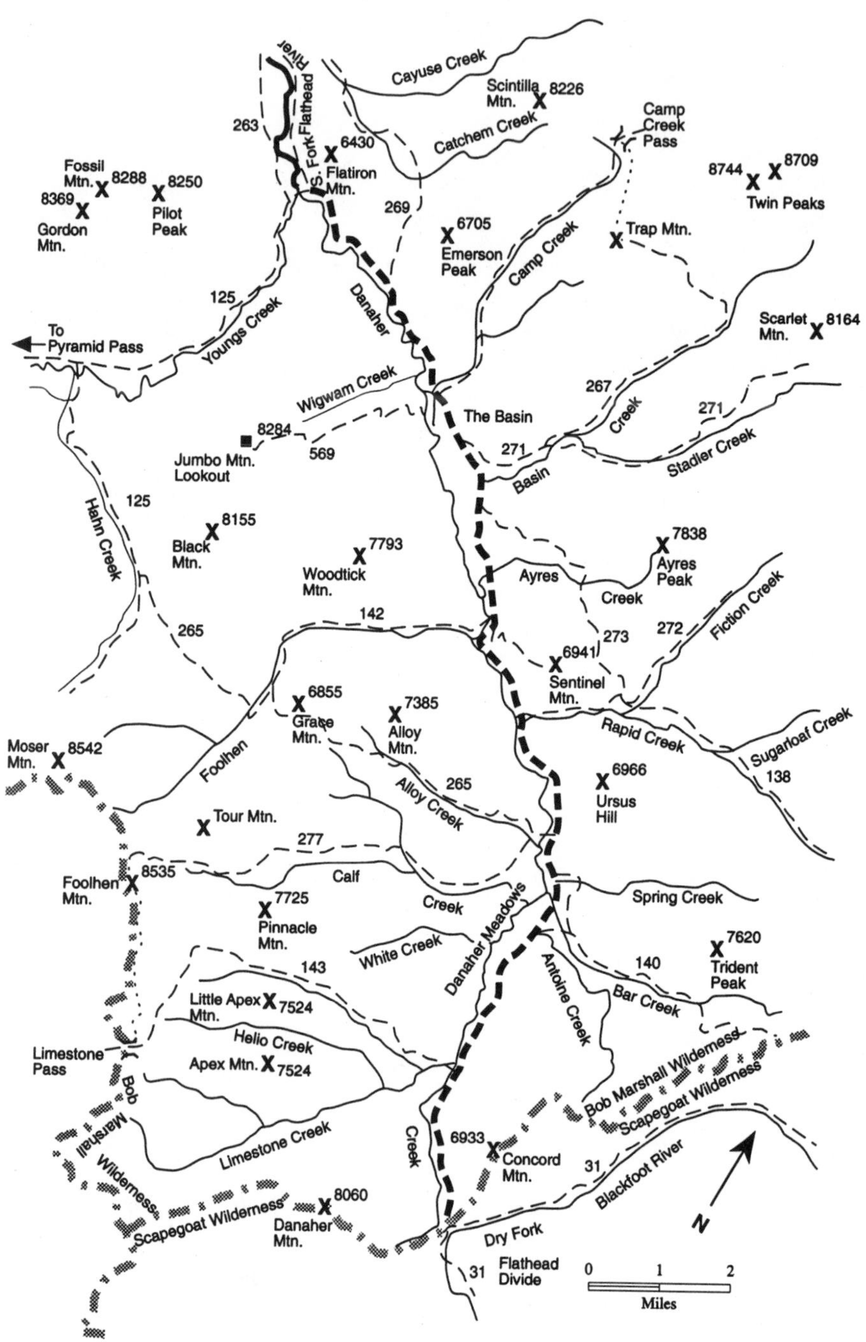

From its beginnings at the south end of the South Fork valley, the Danaher Valley trail follows the dry, timbered hillsides above the east bank of Danaher Creek. The trail climbs steadily, far above the stream, as the forested tailbone of Jumbo Mountain slides by across the valley. After passing the Catchem Creek Trail (269) junction, the Danaher trail descends back to the creek bottoms, where it follows the stream into a wooded canyon. The route climbs to avoid outcrops which overshadow emerald pools, then descends to cross and re-cross a slow-moving side channel. The trail then ascends gently onto the grassy southern slope of Emerson Peak where it remains until its reaches the northern edge of the wide, grassy bowl known simply as "The Basin."

Here, the trail descends to make an ankle-deep crossing of Camp Creek. The junction with the Camp Creek Pass Trail (233) is on the far bank, just north of a marker commemorating a skirmish between Flathead and Blackfeet Indians in 1840. In the open meadows just beyond this sign, a heavily blazed tree marks the spot where the Jumbo Mountain Trail (569) takes off toward its ford of Danaher Creek. The Danaher trail continues southeastward, passing into a stand of lodgepole and crossing a small stream before reaching the edge of a large, grassy expanse of meadow. Looming across the creek are the impressive edifices of Woodtick and Jumbo mountains, while the ruddy summits of Scintilla and Trap mountains rise from low foothills to the east. At the near edge of the meadow is a signpost indicating the point of departure for the Hoadley Pass trail (referred to on the sign as "Stadler Creek Trail 271"). The main trail braids out into four or five deep-rutted tracks across the grass as it makes for the far side of the meadows. Just inside the trees, the trail reaches the Basin Creek Cabin, on the north bank of Basin Creek.

After making a calf-deep crossing of this stream, the trail continues up the flat valley bottom, now dominated by smaller dry meadows that are dotted with sagebrush bushes. The forests surrounding these openings have a few aspen scattered among the lodgepole. As the trail skirts the base of Sentinel Mountain on the south end of The Basin, it passes the unmarked junctions with the Sentinel Mountain and Foolhen Creek trails (142). The Danaher trail follows the creek as it issues from a tight place between the hills, climbing to treetop level as it crosses the rocky slopes above the rushing waters. The trail drops into the cool spruce bottomland of a side valley as it approaches the ford of Rapid Creek, which is crossed via a calf-deep wade. The trail to Observation Pass (139) departs a quarter mile beyond this crossing.

The Danaher Valley trail continues along the bottomland, then climbs onto the grassy slopes named for the scientific name of the bear clan: Ursus Hill. The narrow canyon opens up into a broad valley, revealing the brushy flats of Danaher Meadows, with the sinuous curves of Danaher Creek running placidly down its center. As the trail passes a last, wooded hump, the Alloy Creek Trail (265) fords the creek and runs westward. Look for muskrats in the swampy backwaters of the creek and signs of beaver activity along the main streamcourse. The trail makes its way across marshy meadows, with copses of lodgepole occupying the well-drained soils of the higher ground. Apex and Danaher mountains rise prominently above the meadows to the south, while the rounded hump of Trident Peaks guards the eastern side of the valley.

After the trail makes a shallow ford of Bar Creek, it enters the Bar Meadows. The cliffy caprock to the east is the top of Flint Mountain, visible beyond the verdant foothills that surround the valley. The trail crosses the grassy meadow to reach a signpost marking the trail to Triple Divide, here labeled "Bar Creek Trail 140." From this point, the main trail angles southeast, crossing Antoine Creek and passing a sign that marks the site of the old Danaher Homestead. Looking northeast from this meadow, the limestone block of Sugarloaf Mountain can be seen above a collection of low, forested hills. The trail then works its way through some timber to return to the edge of the main meadow that borders Danaher Creek. The upper part of the meadow is, for the most part, flooded by the activities of beaver and is choked with shrubby dwarf birch and willow.

After skirting the edge of the swamp for several miles, the creek swings close to the trail. Look for the beavers that have impounded much of the upper reaches of Danaher Creek behind sturdy wicker dams. The trail passes the Limestone Pass Trail junction (143), and then moves into the forest. It soon emerges onto grassy slopes dotted with isolated copses of aspen, which turn a brilliant gold during late September. The trail returns once more to the creekside before disappearing into the lodgepole for good. The last 1.5 mile of the trek runs through the silent forest to reach its terminus at the Dry Fork Divide. This low pass could hardly be discerned from the rest of the valley bottom if it was not for the signpost marking the Dry Fork trail.

TRAIL 50 *TRIPLE DIVIDE*

Trail 140

General description: A spur trip from the Danaher valley to the summit of Observation Point, 5.4 mi. (8.7 km).

Difficulty: Strenuous.

Trail maintenance: Occasional.

Traffic: Very light.

Elevation gain: 3,393 ft.

Elevation loss: 70 ft.

Maximum elevation: 8,523 ft.

Topo maps: Danaher Mountain, Flint Mountain.

Finding the trail: This trail takes off from the Danaher Valley Trail (126) in Danaher Meadows, just north of its crossing of Antoine Creek.

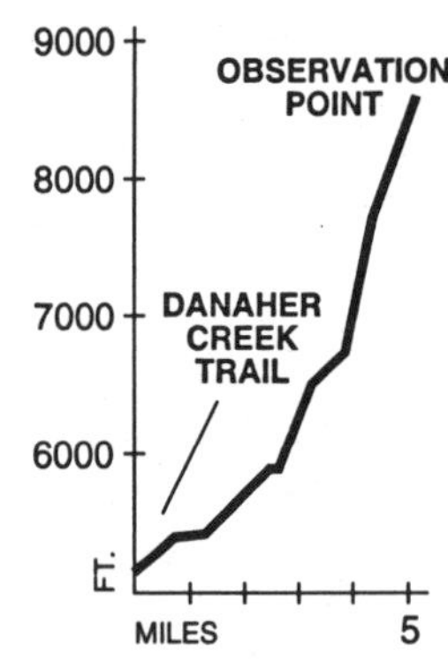

0.0 Junction of Danaher Valley (126) and Triple Divide trails.
0.6 Junction with spur trail to Danaher Cabin. Bear right.
1.4 Trail reaches the end of Bar Meadows.
2.6 Trail fords Bar Creek and begins to climb.
5.2 Triple Divide Point.
5.4 Observation Point.

The trail: This trail offers a rather rigorous side trip for travelers visiting Danaher Meadows. The trail offers a microcosm of the wilderness itself. From its beginnings

TRAIL 50 *TRIPLE DIVIDE*

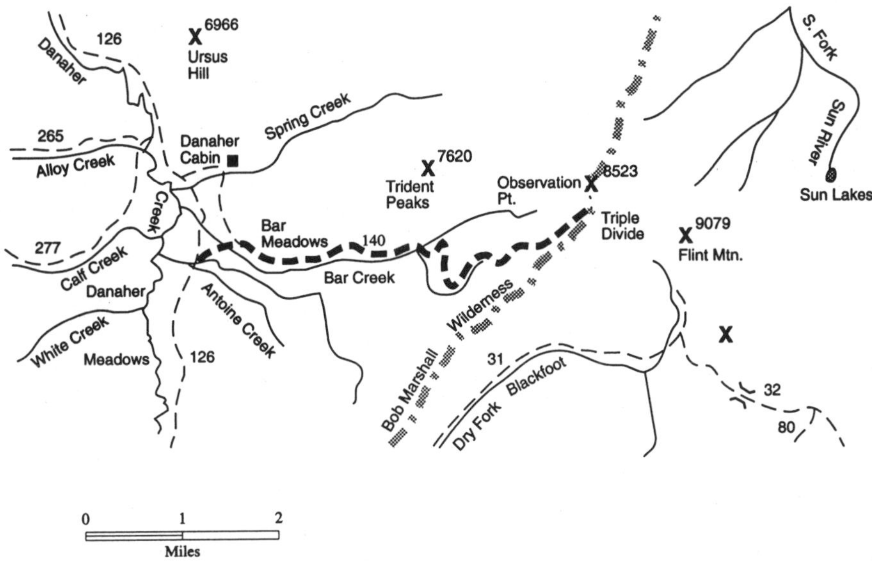

in the Bar Creek Meadows, it climbs through verdant forests to reach the summit of an 8,000-foot peak with views in all directions. The highlight of the trail is a stunning view of Flint Mountain, truly one of the most inspiring peaks in the area. The last half of the trail is extremely steep and will probably cause problems for parties that attempt the trail on horseback.

The trail begins its journey on the grassy flats of Bar Meadows, which is surrounded by a forest of lodgepole pine. These wide meadows dominate the first 1.5 mile of the trek, as the trail makes its way eastward toward the Continental Divide. There are several cutoff trails that run to the left toward the Danaher Cabin; stick to the right fork of the trail for Triple Divide. Upon reaching the end of the meadows, the trail enters a primeval forest and climbs onto a low ridgetop. About a mile later, a short ascent onto a grassy slope precedes a rather steep drop into the narrow bottomlands of Bar Creek. A quarter mile farther on, the trail makes a shallow ford of this small woodland stream and continues its journey on the south bank.

The trail soon departs from the streamside for a steep ascent up the hillside to the south. After a brisk climb, the trail crests the hilltop and reaches a high, flat valley that contains a tiny streamlet. The trail runs northeast across this wooded shelf to reach the base of Triple Divide Point, where it begins to climb steeply. The route runs nearly straight uphill, pausing for a brief respite in the meadow of a flat ridgetop before resuming its steep quest for the summit. The forest becomes sparser near the summit, and lodgepole pine are replaced by subalpine fir and whitebark pine. The trail peters out 150 yards south of the top of Triple Divide, amid scruffy limber pines and eroded soils.

A short jaunt to the north lands that traveler at the summit of Triple Divide Point, from which waters flow into the Flathead, Blackfoot, and Sun River drainages. Flint

Flint Mountain viewed from the summit of Triple Divide Point.

Mountain rises just 0.25 mile to the east, an astounding edifice of towering walls that supports a vigorous population of mountain goats. At its foot, the upper basin of the South Fork of the Sun River is hemmed in by the sheer cliffs of the Scapegoat Massif. A faint path runs northward for 0.25 mile to the slightly loftier Observation Point, where an enormous cairn of cunning stonework overlooks the massive block of Sugarloaf Mountain squatting along the Continental Divide to the north. In the east, the tawny spread of Danaher Meadows sits among forested foothills. Look south into the Scapegoat Wilderness to see the wooded slopes that rise to graceful points like the swells on a storm-tossed sea.

TRAIL 51 *JUMBO MOUNTAIN LOOKOUT*

Trail 569
General description: A spur trip from The Basin to Jumbo Mountain Lookout, 3.8 mi. (6.1 km).
Difficulty: Strenuous.
Trail maintenance: Yearly.
Traffic: Very light.
Elevation gain: 3,394 ft.
Elevation loss: 26 ft.

Maximum elevation: 8,284 ft.
Topo maps: Trap Mountain, Pilot Peak.
Finding the trail: This trail takes off to the south from the Danaher Valley Trail (126) at a blazed tree, just south of the Camp Creek ford.

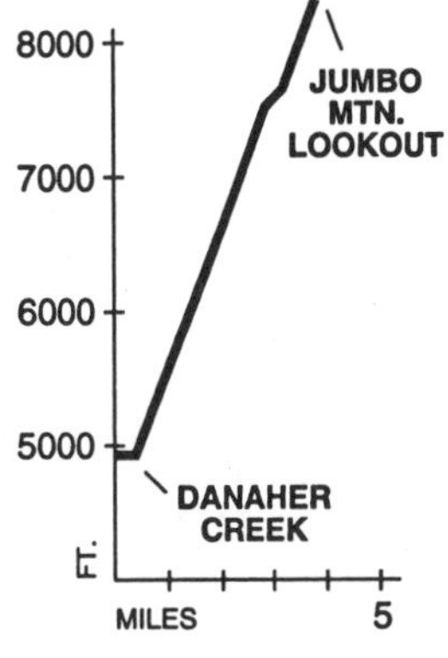

- 0.0 Junction of Danaher Valley and Jumbo Moun tain Lookout trails.
- 0.1 Trail fords the first channel of Danaher Creek.
- 0.3 Trail fords the second channel of Danaher Creek and begins to climb.
- 2.8 Trail crosses the ridgeline and enters the Wigwam Creek basin.
- 3.8 Jumbo Mountain Lookout.

The trail: This trail provides a spur trip to the top of a high peak overlooking The Basin in the Danaher Valley. From the Danaher Creek Trail, the trail to Jumbo Mountain Lookout runs due south, soon reaching a knee-deep ford of the main channel of Danaher Creek, which babbles swiftly over its bed of bright cobbles. The trail then crosses a substantial island in the stream to reach the deep, slow-moving west channel of the stream. Hikers can avoid this ford by following the streambank southward into the woods, where the stream is much shallower and can be crossed on logs that span the waters. Once on the far bank, the trail immediately begins climbing up the forested eastern slope of the mountain. As the trail winds onto grassy south-facing slopes, it offers sweeping views of The Basin, with its tawny grasslands stretched out amid the verdant carpet of the forest.

TRAIL 51 *JUMBO MOUNTAIN LOOKOUT*

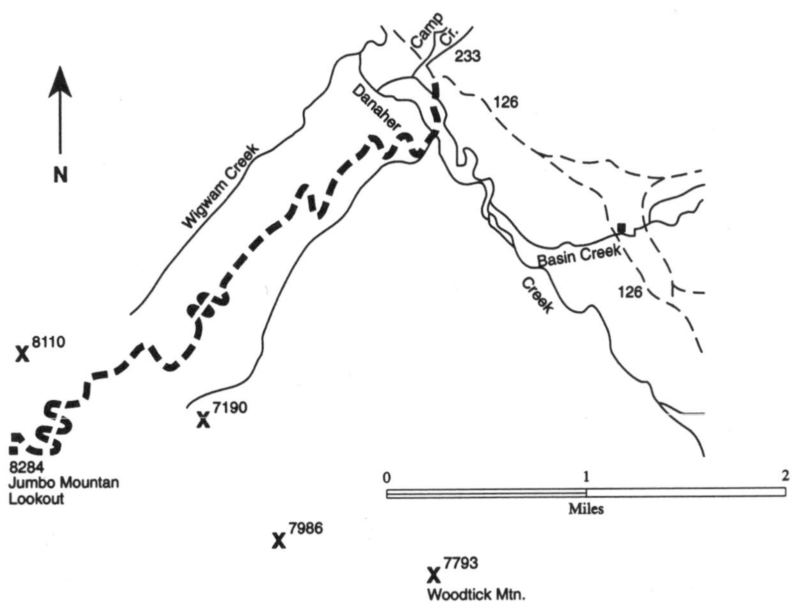

View of Sugarloaf Mountain from the Jumbo Mountain Lookout.

After 0.5 mile of open country, the trail turns northward toward the ridgeline, where it re-enters the forest. When the ridgetop becomes too steep for a straight-line ascent, the trail begins to zigzag across its eastern face. The trees begin to thin out with increasing altitude, revealing the rocky crest of Sugarloaf Mountain atop a wave of green to the east. The trail then passes once again onto the grassy southern slopes of the ridge, high above the valley of a nameless stream. A sheer obelisk of rock guards the entrance to an alpine cirque at the head of the valley, and the convoluted rock faces of Woodtick Mountain rise along the southern rim of the vale. The trail approaches a dry ravine, then switches back to the east to return to the ridgeline.

Once it reaches the ridgetop, the trail continues over it and into the cool, forested bowl to the north. The trail passes through a loose forest of whitebark pine, which are draped with old man's beard. The trail climbs steadily to the head of the bowl and then begins to ascend its west wall, where it begins to climb in earnest. The protected forest of the bowl soon gives way to a scattering of windblown subalpine larch and fir. The going gets quite steep as the trail switchbacks across rocky slopes to reach the lookout at the summit. This aerie overlooks the Youngs Creek valley, and hulking summits rise in all directions. Most prominent among them are Junction Mountain to the north, as well as Sugarloaf and Flint mountains rising from the Continental Divide to the southeast.

TRAIL 52 *WHITE RIVER*

Trail 112
General description: An extended trip from the South Fork of the Flathead to Wall Creek Pass, 18.1 mi. (29.1 km).
Difficulty: Moderate.
Trail maintenance: Yearly.
Traffic: Heavy to the South Fork of the White River; moderate beyond.
Elevation gain: 2,628 ft.
Elevation loss: 218 ft.
Maximum elevation: 6,880 ft.
Topo maps: Big Salmon Lake East, Haystack Mountain, Amphitheatre Mountain, Bungalow Mountain.
Finding the trail: This trail takes off from the east side South Fork Trail (80) just north of its ford of the White River.

- 0.0 Junction of the east side South Fork and White River trails.
- 4.4 Trail fords the White River as the valley bends to the north.
- 4.6 Junction with the White River Pass Trail (138). Keep going straight.
- 4.7 Trail fords the South Fork of the White River.
- 7.1 Needle Falls overlook.
- 8.5 Trail crosses Peggy Creek.
- 9.6 Trail crosses Cliff Creek.
- 10.2 Trail fords the White River to reach its western bank.
- 11.7 Junction with the Pagoda Mountain Trail (100). Keep going straight.
- 12.8 Brushy Park. Trail fords Seep Creek.
- 16.0 Junction with the Larch Hill Pass Trail (112). Bear left for Wall Creek Pass.
- 16.2 Trail fords Juliet Creek.
- 18.1 Wall Creek Pass.

The trail: The White River is born from the glaciers of Silvertip Mountain, meanders through a high, flat basin, and then rushes down a wooded canyon to reach its confluence with the South Fork of the Flathead. The trail that follows its banks pro-

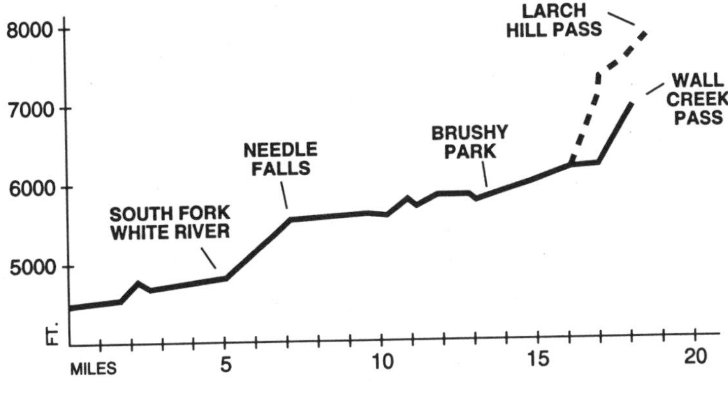

Needle Falls.

TRAIL 52 *WHITE RIVER*

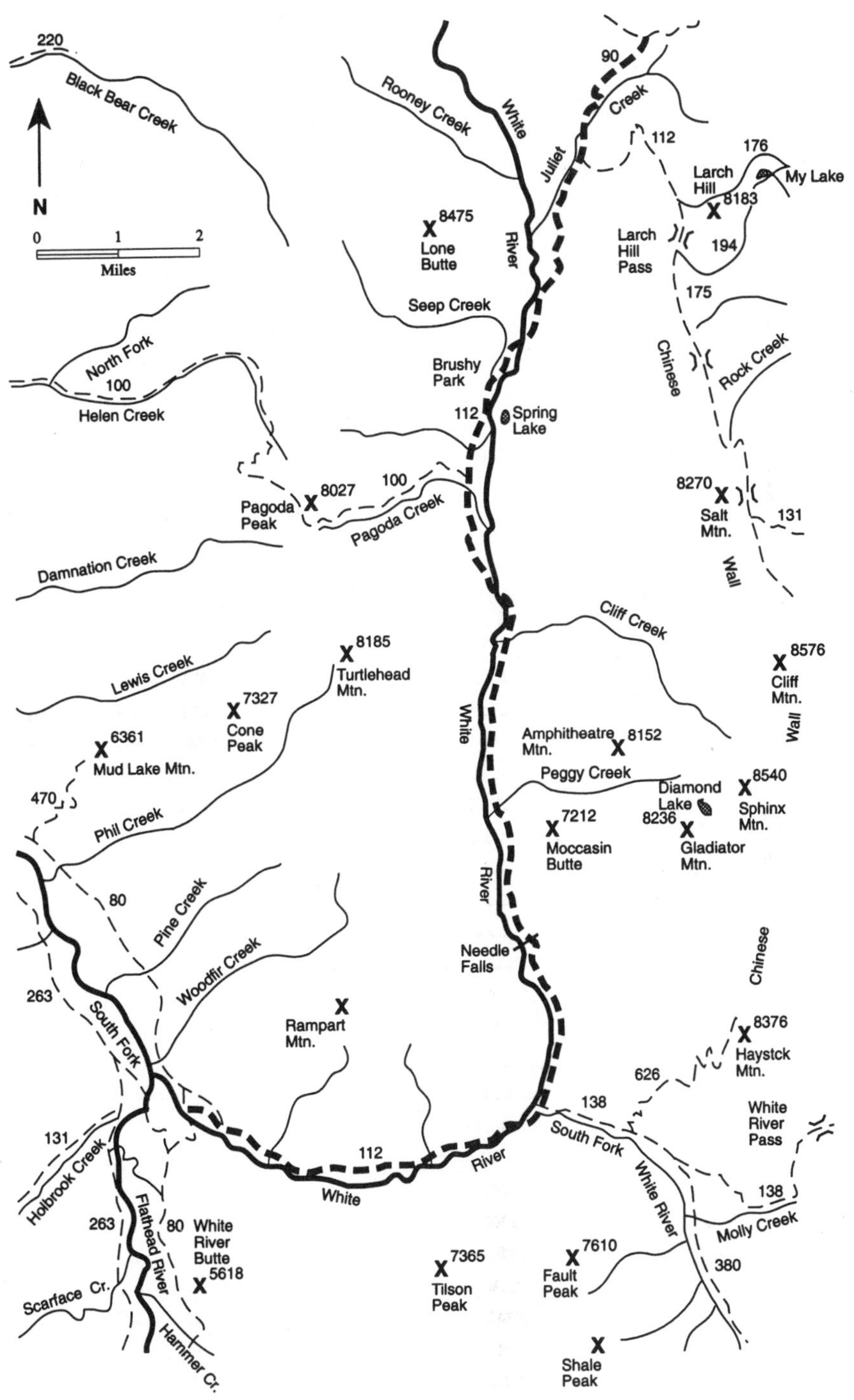

vides a major access route to the Flathead Alps, as well as to the Chinese Wall via Larch Hill and White River passes. The river provides some of the best fishing in the state in its lower reaches below Needle Falls, itself one of the scenic highlights of the trip.

The trail begins amid the broad, flat meadows that line the South Fork of the Flathead. It bears eastward as it traces the north bank of the White River in its wandering curves across the valley floor. The open parkland of Douglas-fir and ponderosa pine allows excellent views of Scarface Mountain and Charlotte Peak, which rise across the valley to the west. The views close in as the trail follows the riverside up into a narrow canyon lined with steep, forested ridges. The canopy is dominated by Douglas-fir, which grow sparsely on the well-drained slopes of the canyon. The forest floor is dotted with snowberry, wild rose, and Oregon grape. As the trail climbs gently on the wooded benches above the river, occasional openings reveal the braided channels of the river running across the bed of white cobbles. As the trail nears the point where the valley bends to the north, it crosses a half mile of muddy bottomland. The forested slopes of Fault Peak rise across the river.

After rounding the bend to the north, the trail runs onto the gravel bar of the river in preparation for a knee-deep ford. Gladiator Mountain rears if sheer face to the north, while the rounded form of Haystack Mountain looms to the east. The rocky summit of Fault Peak overlooks the ford to the south, and the rugged face of Rampart Mountain overlooks the west bank of the river. This latter peak will be a constant companion for the next several miles. After crossing these cold and swift-flowing waters, the trail follows the east bank of the stream. Just before reaching a ford of the South Fork of the White River, the trail passes a junction with the White River Pass Trail (138), which takes off to the east. The main trail continues northward, making a ankle-deep crossing of this tributary and continuing to follow the riverbank through a forest of lodgepole pine.

The trail soon climbs the wooded bluffs that rise several hundred feet above the east bank of the river. The trail then crests a grassy hillock that allows views back down the rivercourse toward Fault Peak. It then disappears into the forest, climbing steadily as it winds its way across several incoming gullies. After crossing the second coulee, the trail climbs to a sparsely wooded point that overlooks Needle Falls. For a better view of the falls, stay on the trail for several hundred yards to reach a second such overlook. This waterfall cascades beneath a natural bridge of bedrock during low water, tumbling over one hundred feet across a mortised rock face into the glimmering depths of an emerald pool. A scramble of several hundred vertical feet down unstable cutbanks is required to reach the base of the falls; this course of action is strongly discouraged.

Beyond the falls, the trail disappears once again into a forest of lodgepole pine as it crosses the flat valley bottom. Several miles beyond the falls, the trail wanders beside some riverside openings that allow views of Turtlehead Mountain to the west. The trail then returns to the depths of the forest and soon fords the river. After the knee-deep crossing of the now rather placid White River, the trail turns inland to cover the next several miles in viewless forests. After several miles of rather muddy traveling, the trail passes a junction with the Pagoda Mountain Trail (100). It then continues north, soon breaking out onto the low bluffs that border Brushy Park. From here, the bulky mass of Lone Butte rises immediately to the south like a lone sentinel over the valley. The trail follows the western bank of the meandering stream for 0.25 mile, then begins a series of fords across the braided channels near its confluence with Seep Creek. The trail crosses a side channel four times, then travels 0.25 mile northward to ford the main channel and arrive at an outfitter's camp.

The trail then enters a spruce-fir forest with scanty views and assumes the form of a wide, sometimes muddy track. After 1.5 mile, the forest opens up into a lodgepole pine savannah, interspersed with dry meadows and overlooked to the northwest by the regal summit of Silvertip Mountain. The trail soon reaches the dry bed of Juliet Creek, which it follows at a steady uphill pace. Soon, the views disappear as the trail enters thicker woods, and the waters can be heard babbling in their stony bed to the west. The trail soon passes the junction with the trail to Larch Hill Pass (112), which will be discussed separately at the end of this trail description.

The main trail continues northward and soon crosses Juliet Creek. It follows the west bank of the creek into an open subalpine basin, where it seems to dead-end at a hunter's camp. The north face of Lone Butte rises prominently to the south. Turn west at this point, following a faint path that angles up the hillside. This track soon merges with a more well-developed trail, which runs north as it climbs the hillside above the Juliet Creek basin. After a steady climb, the trail reaches the pass at the head of Wall Creek. From this point, the Wall Creek Trail (90) and the Bungalow Mountain trail (243) run northward to reach the Spotted Bear River.

Larch Hill Pass Option. This side trail links the White River trail with the Chinese Wall over a high pass in the Continental Divide. From its beginning on the banks of Juliet Creek, this trail climbs quickly through the lodgepole pine, then bends northward through a forest of old subalpine fir underlain by a dense underbrush of false huckleberry. The trail can be quite muddy on this northward leg, which lasts for about one mile. Breaks in the forest canopy allow brief glimpses of Lone Butte and Silvertip Mountain to the west. The trail then doglegs back to the south, slowing its climb a bit as whitebark pine begin to take over the forest.

After another 0.5 mile, views open up as the trail enters an old burn, which contains only young saplings. When the trail crests the ridgeline, Mount Field can be seen on the northwest horizon, in addition to the unimpeded views of Silvertip Mountain and the White River Syncline to the west. This unusual geological formation tilts westward, counter to other rock strata in the overthrust belt. The formation is an upwarping of the rock, which occurred under the intense pressure created by colliding land masses during the most recent mountain building phase. The trail clings to this ridgeline for 0.25 mile of climbing before reaching an unmarked junction with a connecting trail (176), which runs northeast toward Spotted Bear Pass. The main trail continues southeast, climbing through a final stand of old whitebark pine before reaching Larch Hill Pass. This pass sits at the northern terminus of the Chinese Wall, and a short descent to the trail running along its foot reveals excellent views of the cliffs southward to the horizon.

TRAIL 53 *HAYSTACK MOUNTAIN*

Trail 138, 626
General description: A spur trip from the White River to the summit of Haystack Mountain, 4.2 mi. (6.8 km).
Difficulty: Strenuous.
Trail maintenance: Frequent.
Traffic: Moderate.
Elevation gain: 3,629 ft.
Maximum elevation: 8,376 ft.
Topo map: Haystack Mountain.
Finding the trail: Start from the White River Pass junction on the White River Trail (112) on the south bank of the South Fork of the White River.

HAYSTACK MTN.
8000
7000
6000
5000
FT.
MILES
5

0.0 Junction of White River and White River Pass (138) trails.
0.2 Trail fords the South Fork of the White River.
1.0 Junction with the Haystack Mountain Trail (626). Turn left.
4.2 Summit of Haystack Mountain.

The trail: This spur trail climbs steeply up the sloping west wall of Haystack Mountain to reach its lofty summit, which commands sweeping views including the south-

Looking north along the Chinese Wall from Haystack Mountain.

ern marches of the Chinese Wall. The trail is maintained primarily by the efforts of outfitters and guides, who keep the trail bed clear of logs and other debris. This route offers the best observation point in the entire White River valley and makes a good day trip for travelers visiting the area for an extended period of time.

From the White River trail, take the trail to White River Pass, which crosses the South Fork of the White River and climbs onto the high bluffs above its north bank. This trail climbs steadily for one mile, finally reaching a marked trail junction with the Haystack Mountain Trail (626). Turn left onto this trail, which climbs through the forest and onto open slopes. Early views include Fault Mountain and the rest of the Flathead Alps, which rise to sharp pinnacles above the South Fork of the White River. Rampart Mountain rises to the west, beyond the main channel of the White River. Looking downriver, Scarface Mountain can be seen far to the west. The trail soon passes through another stretch of lodgepole pine forest, which harbors a few muddy spots in wet weather.

The trail then emerges onto a broad, grassy slope dotted with occasional Douglas-fir. It climbs steeply, zigzagging its way across the broad western face of Haystack Mountain. Views continue to expand, with the Swan Range emerging above the western horizon, and Sphinx and Gladiator mountains raising their sheer walls to the north. After traveling to the northern rim of the slope, the trail makes a final turn to the south for its final ascent to the summit. To the north, the cliffs of the Chinese Wall stretch away to the edge of sight, while Slategoat Mountain dominates the northeastern horizon. To the south, Junction Mountain and Twin Peaks rise regally above the crest of the Continental Divide.

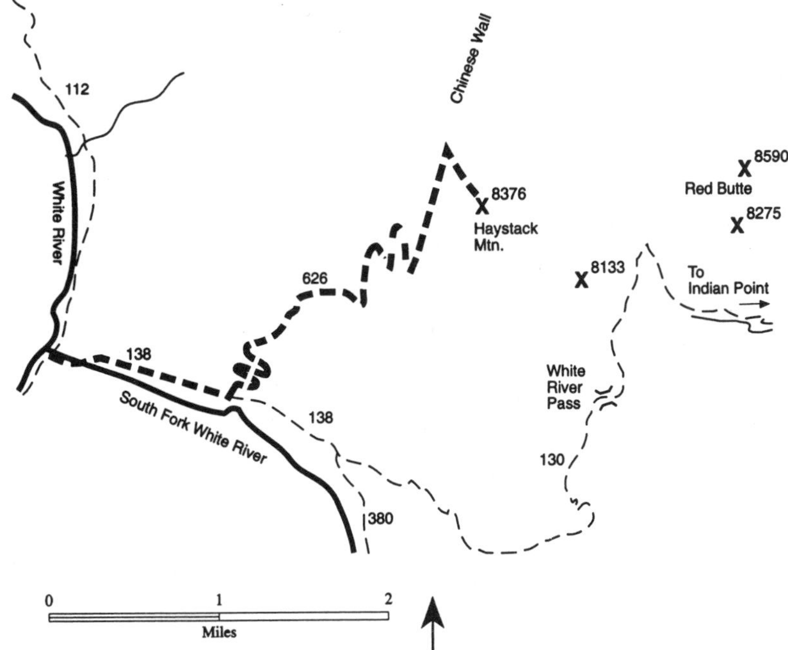

ADDITIONAL TRAILS

Tango Point (455) and **Albino Basin** (118) trails have been abandoned and are a real challenge to find.

Lena Peak is more route than trail; just pick an open ridgeline and start climbing.

Holbrook Creek (131) and **Bartlett Creek** (129) trails are maintained frequently, and provide good alternatives to the muddy and over-used **Gordon Creek Trail** (35) for travelers bound for the South Fork.

George Creek Trail and the upper reaches of the **Doctor Lake Trail** (291) are rarely maintained and are difficult to follow, as are the **Kid Mountain** (628) and **Una Creek** (246) trails.

Butcher Mountain Trail (133) is maintained on an occasional basis and can usually be followed once the beginnings of the trail are found.

Babcock Creek Trail (130) fades out after the first six miles or so; the **Marshall Creek Trail** (137) is only passable for the first two miles.

Youngs Creek Trail (283, 141, 125) is a major access route that receives especially heavy traffic during the fall hunting season.

Ross Creek (284) and **Spruce Creek** (221) trails receive sporadic maintenance; expect lots of blown-down timber.

Youngs Pass (13, 141) is rather steep but is maintained annually. The trail in upper Jenny Creek is washed out and impassable.

Dunham Creek Trail (400) is well-maintained up to the outfitters camps in the headwaters; beyond this point, maintenance is sporadic.

Camp Pass Trail (16) is maintained annually and is easy to follow.

Alloy Creek (265) and **Foolhen Creek** (142) trails are maintained infrequently but can be followed by an experienced hiker.

Calf Creek (277) and **Foolhen Mountain** (278) trails are not maintained and are extremely hard to follow.

Ayres Creek (273) and **Cayuse Creek** (269) trails are maintained frequently and can be followed with little difficulty.

Trap Mountain (267) and **Shale Peak** (127) trails are maintained only occasionally. The Shale Peak trail boasts especially good views.

Brownstone Creek (465), **Sandstone Creek** (743), and **South Fork White River** (380) trails receive little maintenance and fade out quickly.

White River Butte Cutoff Trail (193) runs parallel to the main South Fork trail, is maintained infrequently and has lots of blowdowns.

SCAPEGOAT MASSIF

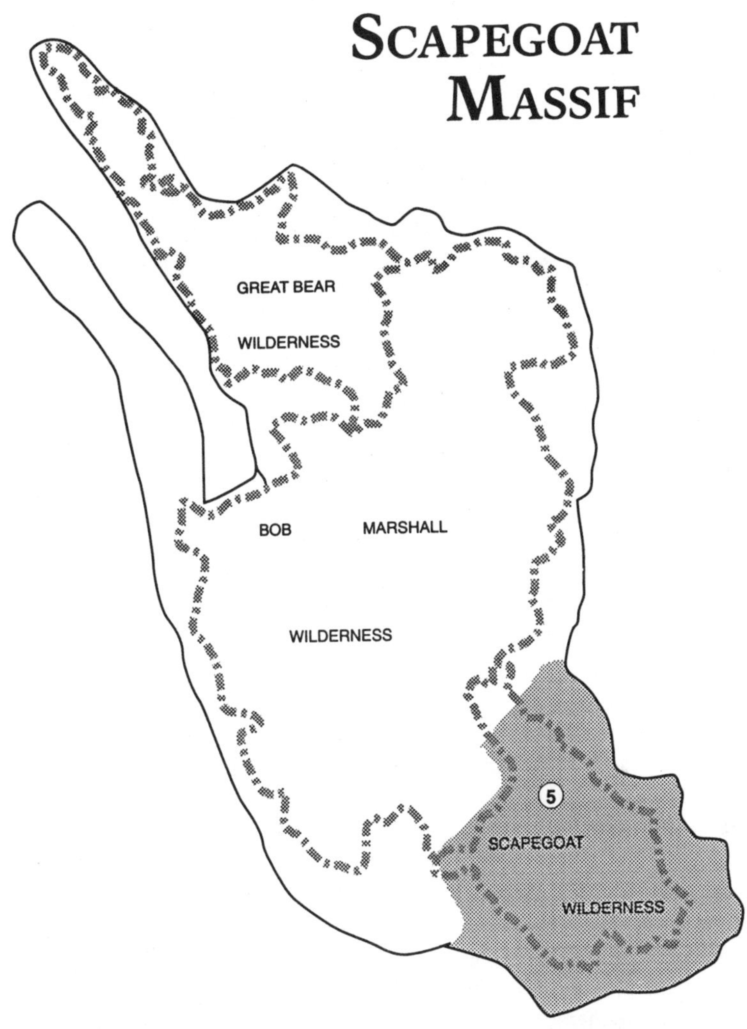

The Scapegoat Wilderness was created in 1972, protecting the upper watershed of the North Fork of the Blackfoot, as well as a southern section of the Rocky Mountain Front. The centerpiece of this region if the Scapegoat Massif itself: an enormous, lofty plateau of rock surrounded on all sides by sheer cliffs. The peak of Scapegoat Mountain (9,202 ft.) rises at the eastern edge of the massif, while Flint Mountain (9,079 ft.) guards its western end. This dramatic assemblage of sheer rock faces serves as a playground for numerous bands of mountain goats and provides aeries for golden eagles. To the south of the massif, rounded mountains overlook the upper drainage of the North Fork of the Blackfoot, while to the east, arid reefs rise to sheer cliffs that face the high plains.

Scapegoat Mountain as seen from the Cave Creek cutoff trail.

Most of the Scapegoat Wilderness burned during the Canyon Creek Fire of 1988. The fire started in the Canyon Creek valley, near the western edge of the Scapegoat Wilderness, and high winds from the west fed the flames as they rampaged through the forest as far east as Haystack Butte on the edge of the high plains. The Forest Service currently has a "let burn" policy for its wilderness areas, so that some lightning-started fires can take their natural course as long as they do not threaten human lives or property. Fire has always been a natural part of forest succession; indeed, some trees such as lodgepole pine and larche are dependent on fire to provide openings in the forest for their shade-intolerant seedlings. Some experts believe that Native Americans deliberately set fires in the Bob Marshall country in order to open up the forest and thus provide forage for the game animals that they depended on for food.

In pre-Columbian times, small fires created a forest mosaic with timber stands of varying ages. Old stands tend to build up lots of dead fuel on the ground (a process called *fuel loading*) and burn readily during dry weather. Young stands, by contrast, will not carry a flame. Because the natural state of the forest is a mosaic of old stands that can burn and young ones that will not, fires that got started in pre-Columbian times would soon reach the limit of the old timber and burn out. With the advent of fire fighting in the twentieth century, the natural cycle of small fires was broken and all of the stands were allowed to grow to an old age. Thus, there were vast tracts of fuel-rich old timber that could blow up into devastating conflagrations like the Canyon Creek and Gates Park fires of the Bob Marshall country, and the Yellowstone fires of the same year. Hopefully, with the new let-burn policy, the forest will return to a mosaic of different-aged timber, and these large wildfires will be averted in the future.

Access to the Scapegoat country can be had via several trails from Kleinschmidt Flats on the North Fork of the Blackfoot, as well as more remote trailheads at Indian Meadows near Lincoln and on the Rocky Mountain Front. From the south, supplies and information can be gathered at the town of Lincoln, while the town of Augusta serves a similar function for the eastern approaches to the Scapegoat. Administration of the area is divided fairly evenly between the Lolo, Lewis and Clark, and Helena national forests.

TRAIL 54 *HOBNAIL TOM TRAIL*

Trail 32
General description: A backpack from the North Fork Blackfoot trailhead to Dobrota Creek, 13.7 mi. (22.0 km).
Difficulty: Moderate.
Trail maintenance: Yearly.

Traffic: Heavy to North Fork Falls; light to moderate beyond.
Elevation gain: 1,530 ft.
Elevation loss: 200 ft.
Maximum elevation: 6,080 ft.
Topo maps: Lake Mountain, Olson Peak, Scapegoat Mountain.
Finding the trailhead: Take the gravel trunk road that runs north through Kleinschmidt Flats from Montana Highway 200, about 6 miles east of Ovando. Follow the signs for the North Fork trailhead, taking a right turn after 2 miles and then resuming a northward course 2 miles farther on. This road follows the North Fork of the Blackfoot into the mountains for 4 miles to reach the trailhead at the end of the road.

- 0.0 North Fork Blackfoot trailhead.
- 0.6 Junction with the Lake Creek Trail (61). Stay right.
- 2.4 Trail crosses the Scapegoat Wilderness boundary. Junction with the former footpath along the west bank of the river (364). Bear right.
- 3.2 Trail crosses a pack bridge over the North Fork of the Blackfoot.
- 3.2 Junction with the Bear Creek Trail (17). Stay left.
- 5.3 Junction with the Sourdough Flats Cutoff Trail (364). Stay right.
- 6.0 Pack bridge over the North Fork leading to the North Fork Cabin.
- 6.1 Junction with the Dry Fork Divide Trail (31). Turn right for the Hobnail Tom Trail.

TRAIL 54 *HOBNAIL TOM TRAIL*

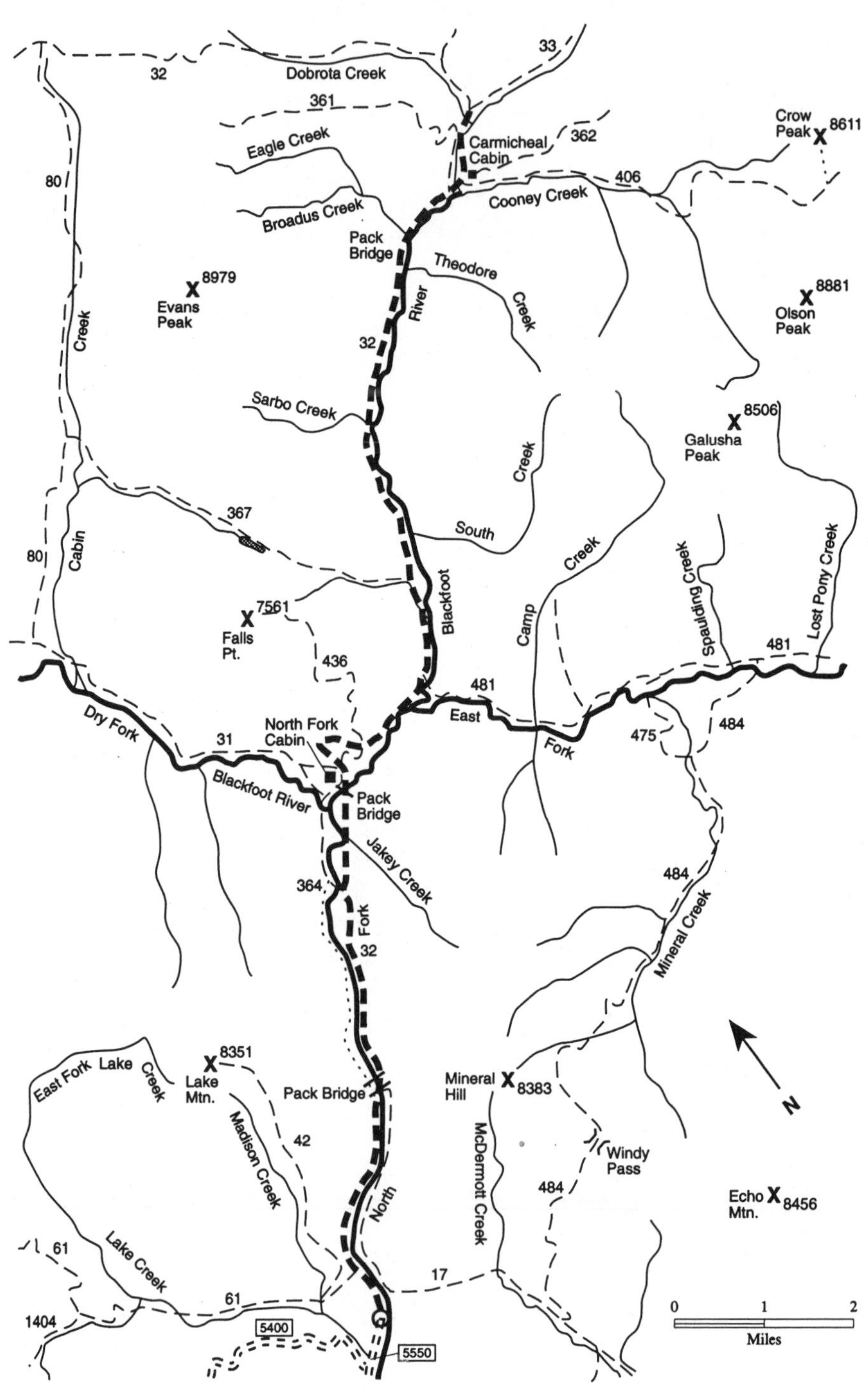

6.15 Steeper cutoff trail takes off to the right. Stay left for a gentler climb.
6.4 Cutoff trail rejoins the main trail.
6.5 Junction with the Falls Point Trail (436). Stay right.
6.6 North Fork Falls.
7.4 Junction with the East Fork Trail (481). Stay left.
10.2 Trail fords Sarbo Creek.
12.3 Bridge over Broadus Creek.
12.9 Junction with Trail 361. Turn right and ford the North Fork for the Hobnail Tom trail.
13.1 Carmichael Cabin. Junction with trails 406 and 362.
13.4 Trail fords the North Fork to return to the west bank.
13.6 Trail crosses Dobrota Creek.
13.7 Junction with the Flint Mountain Palisades (32) and Tobacco Valley (33) trails.

The trail: This trail follows the North Fork of the Blackfoot River to its headwaters deep in the Scapegoat Wilderness. It was named in honor of a longtime local guide who was a strong advocate for the preservation of the Scapegoat Wilderness. The entire North Fork valley burned in 1988, leaving only scattered patches of surviving trees. The fire opened up views from the trail, but the surrounding mountains are rather low and lack the scenic splendor of the ranges closer to the Continental Divide. Blackfoot Falls provides the only real attraction along the trail.

The trail begins by climbing onto the flat bluffs that border the west bank of the North Fork. As the route passes beneath Lake Mountain, travelers will note that large parts of the east-facing slopes were spared by the blaze, while the entire face of the hill across the river was razed by fire. As the fire spread from its origin in the Canyon Creek valley, it was blown eastward by strong, sustained winds. The blaze leapfrogged over the slopes that were on the lee sides of steep hills, and the surviving timber there has provided a seed source for the regeneration of the surrounding burn. Just before reaching the wilderness boundary, the trail passes across the river from The Big Slide, an enormous landslide that has erased the entire western slope of Mineral Hill. Upon reaching the boundary of the Scapegoat, the trail passes an old, abandoned hiker's trail that continues along the west bank of the river. The main trail descends to reach a pack bridge that spans the rushing waters.

On the far bank, the Hobnail Tom trail soon passes a junction with the Bear Creek Trail (17), then continues its northeasterly course for three miles along the riverbank. The trail passes a cutoff trail to a ford of the river (364), then crosses Jakey Creek before descending gradually to the next pack bridge over the river. On the far bank is the North Fork Cabin, with its numerous trail junctions. Just west of the cabin, the trail forks into the Dry Fork Trail (31) to the left and the Hobnail Tom trail to the right. Turning north, the path soon splits again; both trails reach the same point, but by different routes. The right-hand trail is steep and direct and follows the crest of the hill toward the Falls Point trail junction, while the left-hand trail swings westward on a much gentler ascent to the junction.

After passing its junction with the Falls Point Trail (436), the Hobnail Tom trail winds eastward around the hillside and passes far above North Fork Falls. A side

The narrow chasm containing the North Fork Falls.

trail descends to the lip of a steep gorge, and the foaming falls can only be partially glimpsed as they roar at the foot of this rocky chasm. In an amazing display of tenacity, full-grown trees grow from the tiniest chinks in the sheer rock walls and lean out over the swirling waters. Once beyond the falls, the main trail descends gradually to the level of the river, where it reaches an intersection with the East Fork Trail (481). The mountains beyond take on a gentler, more rounded aspect, and there are a few boggy spots in the trail. After crossing a nameless tributary, the trail begins an up-and-down passage across the rolling, burned bluffs to the west of the river.

After passing the steep canyon of Sarbo Creek, the trail settles into a steady, gentle ascent of the slopes above the river, and the muddy spots become much less frequent. Broadus Creek is the next tributary to be crossed, and it is spanned by a well-built bridge. The trail continues to climb the slopes beyond, but soon drops down onto the rocky flood plain of the river. In an open meadow, the trail reaches a signpost, which indicates a junction with a dead-end hunter's Trail (361). The sign is misleading, as it points north for the Hobnail Tom trail. In reality, travelers seeking the Hobnail Tom trail must turn east at this point, making a knee-deep ford of the river to reach the Carmichael Cabin. This cabin was built in the 1920s by a thriving sheep outfit that pastured its animals on the grassy summer range along the Continental Divide. There are several trails running east from the cabin (406 and 362); through traffic should turn north as the Hobnail Tom trail follows the east bank of the river.

After 0.25 mile of forest traveling, the trail reaches a second ford of the river. A knee-deep crossing leads to the other side, and a short distance farther north, the trail crosses Dobrota Creek to reach the end of this trek. At a junction on the far side of the creek, the Tobacco Valley trail turns eastward, while the Hobnail Tom trail turns west, following the cliffs of the Scapegoat Massif to reach the headwaters of the Dry Fork. This section of trail is discussed in detail under the heading, "The Flint Mountain Palisades."

TRAIL 55 *FLINT MOUNTAIN PALISADES*

Trail 32

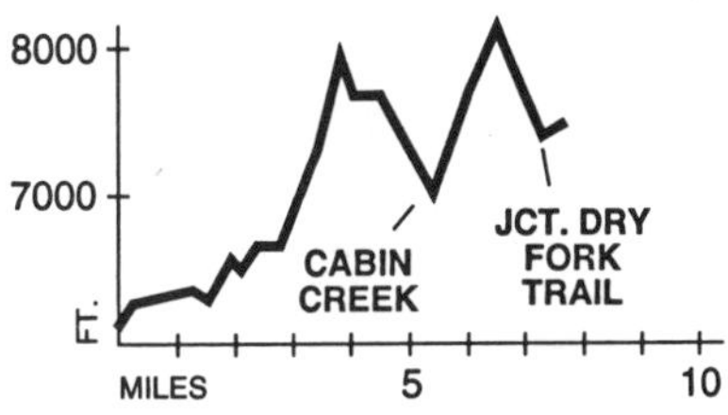

General description: A wilderness route from the North Fork of the Blackfoot to the headwaters of the Dry Fork, 7.6 mi. (12.2 km).

Difficulty: Strenuous.

Trail maintenance: Frequent to Cabin Creek; rare beyond.

Traffic: Light to Cabin Creek; very light beyond.

Elevation gain: 3,150 ft.

Elevation loss: 1,750 ft.

Maximum elevation: 8,120 ft.

Topo maps: Scapegoat Mountain, Flint Mountain.

Finding the trail: This trip begins on the north bank of Dobrota Creek, 13.7 miles up the Hobnail Tom Trail (54).

TRAIL 55 *FLINT MOUNTAIN PALISADES*

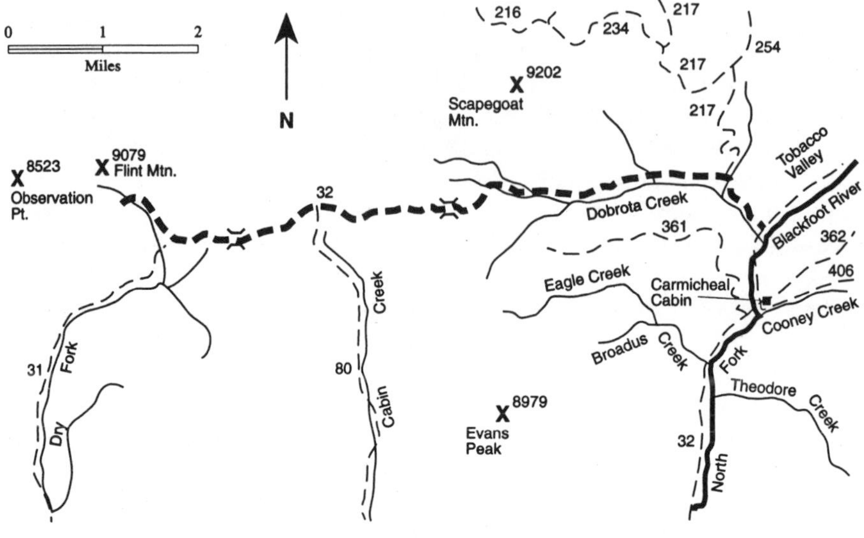

0.0 Junction of Tobacco Valley (33) and Hobnail Tom (32) trails. Turn west.
0.7 Junction with the Cave Creek Cutoff Trail (217). Turn left.
2.8 Trail crosses Dobrota Creek.
3.9 Trail crosses the divide into the Cabin Creek drainage.
5.5 Unmarked junction with the Cabin Creek Trail (80). Bear northwest.
6.6 Trail crosses the divide into the Dry Fork drainage.
7.3 Junction with the Dry Fork Trail (31). Bear right to complete the trip.
7.6 Trail peters out in the headwaters of the Dry Fork drainage.

The trail: This upper portion of the Hobnail Tom trail offers a rigorous route that follows the southern edge of the Scapegoat Massif beneath towering cliff walls. The trail can be found easily as far as Cabin Creek. However, the route from this point onward is poorly marked; expect to use a map and compass on the way into the Dry Fork drainage. Because of the difficulty in finding the trail between the Dry Fork and Cabin Creek, hiking this route from west to east is strongly discouraged. Mountain goats are occasionally seen among the cliffs above the trail, and elk may also be spotted in the headwaters of Cabin Creek.

From its beginnings along the North Fork of the Blackfoot, this trail climbs aggressively through charred snags, cresting a hillside with excellent views of the imposing cliffs that tower above the north rim of the valley. After passing through a copse of live timber, the trail passes a marked junction with Trail 217, which climbs over the Continental Divide and into the Cave Creek drainage beyond. The Flint Mountain Palisades trail runs northwest from this point, passing through several muddy spots as it enters a large tract of lodgepole pine savannah that survived the

Canyon Creek fire. The trail climbs and descends in steep spurts as it makes its way up the hummocky valley, and the gladed forest allows only teasing glimpses of the cliffs that loom to the north.

Nearing the head of the valley, the trail fords the main body of Dobrota Creek and climbs the ridgeline between it and a smaller tributary to the south. The trail becomes stony and washed out as the living trees give way to burned snags, and it ascends mercilessly toward the yellow, miter-shaped peak at the head of the valley. After a crossing of the southerly tributary, the ascent begins in earnest as the trail heads straight uphill at a killing pace. To the east, the summit of Scapegoat Mountain crowns massive walls, while smaller rock pinnacles loom ahead. The trail approaches the base of the yellow spire, then turns south and crosses a flat meadow. On the far side of the opening, the trail begins to climb once more to reach the top of a low hill on the divide between Dobrota and Cabin creeks. This desolate spot commands fine views of the palisades in both directions.

The trail drops into the saddle to the north, then descends steeply across a slope of loose pebbles that roll underfoot like so many ball bearings. Gaining more solid footing, the route runs west, rising and falling as it struggles to maintain its altitude. The trail crosses meadowy benches and steep slopes as it follows the foot of a massive bulwark of the Scapegoat plateau. Distant views to the west reveal the nameless cliffs and crags that crowd the head of the Cabin Creek valley. Upon reaching the west end of the outcrop, the trail descends through subalpine forest to reach the grassy meadow at the head of Cabin Creek. The main trail swings around to the southwest,

The south Palisades above the head of Cabin Creek.

becoming the Cabin Creek Trail (80). The very faint Flint Mountain Palisades route takes off northwestward from a blazed tree on the western edge of the meadows.

From this point on, the trail is devilishly hard to follow; if it disappears, head straight uphill to pick it up again. After passing through a copse of subalpine fir, the route works its way up a steep, boulder-strewn meadow. Look for cairns marking the route. The trail reaches the base of the cliffs and then turns west again, passing through several stands of whitebark pine. The route then crosses a wide, open slope, where springs and seeps are choked with a dense growth of alpine willow. The track climbs high to avoid the springs and makes its way up to the saddle at the base of the cliffs. Here, game trails radiate in all directions; the Palisades route runs straight down the couloir to the west, following blazed trees.

The trail soon jogs northward across the slope, making dangerous crossings of two steep ravines choked with loose debris. Follow the blazed trees as the trail passes into open forest, then loses itself in a grassy meadow. Stay high and the trail will become distinct again as it drops through the trees on the far side of the opening. The trail follows a spur ridge straight downhill for a time, then turns northward through the trees. The trail soon skirts the lower edge of an enormous boulder field that is overlooked by imposing cliffs. As the trail reaches its lowest point, a faint track diverges to the left. A sign identifies this path as the Dry Fork Trail (31). Travelers bound for this drainage should turn off here and look for blazed trees heading straight downhill through the timber; a more well-beaten path bends north again and soon rejoins the Palisades trail. The western tail of the Palisades trail continues to follow the high country for another mile, crossing through subalpine forests before rising into the sunlight of a flat, open meadow. The trail reaches a dead end in this opening, which guards the headwaters of the Dry Fork.

TRAIL 56 *DRY FORK DIVIDE*

Trail 31

General description: An extended trip from the North Fork Cabin to the Dry Fork Divide 8.2 mi. (13.2); to the Flint Mountain Palisades trail 14.5 mi. (23.3 km).
Difficulty: Moderate to the Dry Fork Divide; moderately strenuous beyond.
Trail maintenance: Yearly to Dry Fork Divide; occasional beyond.
Traffic: Heavy to the Dry Fork Divide; very light beyond.
Elevation gain: 520 ft. (to Dry Fork Divide); 2,175 (to end of trail).
Elevation loss: 345 ft. (to Dry Fork Divide); 480 ft. (to end of trail).
Maximum elevation: 5,420 ft. (Dry Fork Divide); 7,400 ft (end of trail).
Topo maps: Lake Mountain, Flint Mountain, Danaher Mountain.
Finding the trail: This trail begins at the North Fork cabin, 6 miles up the Hobnail Tom Trail (32).

- 0.0 North Fork Cabin. The trail to the Dry Fork Divide runs west.
- 0.1 Junction withe the Hobnail Tom Trail (32). Bear left.
- 2.0 Footpath that bypasses the fords of the Dry Fork takes off to the right. Hikers should bear right; stock parties should keep left.

TRAIL 56 *DRY FORK DIVIDE*

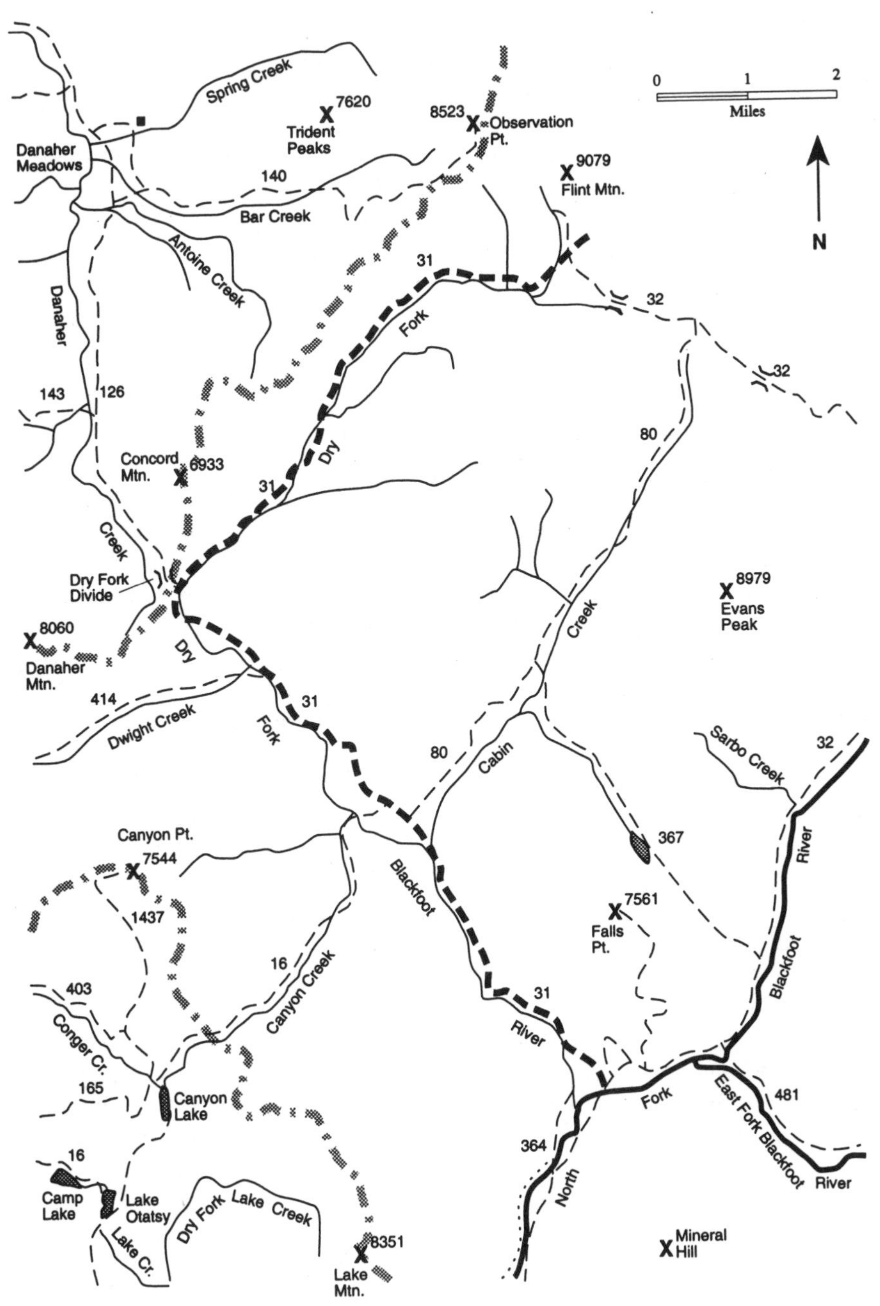

2.4 Footpath rejoins the main trail.
3.6 Trail fords Cabin Creek.
4.0 Junction with the Cabin Creek Trail (80). Keep going straight.
4.3 Junction with the Canyon Creek Trail (16). Bear right.
5.9 First junction with the Dwight Creek Trail (414). Bear right.
7.1 Second junction with the Dwight Creek trail.
7.8 Trail crosses the Dry Fork.
8.2 The Dry Fork Divide. Boundary with the Bob Marshall Wilderness. Straight ahead lies the Danaher Valley Trail (126). Turn right to continue up the Dry Fork.
8.7 Trail makes two fords of the Dry Fork in rapid succession.
10.2 Trail fords the Dry Fork to reach its south bank.
10.8 Trail returns to the north bank of the Dry Fork.
14.2 Trail crosses the headwaters of the Dry Fork.
14.5 Trail reaches the Flint Mountain Palisades Trail (32).

The trail: This popular trail follows the flat basin of the Dry Fork of the Blackfoot River. As the name suggests, this watercourse stops flowing and dries up during midsummer. The lower portion of the trail, running to the Dry Fork Divide, is well-traveled and provides the easiest access route into the Danaher Creek valley. The upper part of the trail is less frequently maintained and is not cleared at a sufficient width to allow the passage of pack stock. This track runs up to the headwaters of the Dry Fork, where it meets the Flint Mountain Palisades trail.

The trail begins from the North Fork Cabin, at a trail junction just west of this complex of buildings. It runs across burned flats for 0.5 mile, then is joined by a second trail that follows the banks of the Dry Fork. The valley narrows into a steep-walled canyon, dotted with sheer outcrops of red shale. As the valley bends around to the north, the bottomlands become a haven for living trees that survived the Canyon Creek fire. After the bend, the trail forks into a horse trail, which makes several fords of the Dry Fork as it continues along the bottoms; a narrow hiker trail climbs onto the steep hillsides to the north. After 0.5 mile, these trails join together again, and the route threads its way through the tall grasses of the valley floor.

The trail crosses a nameless tributary before bending into the Cabin Creek valley. After a few hundred yards, the trail turns west to rock-hop across the eastern channel of Cabin Creek, then makes a knee-deep crossing of the main channel. This ford can be avoided by crossing logjams upstream of the trail. After the crossing, the trail climbs a sinuous ridge of alluvial material to reach the flat top of a high bluff above the Dry Fork valley. From amid the charred wreckage of the burned forest, the rosy summit of Mount Evans can be seen to the northeast, while the Dry Fork lazily meanders through grassy meadows and thickets of willow below. Expect muddy going as the route passes a junction with the Cabin Creek Trail (80) and continues northwest across the burned plateau. A short distance farther on is the junction with the Canyon Creek Trail (16), which splits off on a southwesterly route. After another 0.5 mile of level traveling, the trail descends into the scorched valley of an unnamed tributary, which it follows back to the Dry Fork bottoms.

As the trail follows the Dry Fork through grassy openings, the burned hulks of dead snags are interspersed with stands of living trees. Shortly after passing the junction with the Dwight Creek trail, it enters the entirely unburned country that surrounds the upper meadows of the Dry Fork. The trail hugs the hillside as it passes the edge of this broad, willow-choked opening. Looking back down the valley, Mineral Hill and Falls Point can be clearly seen in the distance. At the far side of the meadows, the trail makes an ankle-deep crossing of the Dry Fork, then runs northwest through lodgepole pine and grassy glades to reach the Dry Fork Divide. Here, beneath the watchful countenance of Danaher Mountain, a signpost marks the junction with the Danaher Valley Trail (126), while the upper Dry Fork trail turns northeast.

The Upper Dry Fork Option. This trail is maintained especially for hikers, which means that the trees surrounding the trail have not been cleared away to provide a sufficient width for the passage of fully laden pack animals. From the Dry Fork Divide, the trail runs northeast through open meadows bordered by lodgepole pine and occasional clumps of aspen. After 0.5 mile, there are two fords of the stream at a spot where it has been dammed by beavers; these crossings are above knee-depth, and it might be worth bushwhacking the hundred yards or so along the west bank of the stream to avoid them altogether. The trail then runs inland, through lodgepole pine and grassy meadows. After climbing up a sidehill, the trail reaches a multi-colored silt bog at the crossing of a small stream. Thereafter, the trail runs out onto the flat, grassy bluffs above the valley bottoms, and the surrounding hills can be viewed to full advantage.

The trail stays high above the stream for almost a mile before returning to the valley floor for an ankle-deep ford among the silent spruce of the bottomlands. The trail then makes its way up the eastern slope beyond, passing through a dry forest of lodgepole pine on its way around an impassable cutbank that runs down to the stream. After crossing the dry bed of a feeder stream, the trail drops down to ford the creek again. The valley soon narrows, and the bottomland forest of spruce is dotted with vest-pocket meadows for the next several miles. As the valley bends to the east, the trail begins to ascend steadily away from the valley floor. After crossing a high meadow, the trail descends sharply to ford a stream at the confluence of two branches. The final 0.25 mile to the Flint Mountain Palisades Trail (32) is straight uphill and quite difficult to follow. Look for blazed trees as the route follows the edge of a steep avalanche slope.

TRAIL 57 *EAST FORK OF THE BLACKFOOT*

Trail 481
General description: An extended trip from the North Fork of the Blackfoot to the Webb Lake Cabin, 10.1 mi. (16.3 km).
Difficulty: Moderate.
Trail maintenance: Yearly.
Traffic: Moderate.

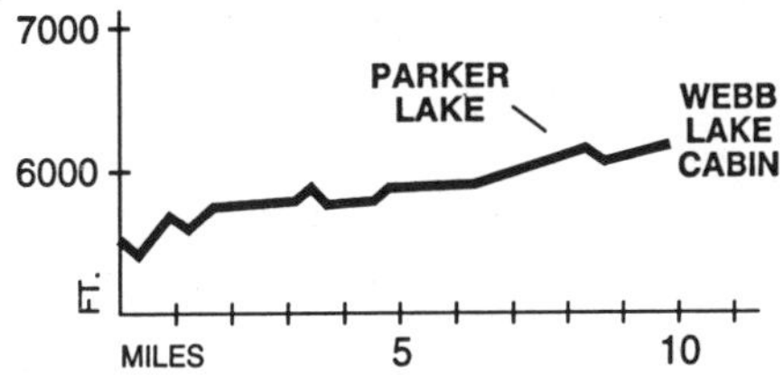

Elevation gain: 950 ft.
Elevation loss: 260 ft.
Maximum elevation: 6,150 ft.
Topo maps: Lake Mountain, Olson Peak, Heart Lake.
Finding the trail: This trail begins at a marked junction 7.4 miles up the Hobnail Tom Trail (32).

0.0 Junction of the Hobnail Tom and East Fork trails.
0.1 Trail fords the North Fork of the Blackfoot.
1.3 Trail crosses Camp Creek.
1.7 Unmarked junction with an outfitters' trail to Camp Creek. Stay right.
2.3 Junction with the cutoff trail to Mineral Creek (475). Stay left.
3.9 Junction with the main Mineral Creek Trail (484). Stay left.
4.7 Trail crosses Lost Pony Creek.
4.8 Unmarked junction with the Meadow Creek Cutoff Trail (480). Bear left.
4.82 Junction with the trail to Twin Lakes (426). Keep going straight.
6.4 Twin Lakes trail returns to the East Fork trail.
6.8 Junction with the Meadow Creek Trail (483). Stay left.
7.0 Junction with the trail ascending the Sourdough Creek valley (427).
7.9 Foot of Parker Lake.
8.5 Junction with the Landers Fork Trail (479). Keep going straight.
10.1 Webb Lake Cabin.

Parker Lake.

The trail: This valley-bottom route, also known as the "Mainline" trail, connects the North Fork of the Blackfoot with the Indian Meadows area. This valley was burned in the Canyon Creek fire, but substantial patches of timber were spared, creating a mosaic pattern on the landscape. The burned patches will be less susceptible to fire in the future and will serve as natural fire brakes to prevent the expansion of fire into the catastrophic proportions seen in 1988. The East Fork trail is very popular with elk hunters and outfitters in the fall, but receives a much lower level of use during the summer.

From its beginnings at the junction with the Hobnail Tom Trail (32), the East Fork trail runs southeast, crossing the North Fork at a knee-deep ford. The trail quickly climbs onto the bluff that separates the two branches of the river, where it turns eastward through burned country. The trail crosses a grassy slope dotted with sagebrush, then enters a severely burned spot, where the old snags have been thrown down and scattered across the slopes like giant toothpicks. A vigorous growth of lodgepole saplings carpets the burn, which will soon return to dense forest. Look back to the west to see the unburned forests of Falls Point that contrast pleasantly with the tawny meadows near its summit. The trail descends into the East Fork bottoms to cross Camp Creek, then climbs back onto the burned bluffs above the river. The scorched helm of Mineral Hill rises across the valley as the East Fork trail is joined by an unmarked outfitter's trail that runs uphill toward a spike camp high in the Camp Creek valley.

Patches of surviving trees interrupt the desolation of the burn here, and the trail soon wanders into a broad stand of surviving timber. Scorch marks at the bases of the trees reveal that this stand was subjected to a low-intensity ground fire, which cleared out the underbrush but failed to kill the mature trees. The trail passes a junction with the Mineral Creek Trail (484), then continues to rise and fall as it crosses the rolling hills. The forest is soon reduced once again to burned snags, and the trail crosses Spaulding Creek on its slow descent to the valley floor. Here it meets the eastern cutoff to the Mineral Creek trail, then crosses the valley floor amid the stark skeletons of the former forest. The valley bottoms make for level traveling, but are often pocked with mud pits in wet weather.

After crossing Lost Pony Creek, a small stream that wanders aimlessly beneath the snags, the trail passes an unmarked junction with the western cutoff for the Meadow Creek Trail (483). Just beyond it is the trail to Twin Lakes (425), which lie half a mile north of the East Fork trail. The trail continues across the flats, passing a second trail to the Twin Lakes before climbing the burned hillside to the north of the valley. The trail soon passes the eastern branch of the Meadow Creek trail, and soon crosses Scotty Creek. Look up the narrow cleft carved by Sourdough Creek across the valley to see the looming mass of Red Mountain that rises above the surrounding hills. As the trail climbs steadily, it passes a charred sign for the Sourdough Creek Trail (427), which has not been maintained since the fire.

After crossing another small stream, the trail enters the unburned forest that borders Parker Lake. This shallow, mud-bottomed lake harbors a few cutthroat trout, and provides an idyllic spot for quiet contemplation. Camping is not permitted on either of the wooded peninsulas that extend into the lake. Passing the wet meadows above the head of the lake, the trail begins to climb gently across burned hillsides.

TRAIL57 *EAST FORK OF THE BLACKFOOT*

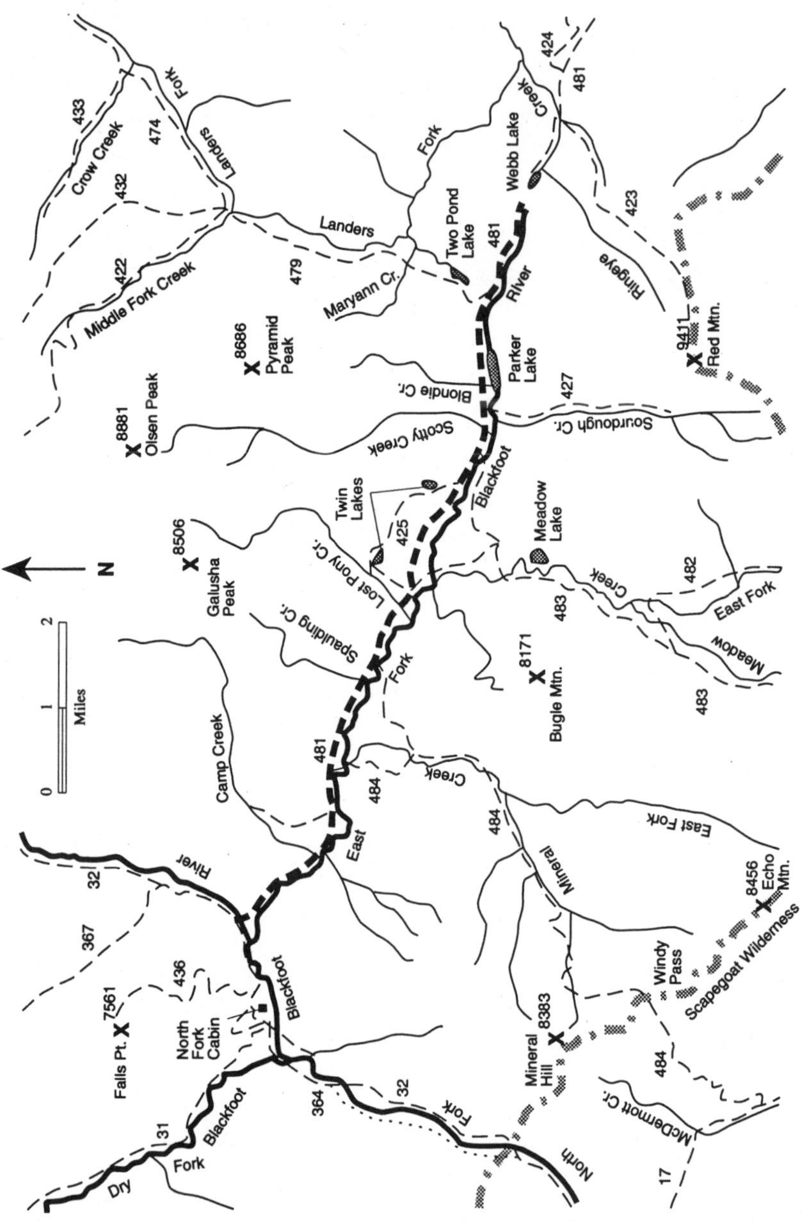

It passes a trail that runs north into the Landers Fork valley (479), then follows a sinuous marshy meadow that bears the headwaters of the East Fork. The trail enters a forest of lodgepole pine just before reaching the Webb Lake Cabin, which marks the end of the trek. The trail continues eastward to reach Indian Meadows, and this part of the route is discussed under "Webb Lake."

TRAIL 58 *MEADOW CREEK*

Trail 483

General description: A backpack from the Dry Creek trailhead to the East Fork of the Blackfoot, 12.9 mi. (20.8 km).

Difficulty: Strenuous (South to North), moderately strenuous (North to South).

Trail maintenance: Yearly.

Traffic: Light to Alpine Park; moderate beyond.

Elevation gain: 3,002 ft.

Elevation loss: 1,492 ft.

Maximum elevation: 6,700 ft.

Topo maps: Coopers Lake, Arrastra Mountain, Olson Peak.

Finding the trailhead: Take the gravel trunk road that runs north through Kleinschmidt Flats from Montana Highway 200, about 6 miles east of Ovando. Follow the signs for the "Dry Creek trail 483." After the road crosses Dry Creek and enters the foothills, a sign marks the spur road to the Dry Creek trailhead.

0.0 Dry Creek trailhead.
0.1 Pack bridge over Dry Creek.
1.0 Trail leaves old logging road and begins to climb aggressively.
5.1 Trail crosses the divide into the Meadow Creek valley. Boundary of the Scapegoat Wilderness.
8.1 Alpine Park.
9.0 Junction with the Arrastra Creek trail. Stay left for the East Fork of the Blackfoot.
10.9 Trail fords Meadow Creek and turns southeast for a short time.
11.2 Junction with the trails (480, 483) to the East Fork Trail (481).
12.8 Trail fords the East Fork of the Blackfoot.
12.9 Junction with the East Fork Trail.

The trail: The Meadow Creek trail provides an alternate route to reach the East Fork of the Blackfoot River. The trail features a long, hard climb over the steep outer ranges of the Scapegoat to reach the headwaters of Meadow Creek. For this reason, it is recommended as a route out of the wilderness, but is a tough haul as an entrance route. However, this trail description will cover the trail from south to north as it runs into the Scapegoat Wilderness. This trail is less heavily used than the nearby Arrastra Creek Trail (482), although it does receive a fair amount of traffic during the fall hunting season.

From the trailhead, the trail makes its way through an old clearcut and then drops

Wet meadows and beaver ponds near Meadow Lake.

into the dark forest of the Dry Creek bottoms. The trail crosses this creek by means of a rickety pack bridge and continues up the north bank of the stream in the form of an overgrown logging road. After 0.5 mile of steady climbing, the trail leaves the road at an old signpost and climbs into the sparse forest of Douglas-fir to the north. The trail reaches the top of an outlying knob after a vigorous ascent of several miles, then turns west through a bit of a low spot to reach the base of Daly Peak. Another long climb awaits, through patches of subalpine fir and more old Douglas-fir. Look for blue grouse along the trail; these birds lead a mostly flightless existence on the forest floor, feeding on pine nuts and other vegetable matter. A few openings in the forest allow distant views of the tawny spread of Kleinschmidt Flats and the Blackfoot Valley to the south.

The trail reaches a high point as it rounds the hillside and turns northeast into the headwaters of Dry Creek. It then descends across a series of wooded shelves defined by the tilted strata of bedrock that rises through the forest floor. Upon reaching the bottom of the grade, the trail runs level across gladed benchlands, crossing several small streams as it passes beneath vast slopes of loose rock. Reaching Dry Creek itself, the trail crosses the stream and follows its course northward to reach a tiny pond. The trail crosses the head of the pond and turns northwest, climbing steadily through a scattering of subalpine fir to reach the pass into Meadow Creek. At this high saddle, closed in by a loose subalpine forest, the trail enters the Scapegoat Wilderness.

TRAIL 58 *MEADOW CREEK*

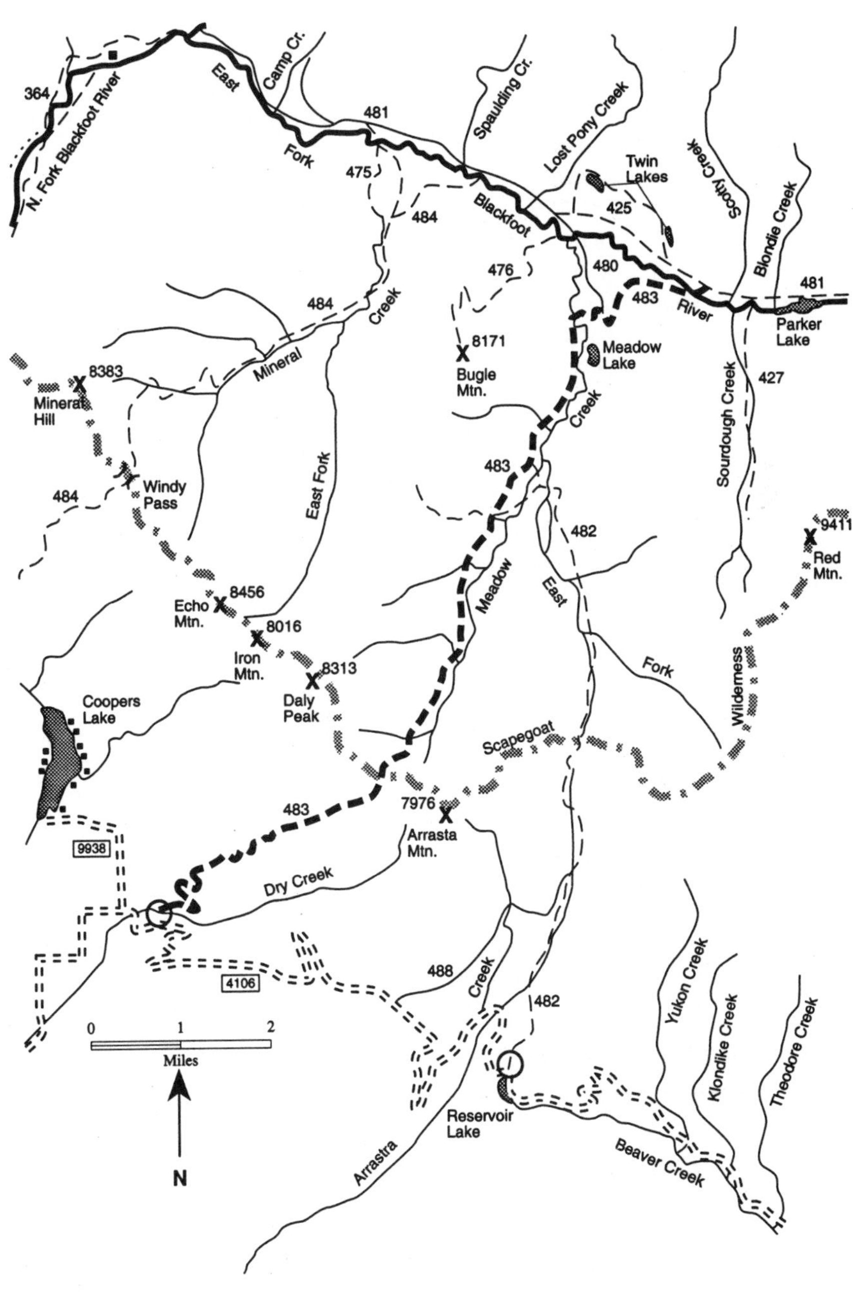

The trail sticks to the west wall of the valley as it descends into the Meadow Creek drainage. After crossing a substantial tributary stream, the grade steepens as the trail drops toward a wide, grassy glade on the valley floor. From this meadow, Arrastra Mountain rises to the south, while wooded hillsides slope away on either side of the valley. After crossing the opening, the trail returns to the depths of the subalpine forest, working its way further inland as it crosses several very small woodland glades. A mile and a half below the upper meadow, the trail passes through the upper fringes of Alpine Park, a gladed meadow dotted with beargrass clumps that stretches downhill to the banks of Meadow Creek. After crossing another tributary stream, the trail reaches an unmarked cutoff trail that connects with the Arrastra Creek Trail (482). The main trail sticks to the high ground, passing through several wide avalanche slopes where lodgepole pine saplings are beginning to make a comeback. The trail then drops steeply to the valley floor, where it reaches the marked intersection with the Arrastra Creek trail.

This junction sits at the western edge of a wide meadow that encompasses the entire valley floor and offers fine views of the summits surrounding Red Mountain. The trail follows the edge of the meadow northward until the trees begin to close in from the west. The route then runs inland through the forest before emerging at a similar but much smaller meadow. Here, the trail splits; the left fork is the more direct (and official) route, while the right fork continues to wander along the edge of the meadow. The two paths converge again at the southern edge of the final meadow, with Meadow Lake lying among the marsh grasses along its eastern edge. The trail sticks to the trees that line the western edge of the opening, finally reaching a ford of Meadow Creek just beyond the northern edge of the opening. The water is knee-deep and sluggish; a much shallower crossing can be made just downstream from the ford.

Once across the creek, the trail doglegs southwest, heading for an outfitter's camp on the shores of Meadow Lake. Westbound travelers should take the first marked trail (480) that takes off to the left toward a junction with the East Fork Trail (481). Travelers heading east must take the next marked trail (283), which turns north and soon enters the burned valley of the East Fork. This trail climbs over some low hills before dropping into the bottomlands of the East Fork. After a shallow crossing of this stream, the trail climbs gently to reach its junction with the East Fork trail.

TRAIL 59 *WEBB LAKE*

Trail 481, 424

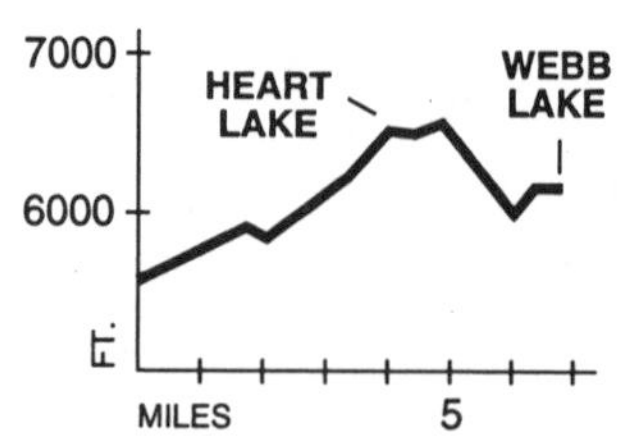

General description: A backpack from the Indian Meadows trailhead to the Webb Lake Cabin, 6.9 mi (11.1 km), or day hike to Heart Lake, 4.1 mi. (6.6 km).
Difficulty: Moderate.
Trail maintenance: Yearly.
Traffic: Heavy.
Elevation gain: 962 ft.

TRAIL 59 *WEBB LAKE*

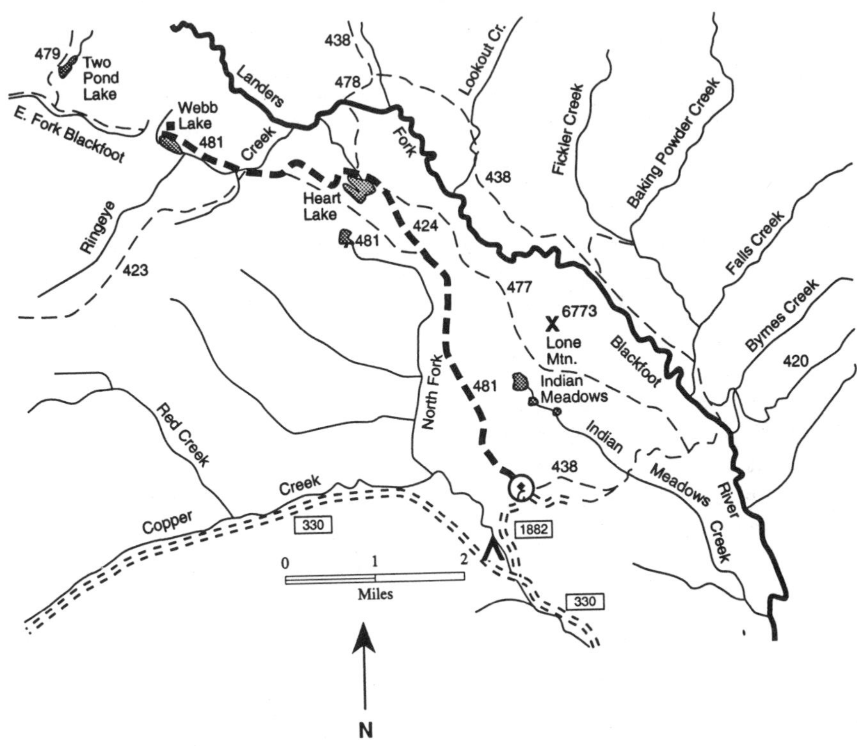

Elevation loss: 410 ft.
Maximum elevation: 6,480 ft.
Topo maps: Heart Lake, Stonewall Mountain, Silver King Mountain.
Finding the trailhead: From Montana Highway 200 take the Copper Creek road (330) for about 11 miles to reach the Indian Meadows trailhead.

- 0.0 Indian Meadows trailhead.
- 2.2 Junction with the Heart Lake Cutoff Trail (424). Bear right to visit Heart Lake.
- 4.1 Foot of Heart Lake.
- 4.2 Junction with the Lone Mountain Trail (477). Keep going straight.
- 4.4 Junction with the Landers Fork Cutoff Trail (478). Stay left.
- 4.7 Trail leaves Heart Lake.
- 4.9 Trail rejoins the Mainline Trail (481). Turn right for Webb Lake.
- 6.1 Footbridge over Ringeye Creek.
- 6.7 Webb Lake.
- 6.9 Webb Lake Cabin.

The trail: This trail offers a taste of what the Scapegoat Wilderness looked like before the Canyon Creek fire of 1988. It features quiet woodland traveling rather than the grandeur of striking mountain scenery. This trail also connects with the East Fork of the Blackfoot Trail (481), providing the most direct access to this drainage.

This trail begins by running northwest, past the pocket-sized meadows in the Indian Meadows vicinity. The trail soon climbs onto a series of low, rolling ridges, and Douglas-fir dominates the rather open overstory. Two and a half miles beyond the trailhead, the trail splits into two forks: The left fork is a more direct outfitter's trail, while the right fork reaches the same destination via a slightly longer route that visits the shoreline of Heart Lake. This latter route is the more popular of the two and is discussed in this text.

This trail continues up the ridgeline, then follows the crest of the hill to reach the eastern shore of Heart Lake. As the trail runs atop the steep bluff overlooking the water, it is joined by the Lone Mountain Trail (477). The bald dome of Red Mountain provides a scenic backdrop for the lake. Its green depths harbor the rather rare arctic grayling. This distant relative of the trout family sports an enormous lobe-shaped dorsal fin, covered with colorful spots. Its iridescent scales send off shimmering blues and violets when struck by the sunlight. The grayling was once more widespread in its range, but is now limited to a few pristine mountain lakes in remote parts of the state. The trail descends to a level spot on the lakeshore, where it meets the Landers Fork Cutoff Trail (478). The main trail continues straight ahead, through a heavily-trampled camping spot complete with a hitchrail, then rounds the western side of the lake. After running southward for a short distance, the trail makes a sharp hairpin to the northwest and descends to the bottom of the bluff.

After a brief westerly trek through a spruce forest, the Heart Lake spur rejoins the outfitter's cutoff, and together they chart a westerly course through a damp forest dotted with marshy openings. The trail soon begins a steady descent, passing the Red Mountain Trail (423) on its way down. At the bottom of the grade, the trail crosses Ringeye Creek via a footlog with a crudely fashioned handrail, then climbs up the south slope of the hill beyond it. The trail passes across meadowy slopes dotted with lodgepole pine and juniper bushes, and Red Mountain can be seen to the south. The trail climbs steadily to reach Webb Lake, which has a shallow water level that is maintained by the activities of dam-building beavers. The head of the lake is bordered by a brushy little meadow. Just beyond it lies the Webb Lake Cabin with its rail fence, which marks the end of this trek. The trail continues westward over an imperceptible divide to enter the valley of the East Fork of the Blackfoot and is discussed in a separate section.

TRAIL 60 *DEVILS GLEN*

Trail 206

General description: A day hike from the Dearborn River trailhead to Devils Glen, 3.5 mi. (5.6 km); to Blacktail trail junction, 6.3 mi. (10.1 km).

Difficulty: Moderate.

Trail maintenance: Yearly.

Traffic: Moderate.

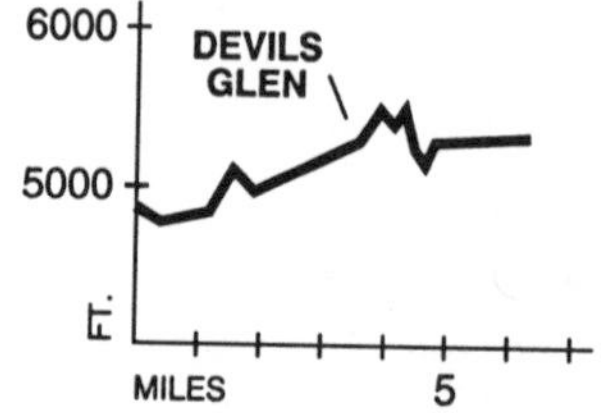

TRAIL 60 *DEVILS GLEN*

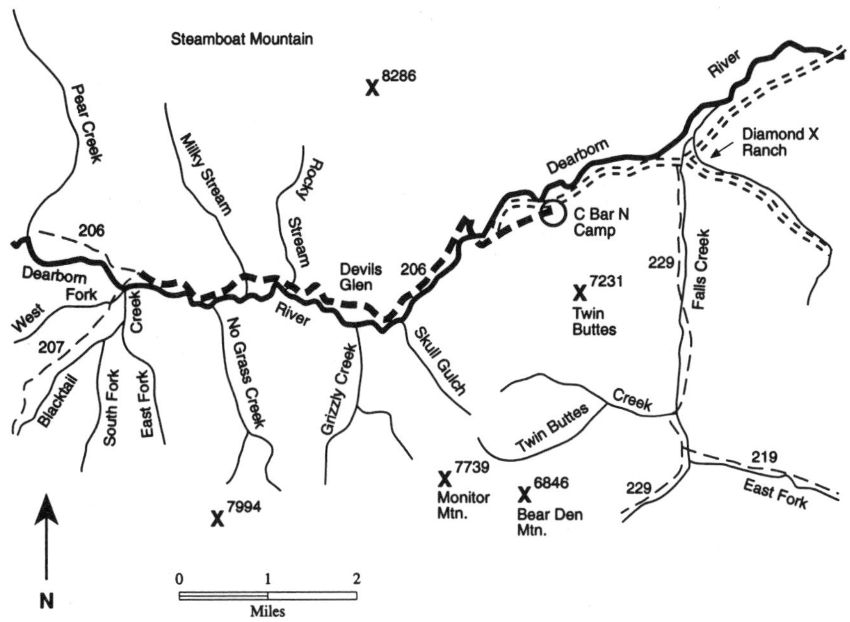

Elevation gain: 940 ft.
Elevation loss: 460 ft.
Maximum elevation: 5,450 ft.
Topo map: Steamboat Mountain.
Finding the trailhead: From County Road 434, take the Dearborn River Road, marked by signs for the Dearborn River Forest Access and Bean Lake. This road runs west, past the Diamond X Ranch and the C-Bar-N Camp to reach the trailhead at the end of the road.

- 0.0 Dearborn River trailhead.
- 1.2 Pack bridge over the Dearborn River.
- 3.5 Devils Glen.
- 4.3 Trail crosses Rocky Stream.
- 4.8 Trail fords Milky Stream.
- 5.6 Trail enters the Bob Marshall Wilderness.
- 6.3 Junction with the Blacktail Creek Trail (207).

The trail: This trail provides a moderate day hike through the Dearborn River Canyon, and also serves as one of the primary entrances to the eastern side of the Scapegoat Wilderness. The trail follows a closed gravel road through private land for the first mile. Travelers are asked to stay strictly on the trail as it crosses private land in order to ensure that this access corridor will remain open in the future. After crossing the Dearborn River via a pack bridge, the trail climbs uphill, beneath the rocky brow of Steamboat Mountain. Across the river, the tilted cliffs of the Twin Buttes have been laid bare by the erosive force of the river. Reaching a high point, the trail turns southwest, crossing the forest boundary as it works its way across the sparsely wooded slopes overlooking the river.

The trail soon descends back to the bottomlands, where it enters a grassy park. This meadow borders a low, rocky canyon that bears the swirling eddies and rushing flumes of the river. The forest soon closes in, but not before the narrow rift of Skull Gulch reveals the hidden summit of Monitor Mountain across the valley. As the valley makes a bend to the west, an enormous slab of cream-colored limestone rises to a sharp point above the north side of the valley. Soon, the open forest gives way to the wasteland of fractured rock that is Devils Glen. As the trail winds among piles of debris, patches of vegetation arise from pockets of soil amid the blasted rock. Thick mats of kinnickinnick, an evergreen shrub, grow among the scatterings of juniper bushes. Occasional spikes of wooly mullen rise in spots where the soil is well-formed. Aspen and Douglas-fir have also colonized this barren spot, dotting the gray waste with patches of green.

As the trail leaves Devils Glen, it crosses a steep slope of loose scree and talus. This loose rock runs all the way down to the edge of the river, which is bordered here by an overhanging cliff on the far side. As the trail enters the forest, it passes above a quiet gorge, where emerald pools and lazy runs swirl among limestone walls and grottoes. The trail crosses a charming rill, which flows across rocky shelves and

A nameless mountain above the head of No Grass Creek.

into mossy pools. Soon afterward, the trail makes a rather tricky crossing of the foaming channels of Rocky Stream. A quarter mile farther, the trail wanders out onto the wide gravel outwash of Milky Stream and then climbs into the riverside meadows beyond.

The trail wanders on through a sunlit forest of lodgepole pine and aspen, finally drawing abreast of the incoming valley of No Grass Creek. Look up this valley to see a massive and nameless peak that rises far to the south. The trail splits into a number of channels at this point. The uppermost fork is the Dearborn River trail, while the left-hand branches descend to a dead-end at the riverside. The main trail climbs gradually uphill, then stays high above the river as it dips northward into the ravine of an incoming tributary. On the far side of this draw, the trail reaches the Scapegoat Wilderness boundary. It then continues westward through a lodgepole pine savannah for the final 0.5 mile to the Blacktail Trail (207) junction.

TRAIL 61 *STEAMBOAT LOOKOUT*

Trail 205, 239

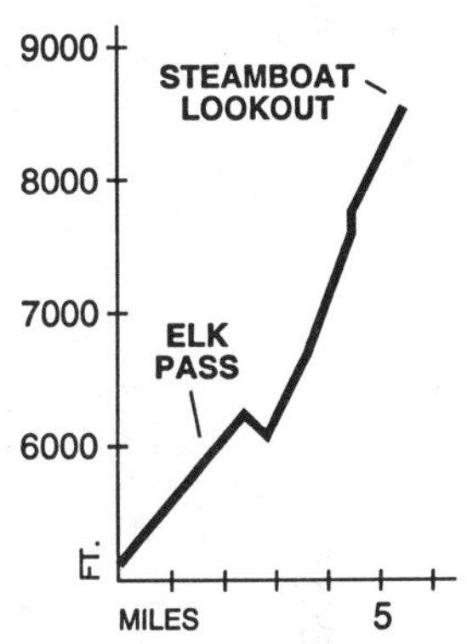

General description: A day hike from the Elk Creek trailhead to the former site of Steamboat Lookout, 5.4 mi. (8.7 km).

Difficulty: Moderately strenuous.

Trail maintenance: Yearly to Steamboat Lookout trail; frequent beyond.

Traffic: Light to Steamboat Lookout trail; very light beyond.

Elevation gain: 3,580 ft.

Elevation loss: 135 ft.

Maximum elevation: 8,565 ft.

Topo maps: Steamboat Mountain, Jakie Creek.

Finding the trailhead: From County Road 434, 6 miles south of Augusta, take the Elk Creek Road, which begins south of the creek. This road runs westward for 9 miles, then crosses through a parcel of private property to dogleg north for 2 miles to reach the trailhead. This improved gravel road is quite slippery when wet and will remind the driver that the term "improved" is, by nature, relative.

0.0 Elk Creek trailhead.
1.8 Elk Pass. Junction with the Smith Creek Trail (215). Turn left.
2.8 Trail crosses Sixmile Creek.
3.6 Junction with the Steamboat Lookout Trail (239). Turn left.
4.5 Trail reaches the ridgeline of Steamboat Mountain.
5.4 Former site of Steamboat Lookout.

The trail: This trail provides an accessible route to a former fire lookout site atop Steamboat Mountain, which commands sweeping views of the eastern side of the Scapegoat Wilderness. Follow the Elk Pass trail westward from the trailhead, across grassy slopes above the north bank of Elk Creek. To the south, the many spires of

TRAIL 61 *STEAMBOAT LOOKOUT*

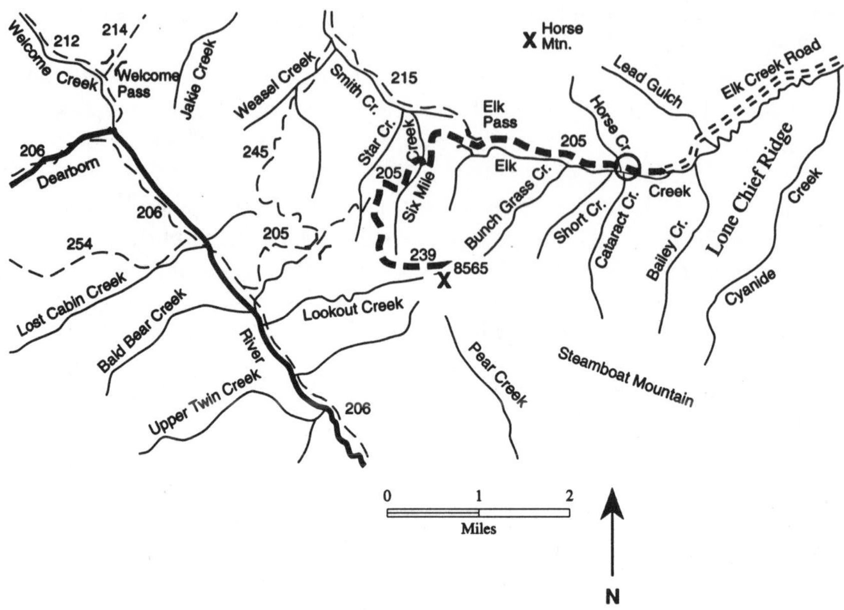

Steamboat Mountain rise above a verdant forest of unburned timber. The trail climbs gently into a flat basin, where it crosses a small feeder creek. The trail then begins to climb vigorously across hillsides burned in the 1988 Canyon Creek fire, finally reaching the low saddle of Elk Pass. At the pass, the trail forks. The right fork descends into the Smith Creek valley, while the trail to Steamboat Lookout turns southwest and continues to climb.

The trail passes above a shallow pond as it continues its ascent, then bends south into the drainage of Sixmile Creek. As it does so, the path begins to descend for a time, crossing burned slopes that allow views of the Crown Mountain massif to the northwest. As it nears Sixmile Creek, the trail resumes it ascent and crosses the two forks of the creek in a brief westward jog. The trail then ascends for a time beside the bank of the westernmost fork of the stream. After a short distance, the trail climbs steeply up the hillside to the west and ascends across a wide, grassy clearing. Upon reaching the top of this meadow, the trail reaches a marked junction with the Steamboat Lookout Trail (238).

Turn left here and follow the rather faint trail southward as it ascends across the western slope of the hillside. As the pitch of the slope steepens, the trail becomes more apparent, and openings in the burned timber permit ever-expanding views of Crown Mountain. After a series of switchbacks that take the trail to the ridgeline, the path turns onto the east face of the ridge, beneath the towering countenance of a northern face of Steamboat Mountain. The trail continues to zigzag up this slope, crossing patches of unburned timber on its way back to the ridge line. This point offers the first view of the Scapegoat Massif, a formidable fortress of sheer cliff wall that looms to the west. The trail then turns southeast again, crossing steep slopes with scattered patches of subalpine fir. The trail works its way up to a high, rocky col, and for the first time, travelers will get the sense that they have reached the top of the mountain.

There is plenty of climbing left to do from this point, as the trail runs across the bare bedrock of the mountain's southwestern slope. A few windblown subalpine fir and whitebark pine grow from fissures in the bedrock, and sweeping views to the west are dominated by the folded domes of Crow Peak to the southwest and the cliffs of Scapegoat Mountain farther north. As the trail approaches the next saddle on the ridgeline, the grade lessens measurably, and the trail uses occasional switchbacks to gain altitude. The trail reaches a flat pass below the summit of the peak, and sweeping views of the high plains can be had to the east. The trail then zigzags steeply up the northwest face of the next point to reach the old lookout site atop it. The lookout site commands broad vistas of the entire Scapegoat Wilderness, and a few peaks west of the Continental Divide can even be seen.

TRAIL 62 *WELCOME PASS*

Trail 215, 214

General description: A backpack from the Smith Creek trailhead to the Straight Creek Trail, 6.1 mi. (9.8 km).

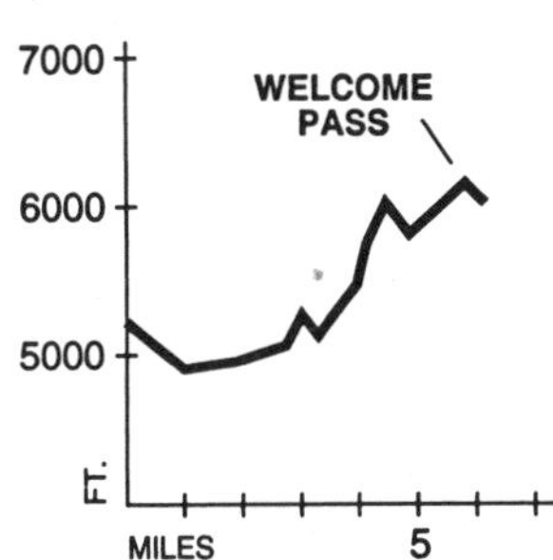

Difficulty: Moderately strenuous.

Trail maintenance: Frequent.

Traffic: Moderate.

Elevation gain: 1,850 ft.

Elevation loss: 1,053 ft.

Maximum elevation: 6,130 ft.

Topo maps: Jakie Creek, Double Falls.

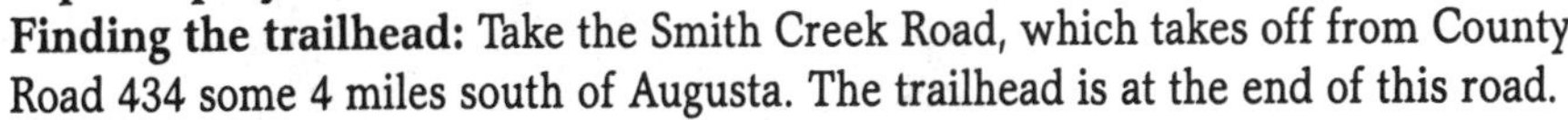

Finding the trailhead: Take the Smith Creek Road, which takes off from County Road 434 some 4 miles south of Augusta. The trailhead is at the end of this road.

0.0 Smith Creek trailhead.
1.0 Trail leaves road and fords Smith Creek. The Petty-Ford Trail (244) runs to the north.
1.4 Trail returns to the south bank of Smith Creek.
2.2 Falls on Smith Creek. Trail fords the creek to reach the north bank.
2.4 Junction with the Moudess Creek Trail (238). Bear left.
2.5 Fourth ford of Smith Creek.
2.8 The Smith Creek Trail (215) turns uphill; keep going straight on the Jakie Creek Trail (214).
3.2 Trail fords Smith and Jakie Creeks in rapid succession.
5.6 Trail crosses the headwaters of Moudess Creek.
5.9 Welcome Pass. Trail enters the Scapegoat Wilderness.
6.1 Trail reaches a junction with the Straight Creek Trail (212).

TRAIL 62 *WELCOME PASS*

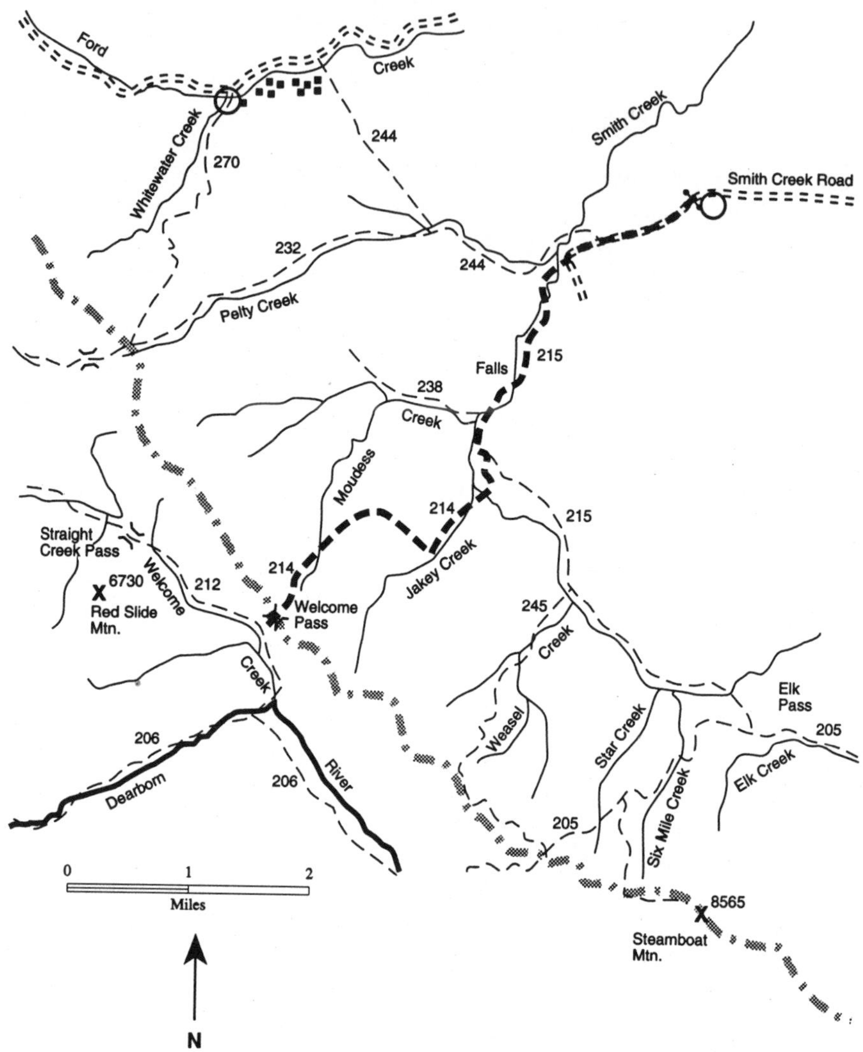

The trail: This trail offers one of the fastest and easiest passages through the Front Ranges to reach the rugged inner peaks of the Scapegoat Wilderness. From the end of the Smith Creek Road, follow a rather new logging road southward, up the Smith Creek valley. After about a mile, the road swings close to Smith Creek at a point near its confluence with Petty Creek. At this point, take the Smith Creek Trail (215), which departs from the road and makes a knee-deep ford of Smith Creek before continuing up the valley. The trail stays in the valley bottom for a short distance, then crosses the creek again and climbs onto the high, grassy hilltop overlooking the east bank of the stream. This meadow allows excellent views of the surrounding foothills, as well as the low peaks at the head of the valley.

Meadows of Smith Creek near the Lewis and Clark National Forest boundary.

The trail passes the forest boundary and continues along the east bank of the stream for almost a mile before reaching a scenic waterfall. The trail makes yet another ford of Smith Creek above the falls, then climbs onto the bluff on the far side of the steam to reach a junction with the rather faint Moudess Creek Trail (238). It then drops back down to the streamside for another crossing of Smith Creek. As the valley bends to the southeast, the Smith Creek trail takes off uphill, while the Welcome Pass Trail (214) continues to follow Smith Creek. The trail then descends for a final set of fords: first down the much-diminished Smith Creek, followed quickly by ankle-deep Jakie Creek.

This trail plots a southwesterly course, climbing through a series of bottomland meadows along the banks of Jakie Creek. After half a mile, the trail climbs out of the creek bottoms and begins a rather steep, zigzagging climb up the hillside to the west. Fire-scarred snags stand naked on the hillsides as the trail reaches the crest of the hill and turns west across gently rolling country. The rocky buttes of the Front Range rise straight ahead. The trail soon crosses a flat hilltop and drops into the scorched upper basin of Moudess Creek. It follows this small stream southwest, climbing steadily up the valley toward Welcome Pass. The trail makes a final brisk climb before passing between low, rugged cliffs and entering the grassy saddle of the pass. This point marks the boundary of the Scapegoat Wilderness; from here, the trail descends gradually for a few hundred yards to reach its terminus at a junction with the Straight Creek Trail (212).

TRAIL 63 *CROWN MOUNTAIN*

Trail 270, 232

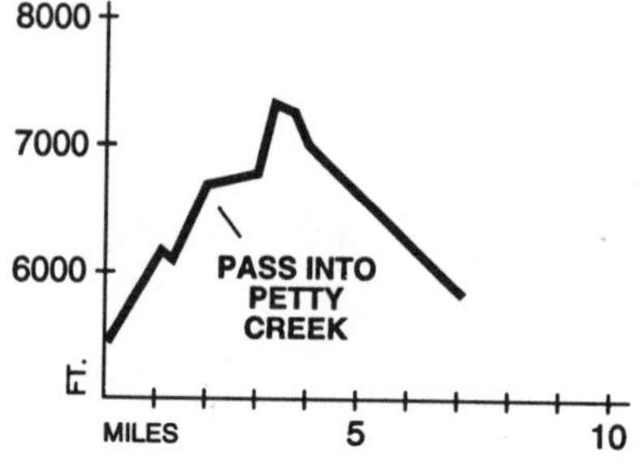

General description: A day hike from the trailhead to the wilderness boundary, 3.4 mi. (5.5 km); or backpack to the Straight Creek trail, 7.2 mi. (11.6 km).
Difficulty: Moderately strenuous.
Trail maintenance: Yearly.
Traffic: Light.
Elevation gain: 1,930 ft.
Elevation loss: 1,490 ft.
Maximum elevation: 7,310 ft.
Topo maps: Double Falls, Wood Lake, Scapegoat Mountain.
Finding the trailhead: From County Road 434 in the south part of the town of Augusta, take the Benchmark Road. This road runs west past Nilan Reservoir to a junction with the Willow Creek Road. Turn left here, continuing toward Benchmark for 5 miles to the sign for the Crown Mountain trail. An unimproved dirt road crosses Ford Creek to reach the trailhead on the bank of Whitewater Creek. The trailhead is marked by small wooden signs and only has parking space for one vehicle.

0.0 Crown Mountain trailhead.
1.8 Trail crosses the divide into the Petty Creek drainage.
3.0 Junction with the Petty-Crown Trail (232). Turn right.
3.4 Trail crosses pass into the Crown Creek drainage and enters the Scapegoat Wilderness.
4.6 Trail makes two fords of Crown Creek.
5.0 Trail fords Crown Creek to reach its south bank.
5.4 Trail returns to the north bank of Crown Creek.
6.0 Fifth ford of Crown Creek.
6.9 Trail makes two more fords of Crown Creek.
7.2 Trail reaches a junction with the Straight Creek Trail (212).

The trail: Without a doubt, this trail offers the most scenic route into the Scapegoat Wilderness. The trail begins on the eastern bank of aptly-named Whitewater Creek, and climbs inland through a loose forest of lodgepole pine as it runs southward. Openings in the trees allow spectacular views of Crown Mountain, which dominates the rugged reefs of the Front Range. The path approaches the creek bottom once more before climbing steadily into the pass that separates the Whitewater and Petty Creek drainages. After crossing this low divide, the trail turns southwest and ascends moderately along the south-facing slope of a spur ridge. The open forest here allows fantastic views of Haystack Butte, which rises like a painted obelisk above the grassy swells of the high plains.

As the trail nears the head of the Petty Creek valley, the sheer rock walls of Crown Mountain and its nameless southern counterpart soar skyward on either side. As the trail approaches timberline, it reaches a junction with the Petty-Crown Trail (232), which rises up from the valley below. Turn right as the trail climbs above timberline into an open bowl flanked with towering walls of stone. After a vigorous ascent, the trail reaches a high pass. Westward views are blocked by the masses of rock that loom to either side of the pass and provide a playground for mountain goats. After passing through an alpine depression, the trail reaches a second saddle and descends into the Crown Creek valley.

The trail drops quickly into wooded ravines, following the watercourse straight downhill. Views are limited as the trail climbs onto the slope to the north of the stream and runs northwest. After descending into a flat-bottomed valley, the trail makes several crossings of the shallow creek, finally climbing onto the south bank to resume its westward progress. Occasional openings in the forest show off a rather stunning set of rust-colored cliffs that rise above the northern side of the valley. The forest then closes in, as the trail makes two more pairs of deeper crossings of Crown Creek. The second set of fords traverses a gravel floodplain, where cairns mark the rather faint path. Immediately after making the final crossing to reach the south bank of the stream, the trail turns west across the valley bottom to reach its terminus at the Straight Creek Trail (212).

TRAIL 63 *CROWN MOUNTAIN*

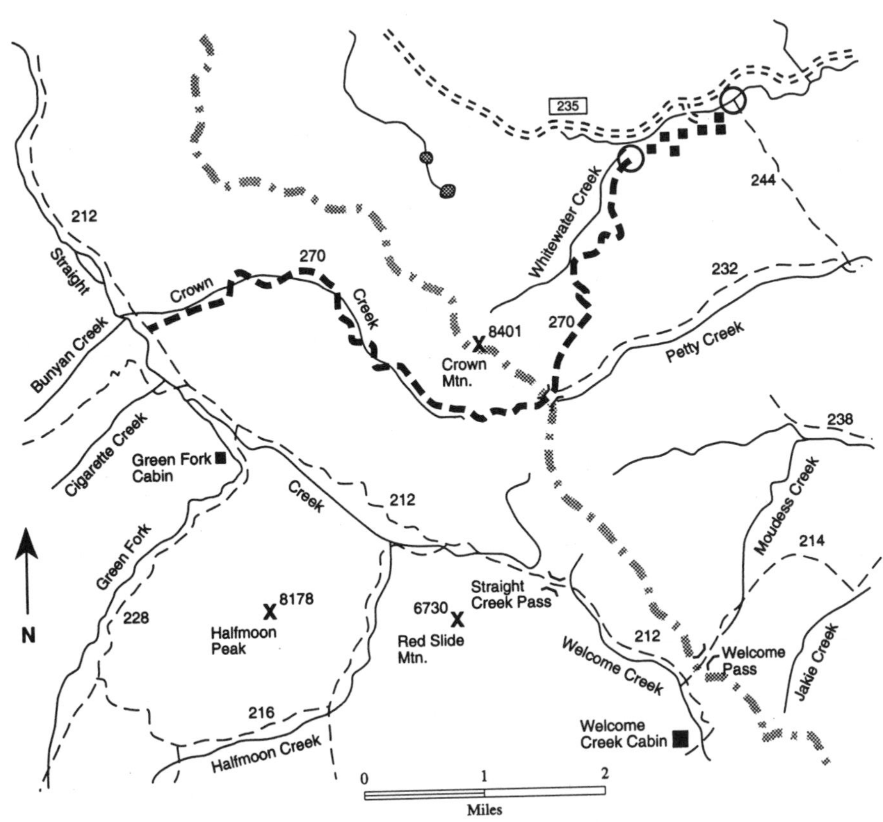

TRAIL 64 *SCAPEGOAT MOUNTAIN*

Trail 228, 270, 216, 234, 217, 206

General description: An extended trip from the Green Fork Cabin to the Welcome Creek Cabin, 11.9 mi. (19.2 km).

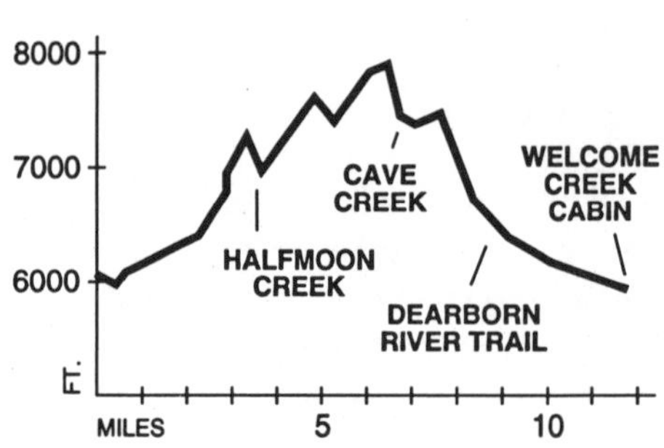

Difficulty: Moderately strenuous.

Trail maintenance: Yearly.

Traffic: Light to Halfmoon Creek; moderate beyond.

Elevation gain: 2,380 ft.

Elevation loss: 2,550 ft.

Maximum elevation: 7,820 ft.

Topo maps: Scapegoat Mountain, Jakie Creek.

Finding the trail: This trail begins at the Green Fork junction on the Straight Creek Trail (212), 1.5 miles southeast of Crown Creek.

- 0.0 Junction of the Straight Creek and Green Fork trails.
- 0.1 Trail fords Straight Creek.
- 0.2 Spur trail to the Green Fork Cabin.
- 2.4 Junction with the Green Fork Cutoff Trail (270). Turn left.
- 3.3 Trail crosses the divide into the Halfmoon Creek drainage.
- 3.6 Junction with the Halfmoon Creek Trail (216). Turn right.
- 3.7 Trail crosses Halfmoon Creek.
- 4.8 Trail crosses the divide into the Dearborn River drainage.
- 4.9 Junction with the Dearborn River Trail (206). Turn right to continue the journey.
- 6.1 Trail crosses the divide into the Cave Creek drainage.
- 6.8 Junction with the Cave Creek Trail (217). Turn left and begin descending.
- 8.8 Junction with the Dearborn River Trail (206). Turn right for the Welcome Creek Cabin.
- 10.1 First ford of the Dearborn River to reach its north bank.
- 11.2 Trail makes two crossings of the river.
- 11.6 Trail returns to the south bank of the Dearborn.
- 11.8 Junction with the Straight Creek Trail (212). Turn left.
- 11.9 Final ford of the Dearborn River to reach the Welcome Creek Cabin.

The trail: This trail is the showpiece of the Scapegoat Wilderness and travels the alpine fields that sit at the foot of the Scapegoat plateau's towering walls. Wildlife is abundant along this route. Elk and mule deer summer among the subalpine fir of the high basins, and mountain goats are at home on the stony walls of Scapegoat Mountain. Marmots and pikas can often be spotted among the loose boulders below the cliffs. Tread with care on the alpine meadows near Scapegoat, as they are easily damaged by off-trail wanderings. There are a number of connecting trails that also provide access to this high route, and these are discussed briefly at the end of the chapter.

From the Straight Creek Trail (212) take the Green Fork Trail (228) westward to begin the journey. This trail runs southeast for a short distance before dropping to the valley floor for a calf-deep ford of Straight Creek. On the far bank, the trail passes several spur trails running to the Green Fork Cabin, which is hidden away in the forest to the north of the trail. The trail passes beneath the foot of Halfmoon Peak as it runs through a forest of young lodgepole pine. The trail follows the south bank of the Green Fork, passing through a burned spot on the creekside that allows views of the stern cliffs that loom to the northwest. The trail then climbs back into the living forest for a short stretch and begins to climb at a moderate pace.

The trail soon enters a second and much larger burn, which represents but a small finger of the great Canyon Creek fire of 1988. The trail works its way across these open slopes for 0.5 mile before reaching a trail junction that overlooks an emerald pond. The Green Fork trail continues westward from this point, finally reaching a dead end near the head of the valley. Travelers bound for Scapegoat Mountain should turn left onto the Green Fork Cutoff Trail (270). Across the valley, a waterfall shoots outward from a hole in the sheer cliff; this unique falls can be viewed from the trail junction as well as from points farther up the cutoff trail.

The path to Scapegoat Mountain makes a series of lengthy switchbacks as it climbs across the steep, burned hillside. To the southwest, the sheer cliffs of a fingerlike promontory jut out toward the trail. After a vigorous climb, the trail enters a series of rolling hills that mark the divide between the Green Fork and Halfmoon Creek. Climbing gently, the trail enters a section of unburned forest, then switchbacks its way up to the divide. From here, a short, meadowy descent leads to a junction with the Halfmoon Creek Trail (216), on the lower edge of Halfmoon Park. Turn right here,

TRAIL 64 *SCAPEGOAT MOUNTAIN*

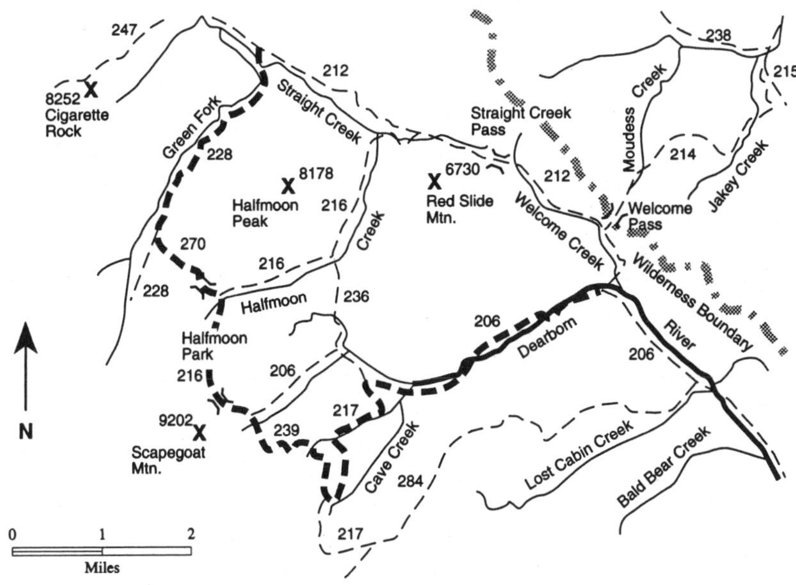

following the Halfmoon Creek trail.

This route crosses Halfmoon Creek, a beaver pond, and assorted mudholes before climbing onto drier ground. The towering cliffs that surround the valley form a natural amphitheater, with the summit of Scapegoat Mountain crowning its northern edge. The trail climbs steadily across what used to be subalpine parkland, but has been transformed by fire into a flowery slope dotted with dwarfed snags. After reaching a high saddle at the foot of the cliffs, the trail turns southward to descend into the next drainage. The path passes a small kettle pond, which was created when a glacier buried a large block of ice in the midst of its debris. The ice later melted to form the depression that bears the pond. After a brief and moderate descent through alpine tundra, the trail reaches a junction with the end of the Dearborn River Trail (206).

Turn right at this junction onto a trail that is now officially known as the Scapegoat Mountain Trail (234). The trail climbs and falls, passing across broken terrain dotted with enormous blocks of stone that have fallen from the cliffs above. Like Halfmoon Park, the head of this basin is also bordered by towering walls of stone. It is interesting to note that the cliffs lining the southern rim of the basin appear to be a different kind of rock from the rest of the formation. In fact, this rock formation is identical with the rock to the west, appearing different only because the formation is viewed from the side rather than head-on. A third of a mile farther on, the trail reaches a junction with the old Dearborn River trail. Stay right, on a trail now known as the Cave Creek Cutoff Trail (234).

This trail climbs gently into a grove of mature subalpine fir, then switchbacks upward to the scree slopes above. The trail then turns east, climbing gently as it crosses the scree, revealing the most stunning views of Scapegoat Mountain of the entire route. After rounding a windswept knob, the trail stays high above the headwaters of a small stream, cresting a low saddle to descend into the valley of Cave Creek. This creek derives its name from the several deep caves that penetrate the cliffs at the head of the valley. These caves have been the subject of several Geological Survey expeditions, but have never been completely explored. From the headwaters of Cave Creek, the summits surrounding Olson Peak can be seen above the spur ridge to the south, and far to the east rise the many summits of Steamboat Mountain.

The trail then descends to the valley floor, where it reaches a junction with the Cave Creek trail. Straight ahead, a trail (217) climbs to the top of Amphitheater Ridge, while travelers bound for the Welcome Creek Cabin should take the Cave Creek trail (217), which descends to the left. This trail works its way northeast through burned timber, descending gently around a spur ridge and then dropping into the narrow valley beyond. The trail crosses the small creek at its bottom, then descends eastward along the far bank as the stream drops away more steeply to the right. The trail arrives at a grassy point on the end of the ridge, yielding unobstructed views of the blunt summit of Red Slide Mountain as well as the scorched valley of the Dearborn River. The trail the drops back toward the creek before turning northward for a long, steady descent to reach the Dearborn River Trail (206).

At this junction, turn right for the Welcome Creek Cabin, following a well-worn trail through the rocky meadows that border the western bank of the Dearborn. After following the valley as it bends to the east, the trail fords the rather shallow beginnings of the Dearborn River, then climbs up onto the bluffs overlooking the north bank of the stream. As the trail makes its way up and down across the bluffs, it passes above a complex of beaver ponds fed by the diverted waters of the Dearborn River. The forest of lodgepole that once covered the area in an unbroken blanket has been reduced to a stark graveyard of charred snags. Look for clusters of cones near the tops of the burned trees. These cones open in response to the high heat of forest fires, and re-seed the burn with lodgepole. Sure enough, the forest floor is carpeted with young lodgepole seedlings. Thus, from the ashes of death rise the next generation of trees, and the old forest renews itself in a younger and more vigorous form. After following the north bank of the river for 0.5 mile, the trail crosses the stream at a calf-deep ford and runs along the far bank to reach a trail junction. To the right, the Dearborn River trail climbs the hillside on its way south, while the left fork is the Straight Creek Trail (212), which fords the river once more to reach the Welcome Creek Cabin.

TRAIL 65 *CIGARETTE ROCK*

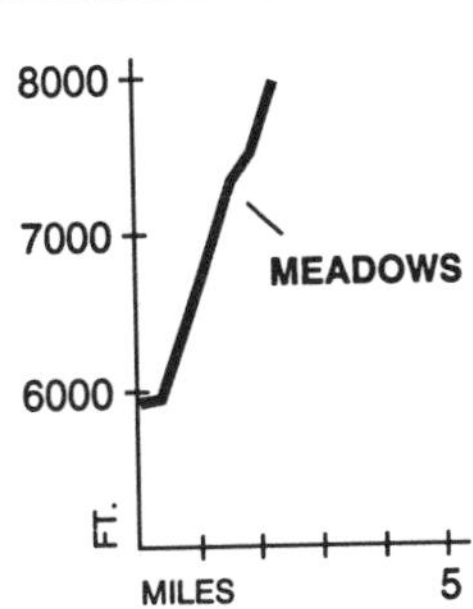

Trail 247
General description: A spur trip from the Straight Creek trail to the Sun River divide, 2.4 mi. (3.9 km).
Difficulty: Moderately strenuous.
Trail maintenance: Frequent.
Traffic: Light.
Elevation gain: 2,080 ft.
Elevation loss: 90 ft.
Maximum elevation: 7,940 ft.
Topo maps: Scapegoat Mountain, Wood Lake.
Finding the trail: This trail begins at the Cigarette Creek Trail junction on the Straight Creek Trail (212), 0.7 miles southeast of Crown Creek.

- 0.0 Junction of the Straight Creek and Cigarette Creek trails.
- 0.1 Trail fords Straight Creek.
- 0.2 Trail crosses Cigarette Creek and begins to climb.
- 1.7 Trail enters Cigarette Meadows.
- 1.9 Trail leaves the upper end of the meadows and runs westward.
- 2.4 Trail reaches the saddle behind Cigarette Rock.

The trail: This trail provides a side trip for travelers in the upper valley of Straight Creek. It climbs across the high, open meadows below Cigarette Rock, then continues westward to a pass into the basin of South Fork of the Sun River. From this pass, a scramble up rocky slopes leads to the top of Cigarette Rock, which boasts excellent views of the surrounding country.

From the Straight Creek trail, the Cigarette Rock trail drops onto a meadowy floodplain, then runs northwest for several hundred yards to reach a knee-deep ford of Straight Creek. After meandering a short distance through a bottomland forest of spruce, the trail crosses tiny Cigarette Creek and begins a shallow climb up the north-facing valley wall. The pitch of the trail becomes steeper as it switchbacks upward and enters a section of the Canyon Creek burn. Halfmoon Peak can be seen to the south through the scattered snags. Upon cresting the ridge, the trail runs along the flat ridgetop before resuming its upward progress through the burn. The cliffs that rise to the north are not part of Crown Mountain, but southern extensions of the Wood Creek Hogback.

The trail soon reaches a burned knob, then drops into the saddle beyond before ascending into a broad expanse of meadow that occupies the ridgeline. This meadow offers outstanding views of Halfmoon Peak, and the summit of Scapegoat Mountain can be seen above the ridges to the south. Cigarette Rock becomes visible for the first time, looming above the meadow to the west. The trail snakes its way up the ridgeline, following scattered cairns. A connecting trail that runs north to Elbow Pass departs from this meadow, but is extremely difficult to find and is probably not worth looking for.

Leaving the upper end of the meadow, the Cigarette Rock trail climbs steeply through the forest, then turns west across the northern slope of the hill as it passes through a forest of subalpine fir. Occasional breaks in the forest canopy allow views of the low, massive strata of Bunyan Peak to the north. As the trail approaches the head of the valley, it climbs steadily into the wooded pass behind Cigarette Rock. From this saddle, Cigarette Rock can be climbed rather easily by scrambling eastward up the ridgeline. The summit of the rock offers outstanding views, featuring Scapegoat Mountain to the south and Crown Mountain to the east.

Gently inclined rock strata form Bunyan Point.

TRAIL 65 *CIGARETTE ROCK*

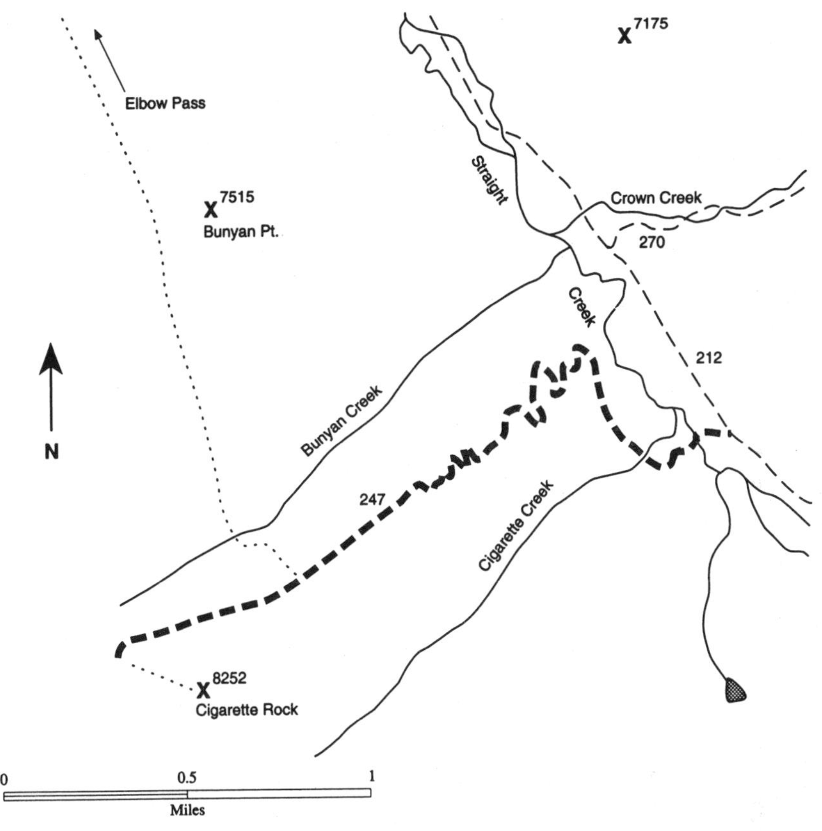

ADDITIONAL TRAILS

Dwight Creek (414), Canyon Creek (16), and **Cabin Creek (80)** trails receive frequent maintenance but little traffic.

Trail 367 between Cabin Creek and the North Fork has not been maintained in years and exists only as a wilderness route.

Trail 361 and **362** access ridgetop grazing near the Carmichael Cabin and are maintained occasionally.

Windy Pass Trail (484) is a frequently maintained trail that crosses a rather desolate pass and follows Mineral Creek to a junction with the **East Fork Trail (481).**

Bugle Mountain Trail (476) is rarely maintained and is quite hard to find.

Sourdough Creek Trail (427) is swampy, heavily burned, and receives infrequent maintenance.

Arrastra Creek Trail (482) provides an alternate route to the Meadow Creek valley. It is heavily used by hunters during the fall. Access **Trail 488** runs from an outfitter's camp to join it.

Red Mountain Trail (423) makes a steep ascent to the summit of the tallest peak in the wilderness complex. Grizzly bears make heavy use of this area during early summer in their quest for biscuitroots.

Lone Mountain (477) and **Bighorn Creek (438)** trails receive little use but are well-maintained.

Landers Fork-Blacktail Trail (479, 207) is a well maintained and level route through heavily burned country.

Crow Creek (433) and **Crow Mountain (432)** trails are not maintained frequently and may be hard to find. No trail exists between Crow Peak and **Trail 422.**

Cooney-Middle Fork Trail (406, 422) receives little use but is maintained regularly on the east side. It is steep and rough on the west side and can be hard to find in the high elevations near the pass.

Landers Fork Cutoff Trail (478) is muddy and has lots of switchbacks.

Silver King Lookout Trail (420) is a well-maintained path that runs to a manned lookout tower.

Continental Divide Trail (440) follows high ridgetops with good views, but is entirely devoid of water. It also accesses Bighorn Lake.

Falls Creek Trail (229) does not have official public access across private land as yet, but travelers are generally allowed to cross. This area was heavily burned and may have lots of blowdowns.

Dearborn River Trail (206) is a main access trail and receives fairly heavy use.

Carmichael Basin Trail (235) is a dead-end hunter access trail.

Tobacco Valley Trail (33, 218) is lightly used and is heavily burned west of the divide.

Trail 254 is hard to find and has heavy blowdown from the fire.

Elk Pass Trail (205) is a primary access route to the Dearborn River trail. It is maintained annually.

Straight Creek Trail (212) is a flat, valley-bottom trail that is a primary access route for horse parties originating at Benchmark.

Petty-Ford Creek Trail (244) is a cattle drive trail that connects Smith Creek with Ford Creek, allowing loop trips using the Crown Mountain and Welcome Pass trails.

Petty-Crown Trail (232) is lightly used between Smith Creek and Crown Mountain, and moderately traveled beyond. See "Crown Mountain."

Elbow Pass Trail (248) is in good shape and allows a long day trip for horse parties connecting the Straight Creek and South Fork Sun River trails. A trail linking Elbow Pass to Cigarette Rock does not exist.

SUN RIVER BASIN

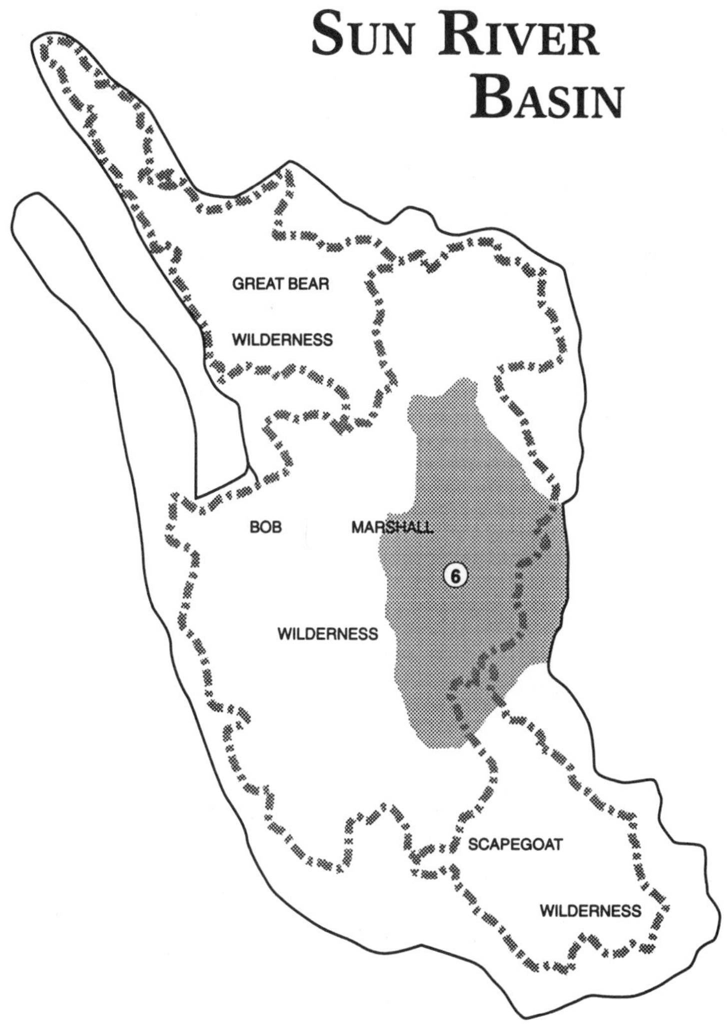

The broad, flat basin of the Sun River extends north and south for forty-five miles, separating the jagged reefs of the Front Range from the sheer walls of the Continental Divide. The northern end of the basin was once carpeted with a continuous forest of lodgepole pine, but the Gates Park fire of 1988 razed all but isolated pockets of the forest north of Rock Creek. Farther south, where the North and South forks join, the basin is typified by large, grassy meadows bordered by lodgepole pine and aspen. The western edge of the basin features such scenic wonders as the Pearl Basin, the Chinese Wall, and the North Wall. Prairie Reef and Beartop Mountains each boast lookout sites that command spectacular views of the Sun River basin and the mountains surrounding it.

The Sun River Game Range encompasses the land between the two forks of the Sun River and the Continental Divide. This area is an important summer range for elk and deer, and hunting in this area is prohibited. Large herds of elk can sometimes be spotted in the alpine meadows along the North Wall during early summer; later on they move to lower elevations as the alpine meadows dry up. Grizzly bears are abundant in the Sun River drainage and have developed a knack for raiding camps where food is in easy reach. Mountain lions also make their home on the dry slopes and wooded valley bottoms of this area. These big cats are quite shy and are rarely seen, but travelers may come across their tracks or kill sites.

The best routes into the basin are via the Benchmark trailhead in the south or over Headquarters or Route Creek passes to the north (see The Sawtooth Range). The route along Gibson Reservoir is narrow and tricky and is not recommended. The towns of Choteau and Augusta both provide goods and services required by travelers, as well as USDA Forest Service information centers.

TRAIL 66 *WEST FORK OF THE SUN*

Trail 202, 203

6000
FT.
BRIDGE OVER WENT FORK
INDIAN POINT MEADOWS
MILES
5
10

General description: A backpack from Benchmark to Indian Point Meadows, 10.5 mi. (16.9 km).
Difficulty: Moderate.
Trail maintenance: Yearly.
Traffic: Heavy.
Elevation gain: 679 ft.
Elevation loss: 539 ft.
Maximum elevation: 5,420 ft.
Topo maps: Benchmark, Pretty Prairies, Prairie Reef.
Finding the trailhead: From Augusta take the Benchmark Road westward. At the junction with the Willow Creek road turn left and follow the road as it enters the mountains and bends north. The trail begins at the South Fork Sun River trailhead, beyond the airfield and at the end of the road.

0.0 South Fork Sun River trailhead.
0.2 Pack bridge over the South Fork of the Sun River.
0.25 Junction with the South Fork Sun River Trail. Bear right for the West Fork.
0.7 Trail crosses Burned Creek.
1.5 Trail fords Deer Creek.
3.6 Unmarked junction with the Bighead Creek Trail (242). Bear left.
4.9 Pack bridge over the West Fork of the Sun River.
5.1 Junction of the South (202) and West (203) Fork Sun River trails. Turn left.
9.1 Trail crosses Reef Creek.
9.6 Junction with the Prairie Reef Lookout Trail (224). Keep going straight for Indian Point Meadows.
10.5 Trail enters Indian Point Meadows.

TRAIL 66 *WEST FORK OF THE SUN*

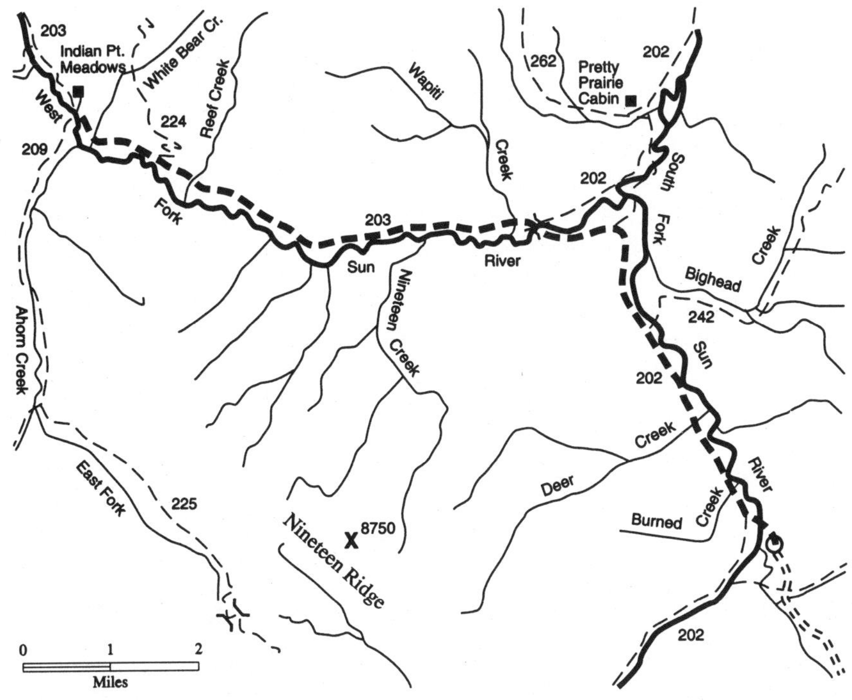

10.6 Junction with the Pearl Basin-Camp Creek Pass Trail (209).
10.9 Indian Point Cabin.

The trail: This route begins at the Benchmark entry point, the most heavily used access point for the Bob Marshall Wilderness. It follows the heavily-traveled Sun River Trail (202) for the first several miles, then turns west along the less frequently traveled West Fork of the Sun. This latter portion of the route offers scenic delights of its own, as well as providing an important access route to travelers bound for the Chinese Wall, the Pearl Basin, and White River Pass.

From the South Fork trailhead, follow the trail northward to a pack bridge that spans the South Fork of the Sun River. On the far side of the bridge is a trail junction; turn right and follow the main trail northward. This wide path crosses lodgepole pine benchlands above the river for the first mile or so, then turns inland. After crossing Deer Creek, the trail slogs through a spruce swamp of incredible bogginess. Poor trail conditions persist for the next 1.5 miles. After the trail crosses the wilderness boundary, it returns to the drier lodgepole forest, and soon reaches a junction with the rather substantial Bighead Creek Trail (242). Stay left for the West Fork of the Sun. The trail then descends as it bends around to the west, rounding the corner of Deadman Hill as it does so. The going gets muddy again as the trail passes through one last spruce stand before reaching a pack bridge over the West Fork of the Sun River.

Once the north bank of the West Fork has been reached, the West Fork Trail (203) bends westward, crossing the rolling prairies that border the riverbank. As the trail mounts a shoulder of Prairie Reef, it reveals in a first glimpse the gunmetal spires atop Nineteen Ridge. As the trail continues its riverside trek, open meadows allow ever-expanding vistas of the sharp spires that cap the verdant shoulders of Nineteen Ridge like the teeth of a saw blade. The trail then enters a low-elevation forest for the next several miles, emerging briefly at isolated glades. After crossing Reef Creek, the trail climbs onto the grassy slopes of Prairie Reef, allowing the first views of Red Butte far to the west. The trail passes the Prairie Reef Lookout Trail (209), then descends across grassy benches to reach Indian Point Meadows. In the interest of site rehabilitation, pack and saddle parties may not camp in these meadows; there are plenty of suitable sites both up- and down-river from these meadows. The junction with the Camp Creek Pass Trail (209) marks the end of this trip; the trail beyond this point is covered in the section titled, "The Chinese Wall."

Looking down on the West Fork Valley with the peaks of Nineteen Ridge rising beyond.

TRAIL 67 *HOADLEY PASS*

Trail 202, 226, 271

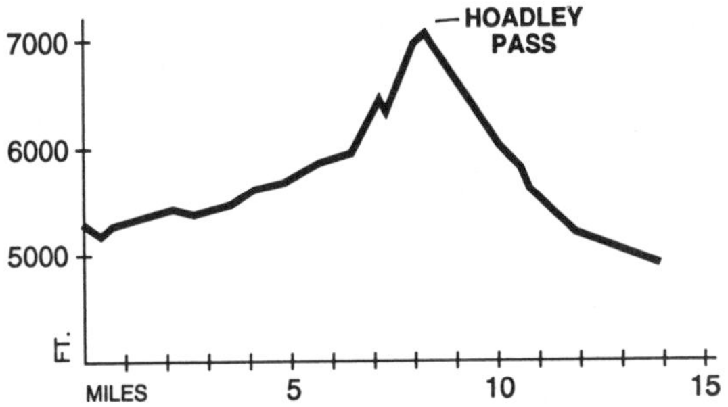

General description: A backpack from Benchmark to The Basin, 13.8 mi. (22.2 km).

Difficulty: Moderately strenuous.

Trail maintenance: Yearly.

Traffic: Moderate.

Elevation gain: 1,930 ft.

Elevation loss: 2,283 ft.

Maximum elevation: 7,090 ft.

Topo maps: Pretty Prairie, Benchmark, Trap Mountain.

Finding the trailhead: The trail begins at the South Fork Sun River trailhead. See the West Fork of the Sun.

- 0.0 South Fork Sun River trailhead.
- 0.2 Pack bridge over the South Fork of the Sun.
- 0.25 Junction with the South Fork Sun River Trail (202). Turn left for Hoadley Pass.
- 0.8 Junction with the cutoff trail from the Benchmark administrative site. Bear right.
- 3.4 The South Fork Sun Trail (202) takes off to the left. Keep going straight on the Hoadley Creek Trail (226) for Hoadley Pass.
- 3.6 Trail turns southwest up the Hoadley Creek valley.
- 6.4 Trail fords Hoadley Creek.
- 6.5 Junction with the Grizzly Basin Trail (225). Keep left for the pass.
- 8.2 Hoadley Pass.
- 11.3 Trail crosses Stadler Creek.
- 12.2 Trail fords Basin Creek.
- 12.4 Unmarked junction with the Trap Mountain Trail (267). Stay left.
- 13.2 Trail enters The Basin. A connecting trail runs straight ahead to the Basin Creek Cabin, while the main trail arcs to the west.
- 13.8 Trail reaches a junction with the Danaher Valley Trail (126).

The trail: This trail lacks scenic value, but does provide the fastest and most direct route to The Basin on Danaher Creek. It receives especially heavy horse traffic starting in mid September, when the elk hunting season begins. From the South Fork Sun River trailhead follow the main trail northward to reach a pack bridge over the South Fork of the Sun. On the far bank, turn left onto a lightly-used trail that runs southward along the river. This trail passes across flat benches and through quiet forests of lodgepole pine. Three quarters of a mile beyond the bridge, the trail is joined by a well-beaten cutoff path that originates at the Benchmark administrative complex. The now wide and rather muddy trail bends southwest, following the South Fork of the Sun toward its headwaters.

TRAIL 67 *HOADLEY PASS*

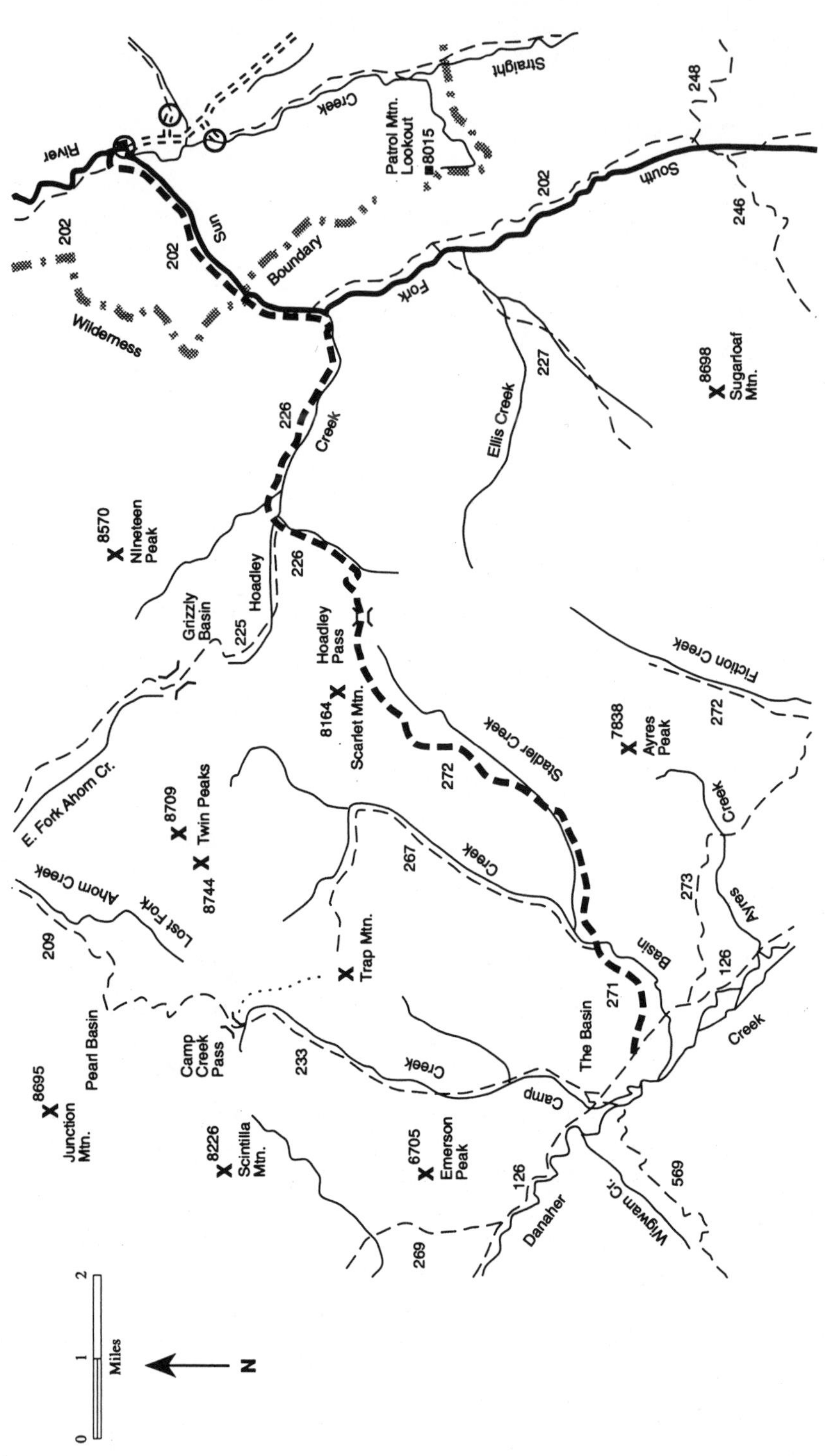

The trail soon climbs above the river to avoid a cutbank and the resulting opening reveals pleasant vistas of the valley ahead. The trail soon returns to the forest and plods along upstream, with occasional lowland meadows to break up the monotony. Two and a half miles beyond the cutoff trail, the Sun River Trail (202) takes off southward to ford the river, while the Hoadley Pass Trail (226) continues to follow the west bank of the stream. After a short distance, this latter trail turns westward up the narrow canyon of Hoadley Creek. The trail climbs steadily up the rocky scarps above the creek's north bank. Below, the foaming waters of the stream course through a gauntlet of mossy bedrock. As the trail returns to the forest, the bogs return with a vengeance and are particularly mucky on level sites for the next two miles.

Just prior to reaching a major tributary stream, the trail bed dries out, and the lodgepole pines give way to a lowland spruce forest dotted with occasional glades of beargrass. The trail makes a shallow ford of the tributary, then turns south to make a similar crossing of Hoadley Creek several hundred yards later. The trail then climbs up a spur ridge on the opposite bank to reach a junction with the Grizzly Basin Trail (225). Stay left and climb along a southern fork of Hoadley Creek. This streamside ascent lasts for about half a mile before the trail abandons the stream and begins to climb a forested, south-facing slope. After a brisk climb, the trail levels out and runs westward through a long and narrow pass cloaked in whitebark pine and subalpine fir.

There is little to see from the pass itself, but as the trail enters the Stadler Creek drainage, the yellow summit of Scarlet Mountain towers above the trail to the north. The trail maintains its elevation as it passes along the southern slopes of Scarlet, and grassy avalanche slopes allow distant views of Foolhen and Woodtick mountains on the far side of the Danaher Valley. The trail then commences a tedious and often muddy descent along the north wall of the Stadler Creek valley. The rounded slopes to the south crowd out all distant views. The trail crosses several extensive meadows on its descent to the north bank of the creek. The trail follows the stream for 0.5 mile before making a shallow ford to reach the dry benches on the south side of the creek. The trail then passes through copses of lodgepole pine dotted with beargrass blossoms as the descent becomes quite gentle.

As the trail approaches its crossing of Basin Creek, it passes through several small meadows bordered by slender, graceful aspen and lodgepole. The trail then crosses the knee-deep and sluggish waters of Basin Creek, and makes its muddy way to a savannah of Ponderosa pine. In this open forest, the trail passes an unmarked junction with the Trap Mountain Trail (267). Three quarters of a mile later, the trail enters the broad meadows of the basin, where Woodtick and Jumbo mountains rise regally on the far side of the valley. A cutoff trail runs toward the Danaher Cabin, while the main trail bends northwest to reach a junction with the Danaher Valley Trail (126) half a mile later.

TRAIL 68 *GRIZZLY BASIN*

Trail 202, 226, 225

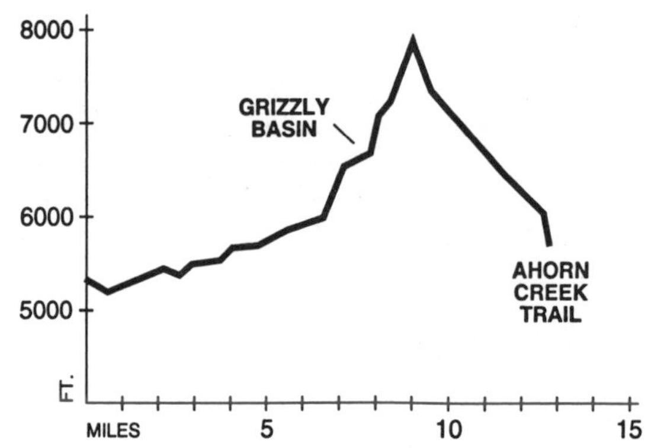

General description: A backpack from Benchmark to the Grizzly Basin, 8.2 mi. (13.2 km); to Ahorn Creek, 12.7 mi. (22.4 km).
Difficulty: Moderately strenuous.
Trail maintenance: Yearly to Grizzly Basin trail junction; frequent beyond.
Traffic: Moderate to the Grizzly Basin; very light beyond.
Elevation gain: 2,630 ft.
Elevation loss: 2,275 ft.
Maximum elevation: 7,820 ft.
Topo maps: Benchmark, Pretty Prairie, Prairie Reef, Trap Mountain.
Finding the trailhead: The trail begins at the South Fork Sun River trailhead. See the West Fork of the Sun.

0.0 South Fork Sun River trailhead.
0.2 Pack bridge over the South Fork of the Sun.
0.25 Junction with the South Fork Sun River Trail (202). Turn left for Hoadley Pass.
0.8 Junction with the cutoff trail from the Benchmark administrative site. Bear right.
3.4 The South Fork Sun (202) trail takes off to the left. Keep going straight on the Hoadley Creek Trail (226) for Grizzly Basin.
3.6 Trail turns southwest up the Hoadley Creek valley.
6.4 Trail fords Hoadley Creek.
6.5 Junction with the Grizzly Basin Trail (225). Turn right.
8.2 Trail enters the Grizzly Basin.
9.1 Trail crosses the divide into the East Fork Ahorn Creek drainage.
12.7 Trail reaches a junction with the Pearl Basin-Camp Creek Pass Trail (209).

The trail: This trail accesses a remote and beautiful alpine basin at the foot of Scarlet Mountain's massive walls. It also connects the Hoadley Pass Trail (226) with the Camp Creek Pass-Pearl Basin Trail (209). The first part of this trip is covered in detail in the section on Hoadley Pass. From the junction with the Hoadley Pass trail, just beyond the ford of Hoadley Creek, the Grizzly Basin Trail (225) climbs steadily through subalpine forest. This trail runs above the main fork of Hoadley Creek, crossing a number of mossy rivulets. The trail then makes its way into a gladed forest of enormous subalpine fir, underlain by a dense carpet of beargrass. The trail bends

TRAIL 68 *GRIZZLY BASIN*

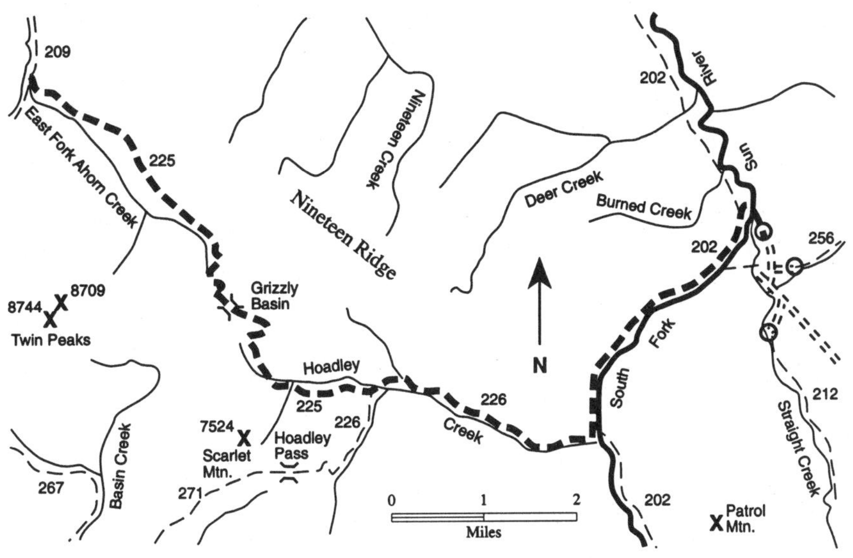

around to the north, beneath the foot of the imposing eastern facade of Scarlet Mountain, as the forest becomes progressively more open. Ultimately, the trees give way to the rolling alpine meadows of the Grizzly Basin, and the trail peters out amid the lush greenery.

From this point, the route takes an uphill tack, angling away from the cliffs. The trail reappears again just before crossing the stream at the edge of the meadows and then takes a sharp eastward bend as it ascends the hillside opposite the cliffs. Upon reaching the ridgeline, the trail turns northwest again, climbing moderately along the crest of the ridge. Openings in the groves of whitebark pine offer views of the knobby ridgecrest of Nineteen Point. The trail then crosses the ridgetop and angles westward across an open beargrass slope to reach a saddle at the foot of the cliffs. This section of the trail boasts excellent views of the Grizzly Basin and the sweeping curve of vertical rock towering above it. Looking north from the pass, a sharp northern bastion of the Twin Peaks thrusts its tilted strata skyward.

From the pass, the trail descends rather steeply into a forested bowl, then runs northward. The route crosses dry hillsides above the valley floor as it makes its way toward Ahorn Creek, and an open forest of subalpine fir and lodgepole pine allow clear views of the Twin Peaks to the west. The steady descent becomes quite steep as the trail makes its way into the valley of Ahorn Creek, and several extensive bogs hinder the passage of hikers and horses alike. At the bottom of the grade, the trail reaches a marked junction with the Camp Creek Pass trail, which runs beneath the overflowing waters of Ahorn Creek's East Fork.

TRAIL 69 *PRAIRIE REEF LOOKOUT*

Trail 224
General description: A spur trip from the West Fork Sun trail to Prairie Reef Lookout, 4.7 mi. (7.6 km).
Difficulty: Strenuous.
Trail maintenance: Yearly.
Traffic: Very light.
Elevation gain: 3,518 ft.
Elevation loss: 40 ft.
Maximum elevation: 8,858 ft.
Topo map: Prairie Reef.
Finding the trail: This trail departs from the West Fork Sun River Trail (203) 1 mile south of Indian Point Meadows.

0.0 Junction of the West Fork Sun River and Prairie Reef trails.
2.0 Trail crosses the bed of White Bear Creek.
4.7 Trail reaches Prairie Reef Lookout.

The trail: This hike runs to the loftiest point in the Bob Marshall Wilderness that can be accessed by trail. The hike offers a good side trip for travelers who find them-

Looking toward Sphinx Peak and the Chinese Wall from the slopes of Prairie Reef.

selves in the Indian Point area. The trail used to be quite rough, but recent reconstruction has made the grade much gentler over most of the trip. Even so, the hefty gain in altitude will take the breath away from all but the hardiest hikers. Water is not available along the trail, so it is best to bring an adequate supply for this challenging and sustained climb.

From the West Fork Trail, the route up Prairie Reef climbs steadily across the grassy lower shoulders of the reef. Between scattered stands of lodgepole pine, early views feature the craggy east face of Red Butte. As the lodgepoles gives way to Douglas-fir, the trail turns north for a shallow but sustained climb. The path makes its way across a steep slope of bedrock and boulders, and the secret spires of Nineteen Ridge appear in the south. The views of Red Butte continue to improve as the trail works its way around into a hidden bowl. The route passes through a maze of rocky ravines beneath the grassy upper slopes of the reef, then bears north toward an upthrust scarp of limestone.

Upon reaching the base of this tilted stratum, the trail begins to switchback upward along the northern edge of a grassy slope. The trail eventually reaches a

TRAIL 69 ***PRAIRIE REEF LOOKOUT***

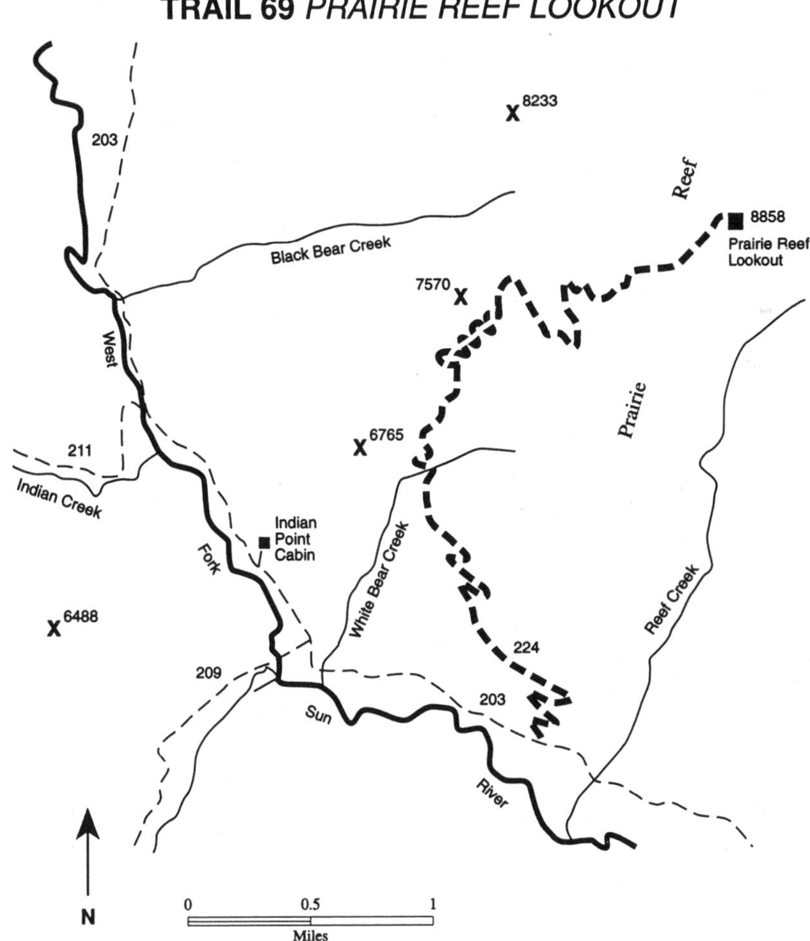

saddle above the uppermost tier of the limestone outcrop, revealing a stunning view of the Chinese Wall, featuring Sphinx Peak and Cliff Mountain. The trail then turns southeast to begin the grueling final ascent to the summit of Prairie Reef. Whitebark pine and subalpine fir eke out a meager existence high on the windblown brow of the reef. Leaving the last of the trees behind, the trail makes a steep final assault through a high alpine desert to reach the lookout.

This lookout, perched atop the 8,864-foot heights that crown the reef, allows a panoramic view of the eastern side of the Bob Marshall Wilderness. The loftiest peaks of the Swan Range crowd the western horizon, while Silvertip Mountain rises above lesser pinnacles to the northwest. Looking northward along the crest of the reef, Slategoat Mountain rises as a lone sentinel over the western edge of the Sun River Basin, while Rocky Mountain and Old Baldy guard its eastern approaches. The brittle reefs of the Rocky Mountain Front stretch away to the southern horizon. The fire lookout is operational throughout the summer months and is staffed by a friendly Forest Service fire guard who welcomes the odd traveler. According to one fire guard, a wolverine includes this structure in its weekly rounds and keeps it free of packrats and other varmints.

TRAIL 70 *PEARL BASIN - CAMP CREEK PASS*

Trail 209, 233

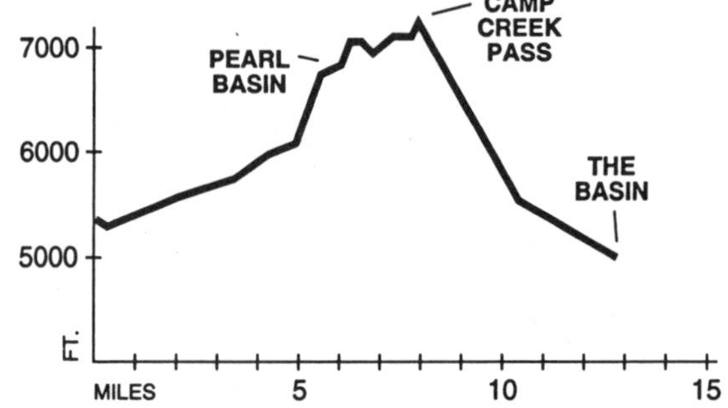

General description: An extended trip from Indian Point Meadows to the Pearl Basin, 5.5 mi. (8.9 km); to The Basin, 12.9 mi. (20.8 km).
Difficulty: Moderately strenuous.
Trail maintenance: Frequent.
Traffic: Light.
Elevation gain: 1,935 ft.
Elevation loss: 2,329 ft.
Maximum elevation: 7,150 ft.
Topo maps: Prairie Reef, Trap Mountain.
Finding the trail: This trail departs from the West Fork Sun River Trail (203) at a marked junction in Indian Point Meadows.

- 0.0 Indian Point Meadows.
- 0.1 Trail fords the West Fork of the Sun River and enters the Ahorn Creek valley.
- 2.0 Trail fords Ahorn Creek to reach its east bank.
- 3.2 Junction with the Grizzly Basin Trail (225). Stay right and ford the East Fork of Ahorn Creek.

TRAIL 70 *PEARL BASIN - CAMP CREEK PASS*

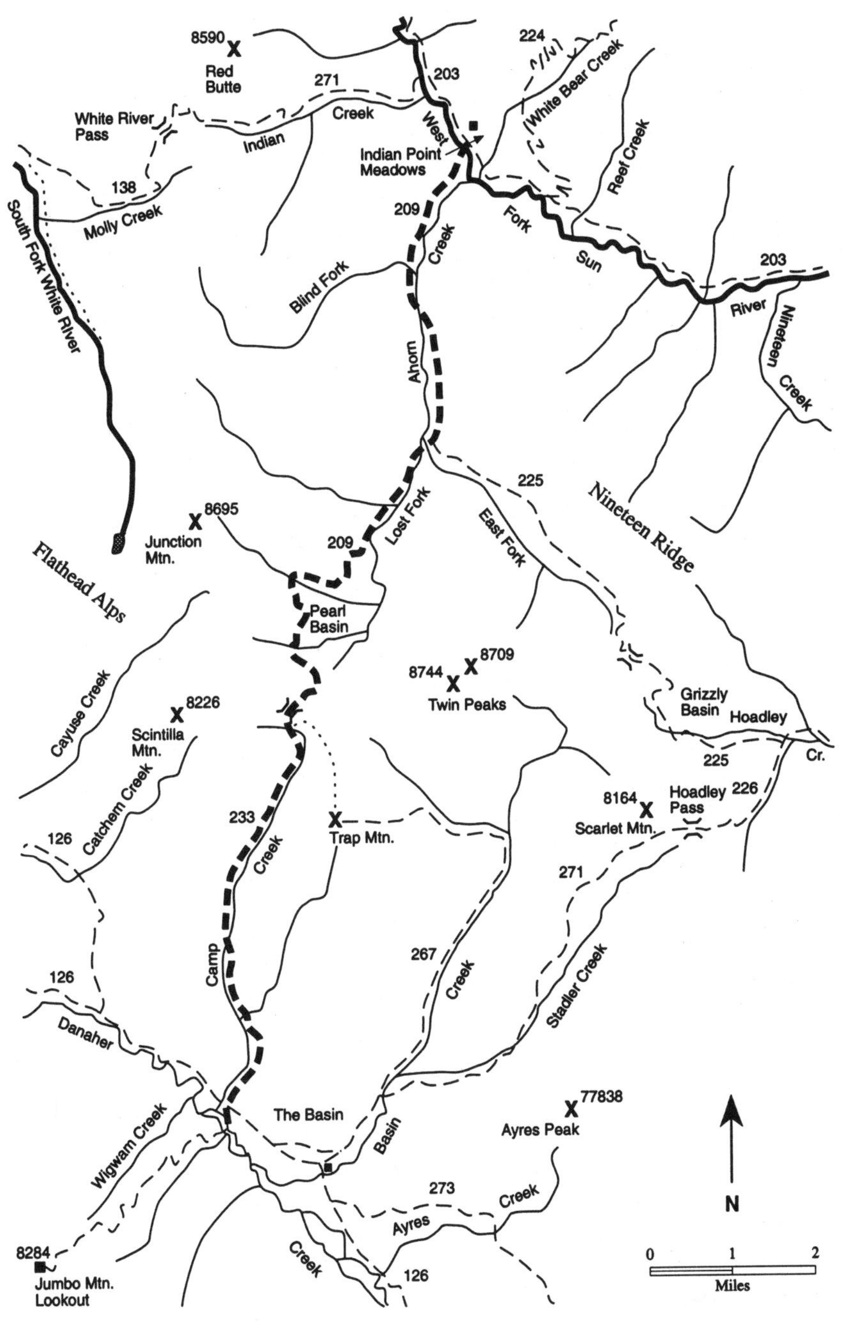

3.4 Trail returns to the west bank of Ahorn Creek.
5.5 Trail enters the Pearl Basin.
8.0 Camp Creek Pass.
8.1 Unmarked junction with a hunter's trail that ascends to Trap Mountain. Stay right.
8.3 Trail fords the headwaters of Camp Creek.
10.5 Trail fords Camp Creek to reach its east bank.
12.9 Junction with the Danaher Valley Trail (126).

The trail: This lightly-used trail connects the West Fork of the Sun River with the basin on the banks of Danaher Creek. On its way, it passes through the Pearl Basin, noted for its spectacular scenery. This high basin is an important summer range for elk, and these magnificent beasts can sometimes be seen from the trail during June and July.

From the signpost at the northern end of Indian Point Meadows, the trail runs southwest into the trees that flank the West Fork of the Sun. Look for blazes as the rather faint trail enters the trees. The path becomes more distinct as it hopscotches across a shallow side channel of the river to reach the main ford. The crossing is knee-deep, but there are plenty of logjams on the upstream side for a dry-footed crossing. Once on the far bank, follow the cairns upstream for thirty yards from the original fording point to reach the spot where the trail ducks through a gap in the willows and enters the forest beyond. From this point on, the trail is quite distinct and hard to miss.

The forest bordering the north bank of Ahorn Creek is dominated by lodgepole pine and is underlain by a sparse cover of pinegrass and snowberry. The trail climbs in fits and starts along the slope bordering the western bank of the creek. Upon reaching a crossing of the Blind Fork of Ahorn Creek, the forest becomes a much richer bottomland community of spruce and fir. Half a mile later, the path reaches a shallow ford of the main body of Ahorn Creek. It then begins to climb gently along the dry hillside overlooking the eastern side of the valley. The forest community on this slope is a loose-knit forest of subalpine fir, underlain by clumps of beargrass. This community is not usually found at such a low altitude; it is more typical of timberline areas. The trail descends briefly to reach a marked trail junction with the Grizzly Basin Trail (226). This junction has been submerged by the overflowing waters of Ahorn Creek's East Fork.

After a thirty-yard wade across the flooded trail bed, the route crosses a strip of dry land before reaching another ford of Ahorn Creek. The trail bends southwest as it passes inland, climbing gently through forested bottomlands on its way to a nameless tributary. After a shallow ford, the trail begins to climb a bit more briskly as it passes along the crest of a series of low hummocks. Upon reaching a clearing created by periodic avalanches, the trail begins to ascend in earnest, and the opening in the forest canopy allows the first of many unobstructed views of the Twin Peaks. After a number of switchbacks, the trail runs southwest along a rocky sidehill. It then zigzags upward to crest the eastern rim of the Pearl Basin.

Entering the basin, the trail passes into a long, narrow dale overlooked on the east by a scalloped finger of rock that projects from the main mass of Junction Mountain. The trail passes around the head of this miniature valley and turns south beneath overhanging cliffs to reach the next spur ridge. Meadows abound as the trail makes its way through fir parkland into the next basin, which is overlooked by a lofty southern spire of Junction Mountain. The trail then runs southeast, climbing gently through a brushy subalpine forest to reach the southern edge of Pearl Basin. The pocket-sized glades found here are shaded by dark forests, and marshy country prevails in the intervening depressions. The trail turns west again as it makes a short but brisk climb to reach Camp Creek Pass. The pass is low and wooded and offers little in the way of scenery.

After crossing the Continental Divide, a steep descent brings the traveler to an overused camping spot among stout subalpine fir and meadows of the upper Camp Creek Basin. Here, an unmarked hunter's trail descends from Trap Mountain to join the main trail. After a shallow, marshy descent through subalpine parks, the valley bends southwest and the descent becomes much steeper. The trail makes its way across boulder fields and through thickets of alder, with views of Woodtick and Jumbo mountains far to the west. Upon regaining the creek bottom, the trail follows its north bank beside laughing cascades and babbling riffles. After crossing a small tributary stream, the trail passes among stately spruce and fir on its way to a crossing of Camp Creek.

After this calf-deep ford, the trail follows the south bank through the woods to cross another tributary stream. Soon afterward, the bottomland forest gives way to a lodgepole pine and Douglas-fir savannah. The trail receives several unmarked

The alpine meadows of Pearl Basin below Twin Peaks.

hunter's paths as it leaves the hills behind and enters the flat expanse of the basin. After passing through several tiny glades, the trail enters the broad meadows that flank the lower reaches of Camp Creek. The trail is joined by a more heavily beaten track that rises from an outfitter's camp by the creekside. Soon thereafter, a cutoff trail splits away southward to meet the southbound leg of the Danaher Valley Trail (126). A fainter path continues southwest to a marked junction with the Danaher Valley Trail on the south bank of Camp Creek.

TRAIL 71 *WHITE RIVER PASS*

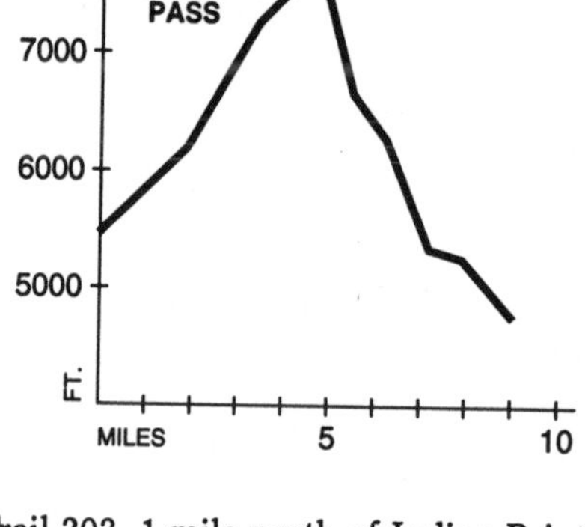

Trail 211, 138

General description: An extended trip from the West Fork of the Sun to the White River, 9.2 mi. (14.8 km).

Difficulty: Moderately strenuous (East to West); strenuous (West to East).

Trail maintenance: Yearly.

Traffic: Moderate.

Elevation gain: 2,186 ft.

Elevation loss: 2,876 ft.

Maximum elevation: 7,626 ft.

Topo maps: Prairie Reef, Haystack Mountain.

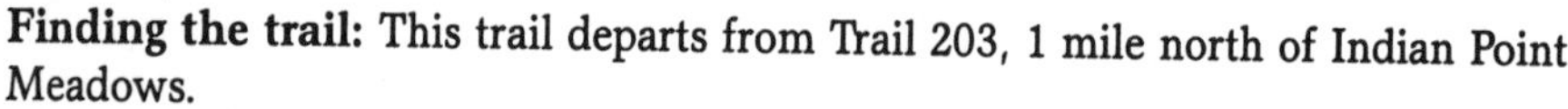

Finding the trail: This trail departs from Trail 203, 1 mile north of Indian Point Meadows.

- 0.0 Trail fords the West Fork of the Sun River
- 4.5 White River Pass.
- 6.3 Trail leaves the Molly Creek valley and enters the valley of the South Fork of the White River.
- 7.3 Unmarked junction with the old South Fork White River Trail (380). Keep going straight.
- 8.1 Junction with the Haystack Mountain Trail (626). Keep going straight.
- 9.0 Trail crosses the South Fork of the White River.
- 9.2 Trail reaches its junction with the White River Trail (112).

The trail: This popular route across the Continental Divide connects Indian Point Meadows with the valley of the White River. Although this route does not offer views of the Chinese Wall, it does reveal stunning vistas of the Flathead Alps and Haystack Mountain. From the shores of the West Fork of the Sun, this trail makes a crossing of this swift, knee-deep river then climbs through the lodgepole pine forest along the north bank of Indian Creek. Crossing the high benches above the stream, the trail runs westward toward the pass. Straight ahead, the blood-colored crags of Red Butte rise above the surrounding hills. The trail climbs steadily as it passes below a talus slope punctuated by scattered groves of aspen.

Upon reaching the southern slopes of Red Butte, the trail crosses a tiny stream

Looking through White River Pass from the east.

that makes its way down from the rugged wastelands above. The path then crosses an open slope above a slender waterfall on Indian Creek. A second tributary lays the bedrock bare, and the stone reveals its origin: Ripple marks have been preserved in the mudstone from the time long past when the rock was a shallow seafloor. The trail continues its moderate ascent across meadowy slopes, climbing into a high basin that was recently laid bare by a forest fire. Subalpine fir are beginning to recolonize the moister depressions, while the drier slopes above harbor only beargrass. As the valley doglegs to the north, the trail crosses it and climbs steeply along its western wall. The rounded western shoulders of Red Butte frame the mottled patterns of timber and grassland on the shoulders of Prairie Reef. The trail then turns west to climb through the narrow defile of White River Pass.

Travelers approaching the pass from the east will be immediately confronted by the massive white monolith that rises beyond the pass. Looking northwest from the pass, the folded ridges of the White River Syncline can be seen on the far side of the White River valley. The trail sidehills to the south, reaching another high saddle at the foot of the limestone edifice. Haystack Mountain rears its tilted plane of rock to the north, and a similar limestone stratum juts skyward to the south. Beyond it lie the pointed teeth of the Flathead Alps. Beyond this second saddle, the trail begins a steep southward descent toward the valley floor. As the trail drops across meadowy slopes, it resembles a washed-out gully more than anything else, and muddy conditions prevail here after rainstorms. The mud continues to be a prob-

TRAIL 71 *WHITE RIVER PASS*

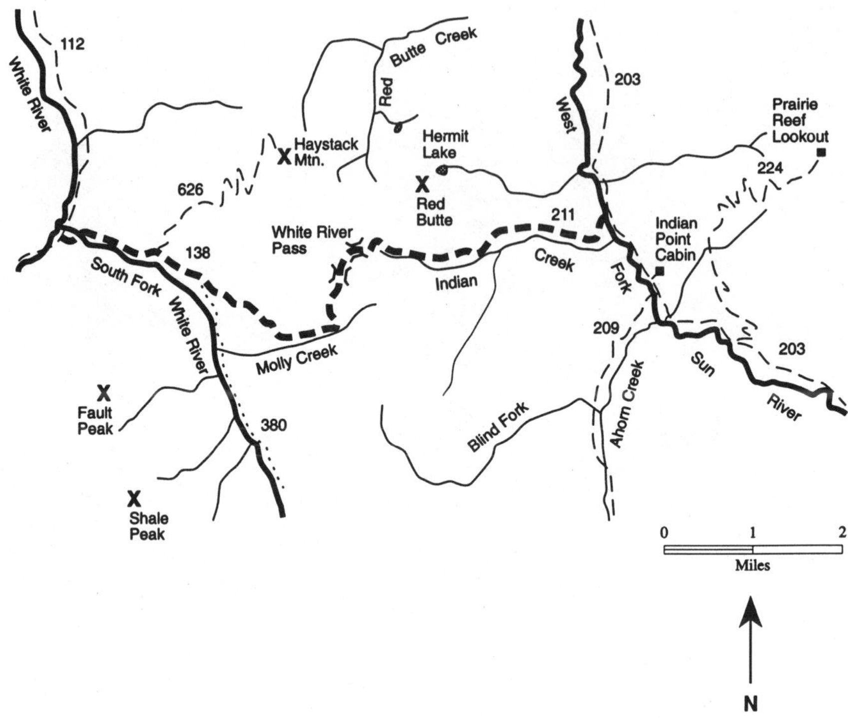

lem as the trail drops into the trees before reaching the north bank of Molly Creek.

Here, the trail turns west again and descends moderately along the creek for 0.5 mile before reaching the valley of the South Fork of the White River. The trail bends northwest into this much deeper valley, crossing a series of open slopes. Shale and Fault peaks crown the Flathead Alps immediately to the south, while the sharp peak that lies straight ahead in the distance is Turtlehead Mountain. When the trail arrives at a broad, rocky wash, it turns straight down the middle of the dry watercourse for seventy-five yards before turning north again; look for cairns marking the way. The trail descends steadily through a forest of lodgepoles crossing a second wash before reaching the junction with the abandoned South Fork White River Trail (380).

After a steady descent punctuated by muddy spots, the trail emerges atop a high cutbank above the South Fork. At this spot, the trail passes a well-marked junction with the Haystack Mountain Trail (626). The trail descends steadily above the gravelly course of the South Fork, which is overshadowed to the south by bluish cliffs. When the trail reaches the level of the stream, it approaches an extensive outfitter's camp. Before entering the camp, the White River Pass trail splits off to the south, making a shallow ford of the South Fork. The trail then continues downstream along the bank of this so-called river to reach its terminus at a junction with the White River Trail (112).

TRAIL 72 *CHINESE WALL*

Trail 203, 175, 194

General description: An extended trip from Indian Point Meadows to the Larch Hill Pass junction, 13.8 mi. (22.2 km); to Spotted Bear Pass, 16.9 mi. (27.2 km).

Difficulty: Moderately strenuous.

Trail maintenance: Yearly.

Traffic: Moderate.

Elevation gain: (to Spotted Bear Pass): 3,748 ft.

Elevation loss: (to Spotted Bear Pass): 2,327 ft.

Maximum elevation: 7,620 ft.

Topo maps: Slategoat Mountain, Amphitheatre Mountain, Prairie Reef.

Finding the trail: This trip begins as Trail 203 in Indian Point Meadows.

0.0 Indian Point Meadows.
0.3 Spur trail to Indian Point Cabin.
1.7 Trail crosses Black Bear Creek.
3.9 Trail fords the West Fork of the Sun to reach its west bank.
4.9 Trail returns to the east bank of the West Fork.
6.0 Final ford of the West Fork of the Sun River.
7.2 Trail fords Burnt Creek to reach its north bank.
8.9 Cliff Mountain.
9.6 Trail crosses the headwaters of Moose Creek.
10.5 Junction with the Moose Creek Trail (131). Stay left.
10.9 Salt Mountain.
11.4 Trail crosses the headwaters of Rock Creek.
13.8 Junction with the Larch Hill Pass Trail (112). Bear right for My Lake.
15.8 My Lake.
16.1 Junction with the Larch Hill Cutoff Trail (176). Bear right.
16.9 Spotted Bear Pass. Junction with the Spotted Bear River (83) and Rock Creek (111) trails.

The trail: The Chinese Wall is easily the most well-known and popular destination for travelers in the Bob Marshall Wilderness. This thousand-foot-high scarp of limestone stretches unbroken for a dozen miles, from Haystack Mountain to Larch Hill Pass. It is arguably the most dramatic manifestation of the Continental Divide be-

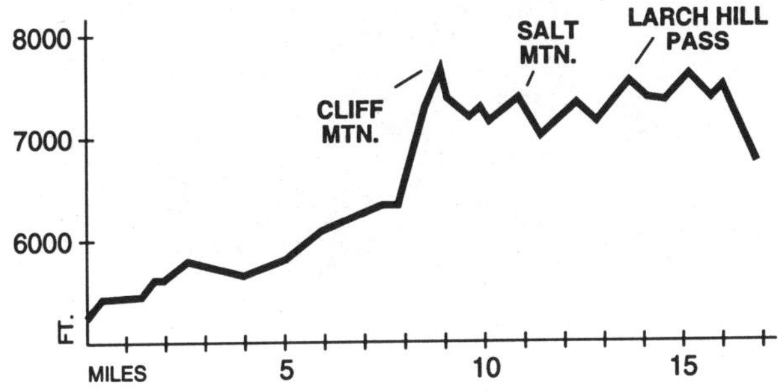

tween Mexico and the Arctic Ocean. The trail crosses fragile alpine meadows at the base of the Wall's northern reaches and offers outstanding wildlife viewing opportunities. Visitors to the Chinese Wall should plan on camping in less fragile areas away from the Wall itself; the meadows at the foot of the Chinese Wall are closed to overnight use. The Chinese Wall receives a very high level of use; travelers looking for a remote wilderness experience will probably be dismayed by the high level of traffic found here.

From Indian Point Meadows, the trail follows the West Fork of the Sun, passing the Indian Point Cabin and climbing gradually through a lowland forest of lodgepole pine. After passing the White River Pass junction, the trail begins to climb briskly. Black Bear Creek provides a break in the trees, revealing the ragged spires of Red Butte across the valley. The trail then climbs to a high meadow that provides even more spectacular vistas. The trail soon descends gradually to rock-hop over No Name Gulch, and crosses timbered bottomland for another 0.5 mile to reach a ford of the West Fork just above its confluence with Red Butte Creek. The trail follows the west bank of the river for about a mile, then makes another ford just below Pine Creek. Looking up the valley of this substantial tributary, the southern marches of the Chinese Wall can be glimpsed for the first time.

Once again on the east bank of the river, the trail wanders for 0.5 mile through a scattering of minor mudholes to reach the final ford of the West Fork. The forest here is dominated by subalpine fir and spruce, and the terrain is quite boggy. Recent efforts at trail construction have failed to defeat the general sogginess of the land-

Looking south along the Chinese Wall from Larch Hill Pass.

scape. The next valley entering from the west carries Burnt Creek, and the trail turns west to follow its course. Almost immediately, the trail makes an ankle-deep ford of this stream, and follows its north bank as the gradient increases to a steady climb. After crossinga minor tributary stream, the trail climbs the hillside away from Burnt Creek, and a solid forest of lodgepole pine opens up into rocky meadows spangled with wildflowers. These meadows offer excellent views of the forbidding cliffs of the Chinese Wall at the head of the valley.

The trail continues its steady ascent, turning northwest to climb into clumps of subalpine fir. The trail reaches a high saddle at the foot of Cliff Mountain, one of the tallest bastions along the Chinese Wall. This spot commands views of the seemingly limitless wall stretching to the north and south, as well as the rugged massif of Prairie Reef to the southeast. The trail then descends steadily through a young stand of whitebark pine to reach the upper basin of Moose Creek. The trail passes below the pond that serves as the source of the creek. Enchanting reflections of the cliffs to the west are mirrored in the still waters of this shallow tarn. This part of the wall is lower than the northern reaches, but numerous turrets and crenellations render it equally inspiring.

The trail continues northward in the shadow of the wall; clouds blown from the west dissipate into thin air as they are blown over the Continental Divide and into the drier air to the east. Alpine meadows dotted with patches of spruce and fir provide ideal summer habitat for elk and mule deer, and the cliffs of the Chinese Wall are a playground for agile mountain goats. The trail passes the junction with the Moose Creek Trail (131), and ascends among house-sized boulders that have been pried loose from the cliffs above by the relentless forces of erosion. The trail crests the next drainage divide, which sits at the foot of Salt Mountain. The swallows that build their nests in the cliffs of the Chinese Wall can often be spotted from these saddles as they perform an aerial ballet in their quest for airborne insects.

The trail then descends in an easterly direction, following the eastward-running spur ridge for a short distance before climbing through a subalpine forest to regain the meadows at the base of the wall. The trail then crests a low rise and braids out into many channels. Stick to the most well-worn path to prevent farther scarring of this fragile landscape. Ground squirrels abound in the grassy meadows, and marmots and pikas inhabit the boulder fields at the foot of this tallest stretch of the Chinese Wall. The trail begins to climb gradually as it approaches the northern terminus of the wall, and crosses a meadowy gulch before turning eastward, away from the towering cliffs. After a few hundred yards of climbing, the trail reaches a junction with the Larch Hill Pass Trail (112).

My Lake Option. The Wall trail continues northward, passing My Lake on its way to Spotted Bear Pass. From the Larch Hill Pass junction, the trail continues to climb in an easterly direction, and openings in the trees afford a last sweeping view of the towering face of the Chinese Wall as it runs southward into the hazy distance. The trail soon bends north, following the contours of the hillside as it climbs through whitebark pine to reach the top of the next ridge. The trail passes across a high, meadowy benchland that is overlooked by the tree-fringed crest of Larch Hill. The alpine larche that crown its summit burst into flaming colors as they lose their leaves in early October. The trail then makes a shallow descent to reach the eastern shore

TRAIL 72 *CHINESE WALL*

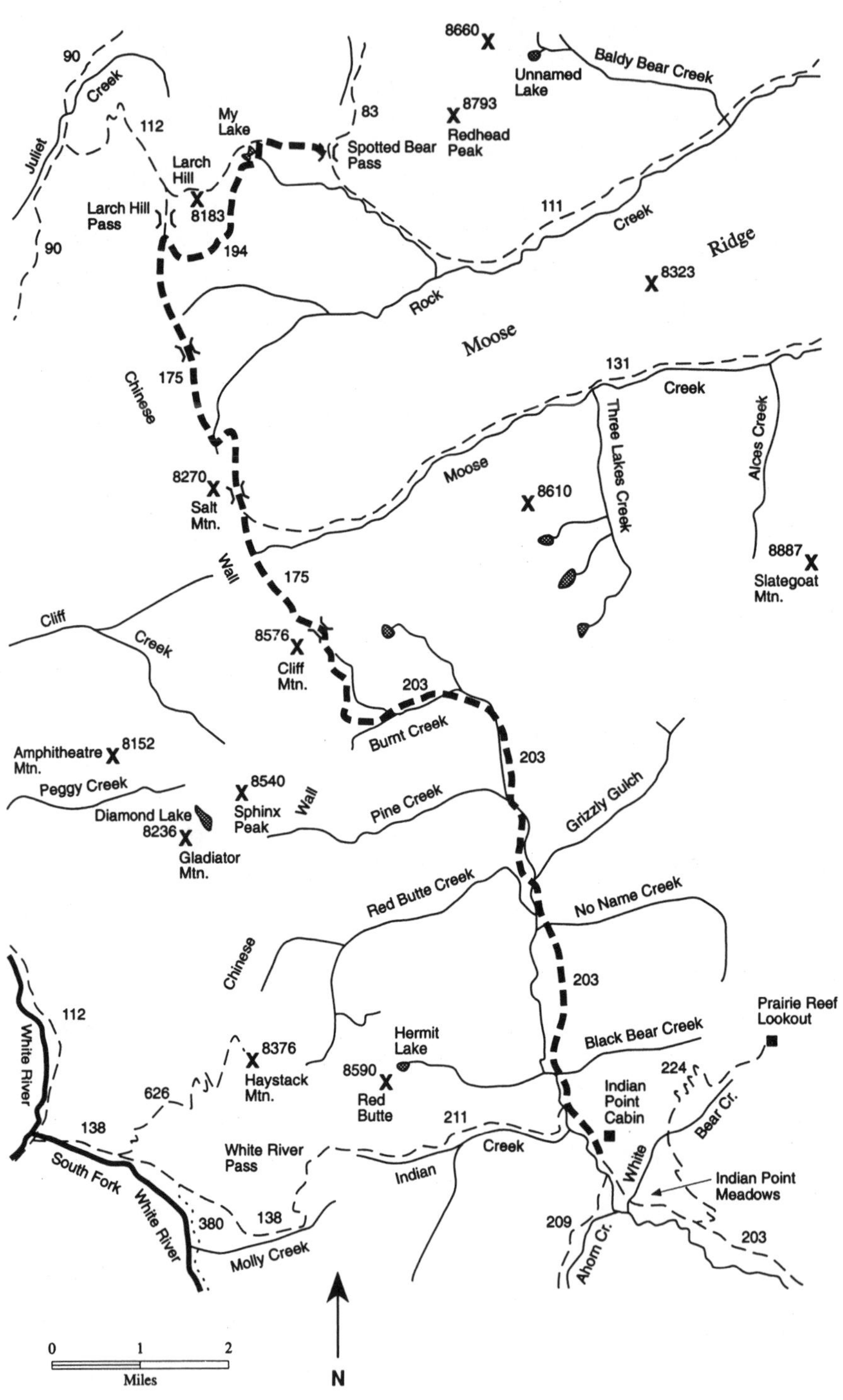

of My Lake. The lakeshore has been heavily impacted by past campers and is closed to overnight use so that it may return to its natural state.

Beyond the lake, the trail begins to ascend steadily and bends eastward again on its way to Spotted Bear Pass. It soon receives the Larch Hill Trail (176), which enters from the west. The main trail then begins to descend steadily as it follows the ridgeline eastward through a forest of whitebark pine. The pine nuts of these trees are a favorite autumn food of grizzly bears. The rocky crest of Moose Ridge is visible to the southeast, through gaps in the forest. As the trail rounds the end of the ridge, Redhead Peak and the Three Sisters reveal themselves to the northeast. The trail then switchbacks steadily downward to reach the wooded saddle of Spotted Bear Pass, where it intersects with the Spotted Bear River (83) and Rock Creek (111) trails.

TRAIL 73 *BEARTOP LOOKOUT*

Trail 129

General description: A spur trip from the North Fork of the Sun to Beartop Lookout, 5.2 mi. (8.4 km).

Difficulty: Strenuous.

Trail maintenance: Yearly.

Traffic: Moderate.

Elevation gain: 2,894 ft.

Maximum elevation: 8,094 ft.

Topo maps: Gates Park, Our Lake.

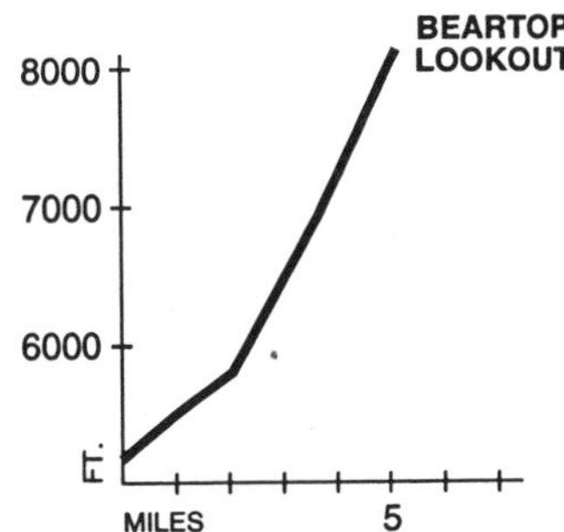

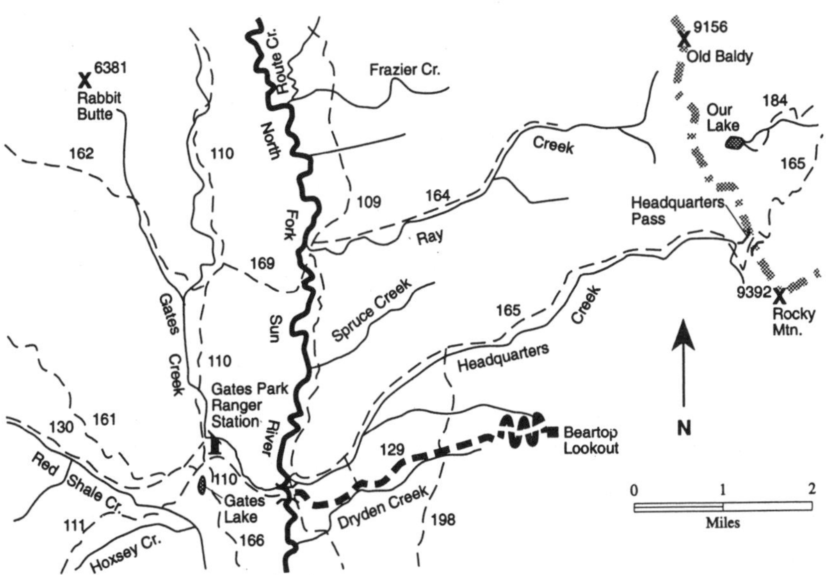

Looking north toward Old Baldy from the Beartop Lookout.

Finding the trail: This trail begins at the North Fork Sun River pack bridge, 1 mile northwest of Biggs Creek Flat on Trail 110.

0.0 North Fork Sun River pack bridge.
1.0 Junction with the Dryden Creek cutoff trail. Stay right.
5.2 Trail reaches Beartop Lookout.

The trail: This trail is used primarily for resupplying the fire lookout atop Beartop Mountain, but also provides a fine day trip for travelers in the Gates Park area. The trail crosses the swampy eastern side of the Sun River basin and climbs steeply to reach the lookout. Hikers who prefer to keep their feet dry will find the first half of the trip quite unpleasant; this journey best suited for semi-aquatic travelers. The hike can also be accessed by Trail198 which connects Biggs Creek Flat with the Headquarters Pass trail, but this route is difficult to find.

The trip begins at the North Fork Sun River pack bridge, just southeast of Gates Park. The trail crosses a boggy hilltop, following the edge of the Gates Park burn on its way to the banks of Dryden Creek. After 0.5 mile, the trail receives a connecting trail that runs north to meet the Headquarters Pass trail. For some unfathomable reason, this short cutoff has been named the Dryden Creek trail. Beyond this junction, the trail climbs modestly through a patchy mixture of habitats that share one common trait: They are all swampy. Through forest, burn, glade, and meadow, the trail slogs eastward through the muck.

The trail leaves the worst of the mud behind as it passes below a boulder field and climbs onto the knees of Beartop Mountain. This part of the trail has been recently reconstructed and switchbacks upward at a mild pace through a pleasant forest of lodgepole pine. After a mile or so of steady climbing, the trail enters the burn again as it winds onto the crest of a spur ridge. Straight ahead the main bulk of Beartop Mountain challenges the willpower of those who would conquer it. Atop the spur ridge lies one last, vast mud hole before the serious climbing begins. The trail steepens to a calf-burning pace as it zigzags up the snag-littered west face of Beartop. The trail emerges from the burn as it climbs southward through loose talus on the final pitch to the whitewashed lookout.

From the lookout, the vast extent of the Gates Park fire can be truly appreciated. To the north of Gates Park, the entire basin of the North Fork of the Sun has been reduced to a grayish sea of snags, interrupted by widely scattered islands of surviving timber. Rimming the western side of the basin is the mustard-colored shale of the North Wall, capped with the bloodstone rock of Hahn Peak. Farther north lies the Trilobite Range, and to the south, bits of the Chinese Wall can be glimpsed through the spur ridges. The rugged western summits of the Sawtooth Range surround the lookout. Rocky Mountain is hidden from view, but Old Baldy rises in plain sight to the north.

TRAIL 74 *RED SHALE MEADOWS*

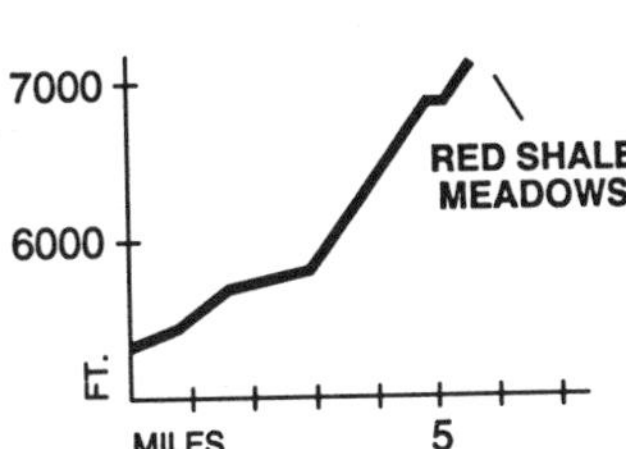

Trail 130

General description: An extended trip from Gates Park to Red Shale Meadows, 5.6 mi. (9.0 km).

Difficulty: Moderately strenuous.

Trail maintenance: Yearly.

Traffic: Moderate.

Elevation gain: 1,778 ft.

Elevation loss: 20 ft.

Maximum elevation: 7,080 ft.

Topo maps: Gates Park, Three Sisters.

Finding the trail: This trail starts on the western edge of Gates Park at a signpost on Trail 111.

0.0 Gates Park Ranger Station.
0.3 Junction with the Red Shale Creek Trail (130). Turn west.
0.6 Junction with the Lick Creek Fire Trail (161. Stay left.
3.0 Junction with the South Fork Red Shale Creek Fire Trail (167). Stay right for Red Shale Meadows.
4.6 Trail crosses Red Shale Creek.
5.6 Red Shale Meadows.

The trail: The trail to Red Shale Meadows provides one of the most direct access routes to the North Wall. From the signpost on Trail 111 on the western edge of Gates

Park, follow the faint track marked by blazes as it runs westward, passing just south of a small finger meadow which has an elk wallow at its lower end. After 0.25 mile, this trail is joined by a much more well-beaten path from the northeast; turn left and head west across a wet meadow of tall grasses. As the trail enters the forest at the far edge of the opening, it reaches a junction with the fire trail that runs north to Lick Creek (161). Stick to the more obvious trail to the left, marked "Red Shale Creek." This trail meanders westward into the Gates Park burn, then turns northwest to follow the burned hills just out of sight of Red Shale Creek.

The trail crosses a number of mudholes early on, but after several miles the condition of the path improves markedly. Early views through the scorched snags are highlighted by the reddish promontory of Lookout Mountain to the west, as well as a buff-colored pinnacle atop the North Wall farther to the north. The trail descends into the Red Shale bottoms to reach a junction with the South Fork Fire Trail (167); stay right for Red Shale Meadows. As the valley bends around to the west, the grade steepens a bit, and the yellow cliffs of the North Wall unfold to the west. Passing the north slope of Lookout Mountain, the burn gives way to unbroken forest. The trail passes among the lush greenery for the next mile or so, crossing a few boggy bottomland spots.

The valley soon becomes a steep-walled ravine, and the trail descends to cross Red Shale Creek and climbs onto the hillside to the south. The trail switchbacks up the crest of this minor spur ridge, then enters a shallow valley of subalpine parkland. The trail wanders westward for another 0.25 mile of gentle but sometimes muddy climbing to reach the flowery expanse of Red Shale Meadows. This pristine alpine

TRAIL 74 *RED SHALE MEADOWS*

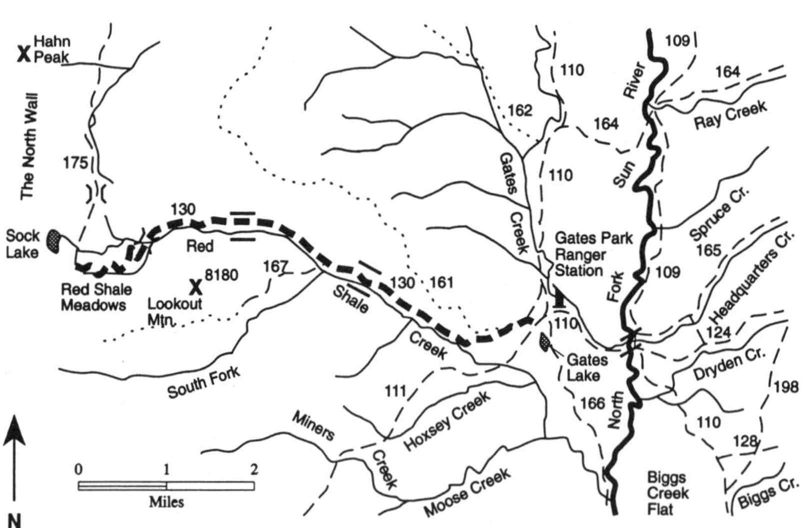

park sits at the base of the towering cliffs of the North Wall. Ground squirrels tumble in the lush meadows, while pikas and marmots can be found in the boulder aprons below the cliffs. Golden eagles ride the thermals in search of their furry prey, and mountain goats can sometimes be spotted among the walls and pinnacles. For adventurous climbers, the hanging cirque at the foot of the northernmost visible peak houses Sock Lake. This lake can be reached via a steep scramble to the south of the headwall below the lake. The North Wall Trail (175) runs northward from a signpost in the meadows. Stockmen are asked not to graze their stock here, but rather to drive them over the divide to the south and picket them in the headwaters of Red Shale Creek's South Fork.

TRAIL 75 *MOONLIGHT PEAK*

Trail 110, 151, 132
General description: An extended trip from the North Fork of the Sun to the North Wall, 6.4 mi. (10.3 km).
Difficulty: Strenuous.
Trail maintenance: Yearly along Lick Creek; occasional beyond.
Traffic: Light to the Moonlight Peak trail; very light beyond.
Elevation gain: 2,500 ft.
Elevation loss: 965 ft.
Maximum elevation: 7,800 ft.
Topo maps: Gates Park, Three Sisters.
Finding the trail: This trip begins from the ford of the North Fork of the Sun on Trail 110, at its junction with the Wrong Creek Trail (117).

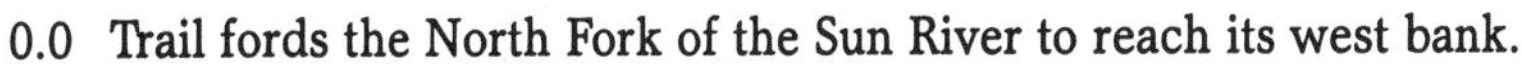

0.0 Trail fords the North Fork of the Sun River to reach its west bank.
0.4 Junction with the Lick Creek Trail (151). Turn left.
0.5 Trail fords Lick Creek to reach its north bank.
1.9 Junction with the Moonlight Peak Trail (132). Turn right.
4.6 Spur trail to Lake Quiet takes off to the left.
5.4 Trail reaches its high point behind the summit of Moonlight Peak.
6.4 Trail reaches its junction with the North Wall Trail (175).

The trail: The Moonlight Peak trail offers a scenic though challenging route to reach the North Wall. The route is a bit sketchy as it leaves the Lick Creek trail to ascend Moonlight Peak, but is quite easy to follow for the remainder of the distance to the North Wall trail. This trail is poorly suited for pack trains, as it crosses a steep and unstable slope of loose dirt high on the shoulders of Moonlight Peak. From the Wrong Creek junction on the North Fork Sun River Trail (110), head south across a knee-deep ford of the river. The trail crosses a shoulder of land before fording Lick Creek and climbing onto the burned bluff that overlooks the creek. Here, the trail reaches a junction with the Lick Creek Trail (151); turn right and descend into the creek bottoms. The trail fords Lick Creek to reach its north bank, where it meets an unmarked dead-end trail. Stay left for Moonlight Peak, as the trail follows Lick Creek upstream through burned bottomlands dotted with fireweed and grassy meadows. The trail runs westward for 1.5 mile, following the meandering course of Lick Creek on its way to the junction with the Moonlight Peak Trail (132).

This trail junction is marked, but the trail itself is difficult to follow for the first half-mile or so. Follow the blazes on the trees as the Moonlight trail angles northwest across the burned slopes of a series of low hills. The trail crosses a substantial stream just before climbing onto a steep hill that is the easternmost spur of Moonlight Peak. Travelers who get lost should head for this point, where the trail becomes well-defined and easy to follow. The trail begins its ascent by climbing up the south face of the hill in a direct manner, heading in a westerly direction. As the trail gains altitude, it begins to switchback upward toward the crest of the ridge. At times the bends in the trail are indistinct, but the straight stretches are easy to follow.

Upon reaching the ridgeline, the trail follows on its northwesterly course, finally arriving at a high knob forested with unburned timber (another good landmark for the lost). A glance to the east reveals the pale summits of Old Baldy and Rocky Mountain. From this point on, the trail is a well-worn path through an unburned landscape. The trail levels off for a short while, then climbs vigorously to the top of the next point. Dropping onto the western side of the ridge, open timber provides a sneak preview of the North Wall. The trail then climbs to the next point only to descend again as the ridgeline dips into a broad saddle. The trail continues to fol-

Looking north toward Kevan Mountain.

TRAIL 75 *MOONLIGHT PEAK*

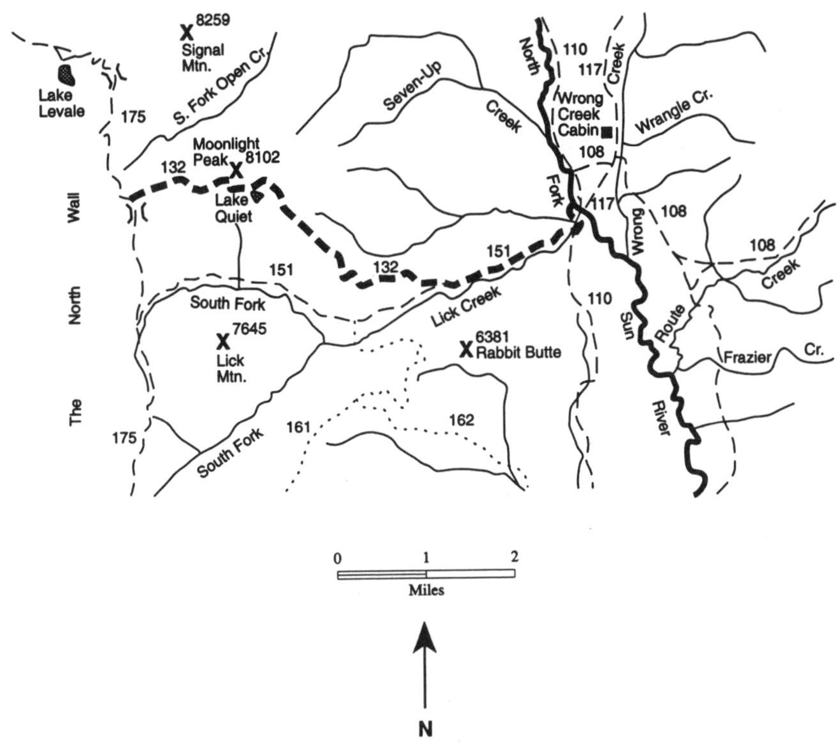

low the ridgeline until it reaches the main bulk of Moonlight Peak.

The trail follows a small stream upward before turning west again to reach a marked trail junction. At this point, a faint track runs south for 0.25 mile to reach Lake Quiet, a shallow woodland pond nestled in the folds of a timbered shelf. Meanwhile, the main trail begins climbing vigorously as it continues westward, crossing a few open ravines but staying mainly within the confines of a closed-canopy forest. After zigzagging upward for a time, the trail continues westward across an eroded slope of loose shale before making the final climb to the flat summit behind Moonlight Peak.

As the trail works its way along the top of the reddish cliffs that comprise the north face of the peak, the rugged blood-red dome of the main peak can be viewed to the east. Meanwhile, an old burn atop the mountain has eliminated the whitebark pine that once stood here; the next generation of pine and fir have only reached the sapling stage. As a result, fantastic views of the North Wall from Hahn Peak to Kevan Mountain can be had from this western platform of Moonlight Peak. The trail continues westward down the ridgeline, descending gently at first and then at a breakneck pace. The Moonlight Pass trail ends at a junction with the North Wall Trail (175) at a high saddle between the Lick and Open Creek drainages.

TRAIL 76 *NORTH WALL*

Trail 175

General description: An extended trip from Red Shale Meadows to Open Creek, 9.1 mi. (14.6 km).

Difficulty: Moderately strenuous.

Trail maintenance: Frequent.

Traffic: Light.

Elevation gain: 2,315 ft.

Elevation loss: 2,585 ft.

Maximum elevation: 7,535 ft.

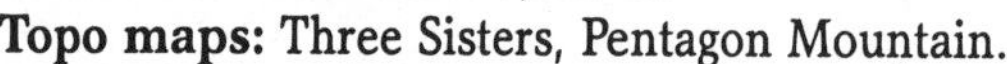

Topo maps: Three Sisters, Pentagon Mountain.

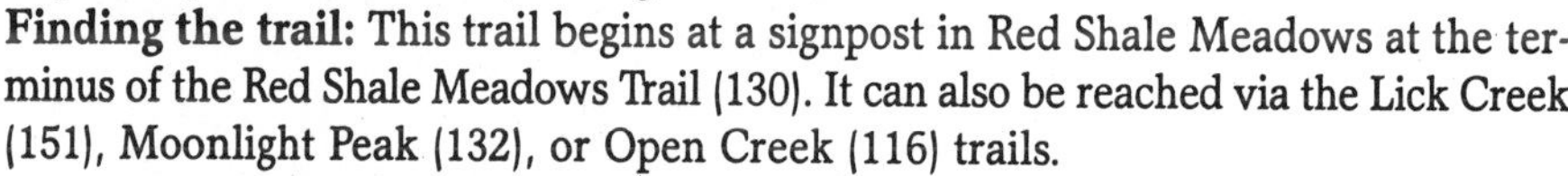

Finding the trail: This trail begins at a signpost in Red Shale Meadows at the terminus of the Red Shale Meadows Trail (130). It can also be reached via the Lick Creek (151), Moonlight Peak (132), or Open Creek (116) trails.

THE NORTH WALL

- 0.0 Signpost in Red Shale Meadows.
- 0.5 Trail crosses the headwaters of Red Shale Creek.
- 1.2 Trail crosses the divide into the South Fork Lick Creek drainage.
- 3.6 Trail enters the North Fork Lick Creek drainage.
- 4.2 Trail crosses the North Fork of Lick Creek.
- 5.8 Trail crosses the divide into the South Fork Open Creek valley. Junction with the Moonlight Peak Trail (132). Stay left.
- 7.4 Trail crosses the pass behind Signal Mountain.
- 8.1 Unmarked junction with the cutoff trail to Lake Levale. Stay right.
- 8.4 Junction with the spur trail to Lake Levale. Through traffic should keep going straight ahead.
- 9.1 Trail reaches a junction with the Open Creek (116) and Kevan Mountain cutoff (732) trails.

The trail: The North Wall is truly one of the secret treasures of the Bob Marshall Wilderness. The wall itself runs for ten miles above the western rim of the Sun River Basin and is followed by a good-quality trail along its entire length. The North Wall is composed of buff-colored limestone and reddish shale of a different origin from the superficially similar Chinese Wall farther south. The trail that follows the foot of this great rampart is as remote and rigorous as it is rewarding, and thus is a good choice for travelers looking for solitude. The basins at the foot of the North Wall provide an important summer range for the Sun River elk herd, and the area also abounds with other species of wildlife.

From the trail junction in Red Shale Meadows, the North Wall trail heads to the north, passing through a lush verdure of grasses and wildflowers at the base of towering cliffs. Entering a subalpine forest at the edge of the meadows, the trail crosses the outlet stream that issues forth from Sock Lake. This alpine body of water lies in a hanging cirque carved into the lofty fastness of the North Wall and can only be reached via a steep scramble. The trail then begins to climb steadily across open

The sheer cliffs of the North Wall near Moonlight Pass.

glades at the foot of one of the loftier bastions of the North Wall. To the south rises the reddish whaleback of Lookout Mountain.

After passing through a broad saddle, the trail descends into the scorched upper reaches of Lick Creek's South Fork. The trail makes a long descent to reach the protected trees that survived the fire in the bottom of the valley. After a number of minor stream crossings, the trail levels out as it passes across the steep slopes that head the valley. To the west, a tiny rill cascades down through a cleft in the wall. The hidden summit of Hahn Peak slides by, and the trail begins its ascent into the saddle behind Lick Mountain. Just before reaching the pass, the trail crosses a tiny hidden meadow, then crests the rise and descends the open avalanche slope into the valley of Lick Creek.

The North Fork of Lick Creek escaped the Gates Park fire, and the verdant forests and flowery meadows of its upper basin are a welcome sight after the scorched devastation of the South Fork valley. The trail descends from the heights into the broken subalpine forest below. After crossing two substantial rivulets, the trail climbs onto a grassy slope to reach the signpost that marks the junction with the Lick Creek Trail (151). Stay left for the North Wall trail, which switchbacks up through the forest and then crosses a meadowy basin. Old Baldy and Rocky Mountain reign over the Sawtooth Range far to the east. The trail then begins a long and steady ascent through open parkland to reach the next saddle, where it reaches a junction with the Moonlight Peak Trail (132).

The main trail bends west as it descends, unveiling a spectacular view of the sheer cliffs stretching northward. The upper basin of the South Fork of Open Creek is kept bare of trees by frequent avalanches, and the trail enjoys excellent views as it sticks to the high tundra at the head of the basin. The next saddle, behind Signal Moun-

TRAIL 76 *NORTH WALL*

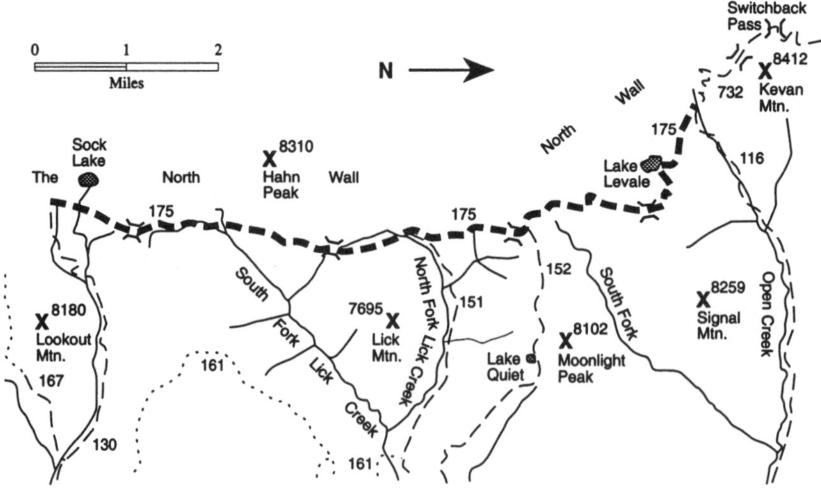

tain, is characterized by a number of washouts and sports a covering of whitebark pine. Beyond this saddle, the trail switchbacks steadily downward, through a dense forest of young subalpine fir that block out all views.

At the bottom of the grade, grassy glades open up the forest, and an unmarked trail heading toward Lake Levale cuts off to the left. The North Wall trail stays right, slowing its descent and crossing a small stream to reach a second, marked trail that covers the short distance to the lake. This turquoise gem lies in a barren cirque at the very foot of the cliffs. Imaginative visitors might find the hints of human faces in the shadowy crags of the walls overlooking the lake. Arctic grayling were recently planted in this lake and in a few years might offer an opportunity for backcountry angling.

After passing Lake Levale, the North Wall trail continues westward, leaving the gladed forest in favor of open avalanche slopes that reveal the full glory of the North Wall. Nearing the head of the next valley, the trail crosses a low ridge and descends toward Open Creek. The imposing bulwark at the northern end of the wall is Kevan Mountain. To the west, Open Creek cascades down sheer cliffs on its way to the valley floor. When the trail reaches its south bank, it reaches the signpost that marks the terminus of the hike. To the right, the Open Creek trail descends toward the North Fork of the Sun River. The Kevan Mountain Cutoff Trail (732) runs straight ahead, making a short but brutal climb that leads to Switchback Pass.

ADDITIONAL TRAILS

Observation Pass Trail (246, 139) is a moderately popular route into the Danaher Valley. It is well-maintained but is rather steep on the west side of the divide.

Patrol Mountain Lookout Trail (213) provides a steep route to a manned lookout. This trail is a fairly popular day hike and offers good views of Sugarloaf and Flint mountains.

Windfall Creek Trail (241, 243) is in poor shape and is slated for reconstruction. The upper end of Gibson Reservoir can only be crossed at low water.

Gibson Reservoir Trail (201) is a main access trail. It is steep and narrow at the present time and will be under heavy construction until at least 1997. Expect delays and frequent closures of the trail.

South Fork Sun River Trail (202) is heavily used and maintained annually. Beyond the Observation Pass trail junction, it becomes a poorly-maintained fire trail.

Prairie-Goat Creek Trail (249, 262) is a loop through the woods that is only in fair shape.

Bear Creek Trail (222) runs to Bear Lake at the foot of Prairie Reef. It is very steep and is slated for reconstruction.

Glenn Creek Trails (221, 250) are old fire trails and receive minimal maintenance.

Cabin Creek complex (231, 268, 208) is a series of hunter access trails lacking scenic value.

Blacktail Gulch Trail (220, 223) is extremely steep in the upper part of the gulch and is not a recommended route to the Sun River.

Biggs-Deep Creek Trail (128) has no public access through the private land to the east but can be reached via the Blacktail Gulch trail. It is popular with horse packers and is very scenic.

Moose Creek Trail (131) is overused and extremely muddy as a result. Avoid it if possible.

Rock Creek Trail (111) provides a well-defined route to the Chinese Wall. It travels through a forested valley bottom with limited views.

Biggs Flat Cutoff Trail (198) is very boggy, and may be hard to find at its northern end.

South Fork Red Shale (167) and **Lick Creek (161, 162)** fire trails receive little maintenance and are hard to follow.

Lick Creek Trail (151) provides a well-travelled route to the North Wall. The lower reaches of the valley burned in the Gates Park fire.

Open Creek Trail (116) is well maintained and was spared the Gates Park fire. It accesses the northern end of the North Wall.

North Fork Sun River Trails (110, 109) are heavily-traveled routes that follow the river.

Wrong Ridge Trail (187) is an old lookout trail that receives fairly frequent maintenance and is quite scenic.

Sawtooth Range

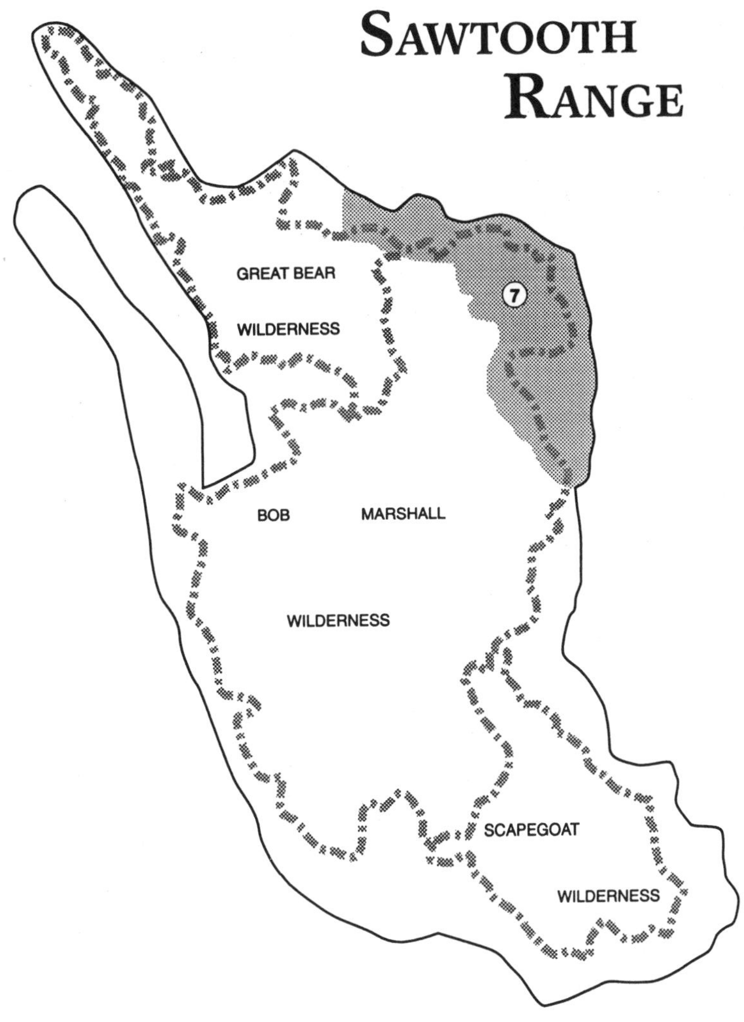

The jagged reefs of the Sawtooth Range provide some of the most spectacular scenery in the entire wilderness complex. Open, semi-arid valleys provide outstanding views of the surrounding cliffs, pinnacles, and hogbacks. The overthrust rock strata that make up the Front Ranges are laid bare of vegetation here. Ridges of resistant bedrock run north and south for twenty or more miles, separated by narrow, steep valleys that have been carved into the softer rock between the ridges by the relentless wear and tear of erosion. The few ancient streams and rivers that existed before the overthrust occurred have worn their way through these north-south ridges, and these old watercourses can be easily identified by their east-west orientation. Such streams are Birch and Dupuyer creeks, as well as the Sun River.

The reefs of the Front Ranges provide critical winter ranges for bighorn sheep, and large numbers of mountain goats congregate on the lofty peaks surrounding Rocky Mountain and Mount Field. Black bears are common in the moister draws and on forested hillsides, while a few mountain lions prowl the arid reef tops in search of mule deer and mountain sheep. There are scattered reports of wolves traveling through the area, and there is some hope that the wolf packs that are becoming established in Glacier National Park will soon begin to colonize these northern reaches of the Bob Marshall Wilderness. Although this arid, rocky country looks like ideal rattlesnake habitat, winters here are too cold to support these poisonous snakes.

Access to the Sawtooth Range is via several long gravel roads that turn muddy and slick during wet weather. The town of Choteau offers a variety of visitor services, while a more limited collection of businesses is located in the tiny settlement of Dupuyer. The area is administered by the Rocky Mountain Ranger District of the Lewis and Clark National Forest, also located in Choteau.

TRAIL 77 *OUR LAKE*

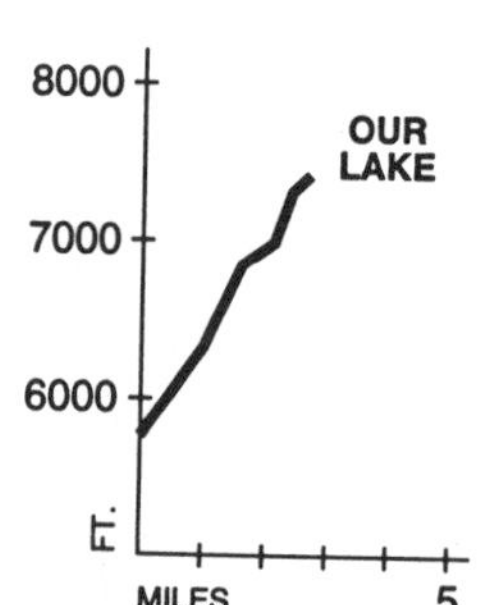

Trail 165, 184
General description: A day hike from the Headquarters Pass trailhead to Our Lake, 2.5 mi. (4.0 km).
Difficulty: Moderately strenuous.
Trail maintenance: Yearly.
Traffic: Heavy.
Elevation gain: 1,506 ft.
Maximum elevation: 7,300 ft.
Topo map: Our Lake.
Finding the trailhead: The trail begins at the Headquarters Pass trailhead. From U. S. Highway 89 take the Teton River Road, which departs the highway some 5 miles north of Choteau. Follow this road to the South Fork Teton Road and turn left on it. The trailhead is at the end of this road.

0.0 Headquarters Pass trailhead.
0.2 Junction with the Our Lake Trail (184). Turn right and begin climbing.
2.0 Trail crosses the outlet stream of Our Lake.
2.5 Foot of Our Lake.

The trail: Our Lake is a popular weekend destination for day hikers from Great Falls. It offers a moderate climb to a high alpine lake set in a rugged basin surrounded by imposing rock faces. Mountain goats scamper along the rocky faces above the lake, and cutthroat trout cruise its placid waters. Horses are not permitted on this trail, and camping should be limited to the basin below the lake. Because the lake receives so many visitors, it is important for each traveler to refrain from activities that might ruin the wilderness experience for others.

The trail begins at the Headquarters Pass trailhead and follows this trail (165) for the first 0.25 mile to reach the junction with the Our Lake Trail (184). There are interpretive signs relating to the ecology of Our Lake on this initial section of trail. Turn right as the Our Lake trail switchbacks northward through a spruce-fir forest,

The final approach to Our Lake.

gaining altitude steadily. The path then turns west, continuing its ascent as it passes among the sturdy boles of Douglas-fir. Openings in the timber reveal the towering eastern spur of Rocky Mountain to the south. As the trail continues upward, it passes onto rubble-strewn slopes below the limestone cliffs that now tower above the trail. Rounding a hillside, the two slender waterfalls of Our Lake's outlet stream dangle down their sheer headwalls. The trail climbs into the basin above the lower falls, where it arrives at a camping spot beside the stream. Livestock are absolutely forbidden beyond this point.

The trail crosses the stream below the foot of the upper falls and climbs the hillside to the south. It passes among groves of subalpine fir and the twisted forms of solitary whitebark pine. Straight ahead looms the twisted formation of limestone that rises to the east of the lake. The trail finally makes its way back to the north, covering the final distance to reach the lip of rock above the upper waterfall. Upon reaching this high point, the quiet waters of Our Lake spread out at the traveler's feet, filling a rugged basin rimmed with sheer rock walls. The west slope and Yellowstone cutthroat trout that cruise the clear waters of the lake are quite wary and provide only fair fishing. The rugged cliffs on both sides of the lake provide a nursery for young mountain goats, while marmots and ground squirrels inhabit the talus slopes at the foot of the cliffs. Adventurous climbers can ascend the avalanche chute west of the lake to reach the crest of the mountain range, then turn south along its crest to reach Headquarters Pass.

TRAIL 77 *OUR LAKE*

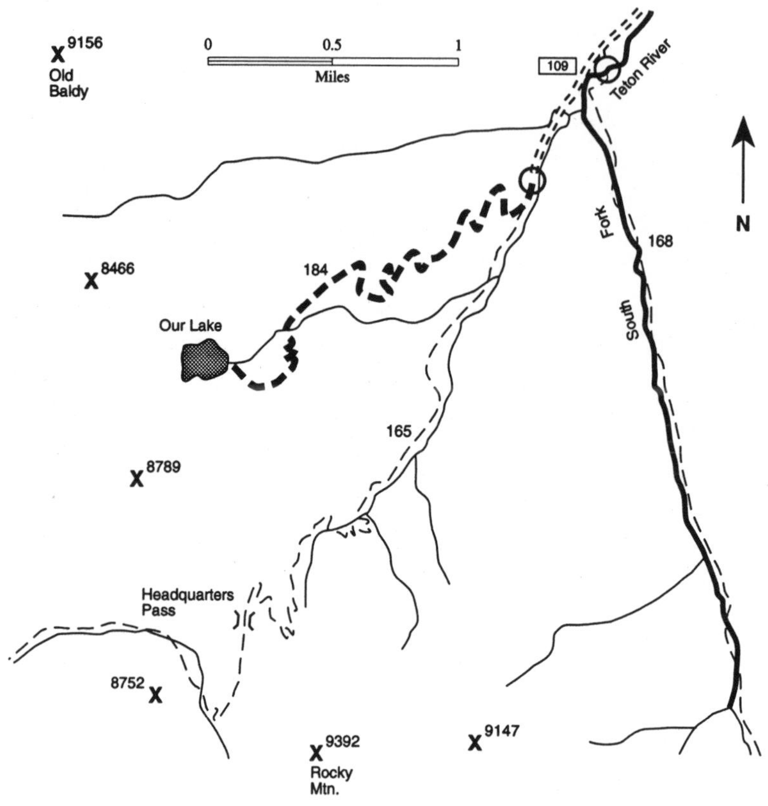

TRAIL 78 *HEADQUARTERS PASS*

Trail 165

General description: A day hike from the trailhead to Headquarters Pass, 2.8 mi. (4.5 km), or a backpack to the North Fork of the Sun, 9.9 mi. (15.9 km).

Difficulty: Moderately strenuous.

Trail maintenance: Yearly.

Traffic: Moderate.

Elevation gain: 1,949 ft.

Elevation loss: 2,534 ft.

Maximum elevation: 7,743 ft.

Topo maps: Our Lake, Gates Park.

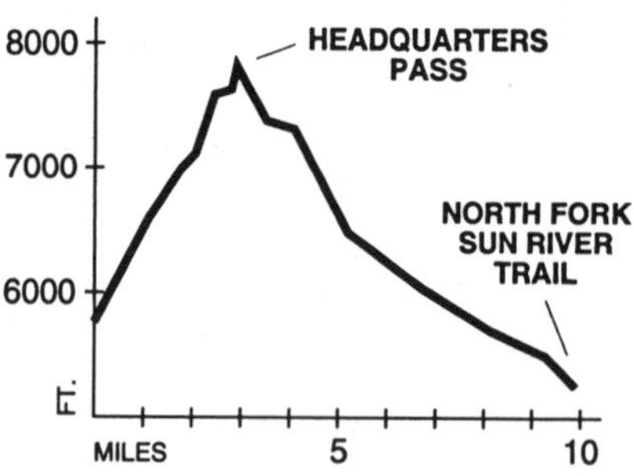

Finding the trailhead: The trail begins at the Headquarters Pass trailhead (see Our Lake, p. 248).

0.0 Headquarters Pass trailhead.
0.2 Junction with the Our Lake Trail (184). Stay left.
1.4 Trail crosses a nameless stream to reach its south bank.
1.9 Trail returns to the north bank of the stream.
2.8 Headquarters Pass. Trail enters the Bob Marshall Wilderness.
7.8 Junction with the Biggs Flat Cutoff Trail (198). Keep going straight.
9.3 Junction with the Dryden Creek cutoff trail. Keep going straight.
9.9 Trail reaches a junction with the North Fork Sun River Trail (109).

The trail: This heavily-traveled route crosses a lofty pass at the foot of Rocky Mountain, the tallest peak in the Bob Marshall Wilderness. It offers the easiest access to the Gates Park region in the Sun River Basin, and the pass itself is also a popular day hike destination. The latter part of the trail, to the west of Headquarters Pass, traverses a particularly heavily burned section of the Gates Park fire. This part of the trail is exceedingly boggy.

From the trailhead, the Headquarters Pass trail runs southwest, following the course of a tributary of the Teton River's South Fork. After passing a cluster of interpretive signs for Our Lake, the trail reaches a junction with the spur trail that climbs to this high alpine tarn. Stay to the left as the main trail continues to ascend gently along the valley floor. After crossing the outlet stream from Our Lake, the trail climbs into open timber that allows a magnificent view of Rocky Mountain. The trail climbs modestly for a mile or so to reach the first headwall, a two-tiered affair featuring elegant waterfalls down both faces. The path crosses the stream above the first falls, then climbs up the slope to the south of the second one, which manifests itself as a tangled skein of delicate silver threads.

At the top of this climb is an open bowl resting at the foot of the towering north face of Rocky Mountain. The trail passes through the bowl and up a finger of talus to mount a second headwall, a steep and arid slope of loose boulders. Above this wall lies a small, protected shelf where subalpine fir and whitebark pine cling to a precarious existence. The trail crosses the shelf and climbs on a northward heading as it ascends the third and lowest headwall. After a stiff climb, the trail reaches a scattering of trees and doglegs back to the south. A gentle climb leads to Headquarters Pass, which boasts excellent views to the east and west. Looking toward the plains, the broad shoulders of Choteau Mountain dominate the reefs of the Rocky Mountain Front, while the blood-red capstone of Hahn Peak crowns the ochre cliffs of the North Wall on the western horizon. Rugged massifs of limestone loom all around the pass.

From the pass, the trail descends southward across a steep talus slope, dropping into the alpine basin that bears the source of Headquarters Creek. The trail makes a sweeping arc around the head of the valley and descends steadily to the north, crossing alpine tundra and small copses of fir. The path reaches the lower edge of this hanging basin, and drops into the scorched valley beyond. This country burned during the Gates Park fire of 1988 and is now in the first stages of regeneration. Grasses and flowering plants, such as beargrass and fireweed, predominate while

TRAIL 78 *HEADQUARTERS PASS*
TRAIL 79 *ROUTE CREEK PASS*

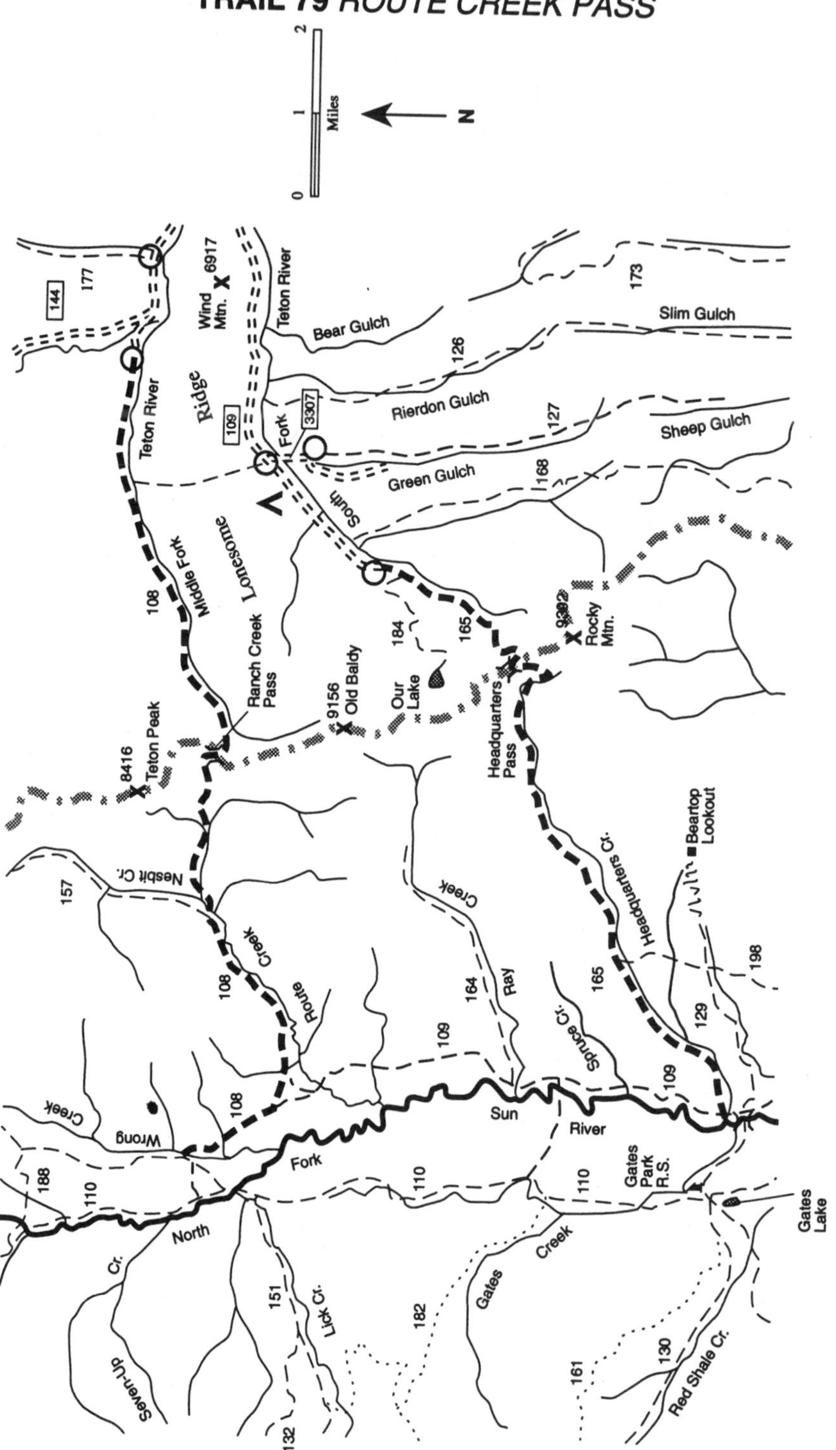

small shrubs are just beginning to colonize the burn site. The trail is a bit muddy at the upper end of the valley, but it soon dries out as it descends across the steep, well-drained hillsides above Headquarters Creek. By removing the forest canopy, the fire has opened up views of the rugged mountains surrounding this narrow valley.

After the trail dips into the creek bottom to avoid an out-thrust limestone cliff, the valley widens into a broad lowland flanked by rolling hills. The trail crosses an interminable series of horse-eating quagmires as it crosses the tablelands above the creek. Expect muddy traveling for the next several miles. One Forest Service researcher estimates that each tree sucks up to ninety gallons of water from the soil each year. Now that the fire has killed all of the trees that once covered this landscape, the water that was once absorbed by the forest now remains in the poorly-drained soil. As a result, formerly damp soils have slid into the creek, and soils that were once quite dry are now saturated with water.

Just before reaching the Sun River, the trail passes a marked intersection with the Dryden Creek trail, which heads toward Beartop Lookout. Staying on the main trail will be easy here because the Dryden Creek trail is quite faint. The last 0.5 mile to the North Fork Sun River Trail (110) is less muddy and boasts views of Moose Ridge far to the southwest. The trail intersects with the North Fork trail just north of the pack bridge that leads to Gates Park.

TRAIL 79 *ROUTE CREEK PASS*

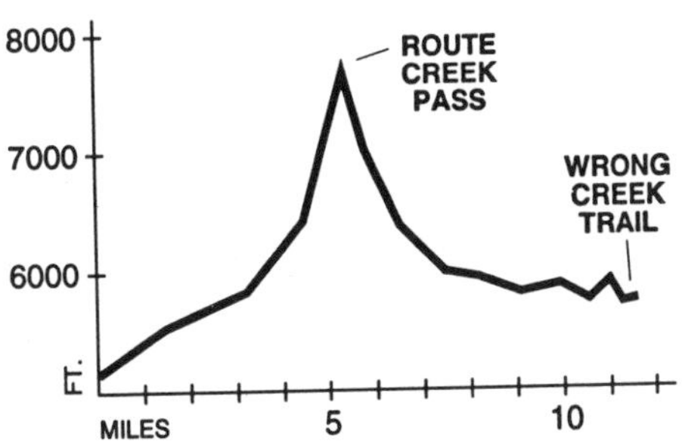

Trail 108

General description: A backpack from the Cave Mountain trailhead to the Wrong Creek trail, 11.5 mi. (18.5 km).

Difficulty: Moderately Strenuous.

Trail maintenance: Yearly.

Traffic: Moderate.

Elevation gain: 2,629 ft.

Elevation loss: 2,109 ft.

Maximum elevation: 7,623 ft.

Topo maps: Cave Mountain, Our Lake, Mount Wright, Gates Park.

Finding the trailhead: Take the Teton River Road, which begins from U.S. Highway 89, 5 miles north of Choteau. Follow this road past the South Fork Road junction and into the mountains. Five miles up the canyon, take a left on the Cave Mountain recreation site road. Bear right until the campground is reached and take the left fork at the campground to reach the trailhead at the end of the road.

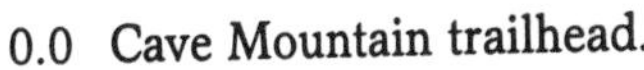

0.0 Cave Mountain trailhead.
1.3 Trail crosses a nameless stream.
1.4 Junction with the Lonesome Ridge trail. Stay right.
2.4 Trail crosses Garners Gulch.
5.3 Route Creek Pass. Trail enters the Bob Marshall Wilderness.

The barren col of Route Creek Pass frames Old Baldy.

7.4 Trail makes two fords of Route Creek in rapid succession.
7.5 Junction with the Nesbit Creek Trail (157). Keep going straight.
10.0 Junction with a cutoff trail to the east side North fork Trail (115). Bear right.
10.3 Junction with the east side North Fork Trail (115). Keep right.
11.4 Trail fords Wrong Creek.
11.5 Junction with the Wrong Creek Trail (117).

The trail: This trail offers a good-quality route into the northern end of the Sun River Basin. The trail has been reconstructed recently, but the old trail bed still remains on the ground, running in tandem with the new trail up to Route Creek Pass. In general, the uppermost trail is the new and currently-maintained version, while the old trail bed stays closer to the Middle Fork of the Teton. Beyond the pass, the valley of Route Creek has largely escaped the rages of the Gates Park fire. A trail that connects the Middle and South forks of the Teton allows for the possibility of a loop trip when combined with the Headquarters Pass trail.

At its outset, the trail passes through a gate, then runs westward along the north bank of the Middle Fork of the Teton. The trail runs along the hillside just above the valley floor, occasionally dipping into the tall aspen of the creek bottom. Early views from the open hillside include a bald dome near the head of the valley, as well as the rugged cliffs of Lonesome Ridge to the south. Look to the north as the trail crosses a dry gulch to get a fleeting glimpse of the ragged summit of Cave Mountain. Two miles up the valley, the trail passes through a second gate and crosses a tributary stream to reach a junction with the Lonesome Ridge cutoff trail. Stay right for Route Creek Pass.

Beyond this junction, the trail continues westward. It crosses a second stream after about a mile then climbs onto a talus slope above a series of beaver ponds. The surrounding country becomes drier and more rugged as the trail makes its gentle upward progress. After crossing a third small stream, the forest is reduced to a scattering of scruffy subalpine fir. The trail begins climbing in earnest as it passes into the barren, rocky canyon that bears the upper reaches of the Middle Fork. As the trail mounts the wall to the north of the river's headwaters, Old Baldy looms to the south like a sleeping giant of stone. The brisk climb continues through a loose grove of limber pine, twisted into fantastic shapes by the fierce winds that roar through the pass on a regular basis.

The trail finally climbs above all but a few hardy alpine plants as it enters the windswept saddle of Route Creek Pass. From the bleak summit of the pass, bald domes of rock block out northward views, while the pointed summits of Wapati Ridge stand guard over the western skyline. The trail then drops into the Route Creek drainage, which was spared the ravages of the Gates Creek fire. The trail zigzags down into a dry gulch filled with scrubby firs, then follows its bottom westward to reach the edge of the much deeper Route Creek valley. Exiting the high ravine, the trail runs north along the north wall of the valley. The trail drops steadily across grassy slopes, as the west face of Old Baldy looms above the lesser peaks to the south.

After crossing a small stream, the trail enters a dense forest of Douglas-fir and lodgepole pine. Thus ends the scenic part of the journey. About a mile further west, the trail fords Route Creek twice in rapid succession to reach a junction with the Nesbit Creek Trail (157). The Route Creek trail continues westward along the creek, descending more gently as it passes through Ninemile and Tenmile parks. These two openings are really nothing more than the lower aprons of steep avalanche slopes. The trail soon makes its way out of the foothills and into the rolling country of the Sun River Basin. The terrain on these flatlands is quite swampy, and mudholes of prodigious size should be expected here.

The trail passes through a section of forest destroyed by the Gates Creek fire, then crests a low ridge bearing the intersection with the East Side North Fork Sun Trail (115). Stay right for Wrong Creek. Half a mile before reaching this stream, the trail moves into a patch of unburned forest. Upon reaching Wrong Creek, travelers can make a knee-deep ford or try a perilous log walk over the stream. On the far bank, the trail reaches a junction with the Wrong Creek Trail (117), a few hundred yards downstream of a Forest Service cabin bearing the same name.

TRAIL 80 *JONES GULCH*

Trail 155

General description: A day hike from the trailhead to the end of the trail, 2.0 mi. (3.2 km).

Difficulty: Moderate.

Trail maintenance: Frequent.

Traffic: Moderate.

Elevation gain: 515 ft.

Elevation loss: 115 ft.

Maximum elevation: 5,775 ft.

Topo map: Cave Mountain.

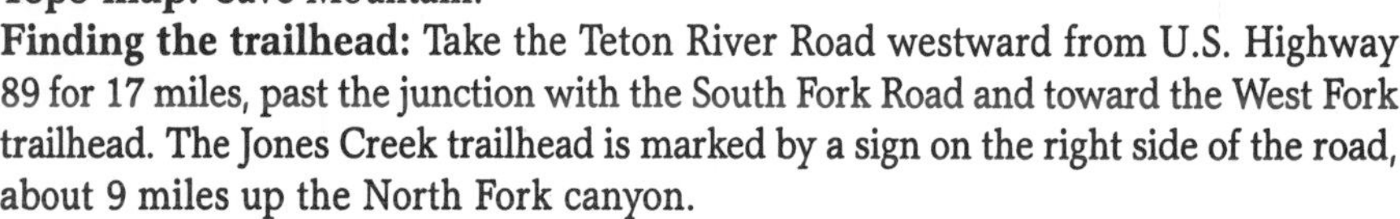

Finding the trailhead: Take the Teton River Road westward from U.S. Highway 89 for 17 miles, past the junction with the South Fork Road and toward the West Fork trailhead. The Jones Creek trailhead is marked by a sign on the right side of the road, about 9 miles up the North Fork canyon.

0.0 Jones Creek trailhead.
1.3 Trail crosses the bed of the West Fork of Jones Creek.
1.4 Junction with the West Fork Jones Creek route (156). Bear right.
2.0 Trail peters out on the gravel bar of Jones Creek.

Reefs rim along the upper valley of Jones Creek.

TRAIL 80 *JONES GULCH*

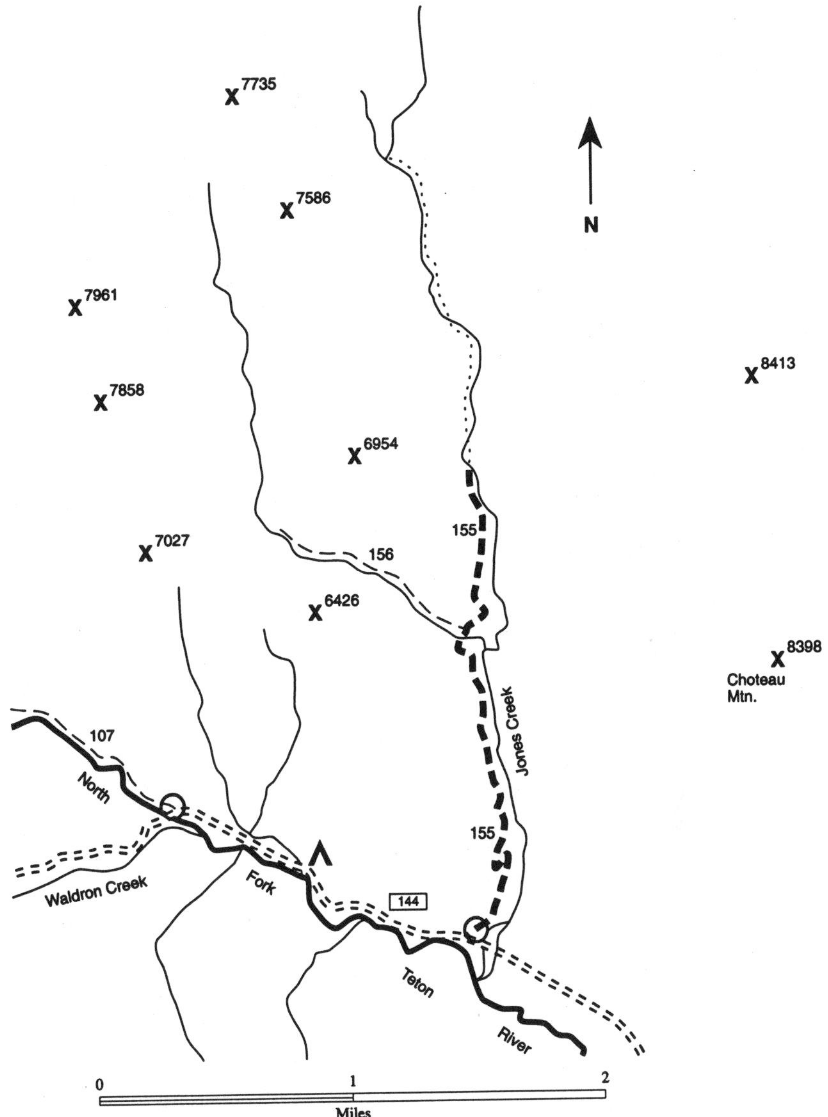

The trail: This trail offers a short day hike that is well-known for its rugged scenery and easy access. The trail leaves the east side of the trailhead parking lot, heading northward past a beaver pond to reach a gate in a barbed wire fence. Pass through and remember to close the gate behind you. The trail climbs gently across an open east-facing slope and a glance southward reveals the sharp points of Wind Mountain as well as the much larger massif of Ear Mountain beyond it. The trail then passes another series of beaver ponds. The evidence of labor by beaver surrounds the ponds; aspens are cut off neatly about a foot above the ground, attesting to the voracious appetite of this oversized rodent. To the east, the hulking mass of Choteau Mountain looms above the lesser reefs of the Rocky Mountain Front. The actual summit of the mountain lies atop the more smooth-sided southerly peak, not the more jagged northern rib.

As the trail climbs across the grassy slopes on the west side of the valley, the tilted reefs of the Front Ranges appear at the head of the valley. The trail then begins to descend through a stand of small Douglas-fir and lodgepole pine. Watch for black bears, which haunt this miniature forest. The trail makes its way down to the gravel wash that represents the West Fork of Jones Creek during spring runoff. Upon reaching the stream bed, the trail turns downstream for twenty-five yards before climbing the aspen-covered slope beyond. A short distance up this hillside, the trail intersects with the West Fork Trail (156), which takes off to the left. This trail is really no more than an abandoned road bed, and does not receive enough traffic to maintain a recognizable path.

The main trail bends eastward, following another old roadbed to the crest of the next bluff. Look south from this high point to see the lofty summit of Cave Mountain above the North Fork of the Teton to the west. The trail then descends gradually to reach the main wash of Jones Creek, where it disappears as a recognizable path. It is easy to follow the creek bed northwest for several more miles, and the views in the upper reaches of the drainage provide an ample reward for hikers that make the trip.

TRAIL 81 *NORTH FORK OF THE TETON*

Trail 107

General description: A backpack from the West Fork Teton Cabin to the South Fork of Birch Creek, 12.2 mi. (19.6 km).

Difficulty: Moderately strenuous.

Trail maintenance: Frequent.

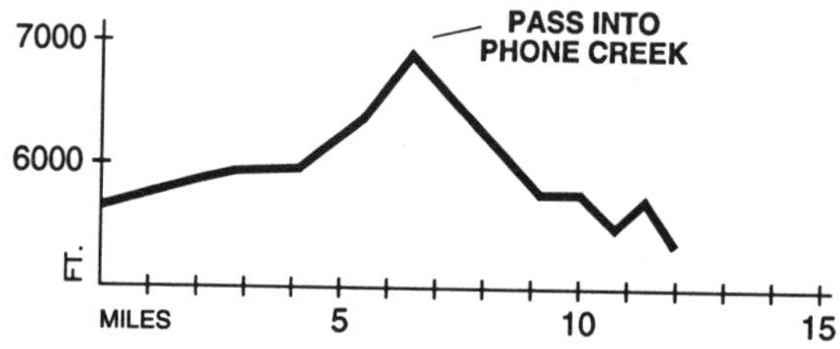

Traffic: Moderate to Bruce Creek; light beyond.

Elevation gain: 1,647 ft.

Elevation loss: 1,985 ft.

Maximum elevation: 6,900 ft.

Topo maps: Mount Wright, Walling Reef, Gateway Pass.

Finding the trailhead: Take the Teton River Road from a point 5 miles north of Choteau on U.S. Highway 89. The pavement ends after 18 miles, and a gravel road then winds northward for 17 miles through the mountains, passing a small ski area on its way to the West Fork trailhead at the end of the road.

TRAIL 81 *NORTH FORK OF THE TETON*
TRAIL 82 *CORRUGATE RIDGE*

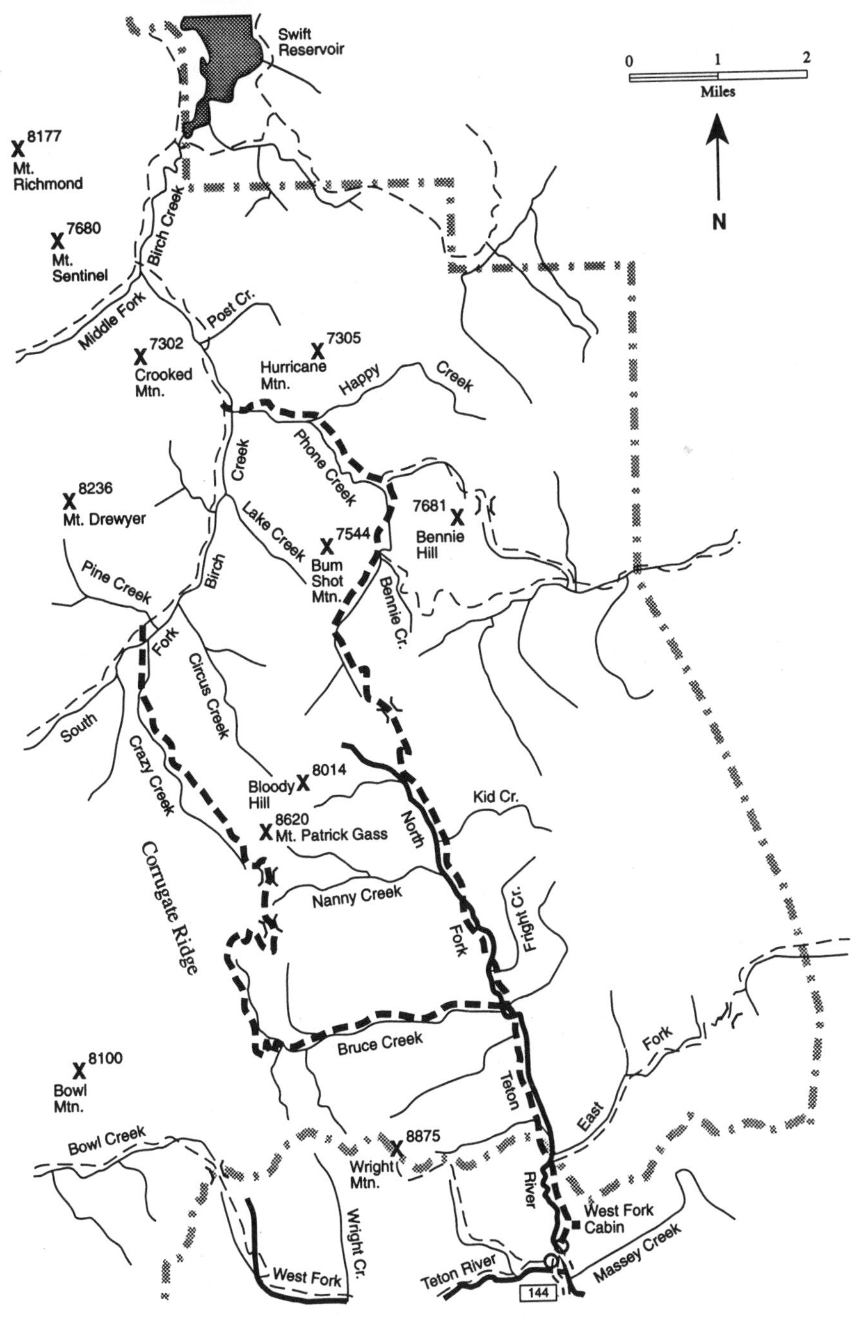

0.0 West Fork Teton Cabin complex.
0.9 Junction with the East Fork - Blacktail Trail (106). North Fork Trail fords the river to reach its west bank.
1.0 Bob Marshall Wilderness boundary.
2.6 Trail returns to the east bank of the North Fork of the Teton.
2.7 Junction with the Bruce Creek Trail (152). Bear right.
3.1 Trail crosses Fright Creek.
3.3 Trail fords the North Fork to reach the west bank.
4.2 Trail makes its final ford of the North Fork.
4.8 Trail crosses Kid Creek.
6.6 Trail crosses the divide to enter the Phone Creek valley.
8.0 Trail crosses Phone Creek to reach its western bank.
9.0 Junction with the North Fork Dupuyer Creek Trail (124). Stay left.
9.4 Trail returns to the east bank of Phone Creek.
9.9 Trail crosses Seedling Creek.
10.0 Junction with the Seedling Creek route (182). Bear left.
11.0 Trail fords Happy Creek.
11.9 Trail crosses Phone Creek to reach its south bank.
12.1 Trail fords the South Fork of Birch Creek.
12.2 Junction with the South Fork Birch Creek Trail (105).

The trail: This trail is an access route to the lower drainage of the South Fork of Birch Creek. It can be combined with the Corrugate Ridge trail to form a two- or three-day loop trip. The trail begins by running through the West Fork Teton Cabin complex, then follows the eastern edge of the bottoms of the North Fork of the Teton. The imposing peak to the west is Mount Wright. After a mile or so, the trail reaches the first ford of the North Fork, a knee-deep affair that also serves as the takeoff point for the rather faint East Fork - Blackleaf Trail (106). On the west bank of the river, the trail crosses the wilderness boundary. It then continues northward, dipping into the forest and emerging at the edge of the North Fork's gravel outwash plain. After a short distance, the trail abandons the forest edge to disappear into the timber. The next opening is provided by the gravel wash of a small stream that descends from the shoulders of Mount Wright. After crossing this stream, the trail fords the Teton again and reaches a poorly marked junction with the Corrugate Ridge Trail (152).

The North Fork trail continues straight ahead, crossing the gravel bed of Fright Creek and then the creek itself before returning to the west bank of the Teton. The trail follows the "river" northward for the better part of a mile through stands of lodgepole pine dotted with grassy openings. The trail then fords the Teton again, and the crossing offers fine views of Mount Patrick Gass and Bloody Hill. The path then disappears into a deep lowland forest of spruce, emerging only briefly to cross the gravel bar of Kid Creek.

After this crossing, the climb begins to stiffen, and the bottomland forest gives way to subalpine fir. A mile beyond Kid Creek, the trail departs the streamside to climb the east wall of the valley. There may be some confusion here, because the old (and abandoned) trail still exists in many places; stay to the right and expect numerous switchbacks on the new trail. Nearing its high point, the trail climbs across a few small openings that allow grand views of the summits to the west. The path then runs north into the pass itself, where subalpine meadows and fir stands are overlooked by the pale walls to the east.

The trail then descends steadily through the forested upper reaches of Phone Creek, which is crowded closely by low hills. The forest opens up 1.5 miles beyond the pass, and the trail drops down to cross Phone Creek and then climbs into the grassy meadows of its west bank. The trails gets a bit sketchy between this ford and Seedling Creek; pay close attention to the trail and its overgrown bed will become apparent. As the valley bends to the northeast, the trail passes through a sort of gateway in the mountains. Sheer, pale cliffs close in on the rushing stream. Once the trail makes it through the narrows, it switchbacks down to the valley floor and continues downstream across the bare gravel of the floodplain.

The route soon wanders onto grassy meadows dotted with copses of aspen. These trees can reproduce by sending up new stems from an existing rootstock. These new "trees" are actually clones of the parent tree, and the clumps of aspen that one often sees here are really the several stems of a single individual plant. After a time, the trail climbs a bit and enters a stand of lodgepole. Here, it reaches a well-marked junction with the trail that runs east to Bennie Hill and beyond to the North Fork of Dupuyer Creek (124). The main trail then descends along the west bank of the creek to reach a ford about halfway between Bennie and Seedling creeks. From this ford, travelers must follow the cairns across the gravel bars on the east side of Phone Creek in order to find the point where the trail leaves the creek bed.

The path then rises onto the hillside, passing through a loose forest of lodgepole pine that offers good views of Bum Shot Mountain. This massif was named in honor of a nimrod hunter who emptied his rifle at a herd of elk at close range and failed to hit anything. The trail bends around to the east as it crosses Seedling Creek, then reaches a small meadow on the north bank of this tributary stream. In this opening, the very faint Seedling-Potshot Trail (182) takes off to the east. The North Fork Teton trail continues northward, passing through the dense lodgepole of the creek bottom and then climbing onto the open slopes beyond. The flood of 1964 ripped huge gashes in the sides of the Phone Creek valley, and the trail wanders high onto the hillside to avoid these slideouts.

After dropping down to cross Happy Creek (watch for cairns marking the route), the trail climbs high onto the slopes of the next hill. From here, the west face of Bum Shot Mountain looms to the west, while Crooked Mountain Rises beyond the South Fork of Birch Creek to the north. After reaching its apex, the trail descends steadily to the valley floor, fording Phone Creek and running north for a few hundred brushy yards to reach the bank of the South Fork of Birch Creek. The trail makes a knee-deep ford, then climbs eastward to meet the South Fork Trail (105) at a marked junction.

TRAIL 82 *CORRUGATE RIDGE*

Trail 107, 152 (see map on p. 259)

General description: A backpack from the West Fork Teton Cabin to the South Fork of Birch Creek, 12.8 mi. (20.6 km).

Difficulty: Moderate.

Trail maintenance: Frequent.

Traffic: Moderate to Bruce Creek; light beyond.

Elevation gain: 2,307 ft.

Elevation loss: 2,185 ft.

Maximum elevation: 7,730 ft.

Topo maps: Mount Wright, Porphyry Reef, Gateway Pass.

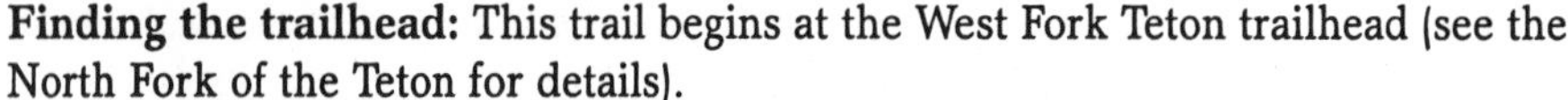

Finding the trailhead: This trail begins at the West Fork Teton trailhead (see the North Fork of the Teton for details).

- 0.0 West Fork Teton Cabin complex.
- 0.9 Junction with the East Fork - Blacktail Trail (106). North Fork trail fords the river to reach its west bank.
- 1.0 Bob Marshall Wilderness boundary.
- 2.6 Trail returns to the east bank of the North Fork of the Teton.
- 2.7 Junction with the Bruce Creek Trail (152). Turn left.
- 2.8 Trail fords the North Fork of the Teton and enters the valley of Bruce Creek.
- 5.5 Trail fords Bruce Creek to reach its west bank.
- 7.3 Trail crosses the headwaters of Bruce Creek.
- 8.5 Trail crosses the pass into the Nanny Creek drainage.
- 9.0 Trail enters the Crazy Creek valley via a lower pass.
- 12.0 Trail crosses Crazy Creek to reach its west bank.
- 12.6 Trail fords the South Fork of Birch Creek.
- 12.8 Junction with the South Fork Birch Creek Trail (105).

The trail: This trail follows the foot of Corrugate Ridge, an imposing rock wall that defines the boundary between the Teton and Sun River drainages. The ascents on this trail are quite gradual due to the shallow grade of its switchbacks. This makes the trail ideal for foot travelers who want to reach the peaks without a steep climb, but may be frustrating for more aggressive hikers. The high alpine areas along the boundary between Bruce and Nanny Creeks are quite susceptible to damage; select a camping spot at lower elevations to avoid damaging the alpine tundra. This trail is typically impassible during early summer, when lingering snowdrifts and spring avalanches block the trail. Travelers should expect muddy conditions along this trail following wet weather.

The trail begins at the West Fork Teton Cabin complex and follows the North Fork

Teton Trail (107) for the first 2.7 miles. After making two knee-deep fords of the North Fork of the Teton, the trail reaches a marked junction on the east bank of the river. The Corrugate Ridge trail is indicated by a sign reading, "Bruce Creek Trail 152." Turn west on this trail and cross the much-reduced flow of the North Fork to reach its western bank. After crossing the "river," the Corrugate Ridge trail climbs gently through the forest as it follows the north bank of Bruce Creek. The going can be muddy on this section of the trail, especially after a rainstorm. However, the views are rewarding: Mount Wright rises majestically to the south, while the bleached spires of a nameless southern spur of Mount Patrick Gass loom to the north.

After several miles, the trail crosses Bruce Creek and climbs gently but steadily up the slopes below the rocky wall of Corrugate Ridge. This impressive reef towers above the western rim of the valley. As the valley bends northward, the trail crosses a series of open avalanche slopes that allow vistas of the whitewashed peaks that surround the Bruce Creek drainage. Soon, the trail passes into the open bowls near the timberline, then turns eastward to cross Bruce Creek a final time. The trail then climbs lackadaisically up the eastern wall of the valley, crossing open slopes that show off the serpentine length of Corrugate Ridge, which terminates in a sharp horn peak at its southern end.

The trail ultimately makes its way onto the eroded wastelands above the timberline, then drops into a beautiful protected basin clothed in tundra meadows and shapely fir. The alabaster slabs of Mount Patrick Gass loom immediately ahead, while the Old Man of the Hills dominates the skyline to the east. The trail runs northward

The summit of Mount Patrick Gass.

along the headwall of this tiny basin, which drains eastward into Nanny Creek. The route then drops through a lower pass and enters the open expanse of the Crazy Creek valley. Mounts Drewyer and Field rise to the north, while the wall of Corrugate Ridge continues in the western side of this new valley. The trail then switchbacks downward across the white rubble covering the western slope of Mount Patrick Gass.

Upon reaching the floor of the valley, the trail follows a tiny rivulet through open meadows and copses of fir, then passes back onto the windswept eastern side of the valley. The power of winter winds can be seen everywhere on these unprotected slopes. Subalpine fir and evergreen shrubs grow prostrate to the ground, and limber pine have been twisted into tortured shapes by the icy gales of winter. Even the aspen growing in the protected coulees seem to crouch down to avoid the wintry blast. As the trail nears the mouth of the valley, it descends through a lodgepole pine forest to cross Crazy Creek, then climbs onto the far bank to complete the final descent. Upon reaching the aspen-choked bottomlands of the South Fork of Birch Creek, the trail fords this icy stream and begins climbing to the northwest. After a brief and gentle ascent, the trail reaches its terminus at a junction with the South Fork Birch Creek Trail (105)).

TRAIL 83 *SOUTH FORK OF BIRCH CREEK*

Trail 143, 105
General description: A backpack from the Swift Dam trailhead to Gateway Pass, 11.6 mi. (18.7 km).
Difficulty: Moderate.
Trail maintenance: Yearly.
Traffic: Moderate.
Elevation gain: 2,843 ft.
Elevation loss: 1,145 ft.
Maximum elevation: 6,478 ft.
Topo maps: Fish Lake, Swift Reservoir, Gateway Pass

7000
6000
5000
FT.
MILES 5 10
JCT. NORTH FORK TETON TRAIL
GATEWAY PASS

Finding the trailhead: From U.S.
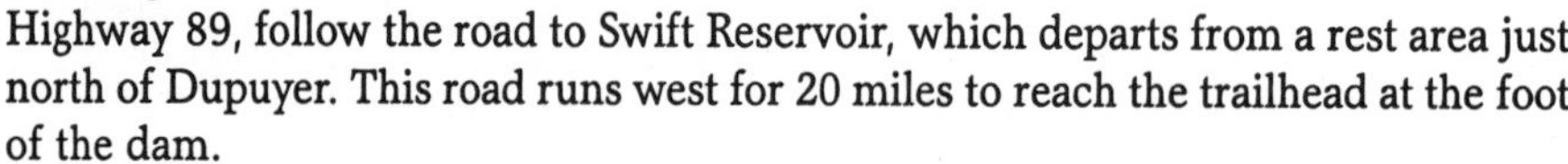
Highway 89, follow the road to Swift Reservoir, which departs from a rest area just north of Dupuyer. This road runs west for 20 miles to reach the trailhead at the foot of the dam.

0.0 Swift Dam trailhead.
1.3 Hellroaring Spring.
2.0 Junction with the Walling Reef Trail (150). Stay right.
2.3 Trail crosses Phillips Creek.
3.0 Trail makes a ford of Birch Creek.
3.1 Junction with the South Fork Birch Creek Trail (105). Turn left.
4.6 Junction with the Middle Fork Trail (123). Turn left and ford Birch Creek.

5.6 Trail crosses Post Creek.

Bighorn Mountain rises above the headwaters of the South Fork.

- 5.7 Trail fords the South Fork to reach its west bank.
- 6.3 Junction with the North Fork Teton Trail (107). Stay right.
- 9.0 Trail crosses Pinto Creek.
- 9.1 Junction with the Corrugate Ridge Trail (152). Keep going straight for Gateway Pass.
- 11.6 Gateway Pass.

The trail: This trail runs up the rugged valley of the Birch Creek's South Fork, an open, windswept basin rimmed with towering peaks. It also provides the most direct access to Gateway Pass, which leads into the headwaters of the Middle Fork of the Flathead. Although the trail begins at a junction on the North Fork Birch Creek Trail (121), it is most commonly reached via the trail around the south shore of Swift Reservoir. This access route sports a tricky ford of the South Fork which is quite hazardous during spring runoff. The trail on the north side of the reservoir crosses Blackfeet Indian land and is currently closed to the public. However, the Forest Service is currently negotiating for a public easement through the reservation lands, and the northern route may soon be open to the public.

From Swift Dam, hike up the access road to the south of the dam to reach the shore of the reservoir. A trail follows the shoreline, rising and falling as it reveals vistas of Major Steel Backbone, Mount Richmond, and Mount Sentinel. After passing Hellroaring Spring, the trail climbs to a high point, then descends toward a junction with the lightly-maintained Walling Reef Trail (150). The trail then drops down to ford Phillips Creek and climbs over a low rise before descending to the banks of Birch Creek. The trail makes a tricky thigh-deep ford of the rushing stream. Soon afterward, the trail reaches a junction with the South Fork Birch Creek Trail (143); turn left here.

After passing southwestward through arid country for about a mile, the trail reaches a junction with the Middle Fork Trail (123). It will be necessary to turn left here, crossing the stream at a thigh-deep ford just below the confluence of the Middle and South forks. The trail then works its way up a muddy gulch to emerge on a grassy

TRAIL 83 *SOUTH FORK OF BIRCH CREEK*

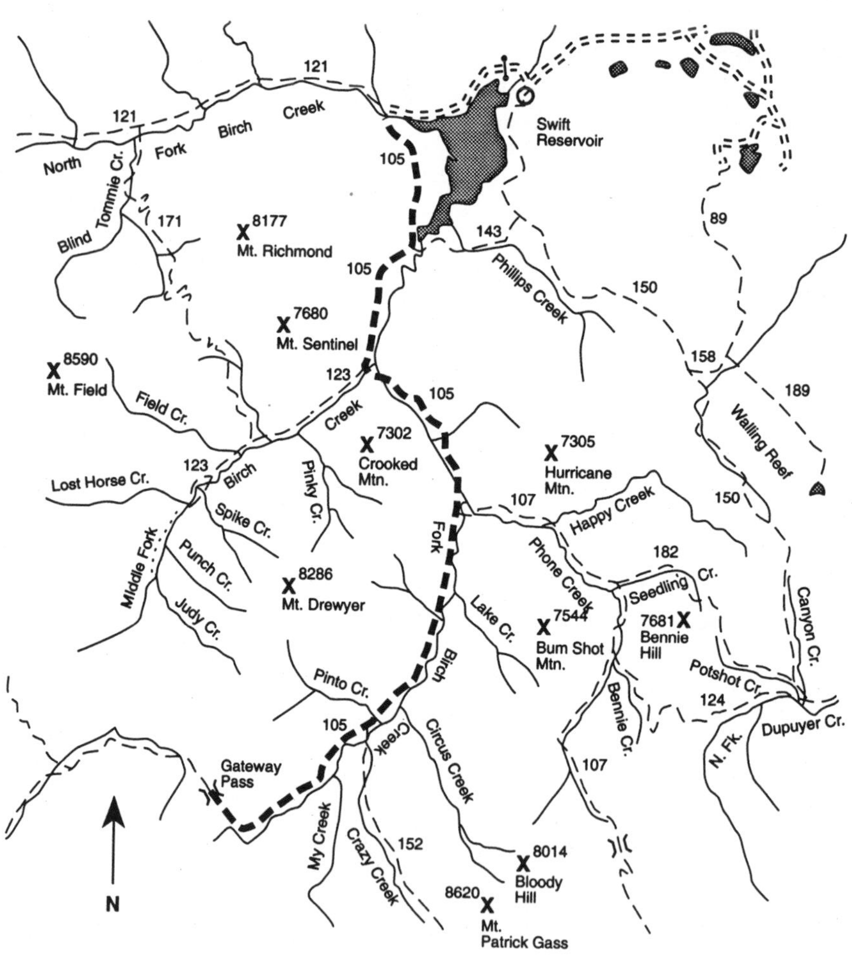

hilltop above the South Fork. Bum Shot Mountain dominates the valley to the south. The rugged face of Crooked Mountain looms across the creek, while a backward glance yields fine views of Mount Sentinel. The trail makes its way beneath the slickrock face of a nameless reef, sporting small waterfalls that descend from hidden basins. As the trail continues southward, the tilted slabs of Mount Patrick Gass reveal themselves further up the valley. This peak, one of the most impressive reefs in the area, was named in honor of a member of the Lewis and Clark expedition.

The trail crosses Post Creek and quickly makes its way down to the shores of the South Fork. After a knee-deep ford, travelers must make a short but muddy slog through the timber. Upon reaching its apogee, the trail passes above a sheer gorge lined with jagged rocks. After emerging on the grassy slopes beyond, the trail reaches a rather confusing junction with the North Fork Teton Trail (107). The latter trail descends to a ford of the creek, while the main trail turns southwest, sticking to the higher ground. Looking southward up the valley of Phone Creek, an unnamed spire towers above the timber to the east. The trail soon drops back into the trees, passing above and out of sight of another narrow gorge. After two thirds of a mile, several hunter's trails descend to the creek bottoms on their way to the Lake Creek valley.

Immediately after this point, the South Fork trail makes its way above the sinuous cleft of yet another twisting canyon. The trail passes through a vigorous forest of aspen and lodgepole pine, and then the forest opens up to reveal Mount Patrick Gass rising majestically above the Circus Creek valley. The trail crosses grassy slopes on its way to the broad gravel fan of Pine Creek, then reaches the Corrugate Ridge Trail (152) in the meadows opposite Crazy Creek. From this junction, the trail continues southwest through the trees, passing above a nameless waterfall on the South Fork. The trail passes through a number of boggy spots before climbing moderately across the open moorland of a south-facing slope. Bighorn Peak and its northern spur loom at the head of the valley, their towering ramparts rising above the virgin forest. The trail follows the valley as it makes a sharp bend to the northwest, climbing through a shallow, wooded ravine to reach Gateway Pass. The trail beyond this point is discussed in the Gateway Gorge section, page 47.

TRAIL 84 *BIRCH CREEK LOOP*

Trail 143, 105, 121, 171, 123

General description: A backpack or long day hike linking the North and Middle Forks of Birch Creek, 17.8 mi. (28.6 km) round trip.

Difficulty: Moderately strenuous (counterclockwise); strenuous (clockwise).

Trail maintenance: Occasional along Blind Tommie and Tubby creeks; otherwise yearly.

Traffic: Very light between the North and Middle Forks of Birch Creek; otherwise moderate.

Elevation gain: 4,545 ft.

Elevation loss: 4,545 ft.

Maximum elevation: 6,860 ft.

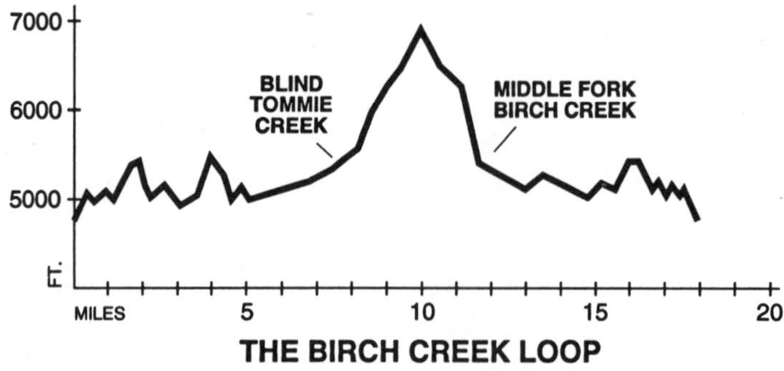

Topo maps: Fish Lake, Swift Reservoir, Gateway Pass.
Finding the trailhead: The trail begins at the Swift Dam trailhead (see the South Fork of Birch Creek).

- 0.0 Swift Dam trailhead.
- 1.3 Hellroaring Spring.
- 2.0 Junction with the Walling Reef Trail (150). Stay right.
- 2.3 Trail crosses Phillips Creek.
- 3.0 Trail makes a ford of Birch Creek.
- 3.1 Junction with the South Fork Birch Creek Trail (105). Turn right.
- 4.6 Trail fords the North Fork of Birch Creek.
- 4.8 Junction with the North Fork Birch Creek Trail (121). Turn left.
- 5.1 Trail makes two fords of the North Fork in rapid succession.
- 6.3 Trail crosses Hungry Man Creek.
- 6.4 Unmarked junction with the Hungry Man Trail (122). Keep going straight.
- 6.9 Trail crosses Killem Horse Creek.
- 7.5 Junction with the Blind Tommie Trail (171). Turn left.
- 7.6 Trail crosses the North Fork of Birch Creek and enters the Blind Tommie valley.
- 8.2 Trail makes two fords of Blind Tommie Creek.
- 10.0 Trail crosses the divide into the Tubby Creek drainage.
- 11.6 Junction with the Middle Fork Birch Creek Trail (123). Turn left.
- 13.2 Junction with the South Fork Birch Creek Trail (105). Stay left.
- 14.7 Junction with the south shore Swift Reservoir Trail (143). Turn right and ford Birch Creek.
- 15.5 Trail crosses Phillips Creek.
- 15.8 Junction with the Walling Reef trail. Stay left.
- 17.8 Swift Dam trailhead.

The trail: This loop trail can be hiked as a two-day trip, or may be attempted in a single day by hikers that are in excellent physical shape. It travels through some of the most scenic landscapes in the Birch Creek country, offering views of such awe-inspiring peaks as Mount Field and Mount Patrick Gass. The trail running along the Tubby Creek drainage is very steep and difficult to follow when approaching it from the south. Hiking this route in a counterclockwise direction is therefore strongly

TRAIL 84 *BIRCH CREEK LOOP*

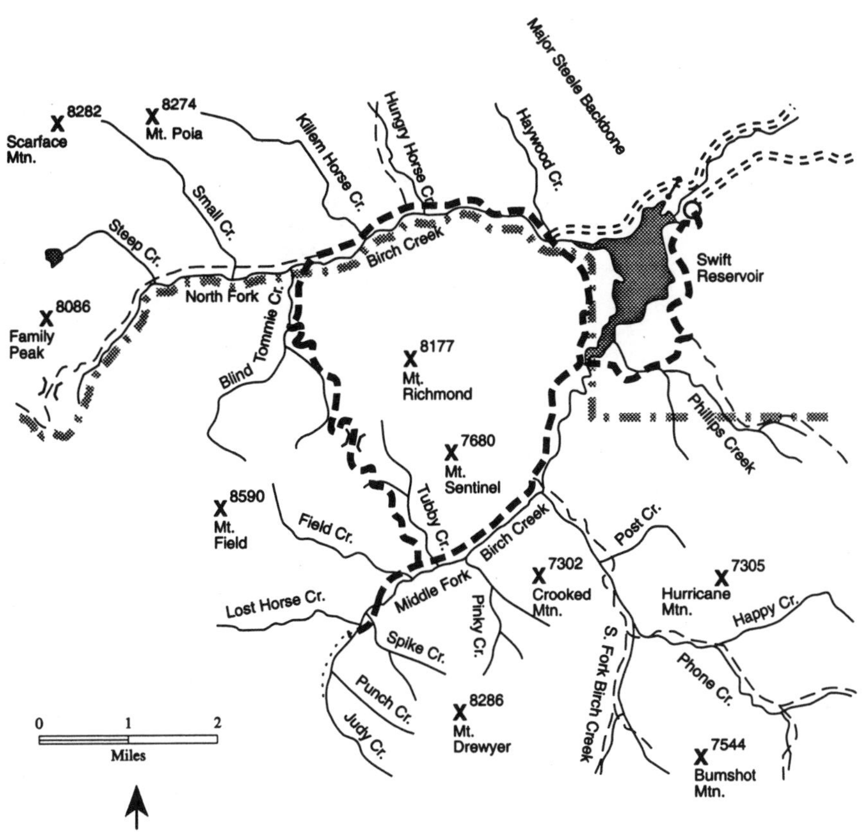

recommended, so that the Tubby Creek trail section can be approached from its upper end. The trail between the North and Middle forks has also been rebuilt, and the topographic maps currently available do not accurately reflect the true position of the trail on the landscape.

From the Swift Dam trailhead, follow the dirt road up to the south side of Swift Dam. This trail rises and falls as it follows the south shore of the reservoir, crossing grassy slopes that afford excellent views of mounts Sentinel and Richmond. After passing Hellroaring Spring, the trail climbs high onto the hillside, where it meets the unmaintained Walling Reef Trail (150). It then descends to cross Phillips Creek and climbs around the shoulder of the next rise before descending to the bank of Birch Creek. After a thigh-deep and rather tricky ford (which may be impassible early in the season), the trail runs north to reach a junction with the South Fork Birch Creek Trail (105).

Turn right and follow this trail as it wanders north beside the stream for a time, then seems to dead-end as the creek reaches a steep cutbank. At this point, the trail runs northeast, climbing the hill beside the cutbank. Upon reaching the crest of the hill, the trail doubles back to the northwest, following above the stream's course as

Looking up at Mount Field from a tributary of the Middle Fork.

it ascends into the arid hills. The trail climbs into a dry gulch as it widens into a washed-out track and runs straight uphill to the top of a bald hillock high above the reservoir. This vantage point affords sweeping views of the reefs of the Rocky Mountain Front, highlighted by Walling Reef to the south and Major Steele Backbone to the northeast. Poia and Morningstar mountains raise their pointed crests far to the north. After crossing another hillock, the trail descends into the dark forest on its way to the North Fork of Birch Creek. After a knee-deep creek crossing, the trail climbs the rocky scarp on the far bank to reach a junction with the North Fork trail (121), just west of Haywood Creek.

To continue the loop, turn left on the North Fork trail, which descends back to the creekside. The trail makes two fords in quick succession; nimble-foot travelers can avoid these fords by skirting the foot of a steep cutbank. The trail crosses numerous tributaries and passes beneath the towering countenance of Mount Richmond on its way to the Blind Tommie Trail (171) junction. The loop trail takes off to the south at this point, departing the North Fork trail to cross the broad gravel wash of the creek, which is often dry at this point during late summer. The massive north face of Mount Field is an intimidating presence as it looms to the south, above the lesser summits of the peaks surrounding it. After crossing the creek bed, the trail runs southward, following the east bank of Blind Tommie Creek. After 0.25 mile, the trail crosses this relatively small stream and makes its way through a lush growth of thimbleberry bushes on the west bank of the stream. The trail soon crosses the creek again and turns southeast, crossing the timbered flats of the valley floor and climbing up the steep slope beyond.

As the trail climbs through openings in the timber, visitors will enjoy spectacular vistas of the surrounding pinnacles that rim the tiny valley. The trail soon winds into the side valley to the east, staying high on the overlooking hillsides. At the head of this side valley is a small, pointed pinnacle; the trail will eventually work its way around to the pass to the south of this sharp point. The trail follows a small ravine for a time, then crosses it and climbs steadily southward, toward the sheer cliffs of Mount Field. A brushy passage through alder and small fir lands the traveler in the alpine parklands at the foot of these cliffs. The trail then switchbacks up to the grassy summit of the pass above, which yields outstanding views in all directions. Look southward to see Crooked Mountain looming in the foreground with Mount Patrick Gass rising in the distance. To the north lie the fantastic sheer faces of the Mount Field massif, while the hulking masses of mounts Richmond and Sentinel loom to the east.

The trail then descends gently across the western slope of the Tubby Creek valley, then switchbacks down a grassy spur ridge for a short distance. Instead of continuing its descent into the valley, however, the trail traverses southward again, crossing a washout (look for cairns) and ascending onto the grassy slopes beyond. These slopes provide excellent views of Mount Drewyer between bushwhacks through seepy spots choked with alder. After crossing a small stream, the trail dives into the lodgepole below, hell-bent for the valley floor. Look for blazes as the trail becomes quite faint in spots, especially where it crosses springs and small glades. The trail ultimately slows its descent as it nears the Middle Fork of Birch Creek, where it meets a trail junction marked, "Tubby-Blind trail." To the right a trail runs several miles up the Middle Fork, and this trail will be discussed in detail at the end of this section. To complete the loop, turn left on the Middle Fork Trail (123).

The trail passes through a forest of lodgepole pine along the streambank, crossing Tubby Creek and then working its way from the woods onto the open gravel banks of the Middle Fork. The trail climbs a grassy rise as it passes beneath Mount Sentinel, then wanders across an open slope dissected by aspen-choked draws. Looking up the valley of the South Fork, Bum Shot Mountain rises above the horizon. The trail descends again to the creekside, passing a junction with the South Fork Trail (105). Stay left, following the stream bank northward through low, arid hills dotted with limber pine and small groves of aspen. After passing the bed of a shallow cove that fills up when the reservoir is full, the trail returns to the junction with the south shore Swift Reservoir Trail (143). Turn left as the loop is completed and follow this trail across Birch Creek and back to Swift Dam.

The Upper Middle Fork Option. The Middle Fork trail continues to follow the Middle Fork of Birch Creek for several miles above the Tubby Creek trail junction. From this spot, the trail quickly leaves the lodgepole forest behind and passes through a stand of quaking aspen to reach the gravel outwash plain of Field Creek. This opening provides outstanding views of the rugged south face of Mount Field. Field Creek itself now flows through the stand of lodgepole to the west of the outwash plain, creating a small lagoon in the trail that is difficult to get around. After passing through the lodgepole, the trail drops down onto the gravel bar of the Middle

Fork and passes through a scattering of aspen and cottonwood.

The trail fords the creek and follows its south bank for a time, crossing more old floodplain. During 1964, the flooding waters of the creek scoured the valley floor clean of all vegetation and topsoil, and only hardy floodplain plants such as cottonwood have been able to recolonize the area. After crossing Spike Creek, the trail becomes a primitive route up the stream course marked by occasional cairns. The route fords the Middle Fork again above its confluence with Lost Horse Creek, then peters out altogether. It would be fairly easy to bushwhack farther up the creek bed from this point by traveling on the gravel bar and making frequent stream crossings.

TRAIL 85 *NORTH FORK OF BIRCH CREEK*

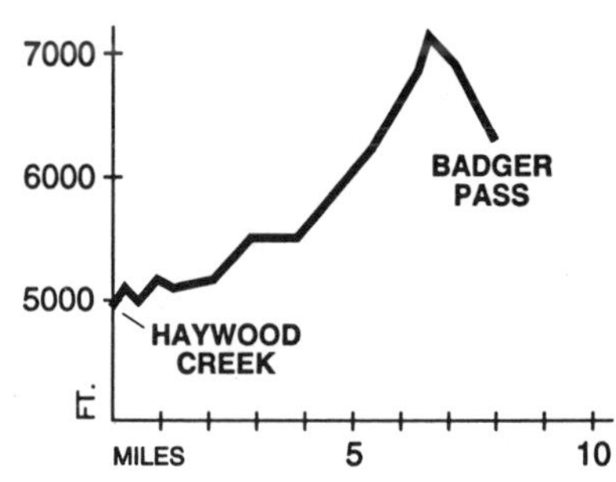

Trail 121

General description: A backpack from Haywood Creek to Badger Pass, 8.1 mi. (13.0 km).

Difficulty: Moderately strenuous.

Trail maintenance: Yearly.

Traffic: Moderate.

Elevation gain: 2,305 ft.

Elevation loss: 995 ft.

Maximum elevation: 7,125 ft.

Topo maps: Morningstar Mountain, Swift Reservoir.

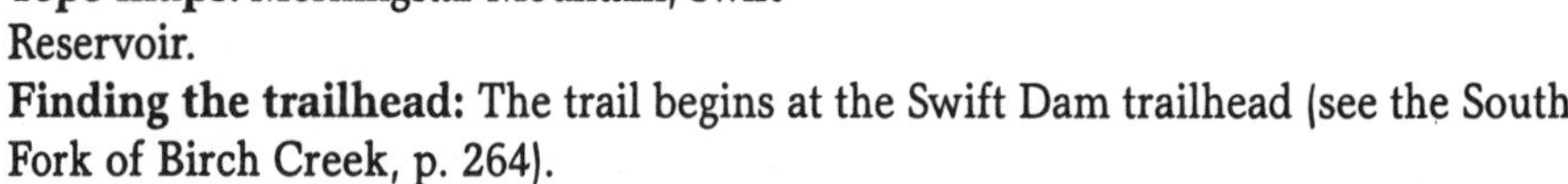

Finding the trailhead: The trail begins at the Swift Dam trailhead (see the South Fork of Birch Creek, p. 264).

- 0.0 Haywood Creek.
- 0.1 Junction with the South Fork Birch Creek Trail (105). Stay right.
- 0.7 Trail makes two fords of the North Fork of Birch Creek.
- 1.5 Trail crosses Hungry Man Creek.
- 1.6 Junction with the Hungry Man Trail (122). Keep going straight.
- 2.2 Trail crosses Killem Horse Creek.
- 2.7 Junction with the Blind Tommie Trail (171). Bear right.
- 3.8 Trail crosses Small Creek.
- 4.7 Trail fords Steep Creek and begins to climb.
- 6.7 Trail crosses the divide into the Badger Creek drainage.
- 7.9 Junction with the South Fork Badger Creek Trail (104). Stay left.
- 8.1 Badger Pass. Junction with the Strawberry Creek (338) and Cox Creek (147) trails.

The trail: This trail penetrates some of the most spectacular scenery of the Birch Creek drainage. It travels through a rather open valley flanked by sheer rock pinnacles on its way over the divide and into the Badger-Two Medicine country. The terminus of the trail is Badger Pass, from which trails descend into the Cox, Badger, and Strawberry creek drainages. The pass below Family Peak is generally free

TRAIL 85 *NORTH FORK OF BIRCH CREEK*

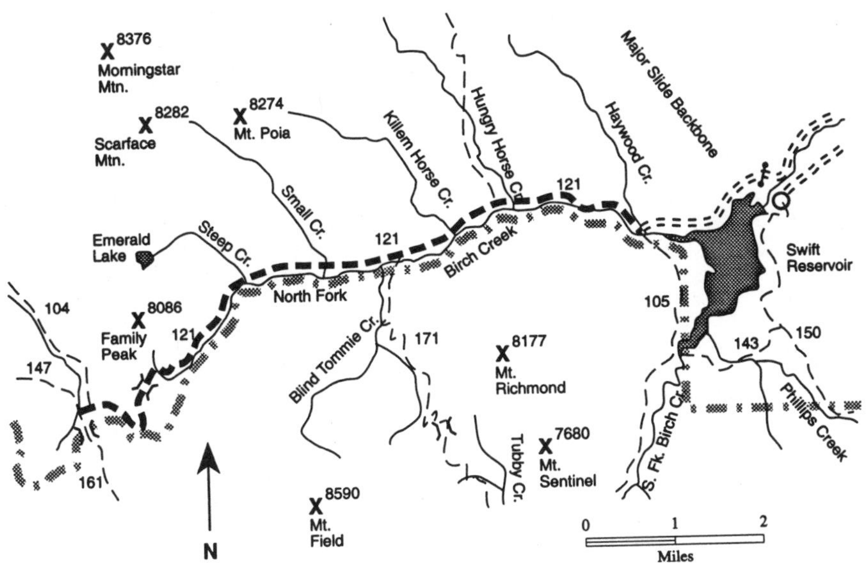

of snow from June on. Access to the trail is a bit tricky, because the trail around the northern shore of Swift Reservoir crosses the Blackfeet Indian Reservation and is currently closed to the public. As a result, it is necessary to traverse the southern shore of the reservoir, then turn north along the South Fork Birch Creek Trail (105) to reach the North Fork trail.

From Haywood Creek, an old dirt road climbs onto a hilltop, where it reaches an intersection with the South Fork trail. Mounts Poia and Morningstar rise to the north, marking the eastern rim of the valley. To the west, Mount Richmond towers above the rushing stream. Bear west as the old road descends to the creek bed and is replaced by a narrow trail. After several hundred yards of creekside travel, the trail completes two fords of the North Fork. These fords are marked by rock cairns and can be avoided by nimble-foot travelers by skirting the foot of a large cutbank. The trail then climbs into a forest of Douglas-fir and lodgepole pine, interspersed with numerous openings that allow ever-expanding views of the surrounding mountains.

The trail soon climbs to avoid a small gorge created by the erosion of the stream through a rising syncline of rock. The vantage point at the top of the rise shows off the jagged northern spur of Mount Field, as well as the more massive summit of Family Peak beyond it. These peaks provide a constant backdrop as the trail ducks in and out of the forest for the next several miles. The trail crosses Hungry Man Creek and then passes an old and faint trail to the high plains (122). In short order, Killem Horse Creek is crossed. Below the trail, the North Fork frolics through a series of small waterfalls as it passes through a ledge of unyielding bedrock. Aspen and spruce

Poia Peak and the North Fork.

begin to dominate the scattered forest as the trail makes its way along the bottomland to reach the next trail junction.

Here, a trail running up the Blind Tommie valley veers off to the left, while the North Fork trail hugs the hillside and begins to climb across a slope of loose talus. To the south, the glorious north face of Mount Field towers above the Blind Tommie valley like a reigning monarch. The trail climbs into the forest for a time, then wanders out onto the gravel bars along the creek on its way to a crossing of Steep Creek. The pointed top of Scarface Mountain becomes briefly visible as the trail fords this stream and then wanders through the clearing on its far bank. The trail then begins a modest but steady climb as it crosses an avalanche slope within sight of a small waterfall. After another stretch of forest, the trail climbs purposefully through a much larger open slope, high above the creek. This slope overlooks a tumbling cascade, with the northern buttresses of Mount Field looming close around the head of the valley.

The trail then climbs into the high, open cirque behind Family Peak, where bighorn sheep can sometimes be spotted as they feed on alpine grasses and forbs. The trail increases its grade as it climbs the headwall of the valley to reach a high pass. Far to the west, the distant peaks of the Trilobite Range rise on the western skyline, while the peaks of the Badger Creek country march away to the north. From the pass, the trail descends steeply for a time, then turns southward to curl around the headwaters of the South Fork of Badger Creek. Just before the trail reaches the trees look north for a view of Goat Mountain and the other high peaks surrounding the lower reaches of Badger Creek. After entering the trees, the trail splits. Both trails run to Badger Pass; the lower fork is more direct but is boggy in wet weather, while the trail to the left sticks to higher, drier ground. The trail passes a junction with the South Fork Badger Creek Trail (104) just before reaching a major trail junction at Badger Pass. Here, the trail to Strawberry Creek and the Middle Fork of the Flathead (161) runs south, while the Cox Creek Trail (147) bears west toward Beaver Lake.

TRAIL 86 *CRUCIFIXION LOOP*

Trail 147, 146, 104, 121
General description: An extended trip to the lower reaches of Badger Creek's South Fork, 12.4 mi. (20.0 km) round trip.
Difficulty: Moderate.
Trail maintenance: Frequent.

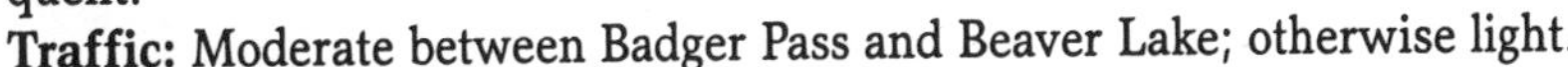

Traffic: Moderate between Badger Pass and Beaver Lake; otherwise light.
Elevation gain: 1,222 ft.
Elevation loss: 1,222 ft.
Maximum elevation: 6,320 ft.
Topo maps: Morningstar Mountain.
Finding the trail: This trail begins and ends at Badger Pass. The most direct route to the pass is via the North Fork of Birch Creek.

0.0 Badger Pass. Bear west on Trail 147.
0.9 Trail crosses the Cox Creek drainage divide and enters the Bob Marshall Wilderness.
1.6 Trail crosses the outlet of Beaver Lake.
1.7 Junction with the Muskrat Creek Trail (147). Turn right.
2.3 Unmarked junction with the cutoff trail that follows the north shore of Beaver Lake. Turn left.
2.7 Muskrat Pass. Trail leaves the Bob Marshall Wilderness.
3.6 Blue Lake.
4.5 Junction with the Muskrat Creek Cutoff Trail (146). Bear right.
5.3 Trail crosses Crucifixion Creek.
6.3 Junction with the South Fork Badger Creek Trail (104). Turn right.
6.35 Trail crosses Crucifixion Creek.
6.8 Trail fords the South Fork of Badger Creek to reach its east bank.
8.5 Trail returns to the western bank of the South Fork.
10.4 Trail makes its final ford of the South Fork of Badger Creek.
12.2 Junction with the North Fork Birch Creek Trail (121). Turn right to complete the loop.
12.4 Badger Pass.

View of Half Dome Crag from Crucifixion Creek.

The trail: The Crucifixion Loop trail offers a day hike for travelers who find themselves in the Badger Pass vicinity. From Badger Pass, follow Trail 147 west toward Beaver Lake. After passing through subalpine forest for a short distance, the trail crosses a series of marshy openings. The trail then crosses the wilderness boundary and becomes much drier on its descent to the shores of Beaver Lake. This marshy pool is surrounded by grassy meadows and is overlooked by rounded hills. In early morning, white-tailed deer emerge from the forest to graze in the lakeshore meadows. After crossing the lake's outlet stream, the trail reaches a junction with the Muskrat Creek Trail (147).

Turn right onto this narrow path, which winds around the western shore of the lake on wooded bluffs. Upon reaching the head of the lake, the trail descends to the edge of the surrounding meadows and passes an isolated beaver pond. Far to the east, the craggy summit of the Mount Field's northern spur rises above the trees. After passing the beaver pond, the trail reaches an intersection with a cutoff trail that skirts the north side of the lake. Turn left and continue up the valley as the trail passes through grassy meadows dotted with occasional clumps of low-growing willows. The trail reaches Muskrat Pass about two-thirds of a mile northwest of the lake. If the pass was not marked by signposts, it would be impossible to tell that one is crossing the Continental Divide.

After crossing the pass and leaving the Bob Marshall Wilderness, the trail descends imperceptibly through more open meadows at the headwaters of Muskrat Creek.

After dipping down through the woods to reach the creek, the trail climbs onto a level terrace overlooked by the twin humps of a nameless hill to the east. The trail passes above Blue Lake, another shallow, marshy pond surrounded by forest. The trail stays high on the hillside as the Muskrat Valley drops away below it, and after a mile it reaches the next trail junction. The rather faint Muskrat Creek trail descends to the left toward Lost Horse Camp, while the Crucifixion Loop trail bears right, bearing the name "Muskrat Cutoff Trail 145."

This trail crosses yet another imperceptible drainage divide, then settles into a gentle descent beside Crucifixion Creek. This tiny tributary of the South Fork of Badger Creek is overlooked by the small but rocky point of Elbow Mountain. To the northeast, the broad shield of Goat Mountain rises in the distance. Upon reaching a slight bend in the course of the valley, the trail dips down to cross the creek and then climbs the bare knoll beyond. All at once, the twin summits of Curly Bear and Spotted Eagle mountains tower to the east, while Half Dome Crag rises in the distance. The trail switchbacks frequently as it descends through the timber, passing a cutoff trail that bears north toward the lower reaches of Badger Creek. Upon reaching a marked junction with the South Fork Badger Creek Trail (104), turn right.

This trail runs southeast as it crosses Crucifixion Creek at the foot of a pleasant waterfall. The trail soon descends to the bank of the South Fork of Badger Creek, which it crosses at a calf-deep ford. On the open slopes of the east bank, a glance

TRAIL 86 *CRUCIFIXION LOOP*

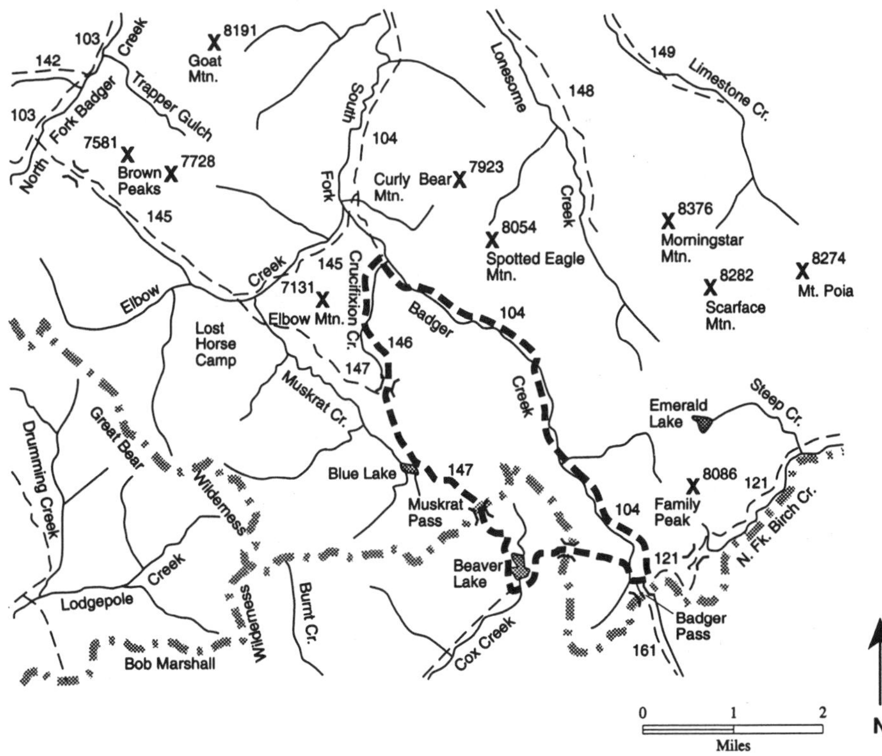

to the northwest reveals the bedrock arc of Goat Mountain, while the peak-lined canyon of the South Fork runs southeast toward Badger Pass. Views continue to be good as the trail crosses the open slopes cleared by avalanches born on the heights of Spotted Eagle Mountain. The trail then wanders out onto the gravel bank of the creek and becomes a bit faint. Subalpine fir replaces lodgepole pine as the dominant overstory tree as the trail fords the creek for a second time, then climbs onto a grassy ledge above the west bank. Look north for a final view of Spotted Eagle Mountain; hereafter the trail alternates between forest and pocket-sized openings that offer little in the way of scenery.

The forest pulls itself around the creek like a cloak, and the trail passes a minor waterfall as it continues its gentle ascent up the valley. Shortly thereafter, the route crosses what appears to be a substantial tributary; in reality, this is the main body of the South Fork of Badger Creek. Fallen logs are on hand for hikers who want to keep their feet dry. The next mile or so is pocked with boggy seeps, until the trail finally climbs out of the valley bottom and onto the slope to the east. After a brief but vigorous ascent, the trail crosses a small tributary and wends its way through subalpine parkland to reach a junction with the North Fork Birch Creek Trail (121). Turn right and descend the short distance to Badger Pass to complete the loop.

ADDITIONAL TRAILS

Mount Wright Trail (160) climbs to an old fire lookout site and is popular with hikers. The trail is hard to follow early on as it crosses an old clearcut, but becomes more distinct as it climbs.

Washboard Reef Trail (117) is very scenic, but is maintained infrequently and is considered a horse killer.

Olney-Nesbit Trail (157) crosses a low, protected pass that makes it a good route for horse parties. The avalanche danger is high on this trail early in the season, and it is not recommended for travel before July.

Teton Pass Trail (114, 324) accesses the upper reaches of the Middle Fork of the Flathead. It is quite boggy on the western side of the divide.

North Fork Dupuyer Creek Trail (124) is maintained annually. The road leading to it crosses Boone & Crockett Club land, and this part of the road is closed to vehicles.

Seedling-Potshot Trail (182) is an old cattle drive trail. It is very steep in spots and generally hard to follow.

Walling Reef Trail (150) is obstructed by some bad washouts and rockslides. It is currently impassable to stock and hard to follow.

Hungry Man Trail (122) is maintained infrequently and is hard to find, but it does exist (so they tell me).

EXTENDED TRIPS

The Bob Marshall Wilderness complex is crisscrossed with a complex network of intersecting trails, which make possible an infinite number of possible trips of varying lengths. Listed here are a few possibilities for hikers who are looking for an extended trip. These routes have been selected to maximize scenic value and minimize travel on heavily-used travel corridors.

TRILOBITE LOOP (51 MILES)

Allow 5 to 7 days

This trip features the rugged and remote scenery of the Trilobite Range, dominated by Trilobite and Pentagon mountains. Beginning at the end of the Spotted Bear River Road, take the Spotted Bear River trail as far as Pentagon Cabin. Turn north here, following the trail up Pentagon Creek beneath the watchful gaze of Pentagon Mountain. The trail crosses into the Middle Fork drainage, descending along Dolly Varden Creek. For a shorter loop, take the Trilobite Cutoff Trail (686); a longer, more scenic route includes the Trilobite trail from its beginning at Chair Mountain. The route follows the Trilobite trail south below the eastern rim of the range, passing Trilobite and Dean lakes on its way to Switchback Pass. From this point, a short descent leads back to Pentagon Cabin and an uneventful return trip along the Spotted Bear River.

Trilobite Peak.

SPOTTED BEAR RIDGE TREK (53 MILES)

Allow 6 to 8 days

This challenging journey describes a great loop around Silvertip Mountain, following good trails from the Gorge Creek trailhead to the end of the Spotted Bear River Road. Because it sticks to the well-drained ridgetops, it is a good choice if the forecast calls for wet weather. Follow the Gorge Creek trail to its unmarked junction with the Picture Ridge Cutoff Trail (226). This trail climbs arduously to reach Picture Ridge, where it meets the trail that follows the ridgetop. Turn south, as spectacular views last until the trail descends into the Hungry Creek valley. Upon returning to the South Fork bottoms turn right to pass the Black Bear Cabin and cross the pack bridge over the river. Continue southward on the far bank of the river to the Helen Creek junction, where travelers will turn east on the Pagoda Mountain trail. The trail climbs over a high divide and then down into the valley of the White River. Turn north, following this valley-bottom trail as it ascends the valley, finally crossing Juliet Creek on its way to Wall Creek Pass. Stock parties should choose the Wall Creek trail, while backpackers should opt for the higher and drier Bungalow Mountain trail. Both routes end up at the same point on the Spotted Bear River trail, from whence one can return to the road network via an easy descent along the river.

CHINESE WALL TRAVERSE (46 MILES)

Allow 5 to 7 days

This route runs from the end of the Spotted Bear River Road to the Benchmark trailhead on the eastern side of the wilderness. It offers fishing along the Spotted Bear and West Fork Sun Rivers, as well as spectacular scenery as it passes along the foot of the magnificent Chinese Wall. Camping is not permitted at the base of this popular terrain feature; plan your trip to camp before and beyond the Chinese Wall. Follow the Spotted Bear River trail as it makes its long and gradual ascent of the valley. After crossing Spotted Bear Pass, the trail turns south along the eastern side of the divide, passing My Lake on its way to Larch Hill Pass, the northern terminus of the Chinese Wall. The trail then climbs and falls as it crosses the alpine meadows at the base of the wall, descending into the lodgepole pine forest after passing Cliff Mountain. The trail then descends along the West Fork of the Sun, passing Indian Meadows and Prairie Reef on its way to the South Fork of the Sun. Upon reaching this larger river, the trail turns south, finally crossing a pack bridge to reach the trailhead in the vicinity of Benchmark.

HEART OF THE WILDERNESS CROSSING (54 MILES)

Allow 5 to 7 days

This route penetrates the very center of the Bob Marshall Wilderness, passing Big Salmon Lake and White River Pass on its way from west to east. From Holland Lake take the trail to Upper Holland Lake. The Pendant Pass trail leads from this high lake to the shores of Big Salmon Creek, where one can pick up the Big Salmon trail heading northeast. After a long slog through the timber, this trail passes along the shores of Big Salmon Lake before turning south for a challenging ford of the South Fork of the Flathead. Turn south after the crossing for about five miles to reach the White River trail. The route follows this trail as far as its crossing of the White River's south fork. Here, take the White River Pass trail as it resumes the eastward trek, climbing over a high, windswept pass and descending to the West Fork of the Sun. Upon reaching this river turn southeast and follow it downstream to its confluence with the South Fork of the Sun River. From this junction, the route turns south for the final uneventful miles to the Benchmark area.

LAKE DISTRICT LOOP (27 MILES)

Allow 3 to 5 days

This route begins and ends at Holland Lake and visits no less than six alpine lakes, with an option to visit Koessler Lake for truly motivated travelers. From the north shore of Holland Lake follow the trail to Upper Holland Lake and beyond, mounting the low divide of Gordon Pass. A steady descent leads past the Doctor Lake trail, where a side trip to Koessler Lake offers good fishing opportunities. At the Shaw Creek Cabin, turn north along the Shaw Creek trail. Atop the next drainage divide is a short spur trail that leads to Lena Lake, a large woodland lake nestled among rounded mountains. The route continues north from here, passing the Pendant Cabin and Big Salmon Falls before crossing Big Salmon Creek. Immediately after the ford, take the Necklace Pass trail westward, passing the Necklace Lakes on the way to a high and windswept divide. After a brief southward jaunt, the trail returning to Holland Lake takes off to the right (although 0.25 mile straight ahead lies Sapphire lake, a beautiful and enticing diversion).

Looking south from Necklace Pass.

OLD BUFFALO TRAIL (53 MILES)

Allow 6 to 8 days

This route was historically used by Flathead Indians on their way to annual buffalo hunts on the high plains. From Holland Lake's north shore follow the trail over Gordon Pass, and all the way down the wooded valley of Gordon Creek. Upon reaching the South Fork of the Flathead, turn south and follow the trail to the Youngs Creek Ford. Turn southeast here, up the Danaher Valley as far as the basin. At an old battleground where Flatheads and Blackfeet once fought over territorial rights turn northeast up the valley of Camp Creek. This trail surmounts Camp Creek Pass and crosses the spectacular Pearl Basin before descending the wooded valley of Ahorn Creek to reach Indian Point Meadows. Here, on the banks of the West Fork of the Sun, the route turns southeast, following the river downstream to its confluence with the South Fork of the Sun River. Turn south here and follow the trail to a pack bridge that leads to the Benchmark trailhead and the terminus of the trek.

DANAHER MEADOWS TREK (35 MILES)

Allow 4 to 6 days

This trip allows relatively easy access to Danaher Meadows, passing over the relatively low Dry Fork Divide and Limestone Pass on its way from the North Fork of the Blackfoot to its terminus on the lower reaches of Monture Creek. Follow the Hobnail Tom trail up the North Fork of the Blackfoot, which is spanned by pack bridges that make river fords unnecessary. At the North Fork Cabin turn west along the Dry Fork, following this trail to the Scapegoat Wilderness boundary. Continue northwest at this point, following the Danaher Valley trail for a short distance into Danaher Meadows, where it meets the Limestone Pass trail. After a ford of Danaher Creek, this trail climbs the narrow valley between Pinnacle and Little Apex Peaks, then turns southwest to Limestone Pass. The trail then descends into the timbered reaches of Monture Creek, which it follows on its downstream journey to the trailhead.

FLINT MOUNTAIN LOOP (42 MILES)

Allow 5 to 7 days

This route provides a challenging trek through some of the more remote parts of the Scapegoat Wilderness. Follow the Hobnail Tom trail up the North Fork of the Blackfoot, passing North Fork Falls and the Carmichael Cabin. At Dobrota Creek, turn northwest along the southern ramparts of the Scapegoat Plateau and follow this trail as it becomes progressively fainter into the headwaters of the Dry Fork. At this point, leave the cliffs behind and follow the narrow upper Dry Fork trail down to the Dry Fork Divide. Here, the route turns southeast, descending gently down the wide and open valley of the Dry Fork to reach the North Fork Cabin and complete the loop.

EAST FORK BLACKFOOT TRAVERSE (23 MILES)

Allow 3 to 4 days

This rather short and easy trip crosses the southern part of the Scapegoat Wilderness, sticking mainly to valley bottoms surrounded by forested mountains. From

Heart Lake and Red Mountain.

Indian Meadows, follow the Webb Lake trail northwest, past Heart and Webb lakes. As the trail turns westward along the headwaters of the East Fork, it is overlooked to the south by the massive mound of Red Mountain, the tallest peak in the wilderness complex. The route descends through the meadowy valley of the East Fork, passing Parker Lake on its way to the Meadow Creek trail junction. Turn south here, passing Meadow Lake and climbing gradually through unburned country to reach a pass that overlooks the broad valley of the Blackfoot. A long and rather steep descent leads to the terminus of the trek at the Dry Creek trailhead at the edge of Kleinschmidt Flats.

BASIN LOOP (38 MILES)

Allow 4 to 6 days

This route allows the easiest access to the basin in the Danaher Valley and also includes the spectacular Pearl Basin. Possible side trips might include the Grizzly Basin, the Jumbo Mountain Lookout, and Prairie Reef Lookout. From the Benchmark trailhead, follow the South Fork Sun River trail southward. The route jogs west at Hoadley Creek, climbing through the mud and forest to reach the pass at its head. The trail then descends into the basin, where it turns north to reach Camp Creek. Turn northeast along this stream, climbing through Camp Creek Pass and into Pearl Basin. A long descent through the forest leads to Indian Point Meadows on the West Fork of the Sun. The route turns east here, following the river downstream to its confluence with the South Fork, where the route turns south to return to Benchmark.

NORTH WALL LOOP (50 MILES)

Allow 6 to 8 days

This trek crosses two spectacular passes in the Sawtooth Range, traverses the Sun River Basin, and runs at the foot of the impressive cliffs of the North Wall. It offers outstanding wildlife viewing opportunities as it passes through prime mountain goat and elk summer range. From the South Fork of the Teton, take the Headquarters Pass trail westward over this spectacular divide, which lies beneath the stony countenance of Rocky Mountain. A long descent through burned country leads to the North Fork of the Sun. Cross the pack bridge and head west to Gates Park, then take the Red Shale Meadows trail to reach the southern end of the North Wall. In Red Shale Meadows, the route turns north, following the foot of the cliffs through forest, burn, and alpine meadows. Follow it all the way to Open Creek, where the route turns east again for a long but gentle descent to the North Fork bottoms. After crossing Fool Creek, follow Trail 110 southward to the Wrong Creek Cabin, and pick up the Route Creek Pass trail just beyond it. This trail runs east, climbing to crest barren Route Creek Pass and descend to the Middle Fork of the Teton. Just before reaching the Cave Mountain trailhead, take the short Lonesome Ridge trail southward to complete the loop. This trail terminates on the South Fork Teton Road, about two miles east of the Headquarters Pass trailhead.

The twisted strata of the North Wall above the headwaters of Lick Creek.

GATEWAY LOOP (37 MILES)

Allow 4 to 6 days

This trail features the most spectacular scenery that the Birch Creek country has to offer, as well as passing such landmark sites as Big River Meadows and Gateway Gorge. From Swift Dam, follow the trail around the south side of the reservoir. After passing its head, take the South Fork Birch Creek trail southward through its open valley flanked with craggy mountains. This trail climbs gradually to cross Gateway Pass and descend into Big River Meadows as the Gateway Gorge trail. Follow this trail through the gorge to Strawberry Creek, where the route turns northward. A long but moderate climb through the forest leads to Badger Pass. Turn east here on the North Fork Birch Creek trail, which climbs over a high pass and then descends into the spectacular valley of Birch Creek's North Fork. The trail passes the spires and pinnacles of mounts Field and Richmond before returning to the western edge of Swift Reservoir. One must then follow the South Fork Trail around the west side of the reservoir to reach the trail that returns along the south shore to Swift Dam.

AFTERWORD

THE WILDERNESS CHALLENGE

By Bill Schneider, Publisher
Falcon Press Publishing Co., Inc.

Many hikers, I suspect, view the "wilderness challenge" as the adventure of braving wild country with only what they can carry on their backs. They briefly flee the comfortable life to risk survival along some austere divide, and they return home the victor.

We've almost come to consider it our right to have the opportunity to visit places on earth that have been affected primarily by the forces of nature, where the imprint of man's hand is substantially unnoticeable.

Yes, we can "challenge" the wilderness. We can climb the highest peak, float the wildest river, seek out the most hidden of the mountain's secrets. In Montana, we can even challenge the mighty grizzly bear, the wilderness king, and temporarily become the most feared creature on the mountain.

This challenge lures us to the blank spots on the map. It seems ingrained in our birthright and most likely will for generations to come.

But today's hikers face an even more fierce, more difficult, more time-consuming, and more frustrating challenge. Now we must rise to the challenge of saving the last wilderness.

Never has the oft-quoted adage of Will Rogers, "They ain't makin' any more of it," been so relevant. Another famous thinker, Aldo Leopold, also emphasized the point by writing "Wilderness is a resource that can shrink, but not grow." How true. But the wilderness must grow to help dilute the rapidly increasing number of hikers.

I suppose the day will come when most wilderness areas have restrictions on the number of human visitors. However, increasing the size of the wilderness resource would certainly make this day a more distant probability.

It's also true that the label "wilderness," when officially designated by Congress, can attract hikers, leading to more crowded conditions. However, limitations on recreational use are undoubtedly preferable to the alternative—gradual destruction.

Knowing this, it hurts to hear politicians talk of "balance" as they prepare to give their guarded support to the destruction of another unprotected roadless area. In the lower forty-eight states, the ratio is now ninety-nine percent nonwilderness to one percent wilderness, as legally defined by the Wilderness Act of 1964.

Yet in almost every speech by wilderness opponents or politicians trying to please everybody, we hear cries for balance. "I'm in favor of wilderness," they predictably say, "but not in this area. We need balance; we can't have all wilderness."

I wonder how many of these podium-thumpers really understand the existing inequity. If every remaining acre of roadless country south of Canada became part of the Wilderness Preservation System (created by the Wilderness Act of 1964), we wouldn't even come close to balance. The pitiful one percent might, at best, climb to three percent.

Herein lies our challenge to make America understand the wisdom of wilderness, to keep the bulldozer out of the last remnants of wild country, to preserve for future hikers a few examples of what the land used to be like.

This challenge can't be taken lightly. Compared to winning congressional protection for a threatened roadless area, climbing the highest peak, or surviving the elements is remarkably easy. In a time when economics dictates most decision-making, pleas to designate wilderness aren't always eagerly received. But wilderness can be an economic bonanza to a community. (In Montana, recreation and tourism are the state's third largest industry.)

Claims that wilderness destroys the local economy illustrate only one of the many myths plaguing wilderness preservation efforts. Other myths include: Only the rich, elite, young, and strong use wilderness. Domestic livestock grazing isn't possible or practical in wilderness. Wilderness locks out sportsmen and other recreationists. Wilderness is bad for wildlife. Wilderness isn't multiple-use. Wilderness locks up vital minerals. We have too much wilderness already.

These are pure myths, and quite the opposite is true in each case. So if you're confronted with these false statements, get the facts and set the record straight. Don't let them pass without a reply; there's too much at stake. The integrity of the last American wilderness is on the line. And even more important, the decisions on what to do with the remaining roadless areas will be made in the next few years.

The conservation groups listed below have the facts to support pro-wilderness claims and dispel myths. They even have detailed information on many of the unprotected areas mentioned in this guidebook. Making the decision-makers listen to these facts is your challenge.

I dislike projecting wilderness as a giant battleground. But in reality that's a fair description. The battle over wilderness has been and will be in the future as bitterly fought as that over any domestic political issue.

Hikers and other people who use and adore wilderness must be the soldiers in this war. Otherwise the day when the last roadless area is protected as wilderness will soon dawn.

Montana Wilderness Association
Box 635
Helena, MT 59624
(406) 443-7350

Alliance of the Wild Rockies
415 N. Higgins Ave.
Missoula, MT 59802
(406) 721-5420

APPENDIX A: MILEAGES OF SOME IMPORTANT TRUNK TRAILS

The Big River Trail (155). Runs along the Middle Fork of the Flathead River.

- 0.0 Nimrod trailhead.
- 0.1 Pack Bridge over Bear Creek.
- 1.0 Trail crosses Edna Creek.
- 1.1 Junction with the Tranquil Basin Overlook Trail (489).
- 2.6 Knee-deep ford of Spruce Creek.
- 2.7 Junction with ford to the Elk Creek - Dirtyface Trail (62)
- 5.4 Spruce Park. Junction with Vinegar Mountain Trail (260)
- 5.8 Junction with ford to the Long Creek Trail (166)
- 9.2 Trail crosses Lunch Creek
- 10.7 Junction with ford to Cy Creek Trail (332)
- 12.3 Junction with Twentyfive Mile Creek Trail (159)
- 13.0 Trail crosses Twentyfive Mile Creek.
- 14.0 Junction with trail to Castle Lake (209)
- 15.0 Granite Cabin.
- 15.5 Junction with Granite Creek Cutoff Trail.
- 15.8 Trail crosses Granite Creek.
- 15.9 Junction with Granite Creek Trail (156).
- 19.7 Three Forks Junction. Miner Creek Trail (81), Morrison Creek Trail (154) junctions.
- 19.8 Three Forks Pack Bridge over Morrison Creek.
- 22.0 Junction with Morrison Creek Trail (154).
- 22.8 Junction with Lodgepole Mountain Trail (337).
- 24.6 Schafer Meadows.
- 25.2 Schafer Meadows airstrip.
- 25.5 Schafer Meadows administrative complex.
- 26.0 Junction with ford to Schafer (327) and Dolly Varden Creek (173) trails.
- 27.4 Junction with Lodgepole Mountain Trail (337).
- 28.5 Trail crosses Surprise Creek.
- 29.5 Trail crosses Calbick Creek.
- 29.6 Junction with Calbick Creek Trail (391).
- 32.1 Junction with Cox Creek Trail (176).
- 32.3 Trail crosses Cox Creek.
- 32.4 Junction with Winter Points Trail (476).
- 36.9 Trail crosses Switchback Creek.
- 39.9 Gooseberry Park Cabin. Junction with Clack Creek Trail (160).
- 42.5 Trail crosses Grimsley Creek.
- 43.7 Trail fords Strawberry Creek.
- 44.0 Junction with Gateway Pass Trail (322).

The East Side South Fork Trail (80). Trail follows the South Fork of the Flathead River.

- 0.0 Spotted Bear Ranger Station.
- 7.7 Junction with Harrison Creek Trail (88).
- 7.8 Trail crosses Harrison Creek.
- 7.9 Meadow Creek airstrip.
- 9.2 Trail crosses Lost Jack Creek.
- 9.3 Junction with Meadow Creek Pack Bridge Trail.
- 13.0 Junction with Mid Creek Trail (103).
- 13.2 Trail makes knee-deep ford of Mid Creek.
- 16.5 Junction with Black Bear Creek Trail (220).
- 16.7 Trail fords Black Bear Creek.
- 17.2 Junction with Black Bear ford of South Fork River.
- 19.2 Junction with north cutoff to Black Bear Pack Bridge.
- 19.7 Junction with south cutoff to Black Bear Pack Bridge.
- 20.1 Junction with Pagoda Mountain Trail (100).
- 20.4 Trail crosses Helen Creek.
- 23.7 Trail crosses Damnation Creek.
- 25.7 Mud Lake.
- 26.4 Junction with Salmon Forks ford of South Fork River.
- 27.0 Junction with Mud Lake Mountain Trail (470).
- 27.5 Trail crosses Phil Creek.
- 29.2 Trail crosses Pine Creek.
- 30.4 Trail crosses Woodfir Creek.

31.0 Junction with White River Trail (112).

31.2 Trail fords White River.

31.9 Junction with White River Park ford of South Fork River.

32.4 Junction with Holbrook ford of South Fork River.

32.6 Junction with White River Butte Trail (193).

34.4 Trail crosses Hammer Creek.

37.5 Junction with White River Butte Trail (193).

37.6 Trail crosses Lime Creek and enters Big Prairie.

38.2 Big Prairie Work Center. Junction with Big Prairie Pack Bridge Trail.

39.5 Trail crosses Brownstone Creek.

39.8 Junction with Gordon Creek ford of South Fork River.

40.0 Trail crosses Cayuse Creek.

40.1 Junction with Catchem Creek Trail (269).

41.1 Junction with Cayuse Mountain ford of South Fork River.

43.5 Junction with Youngs Creek ford of South Fork River and Danaher Valley trail (126).

The West Side South Fork trail (263). Trail follows the South Fork of the Flathead River.

0.0 Black Bear ford of South Fork River.

1.5 Junction with Hungry Creek Trail (105) descending from Picture Ridge.

1.7 Black Bear Cabin.

2.0 Trail crosses Hungry Creek.

2.8 Trail crosses Snow Creek.

6.3 Little Salmon Park.

7.7 Junction with Little Salmon Creek Trail (29).

7.8 Trail crosses pack bridge over Little Salmon Creek.

9.6 Junction with the Big Salmon Trail (110).

9.7 Trail crosses pack bridge over Big Salmon Creek.

10.2 Salmon Forks Ranger Station.

10.3 Junction with Salmon Forks ford of South Fork River.

12.4 Trail crosses Lamoose Creek.

14.0 Junction with White River Park ford of South Fork River.

14.7 Junction with Holbrook Creek Trail (131).

14.8 Trail crosses Holbrook Creek.

14.9 Junction with Holbrook Cabin trail.

15.1 Junction with Holbrook ford of South Fork River.

16.7 Trail crosses Scarface Creek.

17.6 Junction with Burnt Creek Trail (195).

18.2 Trail crosses Burnt Creek.

20.2 Bartlett Meadows.

20.8 Junction with Bartlett Creek Trail (129).

20.9 Trail makes calf-deep ford of Bartlett Creek.

22.5 Junction with Big Prairie pack bridge trail.

23.7 Trail crosses Butcher Creek.

24.7 Junction with Gordon Creek ford of South Fork River.

24.8 Junction with Gordon Creek Trail (35).

24.9 Trail makes knee-deep ford of Gordon Creek.

26.1 Junction with Cayuse Mountain ford of South Fork River.

26.4 Junction with Fossil Mountain - Cardinal Peak Trail (128).

28.2 Junction with Youngs Creek ford of South Fork River and Youngs Creek Trail (125).

The Youngs Creek trail (125, 141, 283). Follows Youngs Creek from the South Fork of the Flathead to Pyramid Pass.

0.0 Inception of trail at the South Fork of the Flathead.

4.4 Junction with the Hahn Creek Pass Trail (125).

5.9 Trail crosses Kid Creek.

6.7 Junction with the Cabin Creek Trail (206).

6.75 Trail crosses Cabin Creek.

6.8 Junction with the Babcock Creek Trail (130).

7.3 Trail fords Youngs Creek to reach the south bank.

7.6 Trail returns to the north bank of Youngs Creek.

9.2 Trail passes the Big Slide.

10.0 Trail fords Youngs Creek to reach its east bank.

10.9 Junction with the Marshall Creek Trail (137).

12.2 junction with the Jenny Creek Trail (141).

12.3 Trail fords Youngs Creek to reach the west bank.

12.6 Junction with the Crimson Peak Trail (468).

13.8 Junction with the Spruce - Ross Creek Trails (221, 284).

16.0 Leota Park.

16.1 Trail fords Youngs Creek to reach its south bank.

18.3 Junction with the Pyramid Lake and Blackfoot Divide trails.

18.6 Pyramid Pass.

The North Fork Sun River Trail (202, 261, 166, 110). Follows the North Fork of the Sun River.

0.0 Pretty Prairie Cabin.

1.4 Trail leaves Pretty Prairie.

3.9 Junction with the Goat Creek Trail (249).

4.0 Trail crosses Goat Creek.

4.4 Trail crosses Bear Creek.

4.5 Junction with the Bear Creek Trail (222).

5.7 Trail crosses Furman Creek.

7.6 Trail fords Freezeout Creek.

9.4 Trail crosses Glenn Creek and reaches junction with the Glenn Creek Trail (221).

12.0 Trail crosses Moose Creek.

12.1 junction with the Moose Creek Trail (131)

16.0 Trail crosses Rock Creek.

18.0 Trail passes Gates Lake.

18.1 Junction with the Rock Creek (111) and Red Shale Meadows (130) Trails.

18.5 Gates Park Ranger Station.

19.2 Trail crosses Gates Creek.

24.3 Junction with the Lick Creek Trail 151).

24.6 Trail fords Lick Creek and the North Fork of the Sun.

24.7 Junction with the Wrong Creek (117) and Route Creek Pass (108) trails.

25.0 Junction with the Wrong Creek Cutoff Trail (108).

26.6 Trail fords Monroe Creek.

27.2 Trail crosses McDonald Creek.

27.5 Junction with the Wrong Ridge Trail (188).

28.2 Junction with the Open Creek Trail (116).

31.3 Sun River Pass.

APPENDIX B: FISHING OPPORTUNITIES

LAKE	SPECIES	FISHING QUALITY
Heart Lake	GRY	G
Parker Lake	CT	F
Webb Lake	CT, RBT	G
Castle Lake	CT	F
Marion Lake	HYB	VG
Stanton Lake	RBT, CT, HYB, WF	P
Elk Lake	RBT	VG
Lower Big Hawk Lake	YCT	VG
Upper Big Hawk Lake	WCT	P
Big Salmon Lake	BTR, CT, HYB, WF	G
Blackfoot Lake	RBT, CT	F
Black Lake	RBT, WCT	VG
Clayton Lake	CT	F
Crater Lake	WCT	G
North and South Jewel Lakes	RBT	P
Koessler Lake	WCT	VG
Lena Lake	RBT	F
Pendant Lakes	CT	P
Necklace Lakes	RBT	G
Sunburst Lake	CT	E
Palisade Lake	WCT	VG
Woodward Lake	HYB	VG
Bear Lake	CT	F
Our Lake	WCT, YCT	F
Lake Levale	GRY	*

STREAM	SPECIES	FISHING QUALITY
Black Bear Creek	CT, BTR	E
East Fork Blackfoot	RBT CT	VG
North Fork Blackfoot	CT, RBT	G
Dry Fork (upper reaches)	CT	E
Dolly Varden Creek (lower)	CT, BTR	G
Dolly Varden Creek (upper)	CT	P
Danaher Creek	WCT, BTR, WF	G
Gordon Creek	WCT, BTR	G
Mid Creek	WCT, BTR	VG
Spotted Bear River	WCT, BTR, WF	VG
White River	BTR, WCT	E
South Fork Flathead	WCT, BTR, WF	E
Youngs Creek	WCT, BTR	G
Middle Fork Flathead	WCT, BTR, WF	G
Dearborn River	RBT, BKT, CT	F
South Fork Sun River	RBT, BKT, CT	P
North Fork Sun River	RBT, BKT, CT	G
West Fork Sun River	RBT, BKT, CT	F
Moose Creek	RBT, CT	F
North Fork Teton River	RBT, BKT, CT	F
South Fork Birch Creek	RBT, CT, BKT	G

** Lake Levale was stocked in 1993 and will not be open to fishing for two to three years after this planting.*

Key: GRY=grayling; CT=cutthroat trout; WCT=west-slope cuttroat trout; YCT=Yellowstone cutthroat trout; BTR=bull trout; BKT=brook trout; RBT=rainbow trout; HYB=rainbow-cutthroat hybrid; WR=mountain whitefish

Key: E=excellent; VG=very good; G=good; F=fair; P=poor

APPENDIX C: WHO TO CONTACT FOR MORE INFORMATION

Lewis and Clark National Forest

Rocky Mountain Ranger District, 1102 Main Ave. NW, Box 340, Choteau, MT 59442. Phone (406) 466-5341.

Flathead National Forest

Hungry Horse Ranger District, Hungry Horse, MT 59919. Phone (406) 387-5243.

Spotted Bear Ranger District, Hungry Horse, MT 59919. Phone (406) 752-7345 (summer); (406) 387-5243 (winter).

Swan Lake Ranger District, P. O. Box 438, Bigfork, MT 59911. Phone (406) 837-5081.

Lolo National Forest

Seeley Lake Ranger District, HC 31 Box 3200, Seeley Lake, MT 59868. Phone (406) 677-2233.

Helena National Forest

Lincoln Ranger District, Box 219, Lincoln, MT 59639. Phone (406) 362-4265.

ABOUT THE AUTHOR

Erik Molvar discovered backpacking while working on a volunteer trail crew in the North Cascades of Washington. A newfound taste for the wilderness experience inspired him to choose a career in the outdoors, and he soon found himself at the University of Montana pursuing a bachelor's degree in wildlife biology. Montana's craggy ranges were to be his playground for the next five years, and his experiences inpired his first book, *The Trail Guide to Glacier and Waterton National Parks.*

An adventurous spirit has led Erik to embark upon backpacking expeditions throughout the Rocky Mountains, the Great Basin, western Canada, and Alaska. Along the way, he earned a master's degree studying moose behavior in Denali National Park, Alaska. Erik has hiked more than a thousand miles in the Bob Marshall country, including all of the trails featured in this book. It is his hope that this book will inspire a greater interest in and appreciation of our wilderness areas, which are fast disappearing in the face of economic development.